RETROFITTING

URBAN DESIGN SOLUTIONS *for* REDESIGNING SUBURBS

SUBURBIA

ELLEN DUNHAM-JONES AND JUNE WILLIAMSON

WILEY

John Wiley & Sons, Inc.

For general information about our other products and services, please contact our Customer Care Department within the United States at (800) 762-2974, outside the United States at (317) 572-3993 or fax (317) 572-4002.

Wiley also publishes its books in a variety of electronic formats. Some content that appears in print may not be available in electronic books. For more information about Wiley products, visit our website at www.wiley.com.

Library of Congress Cataloging-in-Publication Data:

Dunham-Jones, Ellen, 1959–
  Retrofitting suburbia : urban design solutions for redesigning suburbs / Ellen Dunham-Jones, June Williamson.
      p. cm.
  Includes bibliographical references and index.
  ISBN 978-0-470-04123-9 (cloth)
  1. Suburbs--United States--Planning. 2. Sustainable development—United States. I. Williamson, June. II. Title.
  HT352.U6D86 2009
  307.760973—dc22

2008016847

Printed in the United States of America

10 9 8 7 6 5 4 3

CONTENTS

PREFACE

Much of suburbia is due for a retrofit. This book documents the dramatic physical transformations taking place right now in North American suburbia. These changes hold promise for replacing less sustainable development patterns with more valuable, sustainable places. Isolated, privately owned shopping malls and aging office parks surrounded by asphalt are being torn down and replaced with multiblock, mixed-use town centers, many with public squares and greens. Edge city agglomerations of suburban office and retail are being interlaced with residences and walkable streets. Ambitious new public transit networks are being proposed, constructed, and integrated into rapidly redeveloping suburban contexts. Archaic zoning ordinances are being thoroughly overhauled to permit higher-density, mixed-use development, especially near new transit stations. New flats and townhouses are attracting young professionals, empty nesters, single-parent families, and elders, people who historically have had limited housing choices in suburban areas and are projected to comprise 85% of new U.S. households population in the next quarter century. Green parks are replacing parking lots, increasing permeable surface area even as densities increase. Land consumption for development at the periphery is being reduced as growth is redirected inward, where it is regenerating underperforming suburban areas where infrastructure is already in place. This new landscape is evolving, hybridizing, and recombining urban and suburban patterns and practices in ways that are improving sustainability and nurturing urbanism. In short, many suburban areas are evolving into places that are more urban and, we think, more urbane. As historian Robert Fishman quipped, we are rediscovering the "urbs" in suburbs.[1]

Our interest in this rediscovery is both personal and professional. We both grew up in stereotypically suburban environments—leafy enclaves of white upper middle-class privilege, with two cars in the garage, excellent public schools, and nothing much to do as teenagers besides hang out at the mall. It was a good lifestyle, but, as adults, we have not chosen it for ourselves. As architects and urban designers with an intense appreciation for all things urban, we recognize that sprawl has undercut the benefits of suburban living and have been disturbed by our professions' general disregard for the vast landscape we grew up in and which now constitutes upwards of 75% of contemporary development.[2] We also recognize how the sheer quantity of construction in sprawling environments exacerbates the urgent challenges our society faces from climate change, rising oil prices, water shortages, and declining public health. The systematic development of suburban sprawl was the big architectural project for the last fifty years; we believe that the redevelopment of sprawl into more urban, more connected, more sustainable places is the big project for this century.

By documenting the dramatic retrofits to this landscape at a variety of scales, we hope to open the eyes of both professionals and non-professionals to the change that is indeed possible in the seeming stasis of suburbia. More radical in their programming and urban form than in their architectural expression, these projects excite us for their real-world application of new trends in planning, development, economics, policy, and design. Retrofits are responding to significant demographic and behavioral changes in suburban areas and are the first tantalizing steps in the larger project of retrofitting the systems of sprawl itself.

1. Robert Fishman, banquet address at "New Visions of Suburban Life" interdisciplinary conference, Center for Suburban Studies, Hofstra University, Hempstead, NY, March 18, 2005.
2. Ellen Dunham-Jones, "Seventy-Five Percent: The Next Big Architectural Project," *Harvard Design Magazine* 12 (Fall 2000): 4–12.

INTRODUCTION

We intend this book to inform architects, urban designers, planners, developers, public officials, and citizens interested in helping suburbs and metropolitan regions, both aging and booming, to grow in healthy ways. In keeping with the principles of both new urbanism and smart growth, we see these retrofits as an enormous opportunity to direct new growth into existing areas, both the bypassed first-ring suburbs and the bustling outlying nodes. The cases we describe provide vivid examples of attractive, viable alternatives to business-as-usual sprawl.[1] We believe these alternatives promise to make both the existing locations and the larger region more sustainable.

We view sustainability in the broad sense of integrating economic, social, and ecological performance such that current needs are met without compromising the ability of future generations to meet theirs. Beyond the provision of energy-efficient buildings, we advocate for a restructuring of community and government priorities at both the local and regional levels in order to accommodate future population growth within previously developed areas and to ameliorate the detrimental environmental effects of the past sixty years of conventional suburban development patterns. Reducing vehicle miles traveled (VMT) is key to this effort on many counts: reducing household costs, increasing time for social engagement and exercise, and improving air and water quality.[2] We seek to promote ways of understanding suburban retrofits as examples of urbanism whose success is measured in synergistic economic, social, and environmental impacts, rather than viewing them through the lenses of style or as real estate products.

Many of the urbanizing projects that we document in the case studies in this book are large-scale, sited on 40 or more acres. We contend that large projects are needed to achieve the critical mass necessary to induce behavioral change and evolution of the larger transportation, regulatory, and market systems. The zoning codes and land use practices that produced the conventional suburban form of the twentieth century are simply too entrenched and pervasive for piecemeal, incremental projects to adequately improve the sustainable performance of suburbia as a whole. While the case studies are largely singular projects, we envision a future of more systemic changes that will connect the next generation of retrofits into a healthier metropolis. The examples discussed reveal the ample roles for the public and private sectors, usually in partnership, to retrofit individual properties and the governing regulations—both of which are increasingly out-of-date. Before continuing with this argument, which we take up fully in the first chapter, we first define what we mean by the terms *suburb* and *suburban*.

URBAN VERSUS SUBURBAN FORM

In the context of this study of typical suburban real estate products (shopping malls, office parks, residential subdivisions, commercial strips, etc.), we define the terms *suburb* and *suburban* primarily in terms of physical form rather than location or governmental boundaries. The characteristics of suburban form differ markedly from urban form in several important ways (see Figure I–2):

Figure I–1 A dead strip mall in Willingboro, New Jersey, circa 2004. Thousands of similar vacant retail and commercial properties dot the suburban landscape, awaiting retrofitting.

Figure I–2 Whether found within the municipal boundaries of a city or a suburb, typical suburban form (on the left) is low density, segregated by use, and auto dependent, with a discontinuous, dendritic street network and poorly defined public space. Urban form (on the right) is characterized by higher-density, mixed-use, walkable blocks of buildings supported by a continuous street network with well-defined public spaces.

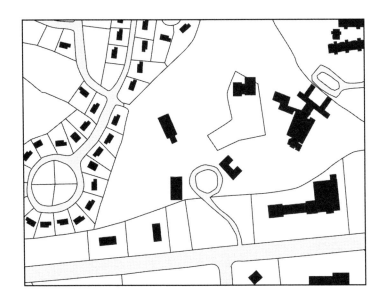

Suburban Form

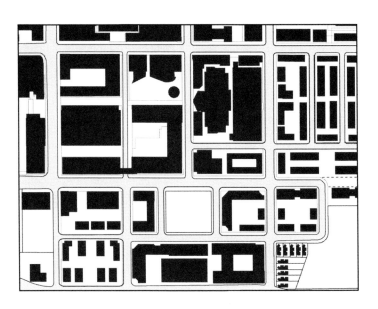

Urban Form

- Suburban form is characterized by buildings designed "in the round" to be viewed as objects set back in a landscape they dominate; in urban form, a clear focus is on the fronts of buildings and how they line up to meet the sidewalk and shape the public space of the street.

- The dominant spatial figures in suburban form are private buildings. Public roadways, schools, and parks exist but are rarely treated as dominant spatial figures or outdoor public rooms, as is the case in urban form.

- Suburban buildings tend to be dedicated to a single use—residential, retail, office, or industrial—while urban buildings are more often mixed in use or may transition in use over the life span of the building.

- Suburban form is almost entirely auto dependent, typically involving surface parking lots surrounding buildings, while urban form is not.

- Suburban roads are often organized in a dendritic pattern with dead ends and culs-de-sac, while urban streets are organized into interconnected networks.

- Suburban form tends to be lower-density and evenly spread out, while urban form tends to have a higher net density as well as a greater range of localized densities. This is true for densities measured by population and by building area.

- Suburban form is predominantly funded by short-term investors interested in volume, such as real estate investment trusts (REITs) and large home-builders, while urban form is more likely to be funded with a combination of short- and longer-term investment vehicles as well as a variety of public-private partnerships.

The suburban retrofits we have chosen to document started out as single-use, stand-alone, private, disconnected, short-term investments on sites characterized by a preponderance of "underperforming asphalt". They have become enduring, horizontally and vertically mixed-use buildings in a connected network of walkable public streets and spaces.

Our emphasis on defining *suburban* in terms of physical form is an important corrective to the stereotypes that have dominated and obscured discussion of suburbia for many decades. In fact, jobs, cultural institutions, and destination retail—once the exclusive domain of the core cities—as well as the residences of Americans of all socioeconomic levels, races, ages, and ethnicities migrated to suburban settings many decades ago.[3] It is no longer useful to talk about center cities *versus* suburbs. The "suburbs" are behaving more and more like center cities, and metropolises embrace both as they become more polycentric. We should no longer consider ourselves players in a zero-sum game wherein a suburb's gain is the city's loss. In fact, our research shows that the areas where suburban retrofits are most thriving—such as Atlanta, Denver, and Washington, DC—have all simultaneously experienced significant center city revivals. The demographic changes driving urbanization are impacting the entire metropolis and while this does not reduce competition, it does allow for systemic sustainable growth.

What concern us here are the areas of suburbs (and cities) that are dominated by suburban form. How can they be adapted to participate in and support the varied needs of interdependent metropolitan regions? And how can architectural and urban design practice contribute to the transformation process?

Figure I–3 A stand-alone office tower on an arterial road in Southfield, Michigan.

Figure I–4 A new, urban mixed-use building, developed by the Buckingham Companies, on a main street in the booming Indianapolis suburb of Carmel.

WHY RETROFITS? WHY NOW?

The conventional meaning of the word *retrofit* is to install parts or equipment not available during the original construction or manufacture. In this study, we intend the term to extend beyond the notions of rehabilitation or adaptive reuse to encompass the idea of systemic, long-lasting, transformative change. The majority of the individual projects discussed in this study go beyond adaptive reuse or rehabilitation to the point of completely redeveloping their sites. Thus the individual projects are examples of suburban retrofits. These redevelopments introduce the components of urbanism that were either illegal, undesired, or missing from much of suburbia; hence the larger project that we are advocating through these case studies is one of retrofitting suburbia itself.

Suburban retrofitting is a process of entirely revamping, and in many cases completely replacing, the conventional zoning that has dominated land-use decision making and development for decades. Formed by concerns about piecemeal development of outlying areas by the unscrupulous and codified by pragmatic adaptations of modernist planning ideology, these methods advocated strict separation of uses in distinct districts, linked together with a hierarchical, automobile-based transportation network. Despite the rational reasons for separating uses and separating people and buildings from cars, the results in suburbia have led to unsustainable automobile dependency and the continued reproduction of development patterns no longer based on contemporary households or workplaces. Instead, we highlight changes in codes and design techniques that prepare for an increasingly urban future.

The future also promises to alter our relationship to place as we continue to shift from an industrial to a postindustrial economy and society. This economy is digitally enabled to be less dependent on geography, making the qualities of individual places matter more in locational decisions. In many of the retrofitting projects we describe in these pages, a primary goal is to build and support an identifiable, durable *place* to which people will be attracted.

In this book we discuss what is becoming a wave of suburban retrofits. The reasons behind it can be summarized as follows:

Aging, Out-of-Date Properties, Often in First-Ring Suburbs

Dead malls and strip retail centers, old industrial parks, and small tract house subdivisions adjacent to transit stops make excellent retrofit sites. A fear of blight often trumps Not In My BackYard (NIMBY) resistance and may lead to the creation of public-private development partnerships and the provision of tax-increment financing (TIF) for regeneration initiatives.

Booming New Agglomerations in Edge Cities or "Edgeless Cities"

Concern over traffic and air quality triggers transit-oriented developments (TODs), planning for mass transit, and a market for more intown locations. "Underperforming asphalt" is replaced with a mix of uses, dwellings, and businesses organized on walkable streets and blocks.

Changing Locational and Economic Identity of the Suburbs

The so-called "bedroom suburbs," peripheral to the core city when first built, now occupy polycentric locations in their vastly expanded regions. Jobs have migrated to locations throughout the metropolitan region and many suburban areas have become economic engines in their own right and now seek to distinguish themselves as destinations.

Changing Demographics and Markets

Between the aging baby boomers and the surge of young echo boomers, increasing percentages of households are without children, even in suburbs. In addition, suburbia is increasingly characterized by diversity in income, race, and ethnicity. These factors are leading to a growing market for a more diverse selection of urban housing types and places.

Smart Growth Practices and Policies

Recognizing environmental limits to unchecked growth, suburban governments are planning for the future by implementing new policies that rethink zoning, anticipate the arrival of mass transit, and encourage the construction of affordable housing.

Our findings are supported by detailed case study analyses of recent suburban retrofits. Our study relates the history of each site and the actors and factors responsible for the retrofitting process, and also examines the underlying morphological structure, or physical form, of each site. To determine the manner in which the morphology has contributed to or impeded the retrofitting effort, we diagrammed the lots, streets, and buildings of each site at three points in time, spaced twenty to forty years apart (depending on the specific development trajectory of each site). A comparison of these diagrams yields insights about those patterns that are resistant to change and those that are more amenable to retrofitting.[4]

Each case study analysis addresses the demographic context for the retrofit, referencing the triggers discussed above, and describing likely future impacts of the retrofit, speculating that retrofits will help the United States accommodate future growth.

ORGANIZATION OF THE BOOK

Part I introduces the drivers of change, the retrofits, and the arguments for their significance. In Chapter 1 we situate suburban retrofitting within contemporary urban design discourse and anticipate and address the criticism that suburban retrofits are shallow "instant cities" and therefore not truly urban. Instead, we argue for the necessity of a large-scale approach, which we term *incremental metropolitanism,* as a way forward in the quest to systemically and sustainably transform suburban form.

A critically important aspect of these large-scale retrofitting projects is the opportunity to introduce compelling public space. While many argue that the necessity of a physical public realm has been superseded by virtual technologies, those of us who dwell in older urban areas, blessed with a physical network of well-used public spaces, know better. We acknowledge, however, that the results of the suburban retrofitting process are hybrid and open to question on many fronts. They will not soon compare to the urbanism experienced in Manhattan or San Francisco.

Part II of the book presents the stories of specific suburban retrofits, how they came to be, and the lessons learned. We discuss various ways in which these projects contribute to sustainability. The chapters are organized by the prototypical "before" condition: garden apartment complex, cul-de-sac subdivision, shopping mall, big box, strip mall, commercial strip, edge city, or office park. Analytical chapters alternate with chapters comprised of a detailed case study. The analytical chapters each focus on a different attribute of sustainable urban design: density, social life, mixed uses, public space, walkability, and interconnectivity. A discussion of the history of each use category precedes analysis of the ways in which that particular use category is being critiqued, redefined, and, ultimately, transformed. We illustrate numerous

examples of notable projects—some exemplary, some flawed—from around the country.

One purpose of writing this book is to demonstrate ways in which suburbs are transformed by developers, urban planners, architects, activists, policy makers, litigators, and financial institutions, as well as through the individual choices of millions of residents of all classes, ages, races, and ethnicities. We hope you enjoy their stories and are inspired to participate yourselves in one of the grand projects of the twenty-first century: the retrofitting of suburbia.

ACKNOWLEDGMENTS

As with many books, this one has had a long and fruitful gestation period. We are grateful to the Graham Foundation for providing us with a grant to support travel to document retrofits around the United States. We are also indebted to Donlyn Lyndon and the journal *Places* for inviting us to guest-edit an issue in 2005 on this topic. Thanks also to the peer reviewers of that issue (you know who you are!) and of course to the contributors to the issue—Renee Chow, Michael Dobbins, Michael Freedman, Paul Hess, Lars Laerup, Christopher Leinberger, Darren Petrucci, Susan Rogers, and Roger Sherman—whose ideas permeate this volume. Editors Nancy Levinson and Bill Saunders of the *Harvard Design Magazine* have also challenged us to hone our arguments with writings that prepared much of the intellectual ground for this book. The Ax:son Johnson Foundation's support of Ellen as a guest professor at Lund University, Sweden in 2006–2007 enabled release time for her to write at a critical time. And thank you to the team at John Wiley & Sons, to John Czarnecki for convincing us we were actually ready to take this on, and to Alda Trabucchi for bringing us to completion.

We also wish to thank the students and faculty of the College of Architecture at Georgia Tech, where Ellen has been at the helm as director of the architecture program since 2001 and where June first taught a course on the history of suburbia. In particular, Ed Akins, Doug Allen, Richard Dagenhart, Steve French, Tom Galloway, Michael Gamble, Ryan Gravel, David Green, Nancey Green Leigh, Sabir Khan, Jude LeBlanc, Fred Pearsall, Stuart Romm, and Catherine Ross have shared our curiosity and their insights about Atlanta's dynamic development. Students Sahnur Bostan, Fred Godbolt, Kristen Halloran, and Renee Hartley provided valuable assistance with graphics and background research. Ellen's earlier students at UVA and MIT offered more inspiration than they know, including Ben Chung, Christine McGrath, Andrew Miller, and Wendy Redfield.

Many of the designers, developers, and planners who contributed to projects featured in this book are members of the Congress for the New Urbanism (CNU). We acknowledge the crucial role that the Congress has played in recent decades in forcing the hand of "business as usual" suburban developers, and in empowering designers and planners to believe that the rules of the game can be radically changed. CNU's seminal publications, *Greyfields into Goldfields* and *Malls into Mainstreets* were important precursors to this book. Among those who encouraged and assisted us in telling these stories of transformation are G. B. Arrington, Jackie Benson, Peter Calthorpe, Don Carter, Hank Dittmar, Victor Dover, Andres Duany, Peter Elmlund, Doug Farr, Will Fleissig, Harrison Fraker, Larry Frank, Ray Gindroz, Ellen Greenberg, Seth Harry, Doug Kelbaugh, Liz Moule, Chris Nelson, John Norquist, Elizabeth Plater-Zyberk, Stefanos Polyzoides, Shelley Poticha, Lee Sobel, Dan Solomon, Galina Tahchieva, Emily Talen, Tim Van Meter, Laurie Volk, and Todd Zimmerman. We also thank Phyllis Bleiweiss and the Seaside Institute for inviting us to opine on suburban retrofitting for professional audiences.

Several urbanists graciously toured us around their regions, including Stephanie Bothwell, Nan Ellin, Joe Kohl, and Greg Tung. Thanks also to interlocutors Marta Gutman, David Kitchens, Paul Lukez, Grahame Shane, David Smiley, Michael Sorkin, and Anne Tate.

Numerous design firms, developers, and municipal officials generously shared information and images with us, too many to list individually here, and we would like to thank them all for their professional generosity. Keep up the good work!

And, of course, we wish to express our apologies to our families for our absence at more than a few holiday gatherings and our deepest thanks for their loving support. To our parents, Alden Dunham, Louise Green Dunham, and Jack and Eunice Williamson, we can't underestimate our appreciation in particular for your willingness to invest in our education and build our confidence. Words are inadequate to express our thanks to David Schiminovich for providing loving encouragement as well as space and time for a busy mother to work, to Theo for being a constant inspiration, and to Phil Jones not only for his unwavering love and patience, but also for his invaluable assistance with the photographic illustrations.

As a final note, we wish to acknowledge the suburbs we grew up in, some of which are featured in these pages: Princeton, New Jersey; Westwood and Needham, Massachusetts; Mt. Lebanon, Pennsylvania; and New Malden, Surrey, UK.

PART ONE
THE ARGUMENT

Chapter 1

Instant Architecture, Instant Cities, and Incremental Metropolitanism

INSTANT CITIES AND SUBURBAN RETROFITS

The goal of urbanizing suburbs calls into question many long-standing cultural stereotypes. If cities are conventionally understood as old places with new buildings versus suburbs as new places with simulations of older buildings, how do we make sense of suburban retrofits?[1] How do these projects challenge expectations of responsible urban design—both in terms of respect for the immediate context and reconfiguring metropolitan areas? How should we evaluate their success? This chapter situates the arguments for retrofitting suburbia within contemporary urban design polemics at three different scales: instant architecture, instant cities, and incremental metropolitanism.

In alignment with democratic ideals, professionals engaged in city making have come to share a pervasive enthusiasm for incremental urbanism—cities that evolve over time through gradual accretions and infill so that the collective form bears the imprint of a broad spectrum of interests. Much as case law is shaped by incremental judicial decisions

to reflect both our past and our current values, urban form that has been continually added to and adjusted is generally perceived as an authentic representation of culture. Organic metaphors further reinforce our perception that urban growth naturally morphs not through the artifice of master plans and government policies but in response to ever-changing conditions.

There is no question that the world's great cities exemplify incremental urbanism and that sensitive interventions that both respect the existing urban structure and advance evolving cultures over time contribute to great places. Much of the motivation behind this book is to encourage more such interventions in suburban areas.

However, love of incremental urbanism can also lead to indiscriminate disdain for that which is perceived as inauthentic. Large new urbanist projects in particular are often derided as "instant cities" and "faux downtowns."[2] This kind of design critique applies to many suburban retrofits, but often fails to distinguish the detrimental effects of "instant architecture" from the potential benefits of "instant cities." At a time when climate change and peak oil prices call for vast swaths of existing suburban areas to be retrofitted on a scale and at a speed that is beyond the capacity of incremental urbanism, it is worth recognizing when the kind of large-scale changes associated with "instant cities" might be welcomed rather than shunned.

The global urgency of reducing greenhouse gases provides the latest and most time-sensitive imperative for reshaping sprawl development patterns, for converting areas that now foster the largest per capita carbon footprints into more sustainable, less auto-dependent places.[3] The transforming of aging and underperforming shopping centers, office parks, garden apartment complexes, and other prototypical large suburban properties into more urban places allows new population growth to be redirected from metropolitan greenfield edges into more central, VMT-reducing, greyfield redevelopment.[4] It also allows for the development of an incremental metropolitanism at a scale far more capable of confronting the problems of sprawl than incremental urbanism is. This jump in scale is more relevant both to the realities of contemporary development practices and to the scope of the challenges confronting us. Ironically, at a time when well over 75% of U.S. construction is in the suburbs, the critiques of faux urbanism often betray more nostalgia for no-longer-as-tenable development practices than the projects' designs do.

Later chapters document the before and after transformations of these low-density, auto-dependent, single-use, suburban formats into urban places, and the roles of the public and private realms in effecting these changes. Some of the changes have in fact been incremental and indicative of both gradual demographic shifts and public efforts to induce change. For instance, every one of the original Levittowns has added not only countless additions to individual houses but also multiunit housing for seniors as inhabitants have aged. A decade after Boulder,

Colorado, revised zoning and setback regulations along suburban arterials, new mixed-use buildings with sidewalk cafés appear cheek by jowl with older carpet-supply stores set behind large parking lots.

Across the country those older stand-alone retail buildings are also increasingly being adaptively reused for community-serving purposes. A dozen Wal-Mart stores were converted to churches between 2002 and 2005. As described in Chapter 4, La Grande Orange in Phoenix is a reborn strip mall whose locally owned restaurants and shops have become so popular that it has its own T-shirts and is regularly mentioned as a selling point in real estate ads for the neighborhood. Daly Genik Architects made an L-shaped mini-mall into an award-winning elementary school in Los Angeles. The addition of sidewalks and pervious public green space figured into both Meyer, Scherer, and Rockcastle's elegant transformation of a grocery store into a public library in Texas, and The Beck Group's award-winning conversion of a Super Kmart into a megachurch in Georgia. Many other vacant big-box stores have been converted to call centers and office space—including the headquarters for Hormel Foods, which includes the Spam Museum in a former Kmart in Minnesota. There are countless additional examples of this kind of recycling that show welcome but minor improvements to the physical and social infrastructure.[5]

However, retrofitting's greater potential goes well beyond incremental adaptive reuse or renovation. By urbanizing larger suburban properties with a denser, walkable, synergistic mix of uses and housing types, more significant reductions in carbon emissions, gains in social capital, and changes to systemic growth patterns can be achieved. On emissions alone, new comprehensive research asserts that "it is realistic to assume a 30% cut in VMT with compact development."[6] The key to achieving this target is the appropriate balancing of uses so that, once on-site, residents, shoppers, office workers, and others can accomplish multiple, everyday trips without getting back in their cars or back on the road. This allows mixed-use new urbanist greyfield retrofits to routinely achieve projections of 25% to 30% internal trip capture rates. In turn, this means that such projects will generate 25% to 30% fewer net external trips on nearby roads than a project of equivalent density but without the same urban qualities. Such capturing of internal trips is dependent upon achieving the critical mass associated with instant cities, not with incremental changes to the suburban pattern.

Are these projections to be trusted? Atlantic Station, an example of compact mixed-use development adjacent to midtown Atlanta on a former steel mill site, is generating far greater reductions in VMT than initial estimates projected. In a region where the average employed resident drives 66 miles per day, employees in Atlantic Station are driving an average of 10.7 miles per day and residents an average of 8 miles per day.[7]

The most dramatic and prevalent retrofits tend to be on dead mall sites, retrofits such as Belmar in Lakewood, Colorado; Mizner Park in Boca Raton; and Cottonwood outside Salt Lake City. The numerous examples have each replaced a typical low-rise enclosed shopping mall surrounded by parking lots with a more or less interconnected, walkable street grid, lushly planted public spaces, and ground-level retail topped by two to eight stories of offices and residences. In Denver alone, seven of the region's thirteen malls have closed to be retrofitted. There are also, however, significant retrofits on the land adjacent to thriving malls. Retrofits such as Downtown Kendall/Dadeland outside Miami incorporate a mall (the Dadeland Mall) and new twenty-plus-story

residential towers, as does Perimeter Place adjacent to Perimeter Center Mall in Atlanta. Both are examples of how thirty-year-old "edge cities," even *bête noire* Tysons Corner, are being repositioned by infilling and urbanizing.

Suburban office and industrial parks are also being retrofitted. The parking lots of an Edward Durell Stone–designed office park of ten-story Kennedy Center–like buildings in Hyattsville, Maryland, are getting infilled with a new Main Street and mix of uses to become University Town Center. The owners of a low-rise industrial park in Westwood, Massachusetts, are taking advantage of its location on a commuter rail line to redevelop it as Westwood Station, a 4.5-million-square-foot, four-to-five-story live-work-shop TOD and the largest suburban development project ever in Massachusetts.

Golf courses, car dealerships, park-and-rides, garden apartment complexes, residential subdivisions, and entire commercial strip corridors are being retrofitted in ways that integrate rather than isolate uses and regenerate underperforming asphalt into urban neighborhoods.

What's driving all this? Several factors: reduced percentages of households with children and a growing market for multiunit housing in the suburbs,[8] continued growth in the percentage of jobs in suburban locations; regional growth patterns that are giving leapfrogged suburban areas a new centrality; rising gas prices making housing on the periphery less affordable; lengthening commutes making leapfrogged suburban locations more attractive; and local smart-growth policies and transit investments that are limiting sprawl and redirecting growth to existing infrastructure. Rising land values; the dearth of good, cheap, undeveloped sites in increasingly built-out suburban markets; and aging greyfield properties with an abundance of surface parking lots are all factoring into a changed suburban market.

Collectively, these market forces and policies are enabling implementation of the principal benefit of projects like these: the retrofitting of the underlying settlement structure itself so as to change unhealthy suburban patterns and behaviors into more sustainable ones. Incremental infill within as-of-right zoning in most suburban municipalities is simply not a feasible path toward achieving diversification or densification. The larger, denser, and more urban the redevelopment, the more ability its designers have to change the existing development pattern and

- reduce vehicle miles traveled and improve public health by creating a transit-served or transit-ready mix of uses in a walkable street pattern connected to adjacent uses
- reduce land consumption and per capita costs of public investment by absorbing growth that without alternatives would otherwise expand in sprawl and edgeless cities
- increase the feasibility and efficiency of transit
- increase local interconnectivity
- increase permeable surfaces and green space
- increase public and civic space
- increase choice in housing type and affordability
- increase diversification of the tax base
- establish an urban node within a polycentric region

The key design challenge to altering the suburban settlement structure is internal and external integration of the parts over time and over multiple parcels. This research has yet to uncover built examples of connected culs-de-sac (a long-standing holy grail of suburban reform) or other perfectly seamless transitions between properties. But designers are producing innovative adaptations to zoning and subdivision regulations to overcome suburban fragmentation. Michael Gamble and Jude LeBlanc have proposed trading the right to build liner buildings within the front setback along arterials for giving up half the width of a new street on the side setback as a means to gradually establish a finer-grained street and pedestrian network on suburban superblocks. Similarly, Elizabeth Plater-Zyberk, Victor Dover, and Joseph Kohl have developed a unique strategy for linking open spaces within Downtown Kendall/Dadeland's 324 acres. Working for Miami-Dade County on new zoning across numerous parcels, they devised a system of points at the corners of property boundaries to which each owner's mandated 15% of open space had to connect. Their suggested, rather than mandated, shapes of public space have been substantially followed by property owners and are far more appropriately sized to the development as a whole than a series of uncoordinated 15% bits would have been.[9]

Internal integration of parts is indeed far easier to control on single-parcel sites—especially sites of 30 or more acres. Projects as small as 15 acres, such as San Diego's Uptown District on the site of a former Sears store, can transform the character of suburban areas and excite local imagination about further change. But larger parcels can more easily justify the inclusion of public space, decked parking, and a fine-grained street network on suburban superblocks.[10] Large sites are also more likely than small ones to be able and/or required to include housing for a mix of incomes. This has not been universally achieved—witness the exclusively high-end residences at Santana Row or exclusively lower-end apartments at CityCenter Englewood—but projects like Mizner Park, Belmar, and Perimeter Place provide a range of housing types, tenures, and costs. While they do not contain the social and physical diversity of incremental cities, the degree of internal integration, diversification, and densification of these "instant cities" deserves commendation.

Large, single-parcel projects also foster integration external to the property. By forcing municipalities to address rezoning and use tax-increment financing to provide infrastructure upgrades for the new density, larger projects are gradually reforming the regulations and financing practices that otherwise continue to favor sprawl. Large projects in particular increase a municipality's experience with and capability to further permit mixed use, mixed incomes, shared parking, form-based codes, context-sensitive street standards, transfer-of-development rights, and other tools, standards, and regulations that foster urban development patterns. As a result, one successful retrofit tends to breed another.

At the same time, the financing and development communities are gaining experience with evaluating mixed-use public-private deals. Gradually, the financial performances of large projects are providing the predictable metrics that lenders require to offer the most competitive rates not only to conventional suburban development but also to urbanizing redevelopment (increasing the feasibility of including affordable housing). Evidence of the magnitude of change in the rules of the game is that the big players have now stepped onto the field.

As detailed in Chapter 7, General Growth Properties, the second-largest mall owner in the country and the second-largest U.S.-based publicly traded REIT, is retrofitting the Cottonwood Mall outside Salt Lake City as a test case for repositioning its underperforming and/or redundant properties into mixed-use town centers. Recognition of the changed market has also led many of the country's high-production single-family home residential builders over the past two years to start "urban" divisions offering lofts, yoga studios, and billiards

lounges.[11] It should not be surprising that these divisions have been the best performers when the rest of the housing market has tanked.[12]

INSTANT ARCHITECTURE, INSTANT PUBLIC SPACE

On the one hand, the urban divisions by K. Hovnanian Homes, KB Homes, Toll Brothers, and Centex Homes, along with smaller "urban" retail formats by Wal-Mart, Target, and Home Depot (their "neighborhood format" is approximately 30,000 square feet in two stories instead of 115,000 square feet on 10 acres, and it incorporates more "do it for me" than "do it yourself" home decor) are a promising indication that even the big guns are recognizing both the market for and the benefits of urbanism.[13] The impact could be enormous if the new divisions perform well enough to shift these companies' focus away from spreading unwalkable, single-use suburban formats across the country. Combining affordability with urbanism in new construction, whether in new developments or redevelopments, has been difficult, and the expertise of these companies in providing affordable products should be welcomed.

On the other hand, their mass-produced "instant architecture," seemingly dropped from a catalog onto land scraped and flattened of distinguishing features, is highly unwelcome. Nor is this a problem limited to the big production builders. The retail and residential buildings of many retrofits are engineered to optimize sales and parking rather than designed to facilitate synergistic interaction between uses and respond to the nuances of place or the complexities of mixed-use building. The time and energy that goes into coordinating the highly varied ground floor footprints for different retailers and restaurateurs with

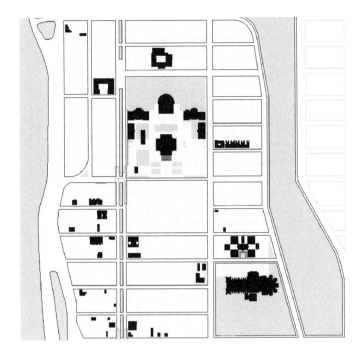
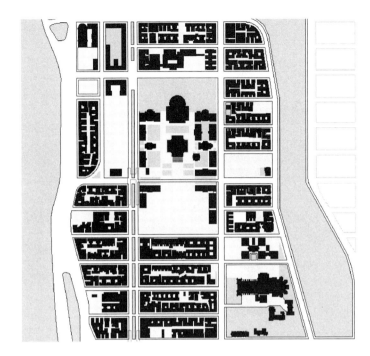

Figure 1–1 A comparison of Morningside Heights in Manhattan from 1897 and 1915 illustrates the astonishing pace of development in the neighborhood. In 1897, when the development of the adjacent Upper West Side had just been completed, the only buildings in Morningside Heights were institutional: colleges, a cathedral, and a hospital. Less than two decades later, the building fabric was entirely filled in with residential buildings. designed and constructed by interconnected groups of investors, architects, and builders. (Source: Bromley Atlas of the City of New York, Manhattan Island.)

a mix of residential unit types above, surrounding a deck of dedicated, shared, and public parking, is far from "instant." But the complexity, especially in the hurried atmosphere of a charrette, tends to default to the formulaic. Despite occasional instructions such as Columbia Pike's "Keep the Pike Funky," form-based codes risk dumbing down design when they are overly prescriptive about style. In their efforts to raise the bar on the design's relationship to the urban context, they can also lower the bar on the designer's ability to incrementally improve the architecture of the place. Designers sometimes self-deprecatingly refer to their "wallpaper" facades. Too much of this uniformity, even in relatively high-density retrofits, results in a pervasive air of predictability and control that is more suburban than urban—at least at first.

Do instant cities age well? How many great urban neighborhoods rolled out repetitive examples of

the "instant architecture" of their day? A surprising number: the brick bow fronts of Boston's South End, Brooklyn's brownstones, and countless others. The entire Upper West Side of Manhattan was graded and rebuilt in one decade, 1885 to 1895. In 1886, the *New York Times* noted, "Thousands of carpenters and masons are engaged in rearing substantial buildings where a year ago nothing was to be seen but market gardens or barren rocky fields." The rapid urbanization of Morningside Heights was next, and so on up the island of Manhattan.[14] (See Figure 1–1.) However, in contrast to contemporary suburban construction, these earlier examples tended to have much better workmanship, materials, and detailing. This is especially important in an urban context, where good detailing contributes to walkability by rewarding up-close pedestrian viewing. At the larger scale, the good bones of these neighborhoods have provided

an accommodating urban structure for ensuing generations, allowing improvement and adaptation over time. The trees have matured, adding varied light, shade, and scale to streets that might have initially appeared stark, monotonous, even "faux." Individual stoop gardens, corner shops, paint choices, additions, repairs, and other responses to needs and opportunities further differentiate the urban experience and its patina of inhabitant participation.[15]

One could argue that many postwar suburban subdivisions have similarly improved. Mature plantings, house additions, and surface treatments have differentiated what were initially mass-produced, repetitive products. In fact, less than 1% of the houses in Levittown, New York, remain in their original state, without additions or remodeling. (The most public part of Levittown, the retail strips on Hempstead Turnpike, is, however, badly decayed.)

While it is extremely difficult to reproduce either the character of individuated inhabitation or high-quality detailing in affordable new construction, retrofits such as Addison Circle and Legacy Town Center outside Dallas (described in Chapter 9) are taking the more urban route by investing in generous, high-quality public spaces. (See Figures 1-3 and 9-11.) Especially in suburban contexts, the parks, amphitheaters, cafés, and street life compensate for the lack of private outdoor space in urban housing. Some

Figures 1-2 & 1-3 The building of Legacy Town Center outside Dallas in the summer of 2007 (below left) looks much like the building of the then middle-class area at 116th Street and Lenox Avenue in Manhattan in 1893 (above left), except that in Dallas the displaced cattle have been sentimentally memorialized in bronze. We may feel sympathy for the shanty dwellers displaced in New York during the rapid urbanization of upper Manhattan, but given the huge disconnect between their makeshift wooden dwellings and the high-density apartments that replaced them, there was never any suggestion that the development might be gradual.

critics scoff at the "pseudo-civilizing" effect of sanitized streetscapes that reference "real" urban places but lack the diversity of urban people. We agree that the diversity of people within public space is a useful measure of urbanity and nurtures the creativity of Richard Florida's "creative class." However, the establishment of public space where none previously existed is the first step. And again, if we look to history, the population of Morningside Heights diversified over time as the buildings aged and their markets differentiated. As its inhabitants and buildings mature, Addison Circle's wide, tree-lined sidewalks and art-filled common green may well accommodate a broader range of incomes and ages. In the meantime, the streetscapes of suburban retrofits accommodate the socializing activities of their many young professionals and shift the focus of suburban outdoor space from playgrounds and ball fields to more urban and public, and less family-centered, spaces. Belmar's avant-garde Laboratory of Arts and Ideas and the museums of CityCenter Englewood and Mizner Park further enhance public life in these "instant cities."

One way to enhance the character and diversity of the public realm of retrofits is to take advantage of the unique adaptive reuse opportunities in redevelopment. Although most aging low-rise suburban buildings lack the systems or construction quality to merit restoration, the most distinctive retrofits tend to creatively retain at least some buildings. Surrey Central City, discussed in Chapter 6, revived a mall by grafting a new five-story galleria of university classrooms on top. The multistory department store buildings of several dead mall retrofits have been converted to housing, offices, and city halls. As counters to "instant architecture," these legacies contribute a sense of history, diversity, affordability (renting for less than new construction), and a reduction of waste.[16] They

also force the master plan to engage with existing conditions rather than lay down an entirely pre-engineered template of formulaic block-sizes based on optimum building footprints for wrapped deck housing.[17] The resulting quirks contribute enormously to the creativity and quality of the placemaking. They can also insert a cool factor to suburban places and help recruit the anticubicle, anticorporate digerati. Upper Rock in Rockville, Maryland, and Cloud 9 Sky Flats in Minnetonka, Minnesota, incorporate modern loft conversions of suburban office buildings. These are but some examples of how retrofitted sites formerly associated with office-park-dads and moms-in-minivans are now also bustling with hipsters, divorcees, and empty nesters.

INCREMENTAL METROPOLITANISM

Bit by bit, beneath the static image of uniform tract houses, many suburbs are undergoing significant physical, social, and cultural change. For the first time in history, suburban municipalities now house more people living in poverty than central cities do.[18] This trend is attributed in part to the increased immigrant populations in "first-ring suburbs" built shortly after World War II. Maps in 2008 showing mortgage foreclosures concentrated in the newer outermost suburbs indicate the likelihood of further decentralization of poverty and an ever-shifting terrain. Suburban retrofits have also contributed to rising property prices. Entire subdivisions in suburban Washington, DC, and Atlanta have been bought up house by house, and as discussed in Chapter 2, one subdivision in Atlanta even self-organized and put itself up for sale for redevelopment. New transit systems, infrastructure improvements, programs to fund planning studies, and new overlay zoning district designations are further incentivizing suburban urbanization.

But all this is not happening everywhere. It is happening at specific nodes and along specific corridors, generally where the transportation infrastructure (usually with some improvements) can support it. The outer rings of new exurban expansion continue to be low density overall, but the densified retrofits and countless revitalized small-town Main Streets are joining the edge cities as increasingly significant suburban activity centers. Arthur C. Nelson, coordinator of the Metropolitan Institute at Virginia Tech, estimates that 2.8 million acres of greyfields will become available in the next fifteen years. If only one quarter is redeveloped into mixed-use centers, they have the potential to supply half the housing required by 2030. As a result, the regional pattern emerging and likely to become more prominent is increasingly polycentric. While we are indeed still decentralizing away from central cities, we are also recentralizing around new and existing suburban centers—and becoming more sustainable in the process. More bottom-up than top-down, these new instant cities are demonstrations of an incremental metropolitanism.[19] And, while it is fair to fault instant cities when their replication of incremental urbanism is unsatisfying, the more relevant issue today is how well each contributes to retrofitting the larger systems of sprawl.

One of the first steps is to recognize the inefficiencies of sprawl development. Most lower-priced houses are at the outer edges but come with higher transportation costs. Jobs and retail are located along arterials, but typically with little transit access. Thoroughfares designed for high-speed travel between centers have become so lined with uses that they do not work well for either access or mobility. And all is designed in isolated pods. Even larger retrofits run the risk of becoming stand-alone fragments unless their urban structure integrates them into both local networks and larger sustainable systems. Only as nodes of a polycentric metropolis can they contribute to regional efficiencies in transit and other civil infrastructure, per capita land and energy conservation, shorter commute distances, lower housing and transportation costs, a jobs-housing balance, and specialized labor agglomeration.

The inclusion of increasingly significant amounts of office space within mixed-use retrofits is particularly important for balancing polycentric growth and reducing VMT. Twinbrook Station in Rockville, Maryland, and Lindbergh City Center in Atlanta are integrating twelve- and fourteen-story corporate office buildings onto the sites of former park-and-ride lots. SkySong in Phoenix and Surrey Central City outside Vancouver are building incubator office space for Arizona State University and Simon Fraser University, respectively, on the site of a dead shopping center and a mall's parking lot.

Far from serving as self-contained villages, today's retrofits simultaneously serve as gathering spaces for the immediate residents, who use the public spaces as extensions of their private space; immediate and nearby office workers for their coffee breaks, lunches, and after-work drinks; nearby suburban parents combining get-togethers with errands; teens and singles seeking friendship and entertainment; and more. In other words, they serve a greater diversity of people than did single-group places like sports bars. They may not yet be as urban as "real cities," but they *are* relatively vibrant nodes.

These efficiencies are not always immediately apparent. A map of contemporary retrofits around Washington, DC, drawn in the same manner as Joel Garreau's maps of "edge cities," reveals a similar peripheral pattern. (See Figure 1–4.) However, whereas edge cities are predominantly located at suburban spoke-and-hub highway intersections, retrofits are

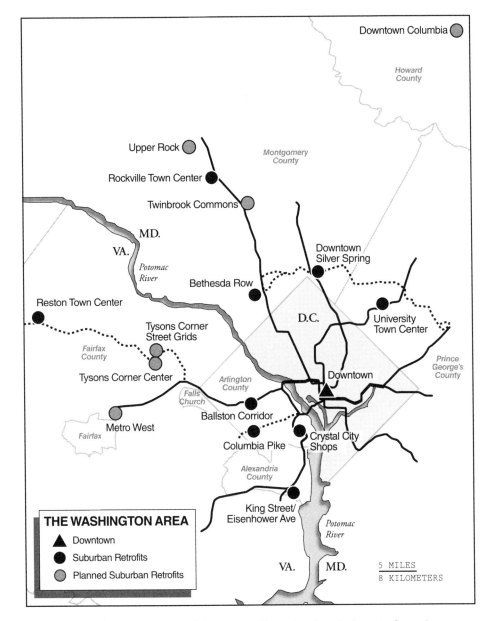

Figure 1–4 Washington, DC, is one of the most prolific markets for suburban retrofits as shown here, where they are mapped in relation to the Metro system. The presence or promise of mass transit, rather than new highways, is a significant trigger for higher-density redevelopment.

predominantly located at the intersection of existing or proposed DC Metrorail stations and suburban arterial corridors. While Garreau's maps of edge cities promised the benefits of a polycentric metropolis, their extreme auto dependency and lack of local or larger interconnectivity other than highways resulted in lengthened commute times, overcrowded roads, reduced access to jobs by those most in need, and a suburban privileging of private space.

Washington, DC's retrofits are far better positioned to deliver on that original promise. Their internal urban structure minimizes auto dependency and values public space and shared commitments to the common good. As important (if not more), their location on transit vastly improves the metropolis's efficiencies. Transit systems also benefit: those in single-center regions are far less efficient than those in polycentric regions, where suburban stations are destinations throughout the day, not only for the evening commute.

Unfortunately, most potential suburban retrofit sites are not on transit lines. And while they can still enhance local conditions, many dots remain to be connected if they are to achieve the benefits of a more sustainable metropolis. There are two principal strategies on the horizon. The first is to add transit to improve access, encourage even greater differentiation between nodes, and reduce VMT. The planned extensions of DC Metrorail through Tysons Corner is an example of this strategy and reveals the high cost and design difficulties of inserting stations and TODs into an edge city not planned for them. The hope is that densification of enough retrofitted sites will make suburban transit feasible. However, the track record so far indicates that more often transit in the suburbs is what makes densification feasible. In fact, examination of over eighty retrofits reveals that the arrival of a rail system is one of the strongest triggers for large-scale suburban redevelopment. In addition to the examples of Washington, DC, and Denver, the availability (or construction) of rail transit in Boston, Dallas, Los Angeles, and Phoenix has stimulated suburban retrofitting at existing and proposed rail stations.[20]

The second strategy for connecting the dots is to retrofit corridors themselves. This is discussed in more detail in Chapter 4. The general argument is that if commercial strip corridors are made more attractive and safer to pedestrians, they can better attract redevelopment. Where nodal development is preferred, transfer of development rights can be used to downzone thoroughfares between intersections and concentrate development at intersections. While this strategy is not in practice yet, there are several examples of public agencies retrofitting corridors either through rezoning or through new streetscaping. In the most ambitious examples, commercial strip corridors are reconstructed as urban boulevards capable of both handling high traffic volume, including streetcars or buses, and attracting dense urban housing, offices, and retail stores.[21] Cathedral City, California, converted four blocks of what had become a commercial strip corridor back into its downtown by retrofitting it into a multiway boulevard. Palm-lined medians separate the high-speed traffic from slower local traffic and wide sidewalks. Now serving as the town's Main Street, the retrofitted corridor has attracted upscale hotels, shops, and housing to join the new city hall on a site that would not previously have been considered attractive.

The more incremental approach for retrofitting corridors is to use form-based codes to require more urban sidewalks, build-to-lines, and pedestrian-oriented treatment of ground floors. As discussed in Chapter 4, Arlington County, Virginia, is using form-based codes, fast permitting, and the promise of a streetcar as incentives for its ongoing redevelopment of low-rise supermarkets and strip malls on Columbia Pike into six- to ten-story mixed-use buildings.

HOW SUSTAINABLE? HOW URBAN?

So how well do instant cities and suburban retrofits live up to their sustainable aspirations? While we are optimistic, each case is unique and merits consideration of at least the following questions.

- At metropolitan and regional scales, does the project make it easier for people to have access to jobs, affordable housing, and affordable transportation while simultaneously reducing VMT and carbon footprints? Or is it gentrifying an important remnant of an affordable landscape and/or draining an existing downtown?
- Are there tangible means, such as transfer of development rights, to link densification at targeted nodes with equally targeted land conservation elsewhere? Or are developers getting a free ride as local communities get overburdened with traffic and displacement and the region as a whole benefits little?
- At the local scale, does the settlement have an urban structure that supports interconnectivity, density, transit, and walkability? Has it triggered further redevelopment?
- Will its design and mix of uses improve with age and endure, or will it remain a fragment of drive-to walkable "product" with a life span driven by its retail and limited to the fashionability of its scenography?

- At the building scale, does it offer a variety of housing choices to accommodate a diverse population with varied needs and ideas about public and private space, or are the choices too similar and the expectations of behavior too conformist?

These are difficult to answer, but they will be at the heart of local and metropolitan politics as we move beyond debates of sprawl versus smart growth and tackle the thorny specifics of implementing real change.

In many respects, the even more difficult assessment is determining how well instant cities and suburban retrofits live up to their urban aspirations. It is easy to compare them to "real" cities and find them lacking the culture, excitement, diversity, conflict, grit, and suffering that coexist in core cities. But this misses the point. Instant cities and suburban retrofits are not core cities. They are urban nodes within a new polycentric metropolis that simultaneously complement the core city's downtown and serve a predominantly suburban population. They are hybrids and reflect aspects of both centeredness and decentralization.

This hybridity is revealed in many ways, including the following:

- suburban parking ratios and urban streetscapes
- ambiguous "public" spaces developed in public-private partnerships and privately owned or leased
- urban building types filled mostly with suburban chain retail outlets
- new, single-ownership parcels deliberately masked to look old and multiparceled
- urban qualities delivered at suburban costs
- transit orientation and automobile dependency

- the appearance of self-contained village/town centers and reliance on larger networks of shoppers, workers, and visitors
- local placemaking by national developers and designers

Hybrid network nodes are neither suburban nor urban. As a result, they are prone to critique from the advocates of both better understood categories. But are cities and suburbs really so different in the polycentric metropolis? The old dichotomy of suburb versus city as the separation of home and work was always oversimplified.[22] Today it is further complicated by continued metropolitan decentralization, new forces of recentralization, the replication of national retailers throughout, and the extended networks afforded by global communications. Over 40% of U.S. office space is now in the suburbs,[23] but many of the same metropolitan regions seeing the most retrofitting in suburban contexts are also seeing population growth in their central cities.[24] Postwar suburbs originally built at the edges of the metropolis have been so surpassed by new growth (often losing property value in the process) that they now enjoy relatively central locations. New instant cities exploit those centralities and activate them as metropolitan nodes in a network increasingly reinforced by mass transit. Retrofitting ushers in networked urbanity in which living, working, shopping, and playing are no longer separated (but neither are they entirely conjoined). The networked urbanity of metropolitanism reinterprets the Aristotelian ideal of the city—living together well—at the larger scale. This bodes well for confronting the challenges of economic and environmental sustainability but is less promising for dealing with entrenched social inequity.

Although instant cities and suburban retrofits are neither as sustainable nor as urban as older established cities, they are more sustainable and more urban than the conditions they have replaced and, as such, have great potential to shape the metropolis. They also have many challenges, not the least of which are constructing the infrastructure to support them and addressing gentrification. Perhaps most important, they need to recognize the significance of their leadership in the new metropolis and the accompanying expectation of representing larger cultural aspirations.

Today, instant cities and suburban retrofits are for the most part more exciting programmatically than architecturally. Serving as conventional background buildings to the outdoor public rooms of the streets they foreground, their buildings express a far greater valuation of placemaking and public space than did the private object buildings they replaced. This is a good thing, but too often, as at Perimeter Place near Atlanta, banal contemporary buildings are aggregated into quasi-urbanistic configurations but are utterly lacking in meaningful architectural expression. At other times, as in many of the projects featured in the pages to come, instead of being instant architecture, the buildings are very well detailed, even within tight budgets, and thoughtfully scaled to transition from the existing context to greater density with careful attention to sustainability.

While many critics fault traditional styling as nostalgic, it should be respected when it is done well and converts a community's fear of change into aspirations for urbanism. Some of us would like to see more stylistic diversity and experimentation exploring hybridity in the architecture of suburban retrofits. And this may come as retrofits become more common and communities less fearful of change. But discussions of architectural style miss the point. *The point is urbanism*.

Americans have an opportunity to retrofit the suburbs into more urban places that reduce VMT, expand public space, diversify housing choices, and conserve undeveloped land at the periphery. We need *both* incremental changes *and* instant cities in order to reshape socially and environmentally destructive sprawling patterns into healthier, polycentric metropolises. We need to better understand the myriad dynamic systems of more sustainable regions, places, and buildings. Above all, we need informed imaginations that can look at entrenched patterns and question alternative possibilities—while working with communities. This is an exciting agenda for all of the professions involved with the built environment. We would do well to heed Michael Sorkin's wise advice to see "the good city as an evolving project."[25]

PART TWO
THE EXAMPLES

Chapter 2

Retrofitting Garden Apartments and Residential Subdivisions to Address Density and the New Demographics

In 2000, U.S. Census data confirmed that more than 50% of the population of the United States was living in urbanized areas outside of central cities—in other words, in suburbs. That amounts to over 140 million American suburbanites. In his groundbreaking 1985 history of suburbia in the United States, *Crabgrass Frontier,* Kenneth Jackson defined American suburbanization as uniquely characterized by low-density residential areas, affluent and middle-class residents, home owner-ship, and long commutes to work.[1] This definition certainly applies to a great many suburban areas, but how representative is it? In what ways is the residential experience of suburbia changing? How might today's retrofits support these changes?

The demographic profile of suburbanites today deviates significantly from the stereotypical imagery in the popular media of affluent dual-parent house-holds—driving child-filled minivans through predomi-nantly white, often gated, neighborhoods. Further-more, recent historical scholarship is bringing to light the ways in which socioeconomic, ethnic, and racial diversity have *always* been characteristic of suburban

settings, despite generations of commentators who assumed otherwise. (See Figure 2–1.) Historian Becky Nicolaides points out how the scathing mid-century critiques of Jane Jacobs, Lewis Mumford, and William

Figure 2–1 The lively scene in a barbershop in Park Forest, Illinois, the prototypical "Organization Man" suburb. Socia-bility persists along with profound demographic change.

Whyte created "a recognizable cultural icon that lives on even in the popular culture of our own day." She cites the "hellish 'burbs" depicted in recent films like *American Beauty* and the popular television series *Desperate Housewives*.[2] Despite these persistent stereotypes and critiques, a close look will reveal that there is a great deal of demographic diversity within suburbs and, with retrofitting, increasing diversity in physical patterns as well.

NEVER HOMOGENOUS? THE NEW SUBURBAN HISTORY

In the conclusion of his seminal 1987 book *Bourgeois Utopias,* historian Robert Fishman observed, "Suburbia was at once the most characteristic product of explosive urban expansion and a desperate protest against it."[3] This observation of the intertwined nature of suburbs and cities was a crucial corrective to the usual descriptions and critiques of suburbia up to that point, which had tended to consider it in a vacuum and had emphasized the white affluent and middle-class bedroom suburb, reified by television sitcoms and movies, over all others. Suburbia was not viewed as a historical construct that changes over time.[4]

The so-called suburban myth, which posited that suburbs are homogenous landscapes of white middle-class conformity and uniformity, was forged in the immediate postwar period when suburban planned development experienced explosive growth. Fishman notes that this rapid growth just made it *seem* as if suburbanization had begun in 1945 when in fact it had been occurring for a century. Suburbs built in the nineteenth century and the first half of the twentieth century—railroad and streetcar suburbs—were not characterized in this way. The residents of earlier suburbs were diverse; despite the mobility offered by regional mass transit and the new "horseless carriages," the wealthy residents of rustic but grand suburban "cottages" required domestic help, who for lack of mobility lived nearby, in neighborhoods made up of smaller, working-class dwellings.[5]

Historians have identified a number of factors that changed and accelerated the pattern of suburbanization in the mid-twentieth century: the wide availability of federally subsidized mortgage loans, the increasing sophistication of large-scale production builders like Levitt and Sons, severe overcrowding in urban ethnic neighborhoods coupled with urban renewal programs that actually *decreased* the number of available dwelling units in cities, and the increasing affordability of private automobiles. The production techniques used by the large builders—70% of the houses built in 1949 were built by only 10% of the builders—led to a fairly uniform product.[6] Many contemporary commentators conflated dwelling with resident and conceptualized a stereotype of suburbanites as mind-numbed conformists (a convenient foil for the cultured urbanite). The experiences, indeed the very presence, of "other" suburbanites who did not conform to the stereotype seem to have been elided from history.

But not completely.

Kevin Kruse and Thomas Sugrue, editors of a 2006 anthology entitled *The New Suburban History,* set out to "challenge an older scholarship that looks at the history of suburbs largely internally and, instead, examine the ideological, political, and economic issues that bound city and suburb together in the postwar world."[7] Essays in the book pay special attention to the lesser-known histories of blue-collar, African American, Latino, and Asian suburbanites and consider how contentious political debates over such issues as taxation, school busing, and immigration have played out in suburban contexts.

An example of a ripe topic for study by a "new suburban historian" is the experiences of the legions of pink- and blue-collar suburbanites who work in shopping malls and office parks, live in garden apartments and trailer parks, and often ride buses on long, inefficient commutes to get from one to the other. It is hardly coincidental that suburbia's history is being revised at the same time that its physical fabric is getting retrofitted. Major changes are afoot and these new histories help urban designers working in suburbia appreciate the rich, layered complexity of these places.

DEMOGRAPHIC CHANGES

Despite the work of these historians, cultural stereotypes depicting suburbia as either commodified conformity or the ultimate attainment of the American Dream stubbornly persist. Therefore, it is vitally important to ask questions about the future of living in suburbia that do not presuppose this imagery: Who are today's and tomorrow's suburbanites? Exactly what kinds of dwellings do suburbanites live in? What kinds of dwellings might they like the *option* to live in? Where, within suburbia, might they prefer these dwellings to be? To address these questions we must examine several demographic trends: the increasing proportion of childless households, population growth through immigration, and the graying of America.

Singles and childless households make up a significant segment of the suburban populace and will continue to do so in coming decades. In the mid-twentieth century, when suburbs experienced a building boom of new single-family house subdivisions, census data indicate that about half of American households included children, but by 2000 only

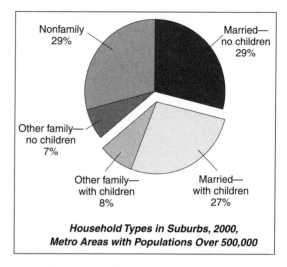

Household Types in Suburbs, 2000, Metro Areas with Populations Over 500,000

Figure 2–2 Households without children outnumber those with children in metro areas, including suburbs. The proportion of nonfamily households is expected to increase in coming decades. (Source: 2000 U.S. Census.)

a third were households with children; meanwhile, the percentage of single-person households (young professionals and elders) had doubled.[8] (See Figure 2–2.) In a provocative analysis based on demographic trends and the results of housing preference surveys, planner Arthur C. Nelson asserts that the United States may already contain all of the large-lot single-family houses required to meet the projected demand in 2025! Despite an expected high rate of overall population growth, he warns that the single-family-house market is dangerously oversaturated, and yet continues to be the sole housing option allowed by zoning regulations in much of suburbia.[9]

Parallel to this trend toward fewer households with children, there is some indication that the ratio of urbanites to nonurbanites in some areas is stabilizing, slowing a decades-long process of decanting population to the periphery. In some metropolitan regions, such as the tri-state metropolitan New York region, the trend is toward population growth in the core urban areas that matches or exceeds growth in the surrounding suburban ring. For example, by 2002 the New York regional core accounted for 39.1% of new housing units permitted, up from only 15.7% in 1994.[10] Even in second-tier cities across the country, such as Kansas City or Tampa, many empty nesters, never nesters, and twenty-something singles—if they can afford it—are flocking "back to the city." In 2004, condominiums accounted for 22% of all home construction in metropolitan Atlanta, more known for its sprawling subdivisions of single-family homes than the fifteen residential towers planned to open between 2008 and 2010.[11] However, despite these highly visible signs of resurgence (and the attendant gentrification) in core urban neighborhoods, the majority of population growth across the country is, and is expected to continue to be, accommodated in the suburbs.

By 2050, the U.S. population will increase by half again what it was in 2000, to around 420 million. With some exceptions, the new immigrants who make up a large part of population growth are now far more likely to bypass gentrifying cities and head directly to suburban areas, especially those in the aging first ring where housing is more affordable.[12] Second homes for retirees and single households made up predominantly of the elderly and echo boomers (the children of baby boomers, born between 1979 and 1996) are also expected to significantly drive future housing demand—especially for condominiums and not just in cities. Marketers emphasize that this new civic-minded, lifestyle-centered, and 24/7 peer-connected generation has different expectations than their parents: 77% plan to live in an urban core and 70% do not think they will move to the suburbs when they have kids, stating a preference for the convenience and connectivity of healthy, walkable, mixed-use communities. They also differ demographi-

cally: one in three is non-Caucasian; one in four grew up in a single-parent household; and three in four had mothers working outside the home.[13]

Meanwhile, their parents are retiring in large numbers. The American Association of Retired Persons reports that the majority of baby boomers would like to "age in place."[14] The auto-dependent nature of suburbia hardly makes this an ideal scenario. Already, more than half of nondrivers aged 65 and older stay home because their transportation choices are limited. Not surprisingly, 71% of older households would prefer to live within walking distance of transit.[15]

How will all present and future suburbanites be housed in a manner that meets their diverse needs? Can established suburban residential districts, single-family subdivisions, and clustered apartment complexes be retrofitted to accommodate an influx of diverse new residents while responding to the changing needs of current ones?

Some possible answers are considered in this chapter and many of them involve increasing residential densities and the benefits well-designed higher density makes feasible: land conservation, transit, a mix of uses within walking distance, and an affordable private realm attached to a desirable public realm. Single-family houses may be remodeled to respond to modern lifestyles, nontraditional family structures, and aging boomers. Alternately, these houses may be expanded with accessory apartments, where zoning is amended to permit it, or entire neighborhoods may be transformed through "connect the culs-de-sac" strategies for remaking dendritic street patterns. Targeted buyouts of groups of individual houses may permit higher-density redevelopment within a subdivision, while in other locations entire subdivisions may be bought out and replaced. Options for retrofitting garden apartment complexes include remodeling and adding amenities for a culturally diverse and economically disadvantaged population and increasing infrastructural support for interconnectivity and walkability, critical where residents cannot afford cars. Alternatively, entire garden apartment complexes may be demolished to transform the zones between commercial property and single-family residential subdivisions from separation buffers into pedestrian-oriented linkages through mixed-use redevelopment and connected streets.

As with the other typologies considered in this book, issues of land cost, difficulty of site assembly, local demand, and entitlements vary the degree of difficulty associated with each of these residential retrofitting strategies. For instance, built examples of connecting the culs-de-sac or other means of interconnecting existing residential subdivisions remain rare. Conversely, ambitious redevelopments of garden apartment complexes raise the specter of gentrification but are providing numerous promising models for meeting future suburban population needs in more urban and sustainable formats. Higher-density residential patterns decrease the collective ecological footprint of the residents. Sustainable urbanism strategies like green roofs, alternative energy systems, rain gardens, and walkability enhance this potential. House-by-house retrofitting can contribute to the "greening" of a neighborhood, such as the recent initiative in the quintessential postwar suburb Levittown to replace inefficient, carbon-emitting boilers and install photovoltaic panels.[16] (For more on changes in Levittown, see Chapter 3.)

RETROFITTING POLICY

The first frontier for implementing many of these promising residential retrofitting strategies is the ring of so-called "first suburbs," where demographics have changed most dramatically and new investment is sorely needed to improve the quality of life. Fascinating data compiled by the Metropolitan Policy Program at the Brookings Institution identify sixty-four aging suburban counties caught in a policy "blind spot" at the federal and state levels. (See Figure 2–3.) These first suburbs, concentrated in the Midwest and Northeast, account for almost one-fifth of the nation's population (45% of New Jersey residents and a whopping 64% of Connecticut's) but have been underserved in recent decades while funding and policy directives have been focused on center cities and new suburban growth areas.[17]

So who lives in first-ring suburbs and how can retrofits attract investment to regenerate their communities in ways that they will benefit from? In the 2000 census, residents of these first suburbs were found to be older, more racially and ethnically diverse, and more likely to be foreign born than the average American. More than half lived in housing built in the period from 1950 to 1970, when these suburban communities grew very rapidly. Today, population growth in first suburbs lags behind the national rate. In general, the percentage of residents over 65 has been increasing, surpassing that of central cities in 2000. One-third of the residents of first suburbs are of racial and ethnic minorities, more than double the percentage in 1980. The two counties that rank first and second in terms of nonwhite residents are Miami-Dade County, Florida (77.6%), and Prince George's County, Maryland (75.7%). Two of the primary case study examples in this book, Downtown Kendall/Dadeland and University Town Center, are located, respectively, in these two counties. Unfortunately, nonwhite suburban residents are twice as likely to be poor and may be found concentrated in pockets of extreme suburban poverty. Since 1980 the foreign-born population in first suburbs

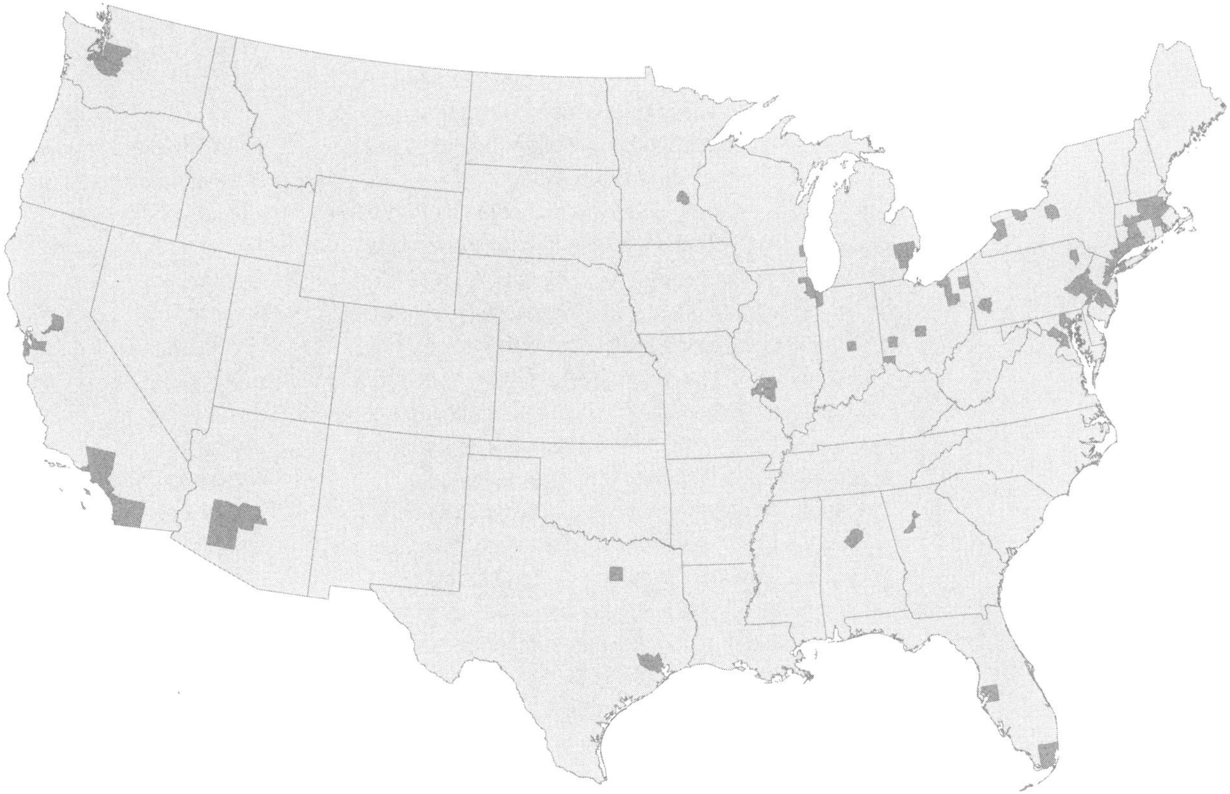

Figure 2–3 Many of the examples featured in this book are located in the sixty-four counties identified by the Brookings Institution as "first suburbs" caught in a federal policy blind spot. These include Norfolk, MA; Nassau, NY; Burlington, NJ; Montgomery and Prince George's, MD; Miami-Dade, FL; Fulton, GA; Cook, IL; Hennepin, MN; Dallas, TX; and San Mateo, CA. (Source: Brookings Institution Metropolitan Policy Program, 2006.)

has grown by 262%, faster than in their central cities and faster than the national rate.

While some are thriving, many of these first suburbs are struggling and failing in their efforts to attract investment, maintain their infrastructure, modernize the housing stock, or support the social needs of aging and diversifying residents. Public investment has been focused on revitalization efforts in urban districts, while both private and public investment in new infrastructure and development has "leapfrogged" these areas. Some of the specific policy recommendations the Brookings Institution advocates to redress the "policy blind spot" include investment in housing vouchers to expand choice,

investment in regional housing corporations to develop and preserve affordable housing, expansion of the HOPE VI program beyond public housing to distressed housing projects financed by the federal government, and funding of metropolitan planning organizations (MPOs) to prepare regional housing strategies that complement the regional transportation plans already mandated by federal law.[18]

The Brookings research identified fragmented governance as a major challenge for these counties; some, as in the Northeast states of New Jersey, New York, and Massachusetts, are comprised of hundreds of local governments with differing land use, zoning, and taxation powers. These small governments often lack the planning and redevelopment expertise that larger municipalities have on staff; in addition, they have been locked in competition with one another to entice tax-paying residents and businesses, leading them to avoid leveraging their land-use powers.

The Long Island Index is one notable effort to provide statistical and survey data at the regional level that can be used to guide decision making in an area with fractured governance. The index, funded by the nonprofit Rauch Foundation, was begun in 2002 with the premise that "good information presented in a neutral manner can move policy." The method is to track progress on issues like housing, land use, jobs, environmental quality, and transit from year to year in order to encourage regional thinking and to inspire action.[19] An example of this approach, highlighting the challenges of fractured governance, is a *New York Times* Op-Ed comprised of a graphic chart comparing Nassau and Suffolk counties on Long Island to the fast-growing suburban counties of northern Virginia. Long Island has 127 separate school districts, 179 fire departments, and 439 government entities, while northern Virginia has, respectively, 3, 4, and 17.[20] The multiple districts and departments throw up roadblocks for redevelopment planning.

With respect to housing and infrastructure, the creators of the Long Island Index hope that efforts to encourage regional thinking will result in increased funding opportunities and decreased local resistance to redevelopment proposals promising to address identified needs: affordable housing, increased housing choice, housing in proximity to existing utilities and transit infrastructure, diversification and expansion of the commercial tax base, conservation of rural land and watersheds, and densification of development in struggling business and retail corridors.

RETROFITTING RESIDENTIAL SUBDIVISIONS

What drives the engines of suburban renewal? There are many factors propelling and differentiating suburban residential retrofits. In many first suburbs, the principal driver may be an alarming increase in the number of aging, run-down properties, creating a fear of blight powerful enough to overcome the more typical NIMBY (Not In My Backyard) resistance to change. In newer, high-priced markets such as Silicon Valley or in booming edge cities, the catalysts may be quite different: the arrival of regional transit, a desire for more affordable housing, or an appreciation for smart-growth plans or policies—themselves empowered by fears that traffic and degraded air and water quality will take the bloom off the boom.

A promising opportunity for increasing residential density is to retrofit residential subdivisions: by altering street patterns with "connect the culs-de-sac" interventions as at Laurel Bay; by demolishing entire subdivisions and replacing them with new, higher-density, mixed-use development, as at MetroWest; or by revising the rules that maintain the auto-dependent, single-family status quo.

Many regulations invite revision—zoning codes that segregate by use, comprehensive plans that place a priority on single-family housing, parking regulations that require off-street parking of at least one space per dwelling unit, and street standards calling for overly wide streets. Revising the rules would allow existing subdivisions to adapt to the new reality without succumbing to the cycle of disinvestment that puts some subdivisions at risk, especially in working-class areas where houses are relatively small. In the postwar period, many predicted that low-cost developments like Levittown would become slums. Levittown did not, but other neighborhoods with a similar housing stock of small ranches or bungalows did, like Compton in South Central Los Angeles.

Homeowners are justifiably terrified that their neighborhoods might deteriorate, lose value, and succumb to gangs. Of course, residential subdivisions at the highest price points do not face these prospects, at least in their immediate future. (Arthur C. Nelson predicts that the enormous houses being built on large lots in exurbs will in the future be subdivided into multifamily units.) Much suburban residential fabric is effectually segregated by income because all the houses in each subdivision are built on similar lots to a standard size and price point. The likelihood that houses of vastly different size and price are co-located is almost nil, except in a small but growing collection of new urbanist towns and neighborhoods.

In many suburbs, almost no new housing at low price points has been built for decades. However, the idea of providing incentives to build new "workforce housing," affordable to the nurses, teachers, and firefighters on whom suburban communities depend, is now politically viable. The technique of "inclusionary zoning" addresses this need by requiring developers to set aside a percentage (often 20%) of new units at prices that this group of workers can afford, often in exchange for zoning variances permitting higher density and smaller lots. David Rusk, former mayor of Albuquerque and proponent of regional planning, has come up with an effective motto, "If you're good enough to work here, you're good enough to live here."

But the notion of providing very low-cost housing for the service workers on whom suburban communities also rely—landscapers, housecleaners, dish washers—is a much harder sell. Service workers present a palpable threat, especially vivid to those just a few steps above them on the socioeconomic ladder. And, as architecture professor Lance Jay Brown says, "Building low-income housing is an act of will."[21] On the income side of the equation, expansion of the Section 8 program and the Earned Income Tax Credit are urgently needed; on the production side, tools include some combination of inclusionary zoning quotas, the Low Income Housing Tax Credit, expansion of the HOPE VI program, pro bono design services, and the use of green design strategies that accrue benefits to the entire community. The best way to address and prevent the conflicts that arise over low-income housing, especially potent in an atmosphere of fractured governance, is to develop regional plans and policies. Why should some working-class communities pay the price for low-cost services that generally benefit the residents of neighboring, more affluent communities?

Revising the Rules: Kansas City First Suburbs Coalition and DADUs in Seattle

Regional thinking is beginning to pay off in some first suburbs. Distressed suburban municipalities in several urbanized regions, including Kansas City, Minneapolis, Norfolk, and northeast Ohio, have banded together into coalitions in order to promote and facilitate reinvestment in their communities, including rehabilitation of aging housing stock. Despite the fact that average household size keeps diminishing, increased demand for privacy and space means that many postwar suburban houses are considered too small by today's standards. And as residents age in place, their houses (and other buildings in the community) may become ill suited to their needs, especially if they develop limited mobility. In addition to facilitating financing for individual remodeling projects, these coalitions encourage retrofitting by promoting the updating and revision of building codes and zoning regulations.

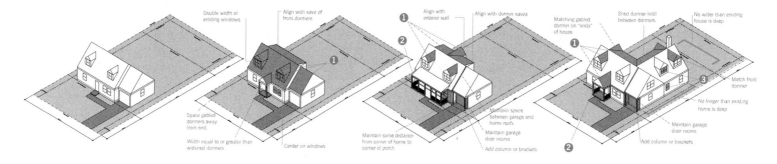

Double width of existing windows.

Align with eave of front dormers

Align with exterior wall

Align with dormer eaves

Matching gabled dormer on "ends" of house

Shed dormer infill between dormers

No wider than existing house is deep

Match front dormer

Space gabled dormers away from end.

Width equal to or greater than widened dormers

Center on windows

Maintain some distance from corner of home to corner of porch

Add column or brackets

Maintain space between garage and home roofs

Maintain garage door recess

Add column or brackets

No longer than existing home is deep

Maintain garage door recess

Add column or brackets

Figure 2–4 This illustrated, step-by-step guide on massing, proportion, and scale for homeowners interested in remodeling their Cape Cod postwar houses is excerpted from the forty-page *First Suburbs Coalition Idea Book*, prepared by architect Eric Piper and MARC. The book examines four common postwar house types—ranch, split level, two story, and Cape Cod—and provides practical tips on enhancing curb appeal and updating floor plans to include master suites, open kitchens, and other plan elements to better compete in resale with newer housing "product." The book also covers considerations such as energy efficiency, financing, and universal design.

The coalitions, while advisory in nature, are generally comprised of town managers and council members who *do* have the authority to revise regulations. Initiatives the coalitions advocate include updating local building codes to provide easy-to-follow guidelines for residential remodeling, revising zoning regulations through overlay zoning or by easing the process for obtaining variances for nonconforming lots, and introducing provisions for accessory dwelling units, often referred to as "granny flats." In addition, municipalities may facilitate financing for rehabilitation through low-interest loans and grants, partnerships with local lending institutions, tax incentives to homeowners and developers, or partnerships designed to take advantage of existing federal and state programs (where they exist, despite the first suburbs policy "blind spot").

In 2005 the Kansas City First Suburbs Coalition, a public-private initiative for innovation formed under the umbrella of the quasi-governmental Mid-America Regional Council (MARC), published a how-to guide for suburban renovators. (See Figure 2–4.) While the staff support for the First Suburbs Coalition is funded by assessments to local town and county governments, the special projects are funded by grants from stakeholder groups such as Fannie Mae and homebuilders and realtors associations.

Recently, the coalition partnered with a local credit union to provide low-interest, fixed-rate home equity loans to fund the remodeling and modernization of qualified homes in participating communities. The Government Innovations Forum director for MARC, Dean Katerndahl, says the role of the First Suburbs Coalition is simply to market the program, which it has successfully done. In the first year of the program, $1.5 million was distributed to seventy-six recipients, half of whom used the funds for upgrading and maintenance while the other half undertook remodels and additions. This may seem like a drop in the bucket, but the incremental effect of individual efforts like these will make a difference in ensuring the vitality and long-term fiscal stability of first-tier suburbs.[22]

Another route toward revitalizing housing stock and choice in aging neighborhoods is through the legalization of accessory apartments within R-1 zones. Illegal accessory apartments in or over garages, often called granny flats, proliferate in neighborhoods lacking affordable apartments or where there are homeowners with limited incomes, such as the elderly, with more space than they need. The city of Seattle is a leader in legalizing these units, which generally increase the affordability of housing for both the homeowner and the renter; its zoning code contains provisions for accessory dwelling units within single-family residential zones, with the following conditions: only one accessory unit no larger than 1,000 square feet per single-family dwelling; one of the dwellings must

Figure 2–5 This detached accessory dwelling unit (or DADU), in the Licton Springs neighborhood of Seattle, was submitted to an ideas competition in 1998 that led to a pilot program to legalize this type of accessory unit in the southwest part of the city. The unit, designed by architect Chad Rollins for his own property, was completed in 2001.

be owner occupied; the total number of occupants must not exceed eight if any of the occupants is an "unrelated person;" and an off-street parking space must be provided.[23] In 2006 an ordinance permitting detached accessory dwelling units (DADUs) was passed with the explicit purpose of providing affordable, alternative housing choices. (See Figure 2–5.) To further enhance choice, Seattle is now proposing to permit cottage housing, consisting of small, detached houses clustered around a common green, in single-family zones.

Many other suburban areas where the cost of living is high and affordable apartments virtually nonexistent, such as Levittown, New York, struggle with resentments brought about by the ubiquity of illegal accessory apartments. Hempstead, the Long Island township in which Levittown is located, issues "Mother/Daughter Use" permits that allow for a second kitchen for the use of a related tenant, and "Two-Family Senior Residence" permits in situ-

ations where one owner-occupant of a house is at least 62 years old. As long as this condition is met, an accessory apartment may be rented to unrelated adults.

Connect the Culs-de-sac: Apollo Beach and Laurel Bay

Older ranch houses, in particular, are out of favor in a market where 90% of new homes are two-story. In their 2004 project for the Florida town of Apollo Beach, Duany Plater-Zyberk & Company (DPZ) provided specific suggestions for retrofitting postwar ranch houses. The DPZ examples are focused on additions that create shaded courtyards, a transformation of the ranch type to better suit the hot, wet Florida climate. The additions are located in the front yard, drastically reducing the setback. By expanding living space toward the street, these prototypes

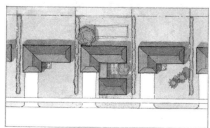

Figure 2–6 A provocative 2004 proposal by DPZ to retrofit ranch houses in Apollo Beach, Florida, by placing an addition smack in the middle of the front yard setback, creating a shaded courtyard and simultaneously recessing the formerly dominant garage entry.

Figure 2–7 A few hypothetical "connect the culs-de-sac" proposals. In 2001 DPZ designed a compelling retrofit plan for the military housing subdivision of Laurel Bay on Parris Island, South Carolina that attempted to convert a monocultural subdivision by introducing a greater mix of housing types and public spaces.

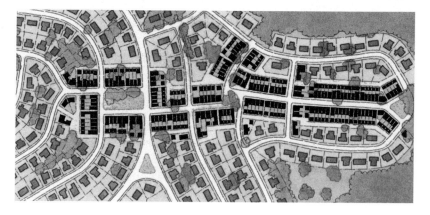

mask garages and help to urbanize the suburban streetscape. (See Figure 2–6.)

It is all very well to retrofit suburban houses by remodeling, building additions, and adding accessory apartments. But what about the subdivision pattern itself? There have been a few hypothetical "connect the culs-de-sac" proposals, but parcel acquisition and fears of increased cut-through traffic tend to make homeowner association approval difficult. In 2001 DPZ designed a compelling retrofit plan

for the military housing subdivision of Laurel Bay on Parris Island, South Carolina. The plan attempts to convert a monocultural subdivision by introducing the greater mix of housing types and public spaces found in a traditional small town. (See Figure 2–7.)

In addition to adding a new neighborhood, they propose demolishing 300 of the original 1,100 houses to allow construction of a new cross street from the subdivision's main entry down to a proposed shoreline park. By improving access to the site's most defining feature, the new street would improve walkability, communal interaction, and orientation to place. It would be lined with 1,200 new town-houses and sideyard houses, many of them facing new common greens. The diversification of dwelling types would significantly augment the housing choices available in the area.

At Laurel Bay, the subdivision provides housing for a nearby military base, and two-thirds of the residents are renters. These conditions avoid the complex process of acquiring individual properties from multiple owners. Nevertheless, the scheme has not been implemented. There is precedent, however, for the purchase of numerous individual single-family house lots in order to form a large, developable parcel. Although rare, a growing number of subdivisions have been acquired in their entirety. The residents of Sunny Brook Meadows, an older subdivision of fifty ranch houses in the rapidly transforming Sandy Springs area of Atlanta, self-organized to put their homes up for sale for redevelopment and found a willing buyer.[24]

From Subdivision to Edge City: Greenway Plaza

An early "down and dirty" example of the strategy of acquiring multiple single-family parcels to amass a larger parcel for mixed-use development is Greenway Plaza, five miles west of downtown Houston, Texas, on the Southwest Freeway (U.S. 59). The lead developer was Century Development Corporation, run by Kenneth Schnitzer, a larger-than-life Texas personality (later convicted and acquitted on charges related to the 1980s savings and loan bank scandals).

In the 1960s, Schnitzer set his sights on the Lamar Weslayan subdivision, a collection of 300 middle-class bungalows, as an ideal location for a major office development. The subdivision had

already been split in two by the construction of the freeway. Because of the lack of zoning regulations in the city, there was no need to worry about the proposed change in use or density. Schnitzer set about acquiring the properties for the fair market value—about $20,000 each. To entice homeowners to sell, he offered to let them stay for several years, rent free; this incentive had the side benefit of preventing rumors from spreading about his plans. But one couple, Jim and Dorothy Lee, held out—not because they wanted to stay in their house, but because they understood the potential profit to be reaped from the ambitious redevelopment deal. By 1974, after a standoff lasting several years, Schnitzer finally agreed to pay their exorbitant asking price of well over $500,000.[25] On the 127-acre parcel Schnitzer built what he called a "new downtown." By 1980 Greenway Plaza had become a classic edge city, as defined by Joel Garreau.[26] (See Figure 9-3.)

From Subdivision to TOD: MetroWest

In 1974, asking $500,000 for one house and lot was tantamount to extortion, but by 2002 it had become the going rate, as demonstrated by MetroWest, a more recent example of the strategy of consolidating house lots to create a large parcel for retrofitting. MetroWest is a planned transit-oriented development (TOD) adjacent to the Vienna Metro Station, a terminus on the orange line, in Fairfax, Virginia. (See Color Plates 1 to 3.) The program calls for a total of 2,250 dwelling units, 400,000+ square feet of office and retail space, and a 30,000-square-foot community and recreation center for public use. Fifty-six acres of the 60-acre site were home to the sixty-nine postwar bungalows of the Fairlee subdivision. The developers, Pulte Homes Development and Clark Realty Capital,

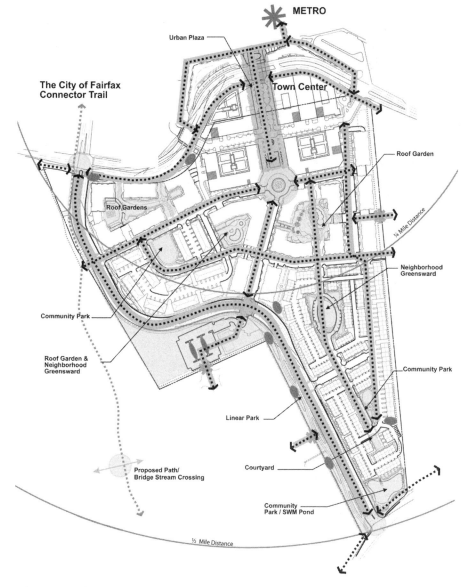

METRO

Urban Plaza

**The City of Fairfax
Connector Trail**

Town Center

Roof Garden

Roof Gardens

¼ Mile Distance

Neighborhood
Greensward

Community Park

Roof Garden &
Neighborhood
Greensward

Community Park

Linear Park

Proposed Path/
Bridge Stream Crossing

Courtyard

Community
Park / SWM Pond

½ Mile Distance

Figure 2–8   The open space plan by Lessard Architectural Group and EDAW for MetroWest in Fairfax, Virginia, shows the proposed street network and connectivity to the Metro station and adjacent residential areas. Failure to acquire the narrow string bean–shaped parcel to the north would have blocked access to the Metro and compromised the entire scheme.

acquired the houses individually in 2002 for $500,000 apiece, a generous increase over fair market value.[27]

The way was paved by various regional regulations and plans in place promoting TOD: MetroWest implements the Policy Plan of Fairfax County by concentrating development next to a Metro station and it furthers the Smart Growth Principles of the Metropolitan Washington Council of Governments.[28] It is hard to argue that replacing sixty-nine homes with more than thirty times the residential density at a transit station is not smart growth, especially in the DC region, where a lack of affordable housing and traffic congestion are widespread concerns.

The remaining 4 acres of the site abut the station in a 150-foot-wide "string bean" shape; the small parcel was purchased from the Washington Metro Transit Authority, but not without a fight. The piece was considered crucial to MetroWest in promoting transit as a convenient alternative to driving because of its shape and location. It is comprised of a long, linear berm, constructed from highway construction fill, that buffered the residences from the transit station; if allowed to stay, the berm would have blocked pedestrians in the new development from reaching the station. Transit-*adjacent* development is not nearly the same thing as transit-*oriented* development, and so intense efforts were made to acquire the parcel. (See Figure 2–8.)

Up to this point the development process required extensive public outreach to quell the opposition of the remaining residential neighbors. Stan Settle Jr., vice president of land acquisitions for Pulte Homes, met with sixty-four area homeowners' associations. As Settle said in an interview, "It used to be that you would talk to the homeowners' associations adjacent to the communities that you're trying to do. With this particular one, we were meeting with HOAs miles away."[29] But after finally receiving approval for an amendment to the Fairfax County

Comprehensive Plan in December 2004, Settle and his team hit the "string bean" roadblock.

Rep. Thomas M. Davis III (R-VA), at the time a powerful chair of the House Committee on Government Reform, lives in Fairfax and opposed the project. He decided to intervene on a local land use issue—a nearly unprecedented maneuver by a member of Congress—by proposing to block a federal funding bill for the DC Metro if the proposed sale went through.[30] The standoff was resolved in October 2005, when the congressman modified the language of the bill, passed later that same day, upon hearing that the Metro's board of directors would hold a public hearing on the proposed $6.5 million land sale. The next month the land sale was approved. The board's chair said the decision to sell came down to two things: the high sale price (a windfall for Metro), and Pulte's $17 million commitment to improving the station.[31]

Before gaining final rezoning approvals from the county's board of supervisors in March 2006, the developers agreed to a series of other negotiated concessions, including a commitment to build convenience retail in the first phase to reduce car trips by new residents; $1.7 million for local schools; a 30,000-square-foot community and recreation center; and strict requirements for monitoring traffic generation. If traffic benchmarks are exceeded, the developer will be forced to pay fines and make changes to the development plan.[32] Besides the notion that some lucky homeowners hit the jackpot, what can be learned from this example? First, smart growth projects approved at the regional scale can still run into serious opposition at the local level. Second, without a plan that truly integrated transit and mixed use, MetroWest would not ultimately have been approved.

These examples illustrate some of the ways in which single-family-house neighborhoods, especially postwar subdivisions, are being retrofitted—at the scale of the individual house and at the scale of an entire subdivision—to address the needs for housing choice and affordability, to respond to demographic change, and to introduce higher-density, mixed-use redevelopment in the right locations, such as at a transit stop.

REINTEGRATING GARDEN APARTMENT BUFFER SITES

Another area of opportunity for residential retrofitting is in garden apartment complexes, typically consisting of three-story walk-ups with through-building apartment units. There are several features of garden apartments that make them ripe for change: first, "attached" units (townhouses and stacked flats) make up more than a third of all housing outside urban cores; second, suburban apartment complexes are typically of higher density and are closer to retail than single-family subdivisions; third, most garden apartment clusters are hostile to pedestrian use, lacking through streets or sidewalks; and finally, they are home to a greater diversity of people—in terms of race, family structure, and income—than is normally found in single-family-house subdivisions.[33]

The systematic use of apartments as buffers around single-family-house subdivisions, to protect them from the encroachment of commercial uses and to limit exposure to the noxious conditions and danger of highly trafficked arterials, is the primary contributing factor for these characteristics. Single-owner garden apartment complexes, often developed on leftover parcels in the zone between residential subdivisions and retail centers at major arterial intersections, could be developed without subdividing the parcel. (See Figure 2–9.) Consequently, the planning and zoning tools put in place

Figure 2–9 Land-use diagram by Paul Hess of Juanita, in the Seattle metropolitan region, showing a typical suburban zoning pattern of apartment complexes acting as a buffer between a retail area and single-family-house subdivisions.

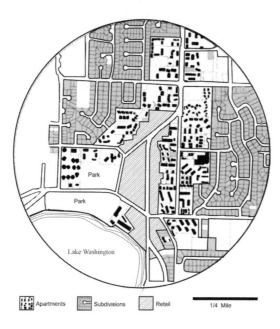

Apartments   Subdivisions   Retail   1/4 Mile

to require developers to make public improvements, such as sidewalks, did not apply. In morphological analyses of several dozen post-1960 apartment clusters around Seattle, academics Anne Vernez Moudon and Paul Hess have shown that apartment complexes of several thousand units covering hundreds of acres were developed with *no net increase* in through streets or number of blocks.[34]

The general planning assumption was that families with children lived only in detached housing in the buffered subdivisions. But in fact many families, often of lower socioeconomic status, live in garden apartments without the benefit of a well-designed, connected pedestrian realm. Residents make do, of course, trodding "desire-line" footpaths and short-cuts through fences and parking lots.

These conditions are starting to change. In some cases, garden apartment complexes are being retro-fitted through remodeling into new complexes better designed to suit large, often immigrant families.

An example is the Brookside Apartments complex outside Atlanta. More commonly, garden apartment complexes, built on large, single-owner parcels, are being razed, rezoned, subdivided, and redeveloped into higher-density (at least in terms of building bulk, if not population), higher-income, mixed-use neighborhoods. The latter approach is occurring in higher-income suburbs where increased land values and population growth suggest intensification of land use. When buffer sites that were once considered less desirable places to live are converted to mixed-use developments, it is the proximity to arterials and existing commercial development that makes new commercial use feasible. Conversely, it is the inclusion of retail and restaurants in the mix that makes the apartments and condominiums attractive. In these cases, such as The Colony in SouthPark, outside Charlotte and Gramercy in Carmel, Indiana, the buffering garden apartment complexes, some with golf courses, have functioned as a community "land bank" of sorts. They are like low-lying fruit to developers seeking redevelopment opportunities because they are single parcel, were not generally built to high standards, and are now aging. As Christopher Jones, a director of planning and development for Beazer Homes in Atlanta, says, the purchase of below-market apartment complexes "affords us acreage we wouldn't normally be able to acquire."[35]

Accommodating New Immigrants: Brookside Apartments and Gulfton

Brookside Apartments in College Park, near Hartsfield-Jackson Airport in Atlanta, began life in the early 1970s as The Windjammer. It was part of a swath of "swinging singles" apartment complexes built for pilots, flight attendants, and their friends. By the 1990s the complex and others like it had become

Figure 2–10 Garden apartment buildings at Brookside Apartments, formerly known as The Windjammer, were rehabilitated in the summer of 2005 to accommodate larger families. The leasing website features Martin Luther King Day essay contests, Easter egg hunts, and "dress for success" workshops for the largely minority and/or immigrant tenants, a far cry from the "swinging singles" parties and cocktails by the pool of the 1970s.

Figure 2–11 Diagram by Susan Rogers of the two primary stages of land development in Gulfton, Texas: a 1950s single-family home subdivision followed by thousands of apartments. Now a thriving immigrant community, Gulfton is the most crowded neighborhood in Houston, with a population density more than five times the city's average.

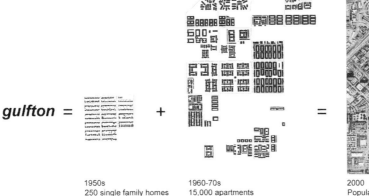

gulfton =   +   =

1950s
250 single family homes

1960-70s
15,000 apartments

2000
Population 45,000+

run down, though still respectable, and home to working-class families. A 1991 article in the *Atlanta Journal Constitution* about the "hidden homeless" among the working poor featured a family evicted from The Windjammer.

In 2005, funded by $14 million in tax-exempt bonds allocated for affordable housing by the Housing Authority of Clayton County, a consortium of private developers rehabilitated the 210-unit complex; apartments were refurbished, shared spaces rebuilt, and new family-friendly amenities provided, such as barbeque grills and a fenced-in playground. The original mix of studio and one-bedroom apart-

ments was reconfigured into two- and three-bedroom units to better accommodate the extended families of new immigrants and day laborers. (See Figure 2–10.)

The neighborhood of Gulfton in the southern part of Houston has experienced a similar transformation at the neighborhood level. The area was built out with 15,000 garden apartments in the oil boom of the 1960s and 1970s. But by 1980 the party was over. Between then and 2000, without the construction of one additional apartment complex, the population of Gulfton nearly doubled. (See Figure 2–11.) What happened? As Susan Rogers has described it, a

Figure 2–12 Flea market at a church in a retrofitted ranch house in Gulfton.

Figure 2–13 Women walking with stroller along the shoulder of a road in Gulfton. Where sidewalks are inadequate or nonexistent, residents make do.

vibrant hybrid community emerged comprised of Latino immigrants. The neighborhood was not designed for families, lacking schools, playgrounds, parks, sidewalks, and other supporting infrastructure, but it is now rich in community social structures that reach out from the neighborhood to the residents' villages in their home countries. Rogers writes, "Gulfton today is simultaneously globally linked, locally severed, socially connected, and physically divided," emphasizing a point made by the new suburban historians: community for these residents is much less place bound than it was a half century ago.[36]

Across the country, areas like Gulfton are being retrofitted *socially* by new population groups. With larger households, these new residents are increasing the population density of auto-oriented developments (despite the new residents' low car ownership rates) as they enrich and diversify the local culture, cuisine, and construction practices.[37] Public investment is needed to further retrofit these places into healthier physical environments—with sidewalks, playgrounds, and transit—but the challenge is to do so without gentrifying a culturally rich community and erasing a needed source of low-income housing. (See Figures 2–12 and 2–13.)

Market Devaluation: Park Forest Courts

A similar story is playing out in Park Forest, Illinois. The pioneering postwar development was planned from the beginning to contain a significant number of garden apartments, following Greenbelt planning principles of the 1930s. These complexes were built in a ring around the retail plaza in the center of town. As documented in William Whyte's *The Organization Man,* the young married couples and families who were the first to move into these apartments, before the sod had even been laid around

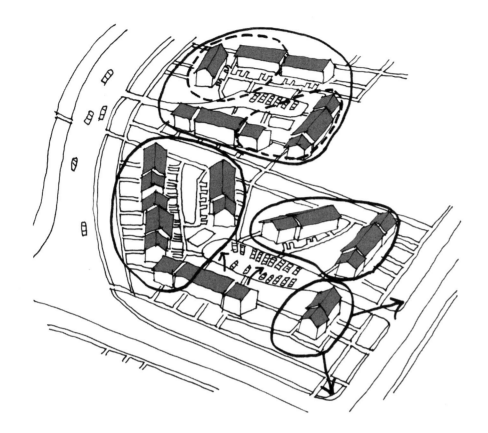

them, were thrilled with the accommodations. "When the doors were thrown open in 1948 the rental courts were islands in a sea of mud, but the young people came streaming out of Chicago," Whyte wrote.[38] He described the convivial social atmosphere in the courts, bubbling with *kaffeeklatsches,* shared lawnmowers, and communal babysitting. (See Figures 2–14 and 2–15.) Later commentators have glossed over the fact that Whyte was describing garden apartment renters, not proud new homeowners.

Over time, most of the rental courts were converted to cooperatives and are well kept and stable, but a few remain rentals. Village leaders blame the negative influence of the apartment courts, "a center of much of the police activity and code enforcement concerns in our Village," for the continuing struggles of Downtown Park Forest, the downsized and retrofitted retail plaza next door, to attract tenants and shoppers. They would like to see the apartment complexes redeveloped. They are ideally located for retrofitting, wedged between the downtown and Park Forest's primary arterial. Similarly targeted for redevelopment or even land-banking is one 336-unit single-family-house neighborhood where crime is described as high and several neglected houses have already been condemned and demolished.

Figure 2–14 "What makes a court clique." In his study of postwar white-collar work and life, William Whyte documented social groupings in Park Forest apartment courts. The early residents he studied were markedly upwardly mobile, treating the apartments as a way station; this is much less true of today's residents. (Source: redrawn from diagram in William H. Whyte, *The Organization Man.*)

Figure 2–15 A recent view of mature gardens at apartment courts in Park Forest, Illinois. The buildings, designed in the late 1940s by Loebl, Schlossman & Bennett Architects, appear well kept, but those that remained rentals rather than becoming cooperatives are reported to have high rates of crime and the Village of Park Forest would like to see them redeveloped.

The completed planning study called for a goal of encouraging the building of fifty new dwelling units per year, preferably multifamily housing in the downtown area and on the western edge of town, within a ten-minute walk of nearby transit stations.[39] (For more on Park Forest, see Chapter 3.)

Gentrification Infill: Gramercy and The Colony

Opportunities abound for redeveloping garden apartment sites in wealthy suburbs, such as Carmel, Indiana. Carmel, a "boomburg" in Hamilton County, north of Indianapolis, prides itself on a notably high median household income of close to six figures. Numerous residential subdivisions, informed by new urbanist principles, have been built on greenfield sites in the area. In this context of wealth, abundant new development, and increasing land values, the impetus to upgrade is great. The Buckingham Companies, a local leader in apartment management, is planning to develop Gramercy, a new mixed-use neighborhood, on the site of Mohawk Hills, a 116-acre, 564-unit garden apartment and golf club complex built in 1970.

Gramercy, master-planned by Looney Ricks Kiss (LRK), is designed to include approximately 2,100 dwelling units, 250,000 square feet of retail and office space, and at least one hotel. The central design conceit is to provide a series of fenced public squares, based on nineteenth-century precedents in London and filtered through the Gramercy Park neighborhood of Manhattan. One of the main accomplishments of the conceptual plan is to increase the street connectivity from a single entrance to eleven intersections. (See Figure 2–16.) This is Buckingham's fifth project in Carmel, and it is by far the largest and most complex. City leaders and planning officials are extremely supportive. The project includes $20 million in tax-increment financing, with an estimated build-out value of $500 million.

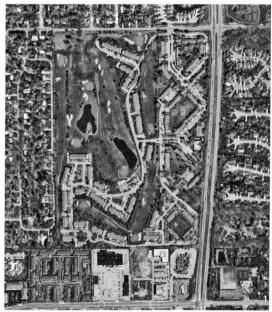 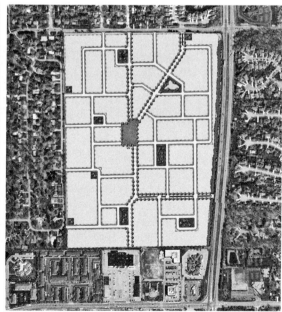

Figure 2–16 From divots to dollars: redevelopment of the Mohawk Hills residential golf community in fast-growing, affluent Carmel, Indiana, into Gramercy. The central design conceit of the retrofit, proposed by the Buckingham Companies and designed by Looney Ricks Kiss Architects, is to provide a series of fenced public squares, based on the precedent of the Gramercy Park neighborhood of Manhattan. One of the main accomplishments of the conceptual plan is to increase the street connectivity from a single entrance to eleven intersections.

There are, however, some thorny issues gumming up the works: namely, density and affordability. In September 2006 the popular four-term mayor, Jim Brainard, was pressured to negotiate a 26% reduction in the project's potential volume, achieved through height limitations, converting 150 townhouse units to fifty single-family houses, and increasing designated open space. The affordability card was played in a front-page article in the *Indianapolis Star* newspaper on Christmas Day 2006. "1 LESS LOW-RENT OPTION" ran the headline.[40] Current tenants paying relatively low rents for outdated apartments will be unlikely to be able to afford units in the new development. To address these concerns, and to permit the development to respond to market changes, the developer will phase construction over a ten- to fifteen-year period, beginning on the golf course portions of the site, so that buildings are not demolished prematurely. The *Indy Star* article drew a flood of impassioned reader responses, ranging from "the war on the working class continues" to "Carmel is hated because it represents what people really want: wealth, security, a symbol of success."

In a wealthy and thriving suburb of Charlotte, North Carolina, a similarly complex scenario is under way. The Colony Apartments, a 353-unit garden apartment complex on 24 acres, lies at the nexus of a hub of high-density redevelopment activity in SouthPark, a district that takes its name from the upscale mall at its center. The master plan, designed by Cooper Carry Inc., calls for 1,100 residential units (60/40 split of for-sale and for-rent units) and 200,000 square feet of retail. The lynchpin of the redevelopment scenario is the introduction of a 60,000-square-foot Whole Foods specialty grocery store.

The inclusion of a Whole Foods store in a redevelopment proposal seems to magically open doors: for project financing and additional retail tenants, for exceptions from zoning and planning officials, and for diffusing neighborhood opposition. Attracting Whole Foods to the mix is like landing an A-list Hollywood actor for a film. A big challenge then for the developer is keeping the star tenant happy; Whole Foods comes into a suburban project with a laundry list of nonnegotiable, antiurban demands, belying their image of supporting sustainability through organic lifestyle choices. In this case, Whole Foods required an exact number of dedicated parking stalls, configured to discourage shoppers from visiting other retailers while parked in their lot.

TOMORROW'S SUBURBANITES

So who are tomorrow's suburbanites? The demographic trends suggest that suburban areas will become even more diverse than they currently are. There will be pockets of the elderly, aging in the same subdivisions where they reared their children. There will be ethnic enclaves of striving new immigrants and there may be pockets of poverty. And we expect there to be many, many new residents, "living, working, and playing," as the cliché goes, in dense nodes of retrofitted properties with walkable, mixed-use buildings and well-defined, shared open space as the norm rather than the exception. Many of these new suburbanites will be living in apartments and condominiums above retail, townhouses, and accessory apartments. And, with compelling places to walk to and better access to mass transit, they will become incrementally less dependent on their automobiles. It is even conceivable that some of the most remote subdivisions will be, over time, demolished and the sites "re-greened" as regional open space.

More clues to the future challenges that will be faced by postwar suburbs, in particular, are unearthed in Chapter 3, an examination of evolutionary change in three pioneering postwar planned residential communities—Levittown, Willingboro, and Park Forest.

Typological studies of suburban housing have tended to focus exclusively on the single-family house.[41] While the single-family house is prominent in the suburban landscape, and continues to represent a key milestone in attaining the American Dream, there are numerous other residential unit types to be found and even more being developed to address changing demographics and preferences for increased density. A key challenge in devising new housing types that allow for urban block configurations in suburban contexts is figuring out where to put all the cars without detracting from the pedestrian experience. Many municipalities have minimum requirements for off-street parking spaces per dwelling unit. Even where these regulations have been revised or eliminated (some municipalities, such as Chicago, are introducing *maximum* parking requirements), market conditions often still dictate the provision of at least one off-street parking space per unit.

Urban designers and architects at the architecture firm Torti Gallas and Partners have extensive experience with the vexing problem of providing urbane parking solutions in urbanizing suburbs. They, and other designers grappling with similar problems, have found it helpful to use a transect concept as an armature for categorizing and analyzing housing types of various densities and recommending appropriate parking solutions for them. A rural-to-urban transect is the organizing framework for the SmartCode, a form-based model zoning code advocated by new urbanists and oth-

ers. (See Figure 2–17.) These tools present a subtly-graded and coordinated set of planning and form relationships for designing the future use in built environments.[42] It should be noted that transect theory does not suggest a constant gradient from zone to zone; there are many fabulous examples of purposefully abrupt transitions between divergent zones, such as Central Park in Manhattan where T1 and T6 zones are juxtaposed.

Figure 2–17 Diagram of the rural-to-urban transect. The transect is an increasingly normative way of using spectrum analysis to describe and ultimately design for a fuller range of settlement patterns than allowed by the simplistic categories of urban, suburban, and rural. The primary zones in the SmartCode transect are as follows:

- T1, the natural zone, consists of lands approximating or reverting to wilderness, including land unsuitable for development.
- T2, the rural zone, consists of lands in open or cultivated state or sparsely settled.
- T3, the suburban zone, consists of low-density residential areas, often characterized by large setbacks and irregular roads.
- T4, the general urban zone, consists of mixed-use but primarily residential urban fabric with a wide range of housing types: single, sideyard, and row houses.
- T5, the urban center zone, consists of higher-density mixed-use building types with a tight network of streets, wide sidewalks, and shallow building setbacks.
- T6, the urban core zone, consists of the highest density with the greatest variety of uses.
- DA, or assigned district, is reserved for such uses as airports, college campuses, or large industrial uses that do not fit into the other transect categories.

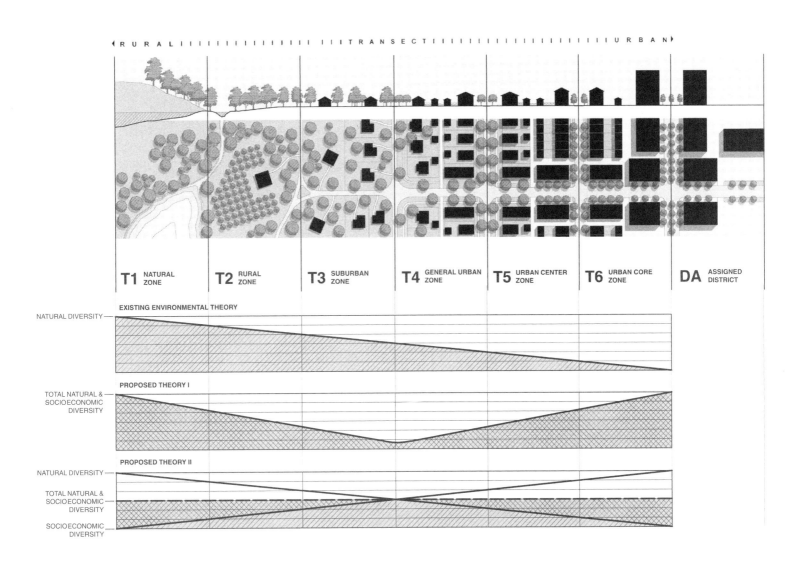

◀ R U R A L I I I I I I I I I I I I I I I I I I T R A N S E C T I I I I I I I I I I I I I I I I I I I U R B A N ▶

T1 NATURAL ZONE   **T2** RURAL ZONE   **T3** SUBURBAN ZONE   **T4** GENERAL URBAN ZONE   **T5** URBAN CENTER ZONE   **T6** URBAN CORE ZONE   **DA** ASSIGNED DISTRICT

EXISTING ENVIRONMENTAL THEORY

NATURAL DIVERSITY

PROPOSED THEORY I

TOTAL NATURAL & SOCIOECONOMIC DIVERSITY

PROPOSED THEORY II

NATURAL DIVERSITY

TOTAL NATURAL & SOCIOECONOMIC DIVERSITY

SOCIOECONOMIC DIVERSITY

The diagrams that follow, prepared by Torti Gallas, map out a range of useful housing types and lot configurations, organized by transect zone. The diagrams describe the physical characteristics associated with each, including useful data about density, relative construction costs, and recommended parking strategies. The final row in the charts lists the minimum block size that can be achieved with each suggested combination of lot configuration, housing type, and parking strategy. Without careful strategizing about where to park the cars, the result is multi-

Transect Zone	T2	T3			T4	T5
Type	1/4 A.C. Large Lot	Neighborhood Lot	Small Lot	Duplex	Townhouse	Townhouse
Lot Configuration	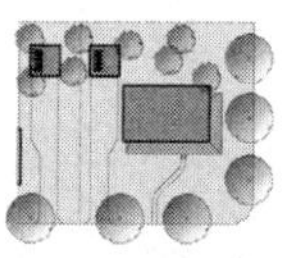	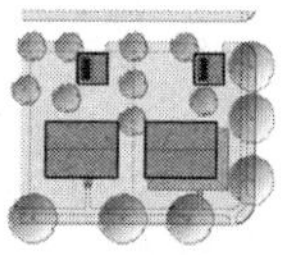	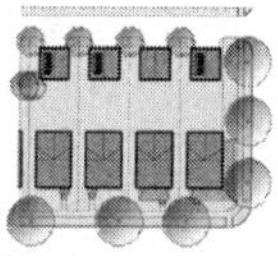	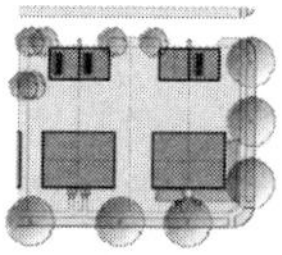	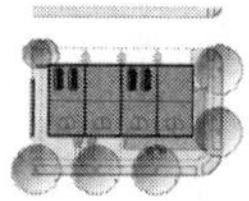	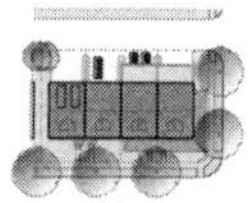
Image	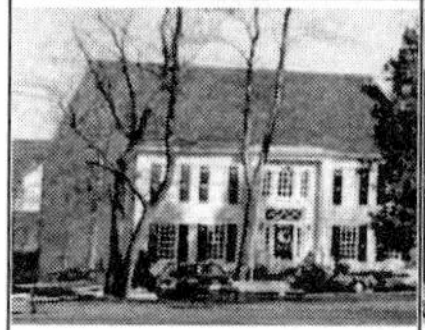	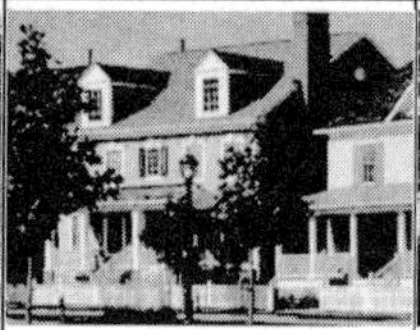	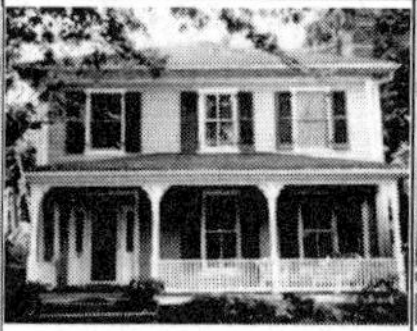	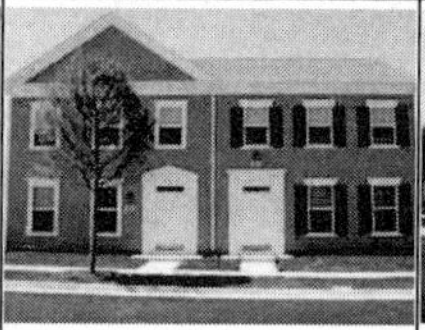	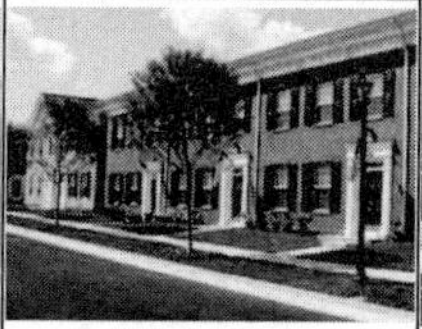	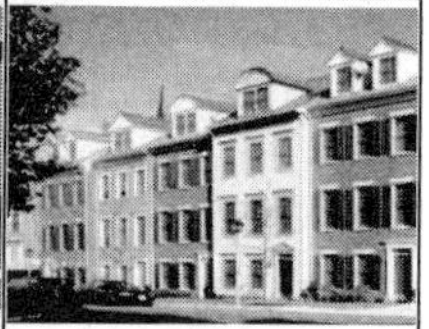
Building Height	2-Story	2-Story	2-Story	2-Story	2-Story	3-Story
Gross Density	3 D.U. /A.C.	5 D.U. /A.C.	7.5 D.U. /A.C.	9.5 D.U. /A.C.	10.5 D.U. /A.C.	17 D.U. /A.C.
Building Construction	Wood	Wood	Wood	Wood	Wood	Wood
Construction Cost (2002)	$195,000/D.U. $60-75/gsf	$175,000/D.U. $60-75/gsf	$140,000/D.U. $60-75/gsf	$119,000/D.U. $60-75/gsf	$119,000/D.U. $60-75/gsf	$185,000/D.U. $60-80/gsf
Parking Location	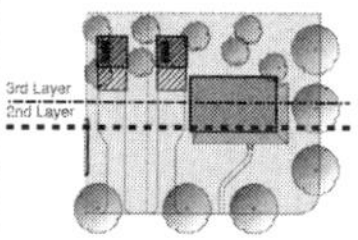	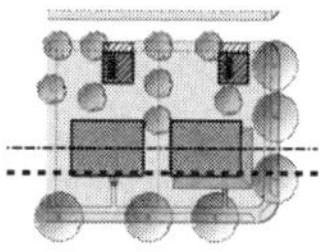	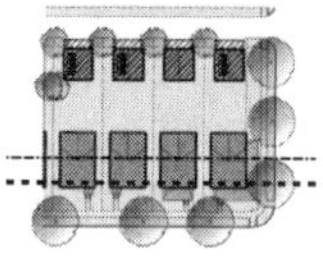	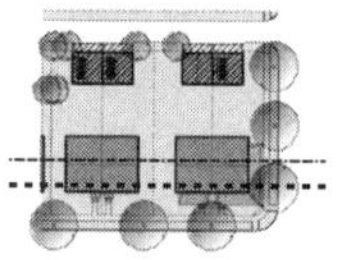	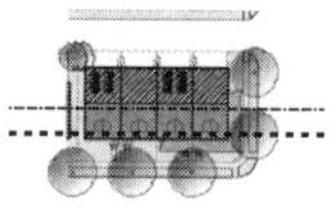	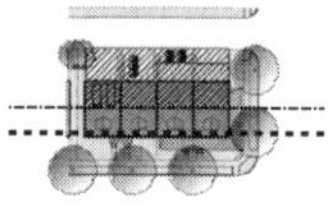
Parking Type	Driveway accessed garages	Primarily alley accessed garages	Alley accessed garage	Alley accessed garage	Alley accessed tuck under	Alley accessed tuck under/ tandem
Parking Layer	3rd recommended	3rd layer	3rd layer	3rd layer	3rd layer	3rd layer
Pkng. Spaces/SF (D.U.)	2 sp / 3,000 sf (1D.U.)	2 sp / 2,500 sf (1D.U.)	2 sp / 2,000 sf (1D.U.)	2 sp / 1,700 sf (1D.U.)	2 sp / 1,700 sf (1D.U.)	2 sp / 3,000 sf (1D.U.)
Cost Per Space (2002)	$9,000-$15,000/sp	$9,000-$15,000/sp	$9,000-$15,000/sp	$9,000-$15,000/sp	$8,000-$14,000/sp	$6,000-$12,000/sp
Minimum Block Size	N/A	130'x220'	100'x220'	90'x220'	70'x180'	70'x180'

Figure 2–18 Residential typology diagrams by Torti Gallas and Partners.

family housing with surface parking lots creating immense superblocks. The block size required to provide surface parking for one typical four-story apartment building is roughly equivalent to three full Manhattan blocks. Parking is a "land hog" when arrayed horizontally in lots, but when stacked vertically in decks it can become quite efficient. Four levels of parking can be provided in the same height at two levels of office over retail, using developer-preferred floor-to-floor heights.[43]

Transect Zone				T5		
		T4				
Type	Stacked Maisonette / 2over 2	Live/Work	Charleston 3 Unit	Manor / Small Apt	Medium Apartment	Texas Donut
Lot Configuration						
Image						
Building Height	3 to 3-1/2-Story	3-Story	3-Story	2 to 2-1/2-Story	3-Story	4-Story
Gross Density	22 D.U. /A.C.	20 D.U. /A.C.	24 D.U. /A.C.	26 D.U. /A.C.	28 D.U. /A.C.	55 D.U. /A.C.
Building Construction	Wood	Wood	Wood	Wood	Wood	Wood
Construction Cost (2002)	$85,000/D.U. $65-85/gsf	$130,000/D.U. $65-85/gsf	$125,000/D.U. $65-85/gsf	$80,000/D.U. $65-85/gsf	$75,000/D.U. $65-85/gsf	$85,000/D.U. $85-100/gsf
Parking Location						
Parking Type	Alley accessed tuck-under / tandem	Alley accessed tuck-under / tandem	Alley accessed tuck-under / tandem	Surface lot / tuck-under	Mid-block surface lot	Embedded 5 level parking deck
Parking Layer	3rd layer	3rd layer	3rd layer	3rd layer w/ streetscreen	3rd layer w/ streetscreen	3rd layer w/ liner
Pkng. Space/SF (D.U.)	2 sp / 1,100 sf (1D.U.)	2 sp / 1,900 sf (1D.U.)	2 sp / 1,900 sf (1D.U.)	2 sp / 1,150 sf (1D.U.)	2 sp / 1,500 sf (1D.U.)	1.5 sp / 1,300 sf (1D.U.)
Cost Per Space (2002)	$6,000-$12,000/sp	$6,000-$12,000/sp	$6,000-$12,000/sp	$6,000-$12,000/sp	$3,000-$8,000/sp	$10,000-$15,000/sp
Minimum Block Size	70'x180'	80'x200'	90'x200'	140'x200'	200'x150'	200'x 200'

Transect Zone	T5			T6		
Type	Mixed-use res. / Retail	Office / Retail	Office / Retail (2 sides) w/ Res. Deck Liner	Mid-rise Apt / Hotel	High-rise res. / Retail	High-rise office / Retail
Lot Configuration						
Image						
Building Height	3 to 4-Story	2-Story	4-Story	6-Story	7+ Story	7+ Story
Gross Density	57,000gsf / A.C.	36,000gsf / A.C.	63,000gsf / A.C.	70 D.U. /A.C.	80+ D.U. /A.C.	100,000+ gsf / A.C.
Building Construction	Wood over conc. podium	Street / bar joist	Street / conc. & wood liner	Proprietary light steel	Steel frame / conc.	Steel frame / conc.
Construction Cost (2002)	$95-110/gsf	$100-110/gsf	$105-115/gsf	$103,000/D.U. $105-120/gsf	$150,000/D.U. $150+/gsf	$145+/gsf
Parking Location						
Parking Type	Parking decks	Freestanding precast 5 level parking deck	Freestanding precast 5 level parking deck	Particularly embedded 6 level parking deck	Underground garage parking	Underground garage parking
Parking Layer	3rd layer w/ streetscreen	3rd layer w/ bldg. liner	3rd layer w/ bldg. liner	3rd layer w/ bldg. liner	Underground	Underground
No. Pkng. Space/SF (D.U.)	2 sp / 2,000 sf (1 D.U.)	2.08 sp shared sp. / 1,000 sf	1.21 sp shared sp. / 1,000 sf	1.5 sp / 1,300 sf (1D.U.)	1 sp / 1,000 sf w/ transit	1.5 sp / 1,000 sf w/ transit
Cost Per Space (2002)	$10,000-$15,000/sp	$10,000-$15,000/sp	$10,000-$15,000/sp	$15,000-$21,000/sp	$27,000-$37,000/sp	$27,000-$37,000/sp
Minimum Block Size	380'x500' or 320'x750'	500'x485' or 440'x550'	495'x515' or 435'x600'	350'x410'	120'x280'	120'x 280'

© 2007 Torti Gallas and Partners, Inc. All rights reserved. SMARTCODE Transect © Duany Plater-Zyberk & Company. Chart compiled by HyoJung Kim and Brian O'Looney.
Cost information purposely antedated from relatively stable 2002 Washington DC market figures - included for comparison only.

The following is a residential retrofitting typology that includes the housing and parking types considered in the Torti Gallas taxonomy, as well as a few additional variants, such as student and senior housing. These types can, and should, be combined on urban blocks designed with generous sidewalks, street trees, and other streetscape amenities. Close attention to providing a mix of housing types and sizes will yield residential neighborhoods able to support a diverse group of residents living well in close proximity to one another. It remains the task of architects and urban designers to continue to devise inventive solutions for combining these types in attractive, efficient, and economical ways.

ACCESSORY APARTMENTS

- Also called granny flats, mortgage helpers, mother-daughter use.
- May be rented to a relative, an elder, a student, or other unrelated adult.
- May be comprised of an addition over the garage, a small ground floor flat carved out of a house or townhouse, or, rarely, a condo subdivided with separate doors to the corridor from each unit.
- Codes usually require a separate kitchen and one off-street parking space for the accessory apartment.
- Codes often limit the square footage of accessory units to around 1,000 square feet.
- Permits may be time limited and subject to reversal.

SINGLE-FAMILY HOUSE WITH PARKING DRIVEWAY

- Average of 3 dwelling units per acre.
- Garage accessed with driveway from street. Garage face should be set back at least 20 feet from the house front.
- Great stylistic variety.
- Typically one or two story.

SINGLE-FAMILY HOUSE WITH ALLEY

- From 5 to 7.5 dwelling units per acre.
- Garage accessed from rear alley, reducing asphalt needed for driveways.
- Alleys allow for narrower lots.

SIDEYARD HOUSE

- Smaller lots and party walls on one side yield an average of 9.5 units per acre.
- Zero lot line setback on one side.
- Garage accessed from street or rear alley.

COURTYARD HOUSING/COTTAGE HOUSING

- Small one- or two-story houses, arranged around a shared common green.
- May be inserted into one or two conventionally sized lots as infill yielding 8 dwelling units per acre.
- Parking on street or in rear garage if accessed via alley.

BIG HOUSE

- Apartment units contained within a single building with shared entry.
- May have tuck-under parking.
- Designed to look like a large single-family house.
- Suitable for infill within a single-family house neighborhood, without looking like "apartments."

TOWNHOUSE

- Two to four levels with a density ranging from 10 to 17 units per acre.
- Side-by-side, zero lot line units.
- Each unit has a separate, clearly visible front entrance.
- Garage accessed from rear alley at ground level, in a tuck-under, or on a shared surface lot.

MAISONETTE OVER FLAT (2 OVER 1)

- Three levels with one-story flat at ground level and two-story townhouse above.
- Unit plans conform to townhouse type.
- May be wrapped around a shared structured parking deck, especially if combined on one block with a "half Texas donut."
- Upper unit accessed from front stoop.

STACKED MAISONETTES (2 OVER 2)

- Four levels with one two-story townhouse above another, yielding 22 units per acre.
- Unit plans conform to townhouse type.
- May be wrapped around a shared structured parking deck, especially if combined on one block with a "half Texas donut."
- Upper unit may be accessed from a rear corridor.

STACKED FLATS/SMALL TO MEDIUM APARTMENTS

- Two to three levels and 26 to 30 dwelling units per acre.
- Shared entryway, walk-up access.
- ADA accessible units on ground floor.
- Parking on surface lot or nearby structured parking.

COURTYARD APARTMENTS

- Three to four levels (maybe five, depending on local code interpretations of Type II construction).
- Apartments arranged along continuous double-loaded corridors arranged around a shared amenity courtyard.
- May have elevator access.
- May have convenience retail on ground level.
- Parking on surface lot, on nearby structured parking, or below grade.
- Unit depths vary from 30 to 40 feet.
- If parking is below grade, optimal building width is 180 feet (three 60-foot bays of parking).

TEXAS DONUT (WITH OR WITHOUT "WINGS")

- Three to four levels (maybe five, depending on local code interpretations of Type II construction) with structured parking; yield 55 dwelling units per acre.
- Apartments arranged along single-loaded corridors, wrapped around an unadorned structured parking deck with two open sides for ventilation.
- May be stacked above a retail level. If so, a fire-rated separation (concrete deck) may be required.
- May incorporate townhouse units at ground level.
- May have elevator access.
- Corridors are continuous on each level for direct access from units to parking.
- Apartment building depth (unit plus corridor) is 35 to 40 feet.
- Optimal block width is 350 feet (three 60-foot bays of parking plus two 30-foot units with 5-foot corridors). Minimal building width is 180 feet (two bays of parking).

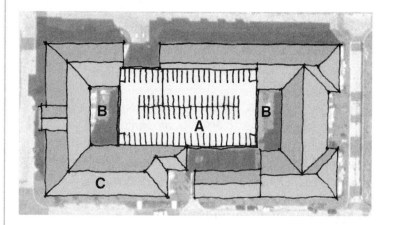

TEXAS DONUT

A. 2-bay parking deck w/ 50% open sides for ventilation

B. Amenity courtyards

C. Apartments on double-loaded corridors

Figure 2–19   Diagram of a typical "Texas donut," an increasingly common apartment housing type in mixed-use suburban retrofits.

LOFTS ("HARD" OR "SOFT")

- Number of levels depends on construction type.
- Higher than typical floor-to-floor heights or double-height living areas permit units up to 60 feet deep.
- Increased unit depth facilitates stacking of residential units over retail or office use.
- Suitable for adaptive reuse of retail or office-use buildings.
- Bedrooms separated from living spaces with low walls and floor-level change in "hard" lofts.
- "Soft" lofts have separate, enclosed bedrooms with windows.

SENIOR HOUSING VARIANT

- Includes a different mix of amenities, such as a shared eating facility.
- May have an assisted-living component.
- Parking ratio (spaces per bedroom) may be lower than typical.
- Convenient access to mass transit is desirable for nondriving residents.

STUDENT HOUSING VARIANT

- Multiple bedroom unit plans differ from standard plans for families.
- Common areas within units are small.
- May have a private bathroom for each bedroom.
- Includes a more generous mix of amenities to support social life, such as game rooms.
- Parking ratio (spaces per bedroom) may be lower than typical.
- Convenient access to mass transit is desirable for nondriving residents.

Chapter 3

Residential Case Study: Changes to "Levittown"
The Earliest Postwar Suburbs Are Sixty Years Old

SUMMARY

Suburbanization accelerated in the United States in the decades after World War II. Levittown, Willingboro, and Park Forest are three prototypical affordable planned suburban communities built during this period. They were "bedroom suburbs," largely comprised of small, single-family houses on winding streets, arranged around schools, playgrounds, and parks, and supplied with auto-oriented shopping centers and strips. What can we learn about the future of later, similar residential communities by studying the current state of the oldest postwar examples?

In the past half century these communities have matured. Residents have aged and diversified while population has decreased due to an increase in the number of households without children. Willingboro and Park Forest are now majority African American. Small, one-story "starter" houses have been extensively added to and remodeled, especially in the still racially homogenous Levittown. All three communities are "built out," such that there is little available land for new construction, except through redevelopment. Nevertheless, recognizing the needs of aging residents, the towns used public money and/or land to support the construction of multiunit housing for seniors, typically on rezoned retail parcels. The retail areas, once cash cows for public tax coffers, have collapsed. In Willingboro and Park Forest, local government assumed ownership of dead mall sites and funded long-term redevelopment efforts geared toward meeting local, rather than regional, needs.

In many ways these communities continue to serve their primary original purpose: the provision of affordable housing. The value of this role to their regions is only likely to grow but will require continued investment in transit and retrofitting opportunities. As morphological theory suggests, the "campus" tissue of large mall sites provides a sizable canvas (40 acres or more) for introducing new uses. But the street and lot patterns in the residential neighborhoods have remained unaltered or "static." These patterns—of small, nearly identical lots supporting similar buildings all from the same time period—are not likely to change unless there is a drastic alteration in the immediate context, prompting a mass cashing in or a wave of foreclosures.

The primary retrofitting strategies are as follows:

- Diversification and modernization of the housing stock, including the introduction of higher-density housing types.
- Publicly funded and initiated redevelopment of failed retail sites for mixed-use town centers.

Figure 3–1 The original 750-square-foot saltbox houses in Levittown, New York, have been extensively remodeled and added to over the past half century such that it is difficult to find an unaltered house.

As recent historical and demographic research has shown, suburbia has always been more diverse than many commentators and critics have assumed. The postwar subdivisions by large-scale merchant-builders in the late 1940s, 1950s, and early 1960s that catered to the housing needs of returning veterans and their new families were subject to particularly harsh criticism for their apparent monotony, homogeneity, and cheap construction. These subdivisions are now a half century old, and much change has taken place in and around them. Indeed, there is much to indicate that Levittown and other planned subdivisions from the era have been undergoing a slow but significant process of evolution since the first starter houses were constructed. We see significant opportunities to direct this ongoing process toward a new set of goals, one based on efforts to retrofit suburbia for even greater diversity, variable density, a finer grain of uses, and improved access to mass transit to systemically enhance the long-term sustainable performance of these places.[1]

Levittown, New York, was one of the first and most highly publicized postwar planned suburbs catering to the needs of the families of returning GIs. In 1947 William Levitt set out to develop a new planned housing development on some 4,000 acres in the existing rural town of Island Trees, twenty-five miles due east of Manhattan, on New York's Long Island. By refining an efficient, vertically integrated, standardized construction process that had first been introduced just before the war, Levitt and Sons rapidly constructed 17,500 houses, of 750 square feet each, on one-eighth-acre lots, 60 by 100 feet in dimension. Young families clamored to put their money down. By 1951, the financial success of Levittown was so clear that Levitt's mass production model for near-instant bedroom suburbs, which took full advantage of government loan programs, was being widely copied by large merchant-builders across the country. Key aspects of the approach continue to dominate suburban development practice, such as the economy of large-scale subdivision, the practice of the subdivider also building the houses, and the use of a limited number of house models all of a similar size or price point in each particular subdivision.

DEMOGRAPHIC DIVERSITY IN LEVITTOWN, WILLINGBORO, AND PARK FOREST

One benefit of examining the challenges facing postwar suburban developments is to forecast the range of issues that will soon confront newer, similarly planned residential developments. Therefore, this case study is comprised of snapshots of three prototypical "Levittowns." One is the original Levittown on Long Island (begun in 1947); second is another, later, Levitt development in Willingboro, New Jersey (1958), which differed from the original in several important respects; third is Park Forest, Illinois (also 1947), an equally influential suburb developed by American Community Builders that shared many of the financial assumptions of the Levitt suburbs, though with more ambitious social goals. (See Figure 3–2.) These particular places were chosen for several reasons. In contrast to typical prewar middle-class and working-class subdivision practice, which was a highly speculative and risky business, and in common with construction practice today, they were built all at once as planned communities.[2] Mortgage loan programs from the Federal Housing Administration and the Veterans Administration made them financially feasible, allowing returning veterans to purchase inexpensive houses with little money down. Also, each has been subject

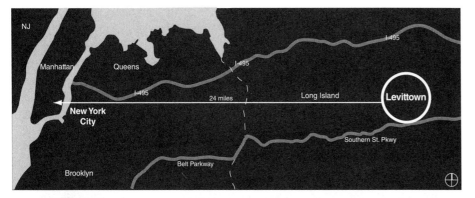

Figure 3–2 Location maps for Levittown, Park Forest, and Willingboro.

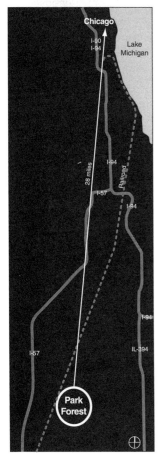

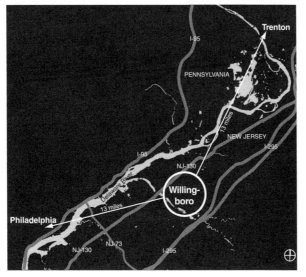

An important shared characteristic of all three places was the speed with which they were developed or "built out," adding to their allure. In the first Levittown, the peak rate of construction was an astonishing thirty houses per day! A second important shared characteristic of all three suburbs is that they were master-planned as full-fledged communities, rather than as simple subdivisions, with the developers taking the responsibility to build not only housing but also schools, pools and parks, shopping centers, and other amenities. Finally, the original demographic profiles of the first residents were similar, consisting of young, white families with children and one primary wage earner, often a returning GI, who commuted to the city to work. In Park Forest, for example, the median age was 28 and fully two-thirds of the heads of families were veterans. Many of these families had previously lived in apartments, often doubling up with relatives, in urban neighborhoods where no new housing was being built.[4]

What has changed? Data from the 2000 U.S. Census clearly indicate that the demographic profiles of the three suburbs have changed significantly over the past half century, particularly with respect to overall population size, race, age, and household structure. By some demographic markers they remain remarkably similar to one another and by others they diverge markedly.

The first Levittown, on Long Island, consisted of a series of subdivision neighborhoods clustered to the north and south of an old country road, Hempstead Turnpike. The neighborhoods were serviced with small shopping centers that residents could walk to, and site drainage was handled in a series of concealed retention ponds. The Levitts donated sites for the construction of schools and added new

to intense media and academic scrutiny; William Whyte's influential 1956 book *The Organization Man* arose from his observations of Park Foresters, while Willingboro was the primary subject of sociologist Herbert Gans's 1967 book *The Levittowners,* in which he vigorously challenged the stereotypical picture of postwar suburbanites living cookie-cutter lives to match their houses.[3] As a result, each became a well-known prototype.

neighborhoods as land was acquired. Privately held parcels along the turnpike that the Levitts did not purchase became retail strips.

The main narrative in the first Levittown is one of low residential turnover and rising equity. Houses in this Levittown, originally two-bedroom models of just 750 square feet priced around $7,000, had a median assessed value in 2000 of $190,000. Twenty-six percent of the current residents moved in prior to 1969, indicating a low rate of turnover. These residents, many of whom consider themselves Levittown "pioneers," are "aging in place." The community, which in 2000 had 53,000 residents, falls into two different municipalities (a complication that the Levitts sought to avoid in later developments). The houses were originally sold with odious whites-only restrictive covenants. While the covenants are

Figure 3–3 Sign of bygone times. A view of children playing below the clock tower at the Park Forest Plaza is the iconic image of the village. These children are retired now and the tower was demolished during renovations to revive the moribund mall.

long gone, Levittown is still, at 94%, predominantly white. The main changes to Levittown in the past half century are physical: less than 1% of the basic starter houses remain unaltered; the Levittown Historical Society was recently dismayed to find that there were no completely unaltered houses to landmark![5]

Park Forest was built by American Community Builders (ACB), also starting in 1947, on 2,400 acres some thirty miles south of Chicago. Elbert Peets, coauthor of *The American Vitruvius* and one of the designers of Greendale, Wisconsin, designed the master plan. Greendale was part of the federal government's idealistic and progressive but short-lived New Deal–era Greenbelt town program of the 1930s. The president of ACB, Philip M. Klutznick, had a long government resume, including a stint as head of the Federal Public Housing Authority. Park Forest differed from Levittown in several ways, reflecting the progressive leanings of its founders. Perhaps most significantly, at least a quarter of the housing units were rental garden apartments, organized in low-rise courts. The courts were grouped around an open-air shopping center, possibly the first example of a suburban pedestrian mall, complete with a Piazza San Marco–style clock tower that became a primary meeting point for Park Foresters.[6] (See Figure 3–3.) Included in the original master plan was a commuter rail spur and station to be located adjacent to the mall, but it was omitted when the Chicago rail authority proved uncooperative. Also notable was the inclusion of a forest preserve and a large park, ideas drawn from the Greenbelt program (which had drawn political fire for exhibiting a "socialist" agenda). The Greenbelt approach advocated clustering housing while maintaining a low gross density in order to provide land for shared open space.[7]

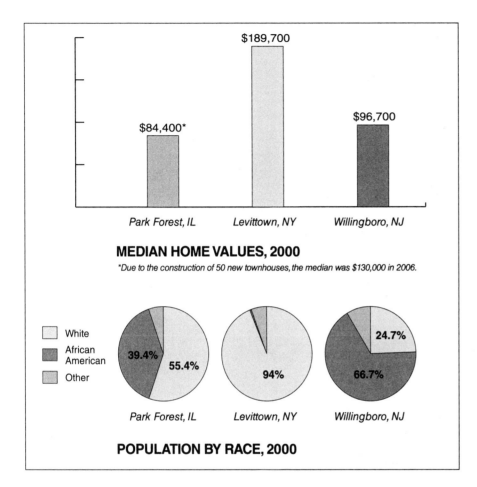

$189,700

$96,700

$84,400*

Park Forest, IL   Levittown, NY   Willingboro, NJ

MEDIAN HOME VALUES, 2000

*Due to the construction of 50 new townhouses, the median was $130,000 in 2006.

White
African American
Other

39.4%   55.4%

94%

24.7%

66.7%

Park Forest, IL   Levittown, NY   Willingboro, NJ

POPULATION BY RACE, 2000

Figure 3–4 Evidence of a "segregation tax"? Comparative demographic profiles of Park Forest, Levittown, and Willingboro in 2000. (Source: 2000 U.S. Census.)

By 2000 the population of Park Forest had dwindled to 23,500, down 29% from its heyday in the 1960s of 33,000, due primarily to smaller household size as residents aged and no longer had children at home. Census data indicate that the population is diverse and fairly well integrated, 55% white and 39% African American. But the average value of the owner-occupied houses, which were originally offered at a much greater range of models and prices than in Levittown, was $85,400, much lower than the Illinois mean value of $130,800.[8] (See Figure 3–4.)

Compared to Levittown, the levels of educational attainment are identical, but the median household income is 30% lower, with almost double the number of female-headed and nonfamily households. The presence of a number of affordable rental units (in the garden apartment courts) may account in part for this difference. But the median home value, a key indicator to national retail scouts, is on the rise due to an influx of new units. Between 2002 and 2006 fifty new townhouses (the first phase of a development on part of a dead mall site that has been reimagined as "downtown") selling for an average price of $190,000 led to an annualized growth rate in median home values of 13.5% in a market that had been completely flat for the previous decade.[9]

Willingboro, partway between Camden and Trenton, was built a decade later; in 1958 the first families moved in, including that of sociologist Gans. It too was named Levittown, although in 1963 the residents, wishing to distinguish themselves from the nearby Pennsylvania Levittown, voted to revert to the name of the original settlement. Learning from earlier Levittowns and from competitors like Park Forest, William Levitt made some major changes in the planning approach. First of all, the community was built to comprise one township; borders were redrawn to achieve this goal. Second, rather than scattered neighborhood shopping centers, Levitt provided one large 600,000-square-foot open-air pedestrian regional mall, located on the main arterial highway, Route 130. Residential neighborhoods were still grouped around elementary schools, built on Levitt-donated land. Third, the houses were designed with three or four bedrooms, ranging in price from $11,500 to $14,500, to accommodate growing families without the need for remodeling and additions. Finally, the site planning was more sensitively and professionally executed with respect to such issues as drainage and wayfinding.[10]

Of all the evolutionary changes that have since taken place in Willingboro, the most significant may be that the 2000 Census indicated that two-thirds of its 23,500 residents were African American and one-quarter white. Willingboro is now the premier African American suburb of Philadelphia, with nice houses, big yards, good schools, and little crime (but no place to shop; see Chapter 6).

Originally, Levitt intended to exclude minority residents, as was his normal practice, which he defended on economic grounds. But when he announced his intentions in a press conference in 1958, the state of New Jersey began legal proceedings against him. He elected to integrate rather than battle in court. He even hired an expert consultant to help with the process! A strategy was implemented intended to prevent the clustering of minority buyers by offering them the choicest lots, backing up to forested space at the periphery of neighborhoods. White buyers were then offered choice lots adjacent to an African American family, or less desirable lots in more central locations.[11] But in the end, many white families left as black families moved in. In 1970 African Americans comprised 11% of the population; that number had nearly doubled by the mid-1970s. An effort to stem the tide of white flight and prevent blockbusting by banning "For Sale" signs was struck down in court. A rash of fraudulent loans to African Americans fleeing central Philly and Camden led to widespread foreclosures (sadly echoed in the subprime mortgage fiasco of 2007) that accelerated white flight and led to home vacancies and drastic reductions in the township's overall population. By 1990 Willingboro was majority African American and the trend has continued.

The median home value in Willingboro, which is now a very stable community with a very low vacancy rate, was $96,700 in 2000, half the median value of homes in Levittown, New York. (See Figure 3–5.)

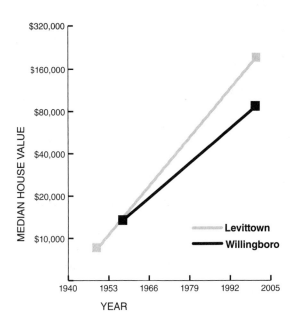

Figure 3–5 The housing stock in Levittown and Willingboro, two communities built by the same developer, is similar, but the mean value of the homes has diverged from 1960 to 2000, a period when Willingboro transitioned to majority black while Levittown remained largely white. (Source: 2000 U.S. Census.)

What accounts for this low median value? The educational levels and median household income figures are similar to those in Levittown, while the houses, by the same builder but bigger with larger lots, are worth half as much. One could argue that the real estate market on Long Island is overheated (which it is) and that the Levittown houses have been substantially improved with sweat equity. But houses in Levittown, Pennsylvania, which is in the same market area but is 98% white, are worth almost 20% more than equivalent houses in Willingboro. Current town and county officials attribute the low median house value in the town to its reputation as a black suburb. They claim that racial bias also negatively impacts efforts to attract national retailers to the retrofitted shopping mall.[12]

The difference in house value may amount to what David Rusk, a former mayor of Albuquerque and New Mexico state legislator, calls a "segregation tax." He calculated home-value-to-income ratios for different communities and found that they drop precipitously as the percentage of minority residents in a neighborhood increases. Rusk asserts that the difference in ratios between the majority-white and majority-black areas constitutes a segregation tax.[13] Further comparative analysis has shown that throughout the 1990s house values in the New Jersey suburbs of Philadelphia grew by 13%, a modest rate compared to the national average of 53%. But in Willingboro, house values rose only a meager 0.3%. When adjusted for inflation, the median Willingboro home actually *lost* 24% of its value.[14]

Finally, there is one demographic factor that is common to all three suburbs: aging. In 2000 the median age in the three census areas was 35.6 to 37.9 and one quarter of the households included at least one senior. This median age is considerably higher than 28, the median age of the first residents of these suburbs a half century ago, and slightly higher than the national median age of 35.3. Suburbanites are getting older, along with the rest of the country, and many want to "age in place." The American Association of Retired Persons (AARP) refers to compact, walkable, mixed-use communities as NORCs (Naturally Occurring Retirement Communities) and recognizes that 71% of seniors would like to have access to mass transportation.[15] Can "Levittown" become a NORC by improving non-automobile-dependent mobility and by providing housing types for seniors to "downsize" to without leaving their valued communities?

FAILURE AND REDEVELOPMENT OF RETAIL PROPERTIES

All three suburbs studied here have experienced notable declines in the amount and caliber of retail activity as newer, bigger malls in better locations (i.e., on new interstate highways) drew customers and tenants away.

In Levittown major retail activity was confined to the strip of Hempstead Turnpike, which both bifurcated the community and connected it to neighboring towns. Along the turnpike were a jumble of small strip malls, stand-alone restaurants, a church, and, eventually, a May's department store. The Levitts built a series of small neighborhood-serving retail areas to which residents could walk, but they didn't thrive and Levitt sold them all off in 1952; some were redeveloped as apartments. The retail tenants in the Hempstead Turnpike storefronts today are decidedly down-market—fast-food joints, low-rent seasonal stores, and a flea market in the old May's building. With a few exceptions, the lots are too shallow in dimension to support the kinds of strip retail centers built since the 1960s (as found elsewhere on Hempstead Turnpike) and they have not been retrofitted to other potential uses. (See Chapter 4 for an extensive discussion of strip retrofits.)

Park Forest, in contrast, boasted an innovative 48-acre open-air pedestrian mall, one of the country's first. (See Figure 6–4.) The centralized complex of shops and offices, with innovative modern architecture, including civic uses along with retail and ringed with plentiful free parking, quickly became the social heart of the town—a setting for community activities like parades, political rallies (Nixon was a favored guest in the 1950s), and arts fairs. In an early use of tax increment financing (TIF) in the mid-

Figure 3–6 Downtown Park Forest in 2004. In a village-led retrofit effort, a new Main Street was cut through the remnants of the pedestrian mall of the Park Forest Plaza, an open-air mall dating from the late 1940s.

1980s, the mall was updated. But by 1995, the Park Forest Plaza was dead. In the absence of any interested developers, the town of Park Forest stepped in, purchased the mall for $100,000, and funded its redevelopment into a downtown. Outer parcels and parking lots were converted to residential use—for senior housing and for-sale townhouses (both new housing types to Park Forest). A new Main Street was cut through the mall. (See Figure 3–6.) One department store that was not demolished has yet to find a tenant and may soon be demolished for more townhouses. Other buildings house an array of local service businesses like beauty salons, accountants, and resale boutiques as well as arts institutions that, while not paying much in rent, do boost civic pride and community spirit. The new downtown isn't exactly hopping, but it isn't dead either. Park Forest has established a second TIF district to redevelop a failed strip center just up the arterial that is adjacent to a possible future transit stop on an existing freight rail line.

In Willingboro, Levitt had built a 600,000-square-foot open-air shopping mall called Willingboro Plaza. Once lively, with a 1,200-seat movie theater, it died in the 1980s soon after a new interstate highway was completed several miles to the east, opening up sites for new retail. No developers were interested in the Willingboro site, not even for big-box use, and so, as in Park Forest, the municipality purchased it for $185,000 (the low price was part of a deal to forgive delinquent taxes) and turned it over to a willing developer interested in sustainable retrofitting. Anchor buildings were adaptively reused as community college classrooms, a mail-order center for a pharmaceutical company, and a new public library. The mall retrofit is not particularly oriented toward pedestrians—the new uses are highly segregated from one another—but, as in Park Forest, the site is now productive rather than fallow. Another large site to the south along Route 130 sits vacant, awaiting retrofitting. There is some hope for a regional turnaround along the aging arterial; a new commuter light rail line between Trenton and Camden has just been opened on an existing rail corridor along the Delaware River. (For more on Downtown Park Forest and Willingboro Town Center, see Chapter 6.)

RESISTANCE TO CHANGE IN RESIDENTIAL PATTERNS

Examining these "Levittowns," one remarkable similarity is the extent to which the original physical patterns, the urban morphology, have remained resistant to change. This is not to say that the places today resemble their original incarnation. The buildings have been substantially remodeled but the neighborhood streets are unaltered, lots have not been combined or further subdivided, and houses have not been demolished or changed to other uses, except for the conversion of most of the rental courts in Park Forest to co-ops.[16]

Several factors have contributed to the high degree of alteration and customization at the building scale. First of all, rates of owner occupancy remain high and residential property has continued to be a repository of owner investment. As Barbara Kelly notes in her thoughtful 1993 study of Levittown, many homeowners applied sweat equity in the form of additions and remodeling to increase the value and utility of their houses, rather than moving to larger houses elsewhere.[17] In addition, local governments are often encouraging this kind of enlargement of older suburban homes to improve their value. The Kansas City First Suburbs Coalition produced a remodeling guidebook encouraging owner upgrades and maintenance (see Chapter 2). In 2006 the Village of Park Forest initiated a similar program, with a guidebook and low-interest loans for remodeling.

Today, one can see the outcome of these trends, particularly in the first Levittown, where houses have changed and diversified in size, style, and, to a lesser degree, in use. But the *type* of housing and its auto-dependency have not changed. Lots have not been subdivided or conjoined, houses have not been replaced with multifamily dwellings, accessory apartments are rare, and detached accessory units are not permitted. Traveling through Levittown today, one sees some new uses on the original retail sites and a large variety of exterior house styles, a marked change from the community's original monotonous appearance, but there has been little change in patterns of residence.[18]

This is consistent with Brenda Case Scheer's proposition about suburban growth. She has proposed three categories of suburban tissue (patterns of block, lot, and building aggregations): "static" tissues, or planned subdivisions; "campus" tissues, comprised of multiple buildings on a single large lot, such as the shopping malls in Willingboro and Park Forest; and "elastic" tissues, the most transformable types, found on arterial strips such as Hempstead Turnpike, where lots are varied in size and irregular in shape, and buildings are of different types and sizes.[19]

In these communities, despite extensive house remodeling in Levittown and racial changes in Willingboro and Park Forest, the "static" tissue, the street patterns and lots, has indeed remained stable. Why? Just as one can still read the street patterns and property lines of ancient Rome in contemporary maps of the city, unless land values change radically—by the proximity of a dead mall or the sudden arrival of transit—street patterns and lot divisions tend to endure and structure later changes. Zoning codes, restrictions of the number of dwelling units allowable, setback requirements, and other legal restrictions intended to protect property values also contribute to the resistance to change. However, even if the original platting had contained more variety, it would still be difficult today to purchase and assemble small, contiguous lots from private owners to convert them to other uses, or even redevelop them as other forms of housing, such as townhouses or small apartment buildings.

The Village of Park Forest, however, is actively encouraging this type of redevelopment. The village has a goal of planning for fifty new housing units per year by attracting a percentage of the 1,400 new units expected annually in the region through 2030, mostly in greenfield developments. In addition to promoting multifamily housing and townhouses

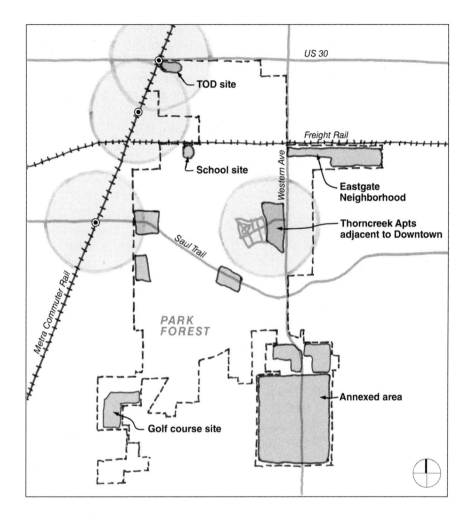

US 30

TOD site

Freight Rail

School site

Western Ave

Eastgate
Neighborhood

Thorncreek Apts
adjacent to Downtown

Saul Trail

Metra Commuter Rail

PARK
FOREST

Annexed area

Golf course site

Figure 3–7 Redevelopment sites identified by Village of Park Forest as suitable for new housing. Planners hope to boost median home values (and attract retailers) by squeezing in fifty new housing units a year over the next two decades. (Source: Redrawn from Report to Village of Park Forest by HNTB, 2007.)

on rezoned commercial sites within walking distance of downtown or existing commuter rail stations, the village would like to rezone, redevelop, and possibly replat the Eastgate neighborhood, an isolated area of ranch houses that have fallen into disrepair through absentee landlord negligence. About 10% of the houses are either already owned by the village, have village liens on them, or are in foreclosure.[20] (See Figure 3–7.)

DIVERSIFYING HOUSING CHOICES

In the first Levittown and in Willingboro, there are few apartments or multifamily dwellings. Singles and seniors who wish to downsize do not have many options. At the same time, because these suburbs are almost fully built out and there is little available land to build on, the focus is on retrofitting existing sites. While the vast majority of the housing (and land use) remains unchanged, efforts have been made to introduce a small amount of variety in the few locations where opportunities exist for new construction.

In Willingboro 220 three-story townhouses were recently constructed on part of the reclaimed parking lot of the mall. Assisted-living apartments were built along Route 130 and the township is actively trying to encourage mixed-use development on other available sites.[21]

In the first Levittown, a small group of townhouses for seniors was constructed using public funding on a small parcel that had been for commercial use. (See Figure 3–8.) Could similar retrofits occur along the primary arterial road, Hempstead Turnpike, where the interface between commercial properties and single-family houses is awkward and abrupt? Morphological analysis suggests that clusters of multifamily residential use tend to emerge at just this type of interface.[22] However, it seems that in Levittown the current residents would prefer to keep the existing down-at-the-heels retail uses along the turnpike for fear of the changes that too much redevelopment might bring, especially in terms of increased traffic. The residents might not be motivated for change because home values are high and Levittown, as a neighborhood within the larger municipality of Hempstead, is not dependent on local retail for tax revenue.

Figure 3–8 Victorian Homes at Levittown, new subsidized housing for seniors, built on the site of a small car dealership. The new buildings fit well into the context.

Figure 3–9 The Victory Center in Park Forest consists of apartments for seniors and an assisted-living center. It was built in 2001 on the cleared site of a Sears store, as part of the retrofit of the Park Forest Plaza into Downtown Park Forest. Residents are within walking distance of municipal services and everyday shopping.

Park Forest, as previously noted, was a wildly successful "starter" community of upwardly mobile young families who relished the opportunity to create their community's political and social networks and institutions.[23] Today, courts that converted to cooperative ownership are well maintained, and there is a stable, if a bit sleepy, air to the town. Senior housing appears to be a pressing need, and an assisted-living facility was recently built on the site of the old Sears store. (See Figure 3–9.) There are more parcels available for housing or mixed-use retrofits on various sites around the downtown as demand develops.[24]

It is likely that in the coming years there will be a shift in ownership of a large block of houses in all three suburbs as the core of long-term pioneers dwindles in size. The houses in Park Forest and Willingboro are a bargain, especially when compared to those in the first Levittown, and seem likely to continue to attract young buyers, especially from new immigrant groups. For example, Willingboro is now home to a small but notable enclave of recent refugees from Liberia.[25] If sizable ethnic enclaves emerge in these suburbs, their presence may help rejuvenate commercial areas with entrepreneurial small businesses.

PATHS TOWARD FURTHER CHANGE

As planners and residents turn their attention to these original "Levittowns," the first wave of affordable postwar bedroom communities, they are reconsidering the role such places ought to play in today's metro areas, where demographic profiles are much changed. Should their primary role continue to be the provision of affordable housing or should they be encouraged to welcome a mix of incomes with a greater range of price points and housing types? Can they be made more sustainable by better integrating walkability and transit? Are new community anchors needed for empty-nesters? Should those with access to rail be encouraged to densify? We suggest that they address these questions by focusing on serving important new demographic niches—affordable homes for the graying and starter homes for minority and new immigrant groups. We also suspect that the greatest opportunities for regeneration lie in areas currently deemed problematic.

One of the issues that plagues postwar suburbs and those who would retrofit them is the reduced vocabulary of uses for which they are zoned, and the forms from which they were built. Bedroom suburbs were meant to be just that—places where families lived while primary wage earners commuted to the city to work. Isolation from toxic industries and nosy neighbors made sense at one point in time but now create limitations, especially for an aging population with reduced mobility and limited opportunities for social interaction. More efforts need to be made to remove the regulatory obstacles to better integration of neighborhood-serving retail, workplace sites, and more varied housing types into suburban communities.

The best opportunities for synergistically incorporating these new uses are on "Levittown's" declining retail sites. Well-designed mixed-use town centers can increase walkable access to retail for all inhabitants, especially seniors. Park Forest's struggling mall added through streets in part to improve its connectivity and accessibility for residents. However, some of its difficulties in attracting tenants stem from its embedded location, too remote from a major arterial road. If town center initiatives are to succeed in retrofits of suburbs, they will have to resolve the dilemma of trying to become the center of their respective communities, while simultaneously attaching to larger transit and traffic networks to attract outside customers. Park Forest's current aggressive efforts to attract new, higher-density housing development both integrated with the downtown and adjacent to existing or proposed transit stops is an excellent step in the right direction. With its walkable downtown, community-minded spirit, affordable housing, and transit access, the village is positioning itself well to compete with new urbanist greenfield developments in the Chicago area.

Schools provide another important retrofitting opportunity. In the 1950s new subdivisions were bursting with children and Levitt anchored neighborhoods around schools. Not so anymore (although a continued influx of new immigrants could restore the school-age population). Residents found it traumatic when Levittown Memorial High School was closed in 1983 due to declining enrollment and converted into an adult- and special-education headquarters for the school district.[26] One of two high schools in Willingboro was closed around the same time and now may be retrofitted into a performing arts center, repurposing a community anchor.

The dearth of civic institutions and truly public space in "Levittown" provides a third opportunity for regeneration. In Park Forest, the Plaza played the role of civic center and when the mall began to fail, the space of public life was diminished. It is now coming back with a focus on the arts. Willingboro Town Center has a new public library, built in the shell of one of the dead mall's stores, which won an AIA-COTE award for sustainable architecture.[27] These are welcome additions to maturing suburbs and provide both the preconditions for democratic citizenship and a means for balancing suburbia's highly valued private space with new places for social activities.

Finally, there is tremendous opportunity to improve the environmental impact of the suburban development patterns that were intensified in the postwar period and continue to this day. Recognizing the pressing need to confront global warming on a local level, Nassau County executive Tom Suozzi introduced an initiative to "green" the most famous neighborhood in his county, Levittown. Residents are provided incentives to replace boilers, add solar panels, and switch to compact fluorescent bulbs so as to improve energy efficiency and decrease carbon emissions. Organizers aim to include 5,000 of Levittown's 17,000 houses.[28] It is not a program that will produce drastic change or address the fundamental impact of low-density development on air and water quality, but it is a commendable and symbolic start.

The snapshot provided here reveals some of the trends in "Levittown" as it celebrates its sixtieth anniversary. Even in such mythologically "frozen-in-time" places, substantial evolution occurs. What changes can we expect and work toward in the future?

■ These communities are almost completely built out. The aggregation of single-family-house sites is unlikely, except in conditions of extreme disinvestment or decay, as in the isolated Eastgate neighborhood of Park Forest. Any new development, especially for multifamily housing, must come from redevelopment, especially of underutilized school and retail parcels or from the legalization and encouragement of accessory apartments. This is an important tool for achieving greater residential density, affordability, and housing choices.

■ Median age has risen more than national norms. Options must be provided for the many long-time residents who are choosing to age in place. These include support for adapting their homes, enabling granny flats, and building new senior apartments and assisted-living facilities in socially supported central locations with access to mass transit.

■ Retail parcels are failing, even when the residential sector remains strong, creating blight and a significant loss of tax revenue. Local government will continue to step in, especially where private developers and national retailers, which remain put off by a high percentage of nonwhite residents regardless of income, are not willing or able. Another strategy to attract new retail is by diversifying and modernizing the housing stock to increase the median home price—a very important indicator to national retail location scouts. This may or may not be combined with attempts to retrofit the retail parcels into mixed-use town centers.

■ Although these places never were exclusively "bedroom suburbs," attempts to diversify and expand workplace opportunities will help them better serve future generations' needs. Opportunities include the conversion of vacant big-box stores to back-office use, permitting live/work use, and encouraging telework and incubator office use.

■ Ethnic minorities will increasingly become the majority. Yet studies show that all else being equal (household income, level of education, quality of housing stock), property values are suppressed where middle-class minority residents, especially African Americans, have increased in number. Efforts must be made to understand and counteract the bias attached to demographic diversity.

■ Regional alliances are being formed to address issues of shared concern, such as retrofitting commercial strips and improving mass transit. Expanded transit options can help revive town centers by improving accessibility and improve community sustainability by making these early postwar settlements, which are already more structured, connected, and compact than contemporary residential developments, into viable, affordable options for suburbanites seeking a smart growth community.

Surprisingly, Levittown, Willingboro, and Park Forest, icons of postwar suburbia, share many significant characteristics of contemporary walkable communities: average net densities of eight dwelling units per acre, small houses, relatively interconnected street grids (fewer culs-de-sac), sidewalks, and access to transit. This is why the retrofit strategies they are employing as they mature—senior hous-

ing, civic uses, and town centers—are so promising as ways to further increase housing choice, density, transit feasibility, and accessibility while maintaining the stock of affordable housing. The allowance of accessory dwelling units (granny flats over the garage or small rental cottages in the back yard) would accelerate these benefits and accommodate even more diverse households. These changes are helping them adapt to new demographic conditions and better position themselves for future markets in ways that similar master-planned residential suburbs should learn from.

Unfortunately, many later such suburbs were developed at even lower densities, with larger houses, less connected street patterns, and no sidewalks or transit. Completely automobile-dependent, they provide many of the same opportunity sites for retrofitting, but with less promise of walkable integration with the whole or systemic improvements to their region's economic, social, or environmental sustainability. Those that are well situated and well loved may endure the demographic changes and rising oil prices likely to come. But others may require more radical surgery to avoid being left behind, as households choose more walkable and more affordable options.

Chapter 4

Retrofitting Social Life Along Commercial Strips

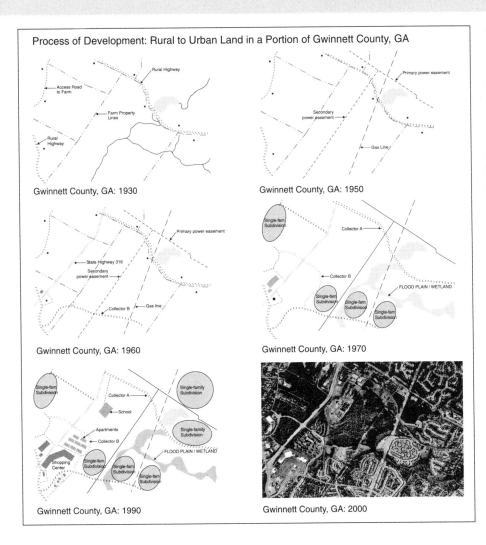

Process of Development: Rural to Urban Land in a Portion of Gwinnett County, GA

Gwinnett County, GA: 1930

Gwinnett County, GA: 1950

Gwinnett County, GA: 1960

Gwinnett County, GA: 1970

Gwinnett County, GA: 1990

Gwinnett County, GA: 2000

The best urban places attract people by the complex and cumulative effect of all of their activities and spaces. In other words, the sum is greater than the parts. Sadly, the opposite is more often true of the aggregation of big-box stores, strip malls, and shopping centers along suburban commercial strips. What strategies are designers using to retrofit these ubiquitous and generic properties into place-specific amenities with community-building potential?

THIRD PLACES IN SUBURBIA?

What is a great, good place? Sociologist Ray Oldenburg uses this term to describe neighborhood gathering places where local people routinely hang out and socialize.[1] Common examples include the corner pub, diner, coffee shop, barbershop or hair salon, and even at times the hardware or general store. Oldenburg argues that as hosts to informal clubs where social bonds and networks are reinforced, these places serve a fundamental role in building community. Private spaces, they nonetheless offer informal public interaction and tend to have minimal restrictions on access (other than gender, which often informally figures

Figure 4–1 The conversion of rural to urban land: a sample from Gwinnett County, Georgia, between 1930 and 2000.

in). Oldenburg describes them as neutral territories where the class distinctions and hierarchical roles that distinguish people at home or work are dropped. The well-off and the struggling, the old and the young (on the television show *Cheers,* the psychiatrist and the postman) can share equally and form strong social ties through banter, gossip, debate, teasing, and dreaming. Oldenburg calls them "third places" and notes that unlike the places of home and work, third places are essential to the growth of social capital and sense of inhabitants belonging to a good place.[2]

Is suburbia generally lacking in "third places"? Oldenburg thinks so and he is not alone in connecting the decline in public forms of sociable behavior with suburban development patterns.[3] Robert Putnam, a Harvard sociologist, has documented the decline in the United States in communal associations, especially in suburban areas. Putnam's book, *Bowling Alone,* documents declining membership in PTAs, Kiwanis Clubs, bowling leagues, churches, and political organizations. While he is hesitant to specifically blame the decline on any single factor, he agrees that the suburban segregation of uses, the substitution of volunteer time by commute time, and the loss of identification of service retail with a specific neighborhood have contributed to the decline. Stephan J. Goetz and Anil Rupasingha have documented similar declines in social capital–generating associations as well as civic participation as a result of the presence of Wal-Mart stores.[4]

This is not to suggest that suburbia lacks social activity—only that such activity has tended to be organized around the home, workplace, or school. In these settings, unlike in third places, hierarchical roles tend to be reinforced and socializing tends to be more exclusive. Suburbia's communal spaces tend to be assigned to very specific forms of recreation that result in age and interest segregation. The soccer entourages, skateboarders, golfers, joggers, bi-cyclists, mall walkers, mallrats, and bird-watchers all have their spaces—just not where they are likely to interact with each other.[5]

This has begun to change with some of the newer private establishments. With its 1996 superstore model, Barnes & Noble responded to the perception that chain stores were impersonal and disconnected from their communities by introducing coffee shops and inviting customers to hang out on lounge furniture. Starbucks's lounge furnishings quickly followed suit and in 2006 the CEO made being a "third place" part of their brand and employee training. It is difficult to say how much of their success can be attributed to encouraging people to sit and gather, but clearly a wide variety of suburban chain stores, including Target and Whole Foods, have similarly retrofitted their store layout templates to incorporate café seating areas and encourage people to linger rather than move on.

The same can only rarely be said for the predominant public space in suburbia—the commercial strip corridor itself. Like earlier generations of retail and fast-food restaurants, the strip is designed for passing through and destination shopping rather than for encouraging social behavior and chance encounters. Instead of the people-filled squares, monument-focused plazas, lushly planted public parks, sports fields, and shop window–enlivened sidewalks of the best urban public spaces, the space for shared experience for most of suburbia is a heavily trafficked commercial strip. Public spaces in cities have traditionally been designed to celebrate the community's collective aspirations of togetherness, memorializing great accomplishments, health, and wealth. These commodious public spaces compensated for citizens' generally small private living spaces. As is well recognized, suburbia in general inverts the equation, providing inhabitants with enriched private realms but a debased public realm. At

ICSC Shopping Center Definitions

Type of Shopping Center	Concept	Typical Acreage/ Square Feet	Anchor Ratio/Typical Anchor(s)	Primary Trade Area
Regional Center	General merchandise; fashion (mall, typically enclosed)	40–100 400,000–800,000 sf	50%–70% Full-line dept. store; jr. dept. store; mass merchant; fashion apparel	5–15 mi
Superregional Center	Similar to regional center but with more variety and assortment	60–120 800,000+ sf	50%–70% Full-line dept. store; jr. dept. store; mass merchant; fashion apparel	5–25 mi
Neighborhood Center	Convenience	3–15 30,000–150,000 sf	30%–50% supermarket	3 mi
Community Center	General merchandise; convenience	10–40 100,000–350,000 sf	50%–70% Discount dept. store; supermarket; drug; home improvement; large specialty/discount apparel	3–6 mi
Lifestyle Center	Upscale national chain specialty stores; dining and entertainment in outdoor setting	10–40 Typically 150,000– 500,000 sf but can be smaller or larger	0%–50% Not usually anchored in the traditional sense but may include bookstore; other large-format specialty retailers; multiplex cinema; small dept. store	8–12 mi
Power Center	Category-dominant anchors; few small tenants	25–80 250,000–600,000 sf	75%–90%	5–15 mi
Theme/Festival Center	Leisure; tourist oriented; retail and service	5–20 80,000–250,000 sf	Restaurants; entertainment	N/A
Outlet Center	Manufacturers' outlet stores	10–50 50,000–400,000 sf	Manufacturers' outlet stores	25–75 mi

Source: Copyright © 2004 International Council of Shopping Centers, Inc., New York, New York. Published in *ICSC Shopping Center Definitions, Basic Configurations and Types for the United States,* dated 2004. Reprinted with permission.

best, the promise of freedom inherent to the road and the promise of self-actualization promoted by consumerism endow the strip with the capacity to satisfy a broad range of individual needs and desires. At worst, the collective aspirations expressed by the commercial strip speak of the willing suppression of local identity by national systems of corporate investment and mass consumption.

Commercial strips' poor performance in community building is but one of the criticisms made of their spaces and building types. At the larger scale, their direct role in extending automobile-dependent sprawl development is responsible for a host of environmental and social problems. At the scale of immediate experience, they have long been disparaged as ugly and been made the focus of beautification efforts, most notably Lady Bird Johnson's campaign against billboards with the 1965 Highway Beautification Act. More recent efforts to be discussed in the forthcoming pages go beyond tidying up signage and burying wires to include efforts to strengthen the social infrastructure of changing suburban communities. Examples to be discussed include adaptive reuse of big-box stores for more community-serving uses, the redevelopment of failed shopping centers into mixed-use neighborhood centers, and the reconfiguration of the strip itself as a walkable, transit-served boulevard attracting a mix of uses.

HISTORY OF THE STRIP AND ITS BUILDING TYPES

Commercial strips can be defined as major city streets lined with commercial activities. They usually host a mixture of retail establishments, office buildings, automobile dealerships, car parks, some occasional residential buildings, and often vacant space. These strips represent typical landscapes in American cities (Clay, 1973). They cut across different urban sections, serving as access routes and travel corridors. Prior to the construction of freeways they were the principal traffic arteries of the city, and they still carry a significant share of vehicular traffic. Inner-city commercial strips can be characterized as the "in-between" spaces of the city. They connect centers with subcenters, and the latter with one another, in the multicentered urban expanse that is typical of the postindustrial American city (Sawers and Tabb, 1984).[6]

— Anastasia Loukaitou-Sideris (1997)

As Anastasia Loukaitou-Sideris suggests, the form and character of commercial strips vary significantly from place to place. However, the variations are less notable from one geographic region to the next and more notable along a single strip between its older and more urban sections and its newer, more suburban lengths. Commercial strips evolved from trunk roads between settlements into streets (some with streetcar lines) serving expanding suburban development and then into today's arterials lined with automobile-oriented strip malls and shopping centers. Each permutation was accompanied by a simultaneously evolving typology of retail establishments, lot size and ownership patterns, and zoning regulations. Chester Liebs documented this story in his 1985 book *Main Street to Miracle Mile,* which he begins with a hypothetical drive outward from "downtown" along the timeline that is traversed by a typical commercial strip. His technique is well worth borrowing and updating in order to understand the different contexts and opportunities for retrofitting.

The Drive out of Town

Our drive starts at a downtown intersection with "Main Street" headed out of town. Within the first mile, traffic rarely moves faster than thirty miles an hour. This older, more urban part of the strip passes late-nineteenth-century linear commercial development clustered at former streetcar stops as well as "taxpayer strips" from the 1920s and 1930s. A few miles out, one finds the branch department stores, banks, and movie theaters that began opening up at major intersections in the 1930s and 1940s. In between the intersections there may still be some surviving single-family homes whose lawns have been paved since they were converted to office or retail use.

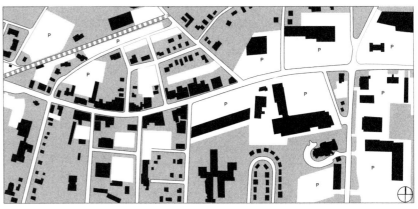

Figure 4–3 Development patterns in many suburban town centers reflect an evolution from older, small lots with buildings near the road in close proximity to a railroad station to newer, larger lots with buildings set behind parking lots in closer proximity to highways.

Figure 4–2 The single-story retail building on the right is a surviving example in Silver Spring, Maryland, of what were called "taxpayer strips." Sometimes incorporating a second floor, this form of development spread quickly on the roads heading out of town as car ownership rates rose. They were typically built right up to the road and relied principally on on-street parking or walk-in customers from nearby neighborhoods (at least before the streets were widened). They were built quickly and at just enough density to cover the property taxes (hence the name) until such time as it would make sense to replace them with larger buildings—such as that on the left.

One also begins to see the early strip malls—a row of shops, often with a simple canopy, on a few acres. In response to the rise in automobile ownership, the early designs provide space for pull-in parking directly off the street. Later, the buildings are set back behind off-street parking lots.[7] The amount of parking has grown over time, now typically taking up 80% of the lot. Many of these survive as contemporary "neighborhood centers," a category the International Council of Shopping Centers (ICSC) describes as serving the day-to-day needs of consumers in the immediate neighborhood.

Along this part of the drive, one also sees that tourists were catered to by locally owned motels with unique, eye-catching neon signs.[8] While few of these reach the glitz of Las Vegas's famous mid-century neon signs, there were many efforts along commercial strips up through the 1960s to attract customers with quirky giant roadside signs and statues that advertised place-specific attributes, from Long Island ducklings to dinosaur fossils.

By the time one arrives at the postwar suburbs, traffic speeds up and the strip centers proliferate, getting larger in size as one proceeds.[9] Even the individual commercial buildings are located on large lots so as to be more visible to passing cars. As early as the late 1940s, pioneering developers began to include full-line branch department stores as anchors and by the mid-1950s enclosed shopping centers provided central air-conditioning and heating. However, the majority of shopping centers at this time were open-air strip centers. The ICSC would refer to the larger ones as "community centers." They were typically arranged in an L or a U and anchored by at least a supermarket, if not another large store in addition to the smaller "in-line" stores. Actively competing with downtowns, the new suburban shopping centers of the 1950s and 1960s often included a post office, bank, church, or other social amenities at the same time that they excluded individuals considered socially undesirable or disturbing to their middle-class, mostly female clientele. By 1964 there

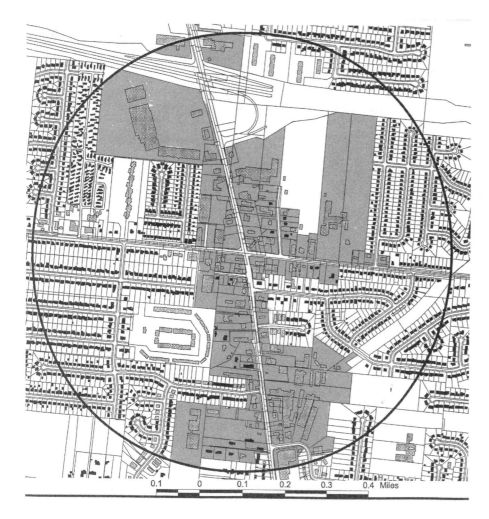

0.1   0   0.1   0.2   0.3   0.4 Miles

Figure 4–4 This map by Brenda Case Scheer of a portion of Colerain Avenue outside Cincinnati, Ohio, shows the larger lots typical of commercial strips developed in the sixties and seventies and the layering of retail activity that results, leading to a greater perception of disorder.

highways and bypasses built as part of the interstate highway system begun in 1956. New residential subdivisions would be visible from our drive, but most would be set enough distance back from the road to install a retail strip and/or an apartment complex as a buffer between the road and the single-family houses. (See Figure 4-4.)

Brenda Case Scheer's revealing morphological analysis of Colerain Avenue, U.S. Route 27, between Cincinnati and Oxford, Ohio, notes how much deeper the commercial lots from the 1960s and 1970s tend to be compared to those developed earlier. This may be due to a desire to install a deeper buffer between the now heavily trafficked road and the new subdivisions bordering it. Sidewalks are no longer common. The oldest buildings, the strip centers, occupy the center of the lot. They are now flanked by newer outparcel buildings along the road (the fast-food restaurants and gas stations, many of which likely came in after 1968 when the parking standards were reduced and owners found themselves able to pack more retail onto their now-oversized parking lots) and even newer strip centers in the rear. Scheer notes that "the need to advertise the 'back row' and the 'middle row' leads to a cacophony of signs" and the mirroring geometry of the relationship of street and building is entirely lost.[11]

The visual cacophony evident in this portion of the drive is compounded by the rapid expansion of fast-food franchises, convenience stores, and discount department stores in the 1970s. Wal-Mart, Kmart, and Target all started in 1962 and established a national presence through the 1970s. From Wal-Mart's expansion in rural areas to Kmart's dominance in suburban markets and the spread of the McDonald's golden arches across the country, successful retailers in the 1970s responded to recession, stagflation, and slumping sales per square foot by focusing on discount prices and scaling up their stores into retail

were 7,600 shopping centers in the United States. By 1972, the number of shopping centers had doubled to 13,174.[10]

The increase can be attributed to the postwar economic boom that the country enjoyed through the 1960s, the 1954 change to the tax code that allowed accelerated depreciation for income-producing buildings, and the suburban development boom (especially in mall construction) that followed the new chains. Eric Schlosser, author of *Fast Food Nation: The Dark Side of the All-American Meal,* points out that there were 1,000 McDonald's restaurants in 1968 and 28,000 by 2002, making it the largest retail property owner in the world. Convenience stores similarly exploded along the strip, growing from 25,000 to 45,000 between 1975 and 1985.[12] Wal-Mart's growth has been similarly astounding, surpassing the number of employees of General Motors, Ford, and Chrysler combined by 1992. As a consequence, between 1972 and 1982, the average American downtown lost one quarter of its retail sales.[13]

At the same time, major institutional investors in real estate such as Connecticut General, Equitable, Prudential, and Teachers Insurance and Annuity concluded that for the same risk they could incur potentially greater revenues by holding equity rather than loans in real estate. With ownership stakes of up to 50%, they significantly influenced the tenant mix toward national retail chains by underwriting requirements calling for "triple-A tenants" (businesses with top credit ratings considered least likely to default on a lease).[14] The chains' national advertising campaigns and standardized designs and products emphasized strategies of mass consumption while disconnecting consumers and passersby from the immediate place. Already by 1975, critics were decrying the uniformity of franchises and chains and the loss of independent retailers as a threat to democracy.[15] Today, 90% of space in large malls is leased to chains.[16] Passing the early stores from this era on the drive, one sees the country's early transition from an industrial to a postindustrial economy as more and more of the landscape is devoted to consumerism.[17]

The visual clutter dies down significantly as the drive passes the enclosed regional malls, corporate campuses, and later edge-city office towers developed in the 1970s and 1980s. Instead of numerous small parcels each with its own direct access and a multitude of signs, the scale of development is now significantly larger. So is the road. With additional lanes and a combination of traffic signals at the landscaped entry points and dedicated exit ramps to the most developed parcels at its arterial intersections, the strip increasingly resembles a limited-access highway. The elimination of any remnant of pedestrian access is now complete, both along the road and at the new complexes. The mall now takes up 40 to 100 acres and serves a trade area of five to fifteen miles. It offers the passing driver marquee signs at each of the limited entrances to its parking lot, with tasteful landscaping in between. The office parks follow a similar typology but with more discreet signage and more extensive landscaping.[18] Neither the mall nor office buildings face the road, let alone face anywhere. They are sheathed in monolithic surfaces, opaque for the mall and most often mirror glass for the office buildings. They are typically object-buildings surrounded by parking with a few outparcels.

A record 16,000 shopping centers were built between 1980 and 1990.[19] Construction did not slow down until the savings and loan crisis in 1989 tightened credit, leading to a 70% decline in shopping center starts.[20] In response, many developers took their companies public, becoming real estate investment trusts (REITs). Shopping center ownership, in particular, shifted from being overwhelmingly a family-run and privately based entrepreneurial business, often with local ties to the community, to becoming a standardized commodity traded on Wall Street.[21] The landscape from the 1990s reflected Wall Street's demand for predictability in increasingly uniform, repetitive building types with little, if any, accommodation to the particularities of place or place-making.[22]

We also see in the strip landscape of the late 1980s and 1990s the proliferation of new retail formats that increased retail specialization and auto dependency. Big-box discount stores like Wal-Mart and "category killers"—warehouse-style stores devoted to a single product type, such as Toys"R"Us— spread rapidly at this time.[23] They were increasingly agglomerated into "power centers"—no-frills open-air strip shopping centers with acres of parking, often displacing older shopping centers and local businesses.[24] Siphoning sales of hard goods, power centers indirectly caused the repositioning of many existing malls into "fashion malls." Not only does this specialization of retail result in consumers making more trips to more places, but research on power centers also suggests that the distances between stores and drab aesthetics result in increased auto dependency as customers drive rather than walk between shops.[25] On our drive, one cannot help but notice that the road has widened with more lanes and the big boxes and shopping centers get bigger and draw on larger and larger trade areas as we pass through lower and lower density development. While a small shop can survive in a visible location in a dense neighborhood, it would be lost in a low-density area that requires a significantly larger trade area to accommodate the same population. Instead, the low-density landscape is dominated by big boxes with short life spans.

Factory outlet centers specializing in discounted or off-season goods also boomed in this period and induced travel to their generally remote locations in resort areas or at the outskirts of town. In 1987 there were 108 factory outlet centers. By 1999 there were 278. Embodying the logic that people will travel further to get both a better price and more selection, all of these types from the 1990s contributed to increased levels of consumer credit card debt and over-retailing (discussed further in Chapter 6 and evidenced by the ghostbox phenomenon discussed later).

As we cross into the twenty-first century and catch up to the present day, we see seemingly contradictory, but intertwined, trends. On the one hand, gigantism continues. For example, instead of the 90,000-square-foot big-box stores Wal-Mart has already blanketed the country with, it is now focused on building 200,000-square-foot supercenters, discount department stores that now include a supermarket and attract an average of 3,300 trips per day. In 1994 Wal-Mart had 147 supercenters; in 2002 it had 1,258.[26] This strategy, which Wal-Mart often refers to as "consolidation," leaves hundreds of former Wal-Mart stores vacant and exemplifies how overretailing contributes to ripening the conditions for retrofitting. At the same time, the construction of enclosed malls has finally ground to a halt, replaced largely by the construction of new upscale, outdoor "lifestyle centers," and "town centers." Discussed in Chapter 6, their walkable Main Streets and, in the best cases, mix of uses, establish pockets of finer-grained urbanism, including a few third places. They reflect the growing diversification of the suburban market that now stretches from supercenters for price-conscious consumers to more urban housing and experiences for a new generation of suburbanites seeking value as well as community. The recent retrofits of big boxes, strip malls, and shopping centers along the strip are adding to this urbanization and diversification while introducing even more fundamental changes: walkability and transit. Are they precursors to massive sustainable change along suburban corridors? Or will the new boulevards and mixed-use neighborhoods be engulfed by ever-widened arterials and supercenters? We can begin to answer such a question by looking at what is happening to those dead 90,000-square-foot Wal-Mart stores.

ADAPTIVE REUSE OF BIG BOXES AND STRIP MALLS FOR COMMUNITY-SERVING ACTIVITIES

At the scale of the single building there is little one can do to affect systemic behavior or VMT. However, as the forthcoming examples show, adaptive reuse is a great strategy for accommodating new activities while recycling old buildings. It is the most sustainable form of growth there is. However, beyond the environmental effects, there are also less measurable but equally significant impacts on the opportunities for social networks when the strip's mini-malls and big boxes are put to more communal uses.

Reviving Ghostboxes

How many ghostboxes are out there? Estimates are in the thousands, but no one knows for certain. Stacy Mitchell of the Institute for Local Self-Reliance reports that Charlotte, North Carolina, had 31 in 2001 and Columbus, Ohio, and Kansas City had 69 and 39, respectively, in 2006.[27] Does every city have a few dozen or only those that were unlucky enough to have had a Woolworths, Montgomery Ward, Bradlees, Ames, or Kmart (some of the losers to Wal-Mart and Target that have gone bankrupt in the last decade and shuttered over 1,500 stores in the process)? Actually, even the cities that had the "winners" are just as likely to have been left with white elephants. Wal-Mart routinely closes fifty to one hundred stores a year in order to "consolidate" four or five stores' trade areas into a larger supercenter.[28] And it is not alone—nor are discount department stores the only big boxes that have cannibalized their profitable stores in order to open even larger formats just down the road. Toys"R"Us, Barnes &

Noble, Circuit City, and Home Depot are just a few of the big-box chains that have also contributed to communities' concerns when they have pulled out. Add to this the thousands of independent retailers killed in their categories—5,000 independent hardware stores alone since 1990[29]—and the scope of the problem becomes clear.

Retail is a notoriously volatile industry, and a good number of vacated properties are soon reinhabited by other stores. (Wal-Mart Realty maintains a website listing their 200–400 available vacant stores at any given time; however, they will not turn over a lease to Target or Kmart.) However, the longer a store sits empty, the harder it is to overcome the perception that retail simply cannot succeed at that site. When a big box anchoring a shopping center goes dark, all of the stores' sales drop. Fears of blight arise amidst the sense of failure that inevitably surrounds a ghostbox. In the successful examples, this has led to "thinking outside the box" and creative reprogramming where adaptive reuse enriches communities' social infrastructure in the process.

The silver lining to the failure of a big box is the availability of cheap space for alternative uses. This is especially important for nonprofit groups, cultural facilities, or local shops that cannot generally afford new construction or extensive site work yet are in need of central locations to best serve their constituents. In *The Death and Life of Great American Cities*, published in 1961, Jane Jacobs criticized how urban renewal and large swaths of "one-age construction" robbed cities of older, affordable buildings—a vital asset for diversity. "Chain stores, chain restaurants, and banks go into new construction. But neighborhood bars, foreign restaurants, and pawn shops go into older buildings. Supermarkets and shoe stores often go into new buildings; good bookstores and antique dealers seldom do. Well-subsidized opera and art museums often go into new buildings. But the unformalized feeders of the arts—studios, galleries, stores for musical instruments and art supplies, backrooms where the low earning power of a seat can absorb uneconomic discussions—these go into ordinary buildings."[30]

While Jacobs's observations were based on urban examples, contemporary observation of aged strip malls and shopping centers reveals the same processes of diversification and gentrification at work. Several first-ring suburbs have new immigrant communities that depend on and support this third generation of uses and would be hurt by the kind of gentrification that redevelopment would likely bring. (See Figure 4–5.)

Empty big boxes have facilitated the same kind of diversification of activities and enrichment of social opportunities along suburban strips. They have been adaptively reused as churches/synagogues/mosques, libraries, courthouses, government offices, community centers, school and university buildings, nightclubs, dinner theaters, multiplex cinemas, gymnasiums, an indoor go-cart raceway, the Spam Museum, call centers, offices, and medical clinics (one example in Savannah reused the heavy voltage from the frozen food section of a former grocery store to power an MRI scanner).[31] The addition of these programs to suburban areas lacking in third places enriches their neighborhoods and adds opportunities for greater communal interaction—even without further changes to the physical context. However, in the best cases, big-box retrofits have also improved pedestrian access, interconnectivity with adjacent neighborhoods, and the amount and quality of public space, as well as their site's environmental performance.

Aside from being reused for retail, the most prevalent reuses have been as places of worship. The congregation of Calvary Chapel of Pinellas Park, Florida, spent seven years meeting in a former Winn-Dixie supermarket before it expanded enough to move across the street into a former Wal-Mart. Bob Corry, an associate pastor with the church, was quoted in the New York Times saying, "The generation we live in today, when they look at an old-fashioned steepled church, there's a fascination but also a little bit of intimidation....If we dolled up our building, we'd be pushing away an element of our community that desperately needs to be welcomed."[32] Are these conversions successful because suburbanites are so accustomed to the architecture of malls, shopping centers, and big-box stores that they are more comfortable in low-slung, deep interiors than the highly articulated and hierarchical sections associated with traditional churches? Or is the rise of the suburban megachurch, with its sanctuaries accommodating several thousand congregants and parking lots to

Figure 4–5 Retrofitting aging strip malls may not always be in a community's interest, especially if its uses are providing spaces for diversification beyond standard retail as in this example in Los Angeles. Because of its cheaper rent, a twenty- or thirty-year-old strip center is much more likely to house public services such as a community health clinic or job center, ethnic specialty shops and restaurants, and places of worship, as well as shoe or bicycle repair shops and thrift stores, than when it first opened. Cheap space, accessible to the larger community, is also vital to incubating immigrant entrepreneurial economies.

Figure 4–6 Many ghostboxes have been retrofitted into suburban megachurches. This is The Beck Group's retrofit of a Big Kmart into His Hands Church in Woodstock, Georgia.

match simply a good fit for the retired properties of the country's biggest megaretailer? In April 2006, Dan Fogleman, a Wal-Mart spokesperson, said that over a dozen Wal-Mart stores had been converted to churches since 2002.[33] Goodman Architectural Services, based in Joplin, Missouri, has a specialization in the conversion of big-box stores to churches. The firm's website, *http://www.goodmanarchitects.com/bigbox.html,* has a "Frequently Asked Questions" page where they point out several of the advantages, including high visibility, ample size, low price, and the message that the church is restoring life to the community.

These factors all came into play when The Beck Group was hired to transform a 123,000-square-foot Big Kmart into the nondenominational His Hands Church on a 13-acre site in Woodstock, Georgia. (See Figure 4–6.) On its home page the church describes itself as a "non-religious, rock music, wear your jeans, bring in your coffee, all-out worship to God kind of church where you can be yourself and know that you are loved." In addition to outfitting the interior with both 1,500- and 500-seat worship halls with comfy chairs and theater lights from the exposed beams, two sides of the box received new, more welcoming facades. The project received two design-build awards in 2007 but Fred Perpall, Beck's Director of Architecture, is particularly proud of its contributions to sustainability. "Not only is the whole building a great example of recycling, we were able to install a new public green space leading to the entry, new sidewalks to the neighborhood, and reduce the amount of impervious surface by forty percent."[34]

Meyer Scherer & Rockcastle paid similar attention to retrofitting both the parking lot and building when they converted a 32,800-square-foot Food Lion grocery store into the Denton Public Library North Branch in Denton, Texas. (See Color Plates 4 to 6.) They removed seventy-five parking spaces to create a tree-lined, pedestrian-friendly xeriscape green zone to front the entry, while additional green spaces and walkways connect to the surrounding neighborhood and an adjacent park. A new glass curtain wall with translucent and transparent glazing gives passersby a glimpse of the public activities within during the day and makes the building glow at night, improving safety and visibility. Along with a series of light monitors and new windows at the old loading dock doors, the new curtainwall brings much welcome light into the deep interior. Café and community rooms are located immediately off the lobby and can be used by the neighborhood after hours.

From Strip Malls to Community Anchors: La Grande Orange and Camino Nuevo

One of the more minimal but effective examples of adaptive reuse has been the La Grande Orange empire created by Bob Lynn and Craig and Kris DeMarco out of three small all-but-abandoned strip buildings clustered at the corner of 40th and Campbell Streets in Phoenix. (See Color Plates 7 and 8.) Without significantly changing the overall structure or parking lots, their conversion of a former laundromat and convenience store into several hip eateries has managed to upgrade the cool factor and social life of the entire Arcadia neighborhood. It started in 2001 with the redevelopment of a former post office in a one-story, brick L-shaped strip mall into Postino Winecafé. Then they opened La Grande Orange Groceria in another strip that shared the same parking lot and faced the corner. An upscale gourmet corner market that also offered breakfast, by

2004 it was expanded to include La Grande Orange Pizzeria. A chic bakery and home furnishings shop joined the mix and in 2007 the owners opened Radio Milano, a cocktail bar and small-plates restaurant in another strip across the street with plans just up the street for a taqueria designed by award-winning architect Will Bruder.[35] In all, they have maintained the buildings' informality and parking in front (which becomes valet in the evenings) while inviting patrons to linger through the addition of outdoor patios, seating, plantings, and lots of bright, shiny paint.

The mixture of casual, family-friendly, retro funkiness combined with sophisticated, urban, foodie trendiness has been immensely popular. Real estate advertisements in the neighborhood routinely advertise their proximity to La Grande Orange and conversations in 2006 with a few "regulars" confirm its standing as a third place where one can expect to run into and chat with both neighbors and local power brokers from the general vicinity. Part of the implicit draw, the added value, of neighborhood centers like La Grande Orange is that they provide the opportunity to increase one's social capital. No longer the inexpensive commodity it once was, people will now pay a premium for it, especially in suburban areas where such informal opportunities to increase social capital are scarce.[36] The owners have capitalized on this value, with Bob Lynn stating he expected sales in 2006 to hit $20 million.[37]

There are several more examples of popular, sophisticated restaurants reviving older buildings on commercial strips as well as the neighborhoods adjacent to them. More renovations than retrofits, they are bringing back older neighborhood centers. The Bank Block in Grandview Heights, Ohio, dating to 1928 and considered by many the first strip shopping center in the country, was a candidate for demolition when a gourmet chef was attracted to its cheap rent. His venue's popularity attracted a coffee shop, fol-

Figure 4–7   The third place created by a grouping of hip restaurants in three strip malls in Phoenix around La Grande Orange Groceria has raised profits, local property values, and neighborhood socializing. The gourmet grocery and cafe attracts an energetic brunch crowd and may be the only strip mall with its own T-shirts.

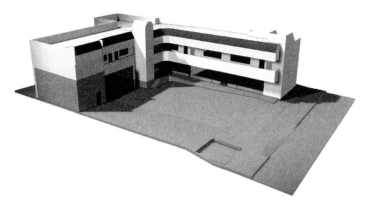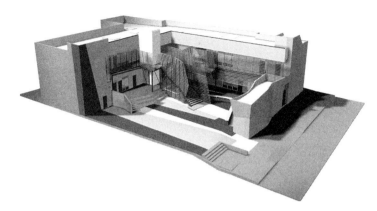

Figure 4–8 These before-and-after diagrams show how Daly Genik Architects retrofitted a dead two-story mini-mall in Los Angeles into the Camino Nuevo Charter Academy. Working with a very limited budget, they changed the building typology from a commercial building fronting a parking lot to a courtyard building with a safe zone protected from the street. They widened all of the exterior stairs and walkways to accommodate hordes of schoolkids and then built a brightly painted addition at the street edge to both establish the school's presence and to make a clear threshold between inside and outside.

lowed by local shops and galleries, to the point where it is now some of the most expensive real estate in the Columbus area—a revival that some credit to the value of its more urban form. From the beginning, the Bank Block fronted onto a sidewalk at the street and placed its 400-car parking lot behind.[38] Several taxpayer strips along West College Avenue in Decatur, Georgia, which similarly front the road and sat vacant for decades, have recently become popular locations for bistros, bakeries, and smoothie bars as the neighborhoods behind them have gentrified.

However, not all new neighborhood centers are upscale or mini versions of lifestyle centers. A final example of adaptive reuse illustrates the role that schools can play as community anchors, and as tenants of former strip buildings. Camino Nuevo Charter Academy approached Daly Genik Architects to transform a dilapidated—and never occupied—two-story, L-shaped mini-mall in the MacArthur Park section of Los Angeles into an elementary school. (See Color Plates 9 to 11 and Figure 4–8.)

After it opened in 2000, Daly Genik was asked to develop a middle school on the same block. This time the firm was asked to fit classrooms into a one-story warehouse and a dingbat office building (a Los Angeles low-rise building type from the 1950s and 1960s that more or less sits on stilts above ground-

level parking that generally rear exits directly onto the road). With the requirements for new stairs and earthquake resistance, it might have been less expensive to build new construction, but the carbon investment would have been much higher and parking requirements would have kicked in. Daly admits to his preference for working with the existing buildings. He likes how the projects reinforce the L.A. stereotype as a place where reinvention is possible and compares the buildings to actors going into rehab.[39]

Nonetheless, the firm's next two projects for the academy, a high school and a prekindergarten building, were in fact new construction. The high school is on the site of a former ice-cream factory that had become a computer distribution warehouse, wedged between a freeway and an arterial, while the pre-K building joins the elementary and middle schools on the original block.

Although Daly Genik did a master plan for the block at the outset (just in case the academy was indeed able to acquire all of the property), in retrospect Daly believes it is better that the development has been incremental. When they first started, it would have been too easy to wall it off into a protected compound. Instead, it has developed as a campus of interrelated parts and allowed for more engagement with the neighborhood as conditions have improved. When a house associated with drug use burned down next to the elementary school, Camino Nuevo was able to turn the lot into a playground. Today, the academy serves over 1,200 students and is sending graduates back into the neighborhood, sponsoring even further change. The projects have won numerous AIA awards for the architects, as well as the Gold Medal from the Rudy Bruner Award for Urban Excellence in 2003.

RETROFITTING SHOPPING CENTERS: THE MIDDLE SCALE

The ICSC uses the term *shopping center* very broadly to refer to any "group of retail and other commercial establishments that is planned, developed, owned and managed as a single property, with on-site parking provided."[40] They estimate that there are more than 45,000 shopping centers in the United States. Approximately 40,000 of those are under 250,000 square feet—the open-air strip centers. We will look at retrofits of the largest shopping centers in Chapter 6; the regional and superregional malls whose 40- to 120-acre size enables them to establish new infrastructure patterns capable of reducing per capita urban carbon footprints. We have also seen the design possibilities of adaptive reuse of the smallest strip centers and individual big-box stores and how even relatively minor changes of use can impact social networks. What of the middle scale—the 10- to 40-acre shopping centers with two or more anchors? What kind of impacts and communities can retrofits build at this scale?

Based on his extensive experience, noted urban designer Andres Duany believes that it is difficult to establish a sense of place or urban synergy on less than 15 acres.[41] However, what smaller shopping center retrofits in relatively urban areas can do very well is *restore* urbanism. Uptown District in San Diego and Kirkwood Station Plaza in Kirkwood, Missouri, both restored street connectivity that had been removed by their prior occupants, a giant Sears store and Target, respectively. At 15 acres in a context with an urban structure, Uptown District both strengthens the neighborhood with a great mix of uses, including a community center, while operating as infill, blending, more or less seamlessly, into the neighborhood rather than being clearly identified as a new "development." (See Figures 4–9 and 4–10.) On only 7 acres, Kirkwood Station Plaza contributes a grand public plaza to its surroundings but is too small to itself constitute a neighborhood.[42]

Regreening: Phalen

Fifteen acres is also the minimum threshold that the Environmental Protection Agency deems necessary to implement the principles of smart growth. In most cases, these are achieved through densification and the design of complete neighborhoods. However, on smaller parcels or in areas of low or negative growth, de-densification and regreening may be more successful strategies. The Philadelphia Horticultural Society's "Philadelphia Green" program has redeveloped hundreds of vacant lots as pocket parks and community gardens, increasing sales prices of homes near the lots by as much as 30% in the process.[43] Several cities and counties have land-banking programs that either renovate or demolish abandoned buildings. Genesee County in Michigan (which includes the city of Flint, whose downward economy was made famous in the documentary *Roger and Me*) has one of the most comprehensive in the country. Working primarily with lots of 1 acre or less, in the past five years it has helped demolish over 500 homes, renovated

Figure 4-9 The Uptown District in the largely gay Hillcrest neighborhood of San Diego restored mixed-use urbanism to a 15-acre site of a Sears department store. The superblock was subdivided into four blocks, many of which are further broken down with courtyards. Housing over retail faces the reurbanizing arterial corridor while a new pedestrian bridge over a freeway connects the project to the University Heights neighborhood. Completed in 1990 for $70 million, it was developed by Oliver McMillan/Odmark and Thelan. The project team included Gast Hillmer Urban Design, Williams-Kuebelbeck Associates Inc. Economic Consultants, and Urban Systems Associates Transportation Consultants.

Figure 4-10 Uptown District provides a wide range of neighborhood-focused uses: a community center, a high-performing Ralph's grocery store (despite having limited visibility from the street and underground parking), small shops (many of which have struggled), and over 300 dwelling units on 15 acres. The Sears site was bought by the city for a library until citizens' groups lobbied for mixed use and residences. Retrofits like Uptown District that are city-led are more likely to be residence than retail driven.

twenty-five to fifty per year, and handed approximately 500 lots over to neighboring residents through its Adopt-A-Lot, Clean and Green, and Side Lot Transfer programs. It has also established demonstration model vegetable and rain gardens and in conjunction with other city, county, and state agencies, hopes to connect its growing inventory of over 3,000 vacant lots into low-maintenance "green infrastructure" systems: open space, trails, community gardens, tree nurseries for neighborhood use, urban agriculture, phytoremediation soil improvement, flood control, and parks.

Regreening has also been successful on greyfield sites. When faced with a failed strip center dating from 1959 on 20 acres in Phalen, a suburban area in St. Paul, Minnesota, the city of St. Paul bought the property, restored the wetlands and lake that had previously occupied the site, and turned it into a public park.[44] (See Figure 4-11.) The plan for the project was developed in 1994 by the University of Minnesota College of Architecture and Landscape Architecture, working with the city of St. Paul and Phalen residents.[45] Called the Phalen Village Plan, it looked at revitalization strategies for the larger neighborhood, with the park playing several key roles: restoring a system of lakes and migratory bird habitat; filtering and retaining stormwater; and fostering affordable

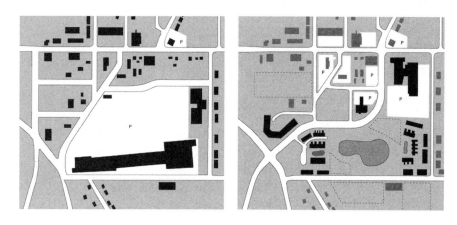

Figure 4–11 These before-and-after diagrams show the regreening of Phalen. The left shows the failed shopping center in 1997. The right shows Phalen Village in 2005 after the lake and wetlands were restored with new road alignments and new housing.

transit-oriented development, as well as serving as a catalyst in economic development. In this case, the retrofit was spurred not by rising property values in the area, but their decline. Bordered by several older public housing projects to the east and declining apartment complexes to the north, market rate densification on the site was not feasible. Rather, the innovative idea was to increase investment in the area by converting much of it to lakefront property and what the designers called "an ecological neighborhood" centered on the Phalen Wetland Park.

By 2005 Ames Lake had been reconstructed in the middle of the block formerly occupied by the parking for the strip center and included a public, educational boardwalk over the reed beds. The reconstructed wetlands, although not as extensive as in the 1994 plan, had demonstrably increased local biodiversity.[46] The adjacent public housing had been renovated but without the new street grid called for in the plan. New Habitat for Humanity homes, new senior housing, as well as several commercial parcels north of the lake were in place along the new Phalen Boulevard. And while the proposed transit center was not built, the project had stimulated the construction of new market-rate houses bordering the lake. A 2007 report estimated the market value of the project

area had increased over $26 million since 2000.[47] In many respects, the project has been a great success. Lee Sobel's 2002 book for the Congress for the New Urbanism, *Greyfields into Goldfields,* concluded that "Through the oversight of the city of St. Paul, Phalen Village Center's ongoing revitalization is leading the revival of an old community with a new identity."[48] Chuck Repke, head of the local planning council, said the project reminded him of a Joni Mitchell song. "She sang, 'They paved paradise and put up a parking lot,'" Repke says. "We did the reverse."[49]

However, not only is the size of the park substantially diminished, its borders have been encroached upon by private development. A market-rate development called Phalen Crossing has been allowed to arrange semirandom bars of suburban front-loaded townhouses, condos, and cottages in four clusters around the lake. (See Figures 4–12 and 4–13.) The fact that this public amenity has been allowed to be privatized is a tragedy. The fact that the designers of the new housing did not even attempt to spatially frame the lake or orient the housing toward it is an insult. Instead of being treated as a public park, a third place for the neighborhood, the lake seems destined to be treated as a suburban retention pond.

Figure 4–12 View of the restored lake and wetlands of Phalen Village with new townhouse clusters "backing" onto the park visible in the background. The size of the park has been substantially diminished from the original plan.

Figure 4–13 View of the rear yard of one of Phalen Village's new townhouse clusters abutting the wetland. This juxtaposition both privatizes and potentially poisons a public asset.

in 2007. Was it asking too much to give more than two-thirds of a 20-acre parcel to a public park in an area prioritizing economic investment? Are publicly driven projects inherently more prone to compromise? What can urban designers do to see that beautiful plans are not degraded by poorly laid out, poorly designed "instant architecture"? It is certainly a reminder that substantial change, such as retrofitting the public realm, requires not only great plans, but also great implementation.

Public Sector Strategies to Support Retrofitting

Unfortunately, implementation of redevelopment projects is usually more difficult—and more costly—than new construction. While the sites have already been flattened and drained, there are often contamination costs to contend with. Add to this the cost of relocating or working around existing tenants and demolition and it can be difficult for a developer to keep costs competitive. More and more, municipalities that want to attract redevelopment have to come up with incentives, including shouldering the cost differential between greenfield and greyfield development. In 2006 the city of Buffalo, New York, joined with its first-tier suburbs (Amherst, Tonawanda, and Cheektowaga) in a regional strategy for combating vacant properties, called "Blueprint Buffalo." Led in large part by the Virginia Tech Metropolitan Institute, it recommends new programs and incentives as well as policy and zoning changes. Colleen DiPirro, president of the Amherst, New York, Chamber of Commerce, said, "It's still more expensive to rehab a property than to build from scratch, and that's why we're trying to level the playing field."[50] One of the advantages of smaller retrofit sites is that the cost differential is that much more manageable for a city

This may be a cautionary tale for the designers of retrofits. Perhaps you can take the shopping center out of the suburb, but you cannot take the suburban mind-set and building typologies out of the developers and city officials. Were the designers' ecologically and urban-oriented visions out of sync with the actual needs and desires of the community? In the later version of the Small Area Plan published in *Goldfields into Greyfields* in 2002, the park is much reduced from the 1994 version but still larger than it stands budget and the limited programs intended to assist cities with redevelopment.

The city of Charleston, South Carolina, engages in what might be called preemptive retrofitting. The city expects to overhaul its zoning to incorporate new urbanist and smart growth principles, but in the meantime beefed up its urban design staff to retrofit developers' design proposals as a free service. Led by Josh Martin, the staff has "urbanized" twenty projects, both residential and commercial, in one and a half years. Martin says that under current practices, civil engineers have become de facto land planners and his staff is augmenting their work with more attention to architectural and urban design, tenant mix, and subarea plans. For example, when the owner of Saint Andrews, a failing strip mall, presented his plans for a "facadectomy," the office asked, "Can we help and play with it?" Within approximately one week, they surveyed the tenants' lease terms and came up with a plan for incremental redevelopment in accordance with the lease expirations that gradually inserted new streets into the superblock, liner buildings facing the streets, and a new park, while showing a better expected rate of return for the owner. While the city does not always get all of the changes that it asks for, developers recognize the entitlement incentives of working with the city on the design up front. Martin credits the deep commitment of Charleston's mayor, Joe Riley, for supporting the three urban designers and two architects on staff but believes that any city could employ the same strategy with a minimum of one well-trained urban designer.[51]

One of the programs that was used to develop Phalen Village was Minnesota's Livable Communities Demonstration Account (LCDA), part of the 1995 Livable Communities Act. From 1996 through 2007, the LCDA made 143 grants to forty-seven communities for $74.67 million. In return for these investments, 7,182 new jobs have been created, with $7.94 million in new net tax capacity resulting from the attraction of $653 million in private investment. In addition to the $1 million invested in helping to demolish Phalen's shopping center, LCDA funds have helped transform several greyfield projects. A retail shopping strip has been converted into three- to four-story housing and neighborhood commercial development at Kensington Park in Richfield. A 4.5-acre site with a failed fifty-year-old shopping center in Falcon Heights has become Falcon Heights Town Square, with three- to four-story senior housing, apartments over retail, and townhouses providing urban edges on a small site. The Village North Shopping Center in Brooklyn Park, a once-thriving subregional mall from the 1970s, has been torn down and construction started on a 27-acre mixed-use, new urbanist community called Village Creek. (See Figure 4–14.)

The LCDA program is not dissimilar to the Atlanta Regional Commission's Livable Centers Initiatives (LCI) program.[52] Started in 1999, the program uses federal transportation funds to support planning studies for improvements to existing centers and corridors that will reduce VMT and improve air quality. Competition for the grants is steep and communities are encouraged to link transportation improvements with land-use development strategies to create mixed-use communities consistent with regional development policies. Over 203 planning studies in 68 study areas throughout the region have benefited from the $10 million committed since 1999. More importantly, $500 million has been committed for priority funding of the transportation improvements resulting from LCI studies. By changing zoning and making the infrastructure investments recommended in the plans, half of the proposed projects have been completed as of this writing. Including those that are being planned, the region expects to accommodate 63,000 residen-

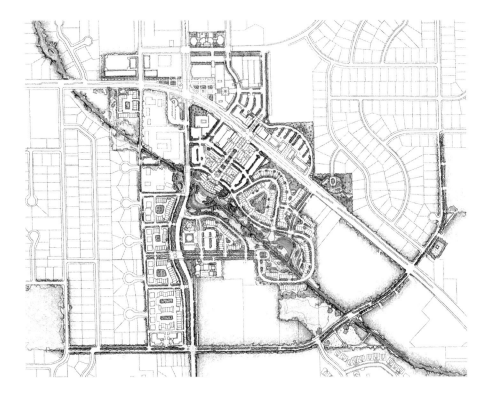

Figure 4–14 The Cunningham Group designed Village Creek as part of a retrofit of a shopping center site in Brooklyn Park, Minnesota, that is linked to a larger landscape restoration project. In addition to facing Brooklyn Boulevard, a commercial arterial, with new mixed-use buildings, the project includes Welcome Avenue, a new Main Street perpendicular to the arterial that leads down to a daylit creek and production-built affordable housing.

the region expects to accommodate 63,000 residential units, 9,000 hotel units, 11.5 million square feet of commercial space, and 40 million square feet of office space within more walkable, more compact development patterns as a result of the LCI program.[53] The notable retrofitting occurring at Perimeter Center and in the area of the Lindbergh MARTA station are both results of this process. Perimeter Place is discussed in Chapter 9 and the BellSouth development at Lindbergh in Chapter 11, although both projects have since triggered considerably more redevelopment of adjacent strip malls and garden apartment complexes.

Additional incentives that Atlanta LCI communities have successfully used to attract redevelopment are tax allocation districts (TADs), a local name

for what is generally referred to as tax-increment financing, or TIF. This method of financing public improvements to real estate is based on future tax revenue that is dedicated to financing redevelopment debt. Its use by cities to induce redevelopment has dramatically increased over the past ten years. However, it is a complex mechanism that requires city council and school board approval, as well as in some cases a local referendum. As such, it is cumbersome to use for small parcels. An exception to this was in Kettering, Ohio, at the vacant 1950s 22-acre, 200,000-square-foot Hills and Dales shopping center. In 1999, the city council bought the site, renamed it Governor's Place, and used the nonschool portion of a TIF to install roads and utilities. Acting as the developer, the city sold all seven parcels on the site and achieved a three-and-a-half-year build-out and seven-year payback, well ahead of schedule. Smaller redevelopment projects can also be induced by the establishment of a TIF over a larger blighted area. In Smyrna, Georgia, just west of Atlanta, an LCI study led to the establishment of a 140-acre TAD to build on the recently redeveloped downtown and to sponsor nodal growth along a major corridor between two intersections. Two aging shopping center sites within the TAD, Jonquil Plaza and Belmont Hills, have since begun redevelopment plans.[54] However, as of this writing, retrofitting of both large and small projects in Georgia has halted due to a successful lawsuit challenging the legality of tying up school-based tax revenue for nonschool-based use. Advocates for TIF argue that in the long run schools benefit from the higher tax revenues that would not have occurred without redevelopment. But the questions of whether redevelopment would occur anyway (without public investment) and whether schools' revenue is being held hostage to support redevelopment remain thorny issues for many municipalities.

Santana Row's Rough Road to Riches

While many suburban retrofits we have studied have benefited from tax-increment financing, it is certainly true that not all retrofits have relied upon public subsidies. Two of the better-known strip center retrofits, Mashpee Commons on Cape Cod, discussed in Chapter 5, and Santana Row in San Jose, received no public funding. In both cases, visionary, tenacious, and optimistic developers led these projects. But the lack of public support cost them dearly in terms of time at Mashpee Commons, and in terms of the CEO's job at Santana Row.

Federal Realty Investment Trust had a successful track record pioneering new urbanist redevelopment at Pentagon Row and Bethesda Row, both outside Washington, DC, when its CEO, Steven Guttman, embarked on a much more ambitious retrofit of a 43-acre strip shopping center. (See Figure 4–15.) To be called Santana Row, the first phase's 22 acres were three months away from opening when a fire in 2002 destroyed more than one hundred apartments,

townhouses, and retail spaces. The delayed opening (and revenue stream), as well as the need to fund the rebuilding before waiting for insurance claims to be settled, was the last straw for Wall Street analysts impatient with the REIT's $500 million investment in the project. Four months later the *New York Times* reported that "Mr. Guttman initiated Santana Row, and he moved here, across the country from corporate headquarters in Maryland, to see it through. Last March [2002], under criticism from Wall Street for putting so much of Federal Realty's money into Santana Row, he announced plans to resign as chief executive, and Federal Realty has indicated that it will back away from projects like this one."[55]

This was confirmed in 2004 when returns on the first phase were running at 5%.[56] Jan Sweetnam, COO for Federal Realty's western region, told attendees at an Urban Land Institute conference that projects like Santana will only be undertaken with public assistance. He claimed that Federal had not wanted public money on Santana because it wanted to maintain private control of the development without strings attached, such as requirements for affordable housing.[57] Plus, the deputy director of planning for the city of San Jose, Joseph A. Horwedel, claimed that it would have been hard to declare the site a blighted area.[58] Sweetnam went on to say, "If you build a grocery-anchored shopping center and reap 9 percent return on costs, how much more yield do you want (for a Santana Row)? I would say close to 13 to 14 percent return." And he said to get that, public dollars must be involved.[59]

However, since its rocky start, Santana Row's financial performance has been enormously successful. Yields on the second phase are expected to be 18%[60] and Federal Realty is contemplating how to develop the remaining 17 acres, on which it has the right to build another hotel, 690 more condominiums, and another 125,000 square feet of shops. By December

Figure 4–15 At its southern end, Santana Row's Main Street becomes a well-furnished and popular outdoor room flanked by upscale shops, condos, and apartments.

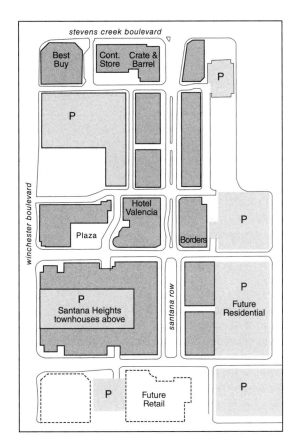

stevens creek boulevard

Best Buy

Cont. Store

Crate & Barrel

P

P

P

Hotel Valencia

P

Plaza

Borders

P

winchester boulevard

P

Santana Heights townhouses above

santana row

Future Residential

P

P

Future Retail

P

Figure 4–16 Santana Row combines a hotel; 1,200 residents; ten spas and salons; over thirty restaurants; high-end fashion such as Gucci, Ferragamo, and Burberry; and more moderately priced local shops, as well as large chains facing the arterial such as Best Buy, Borders, and Crate & Barrel.

2005 the project had reaped record prices for 219 condominiums, selling both of its $2.5 million units, nineteen 2,200-square-foot "villa" units for up to $1.45 million, and received $750 per square foot for its smallest 700-square-foot lofts.[61] By 2007, it was reported that its Hotel Valencia had been getting 150%–180% RevPAR penetration (i.e., that percentage more than its "fair share" of the competitive set). This inspired General Growth Properties to conduct a study that concluded that hotels attached to retail in master-planned communities command 20%–40% premiums while contributing to boosted sales in the other mixed-use components.[62] Certainly this appears

to be borne out by the success of the project's retail. An altogether different measure of its popular success is the 195 videos featuring Santana Row on YouTube and 7,207 photographs on the photo-sharing website Flickr as of January 6, 2008.

Richard Heapes of Street Works designed Santana Row after leaving Cooper Carry, where he was the lead designer on Mizner Park. Like many suburban retrofits, both projects confronted the designer with a fundamental dilemma: How do you follow the principles of good urbanism by relating to the context when the context is an antiurban strip? In both cases, Heapes responded by creating an urban oasis centered on a lushly landscaped street surrounded largely by parking lots and decks. Improving on Mizner Park, the 1,500-foot-long main street, named Santana Row, is perpendicular to Stevens Creek Boulevard, the commercial strip. The main street's four blocks transition from two-way traffic to a pedestrian boulevard lined with arcaded shops and three- to five-story buildings. The result is a very lively, very popular, urban "room" that is open at its ends but is spatially far more compact than anything in its immediate context. (See Figures 4–16 and 4–18.)

However, it is a project one only sees from the inside. The big chain stores front on Stevens Creek Boulevard, albeit right up at the sidewalk rather than set back behind parking as they would be elsewhere along such a strip. The project's "face" on Winchester Boulevard is dominated by a parking garage and large residential buildings without the façade detail that distinguishes the internal main street. A future eight-story residential building on the east side is expected to replace the current surface lot and carports and step down to three-story townhouses where it faces an adjacent subdivision.[63] The fact is that the wide arterials the site is bordered by are not conducive to interconnectivity or pedestrian access. But the result is that Santana Row feels like an interior destination, a

Figure 4–18 Like a mall, Santana Row is privately owned but makes space available for public use. This space is highly programmed with concerts, fashion shows, and farmers' markets such as this one, which included a booth protesting development on agricultural land.

Figure 4–17 The surface parking lots east and south of Santana Row are expected to be developed in future phases. At present they isolate rather than integrate the project with its surroundings.

high-end bubble with a regional draw, disconnected from its neighborhood. Its design is successful at compressing the energy of its hordes of visitors into its well-furnished, well-detailed, amenity-rich, highly programmed, pedestrian-oriented "public" street, but even with a growing number of residents it is a tourist attraction more than a neighborhood center for the local community.

Santana Row's impact on the local community has in fact been controversial. Only three miles from downtown San Jose, there has long been concern that the project would compete with downtown retailers and drain an already struggling market. Not that Gucci was at all likely to open in downtown San Jose—but why should the rest of the retailers open in an "instant city" when there is a real one just down the road? More recently, Santana Row has been credited with demonstrating the market for urban residential living and boosting investment in downtown condominium projects.[64] Philip Nobel, an architecture critic for *Metropolis Magazine,* echoed this point, calling Santana Row (and Easton Town Center) "rehearsal spaces for future urbanites."[65] Arguing that the role of public space in public protest has been eclipsed by digital communication, he appreciates how even "fake downtowns" like Santana

Row provide training grounds for the experience of being with lots of other people on a street at the same time. He argues this alone builds civic health and one can imagine that those future urbanites who cannot afford Santana Row's high rents are the generation discovering downtown.

From Strip Centers to New Downtown: Temple Terrace

Smaller strip centers rarely have the acreage to serve as, let alone compete with, downtown. However, they can be assembled into a larger redevelopment proposal and also begin to transform the strip itself. An ambitious example of this has been planned for Temple Terrace, Florida. (See Color Plates 12 to 14.) Designed as a golf course community in the 1920s, it never had a downtown. The 2005 Temple Terrace plan, "From Bullard to the River," designed by Torti Gallas and Partners and led by Neal Payton, proposes rectifying that situation by redeveloping the four quadrants around a major commercial intersection in the town (already designated as a community redevelopment area) and orienting development toward a redeveloped waterfront as the symbolic gateway to the city.[66] Unlike Santana Row's and

COLOR
PORTFOLIO

Before and after of
Denton Public Library.

▲ Color Plate 1: Perspective night view in the core area.

▶ Color Plate 2: "Before" aerial indicating 69-house subdivision and Metro station.

METROWEST: From 69 Houses to 2,250 Transit-Oriented Residences

PRINCIPAL CLIENT: Pulte Homes Clark Realty Capital
LEAD DESIGNERS: Lessard Architectural Group, EDAW
LOCATION: Vienna, Virginia

Suburban demographics are becoming less family-centered and although retrofits of residential subdivisions are rare, they are growing in number as such properties age. Pulte Homes contracted with each homeowner in the subdivision immediately south of the Vienna Metrorail station for transit-oriented redevelopment to accommodate a dense mix of urban housing and offices. Sandwiched between two apartment complexes and an interstate and a local highway, MetroWest has better regional than local interconnectivity. (See Chapter 2.)

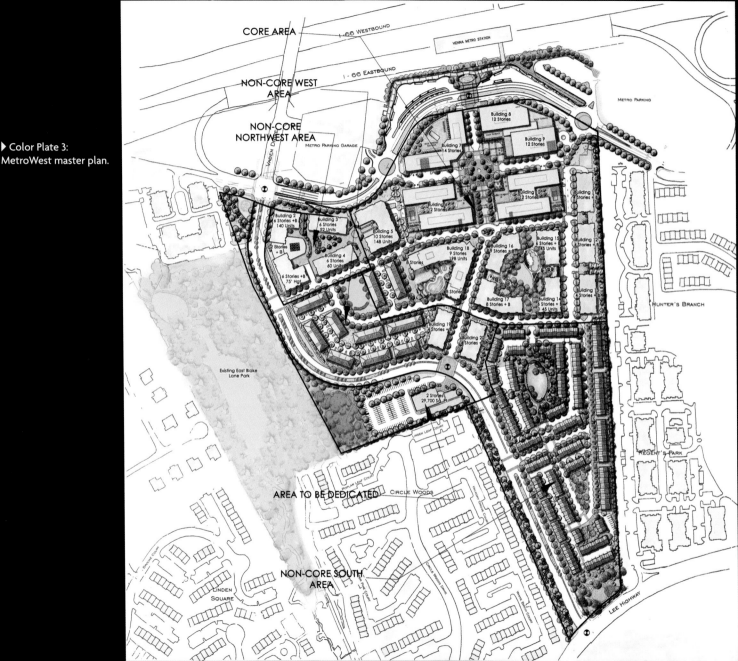

▶ Color Plate 3:
MetroWest master plan.

CORE AREA

I-66 WESTBOUND

VIENNA METRO STATION

NON-CORE WEST
AREA

I-66 EASTBOUND

METRO PARKING

NON-CORE
NORTHWEST AREA

METRO PARKING GARAGE

Building 8
12 Stories

Building 7
4 Stories

Building 9
12 Stories

Building 2
6 Stories + B
140 Units

Building 3
6 Stories
52 Units

Stories
+ B

Building 4
6 Stories
60 Units

Building 5
10 Stories
148 Units

Building
12 Stories

Building 6
2 Stories

6 Stories
2 Stories

Building
5 Stories

6 Stories + B
75' Hgt

8 Stories

Building 18
9 Stories
198 Units

Building 16
9 Stories

Building 15
6 Stories +
45 Units

Building
6 Stories

Building 17
8 Stories + B
45 Units

Building 14
6 Stories + B
45 Units

Building
4 Stories

Building
6 Stories

HUNTER'S BRANCH

Building
5 Stories + B

Building 20
Stories

Existing East Blake
Lane Park

2 Stories
29,700 Sq. Ft.

REGENT'S PARK

LINDEN LEAF COURT

POPLAR LEAF COURT

AREA TO BE DEDICATED

CIRCLE WOODS

NON-CORE SOUTH
AREA

LINDEN
SQUARE

LEE HIGHWAY

▶ Color Plate 4: Denton Public Library façade.

▼ Color Plate 5: "After" view of the retrofitted library.

▼▼ Color Plate 6: "Before" view of the grocery store

DENTON PUBLIC LIBRARY NORTH BRANCH:
From "Ghostbox" to Public Library

PRINCIPAL CLIENT: Denton Public Library System
LEAD DESIGNER: Meyer Scherer & Rockcastle Architects
LOCATION: Denton, Texas

Ghostbox is a term used for vacant big box stores. Those deemed unmarketable for retail are often prime candidates for retrofitting to more community-serving uses. Such was the case for both the parking lot and the building of this former Food Lion grocery store. The library brings a civic presence to the retail-oriented strip. The design welcomes neighbors with the bright colors and light emanating through the new glass façade while the sidewalks, xeriscape planting strips, and run-off filtering gravel beds contribute to a cleaner environment. (See Chapter 4.)

LA GRANDE ORANGE: From Strip Mall to High-End Hipster Hangout

PRINCIPAL CLIENT AND DESIGNERS: Bob Lynn, Kris and Craig DeMarco
LOCATION: Phoenix, Arizona

The cheap rents of older retail spaces can provide entrepreneurial opportunities for reinventing suburban life. With bright paint and upscale food and drink, the owners of La Grande Orange gradually converted a dowdy cluster of three adjacent strip malls into a stylish and bustling social scene. Beginning with the conversion of a post-office into Postino Winecafé, they have created an expanding empire that has triggered further retrofits and added to the popularity of the neighborhood. (See Chapter 4.)

◀ Color Plate 7: Breeze-way at La Grande Orange

◀ Color Plate 8: Night view of La Grande Orange

◀ Color Plate 9: "After" view of the elementary school, an educational oasis in a troubled Los Angeles neighborhood.

◤ Color Plate 10: "Before" view.

CAMINO NUEVO ELEMENTARY SCHOOL:
From Mini-mall to Elementary School

PRINCIPAL CLIENT: Camino Nuevo Charter Academy
LEAD DESIGNER: Daly Genik Architects
LOCATION: MacArthur Park, Los Angeles, California

Cash-strapped school systems and day-care providers have adaptively re-used several Kmarts, Sears stores, etc., into educational facilities. Camino Nuevo is distinguished by its role in retrofitting the larger neighborhood and local children's limited opportunities. The creative conversion of the L-shaped mini-mall into a school centered on a protective courtyard seeded the development of a larger urban campus for all grade levels on a blighted block. (See Chapter 4.)

Color Plate 11: Kids gather in the central courtyard, where cars used to park.

Color Plate 12: "Before" diagram of the street network.

Color Plate 13: "After" diagram of the street network.

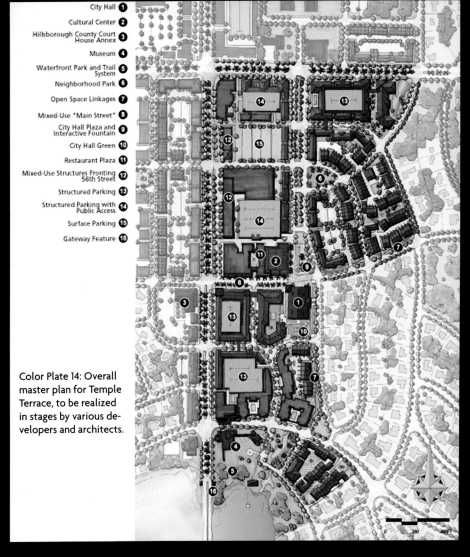

City Hall ➊
Cultural Center ➋
Hillsborough County Court House Annex ➌
Museum ➍
Waterfront Park and Trail System ➎
Neighborhood Park ➏
Open Space Linkages ➐
Mixed-Use "Main Street" ➑
City Hall Plaza and Interactive Fountain ➒
City Hall Green ➓
Restaurant Plaza ⓫
Mixed-Use Structures Fronting 56th Street ⓬
Structured Parking ⓭
Structured Parking with Public Access ⓮
Surface Parking ⓯
Gateway Feature ⓰

Color Plate 14: Overall master plan for Temple Terrace, to be realized in stages by various developers and architects.

TEMPLE TERRACE: From Strip Shopping Centers to New Downtown/Town Center

PRINCIPAL CLIENT AND LOCATION: City of Temple Terrace, Florida
LEAD DESIGNER: Torti Gallas and Partners

While developers often seek out "underperforming asphalt" on greyfield sites to densify development opportunities, municipalities also often initiate retrofits as a way to stem declining property values, increase housing options, and, in some cases, to create a downtown where none existed. This is the case in Temple Terrace where the designers propose retrofitting four quadrants around a major intersection. New streets break up the superblocks of two aging shopping centers allowing for a more walkable network with mixed-use buildings, parking at the center of blocks, and a new Main Street connecting civic buildings, shown in blue. (See Chapter 4.)

CATHEDRAL CITY: From Commercial Strip to Boulevard

PRINCIPAL CLIENT AND LOCATION: City of Cathedral City, California
LEAD DESIGNER: Freedman Tung and Bottomley Urban Design

The first constructed retrofit of a commercial strip to a multiway boulevard is reviving Cathedral City's down-town. The boulevard separates fast-moving through traffic in the center from slower, local lanes with bus stops and parking at the sides, resolving the conflict between mobility and access so common to suburban arterials. The tree-lined medians improve the aesthetics, safety, pedestrian experience and walkability (See Chapter 4.)

▲ Color Plate 15: A bus travels down the multiway boulevard lined with new palm trees.

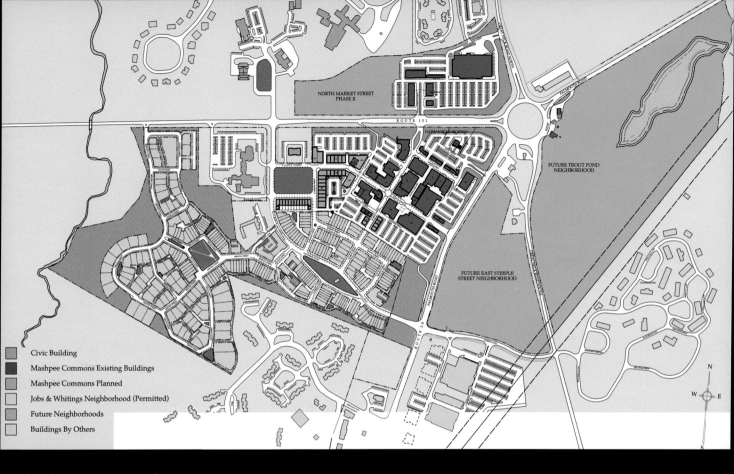

Legend:

- Civic Building
- Mashpee Commons Existing Buildings
- Mashpee Commons Planned
- Jobs & Whitings Neighborhood (Permitted)
- Future Neighborhoods
- Buildings By Others

Map labels: NORTH MARKET STREET PHASE II · ROUTE 151 · FUTURE TROUT POND NEIGHBORHOOD · FUTURE EAST STEEPLE STREET NEIGHBORHOOD · ROUTE 28

▲ Color Plate 16: 2007 master plan for Mashpee Commons, indicating approved street and block locations for the Jobs and Whitings residential neighborhoods.

MASHPEE COMMONS: From Shopping Center to Walkable Village

PRINCIPAL CLIENT: Cornish Associates Limited Partnership
LEAD DESIGNERS: Imai Keller Moore Architects, Duany Plater-Zyberk & Company
LOCATION: Mashpee, Massachusetts

While the suburban properties they replace tend to resist significant growth, the urban patterns established by retrofits allow for incremental adaptation. Mashpee Commons, the first suburban retrofit of a strip center, is a case in point. Inspired by Cape Cod village centers, the family-owned development company partially demolished the shopping center on the site and pioneered the legalization and return to open-air shopping with on-street parking and apartments over retail. The configuration has evolved through lengthy permitting processes and modifications along the way, including the latest addition of residential neighborhoods connected across major arterials. (See Chapter 5.)

◀◀ Color Plate 17: "After" view showing traditional urban configuration of varied buildings with apartments and offices above shops fronting the street.

◀ Color Plate 18: "Before" view of the New Seabury Shopping Center, 1968–1986.

▼ Color Plate 19: Typical view of the pedestrian street at the center of the Commons.

◀ Color Plate 20: "After" view shows the publicly owned and maintained linear park at the heart of Mizner Park.

▲ Color Plate 21: "Before" view of the short-lived Boca Raton Mall.

MIZNER PARK: From Dead Mall to Town Center

PRINCIPAL CLIENTS: Boca Raton Community Development Agency and Crocker & Company
LEAD DESIGNER: Cooper Carry Inc.
LOCATION: Boca Raton, Florida

The most prevalent sites for suburban retrofits are dead malls. Many hope to emulate Mizner Park's success at proving the value of investing in public space. The mall was replaced with a lifestyle center with shops and restaurants centered on a verdant plaza. Significantly, the inclusion of housing and offices both above the retail and lining the parking garages, as well as several cultural institutions, has enabled it to take on the role of Boca's downtown. (See Chapter 6.)

▲ Color Plate 22: Apartment liner buildings wrap around the parking decks and make a well-scaled transition to the adjacent single-family house neighborhood.

► Color Plate 23: The many restaurants contribute to a lively nightlife that reflects suburbia's growing population of singles and young professionals.

◀ Color Plate 24: "After" street view, looking south to central green and civic center.

▲ Color Plate 25: "Before" aerial view of Cinderella City Mall, a three-story retail extravaganza.

CITYCENTER ENGLEWOOD: From Dead Mall to City Hall

PRINCIPAL CLIENTS: City of Englewood, Miller Weingarten Realty, and Trammell Crow Residential
LEAD DESIGNERS: David Owen Tryba Architects, Calthorpe Associates
LOCATION: Englewood, Colorado

Retrofits appeal to a variety of markets and their realization often requires public-private partnerships. Faced with a dead mall and the arrival of transit, the City of Englewood partnered with private developers to center a new neighborhood of affordable apartments on art-filled public streets that connect the transit station and new town green at one end to big box development at the other. Instead of anchoring the mall, the former Foley's department store has been retrofitted into a new city hall and anchors the new civic center. (See Chapter 6.)

Color Plate 26: Englewood's civic center includes an art-filled public park, city hall in a retrofitted anchor store, and a pedestrian bridge linking to the light-rail station.

◀ Color Plate 27: "After" aerial model of new construction atop an older mall.

SURREY CENTRAL CITY: From Dying Mall to High-Rise Hub

PRINCIPAL CLIENT: ICBC Properties Ltd.
LEAD DESIGNER: Bing Thom Architects
LOCATION: Surrey, British Columbia

As metropolitan regions have expanded, many suburbs have grown into significant destinations with ambitions for a more urban identity. Surrey's leaders chose to encourage building up rather than out, grafting an unusual mix of uses onto their dying, transit-served mall. A five-story galleria of classrooms for Simon Frasier University was built on top of the mall, both of which share a plaza, lobby, and abundant use of recycled materials, with a new 25-story office tower. (See Chapter 6.)

◀ Color Plate 28: "Before" view of the mall and transit line

▶ Color Plate 29: The public plaza links transit riders to the new and old uses at Surrey Central City.

▶ Color Plate 30: "After" rendering of Cottonwood looking east.

◢ Color Plate 31: "Before" view of Cottonwood Mall looking east.

COTTONWOOD: From Dying Mall to Mixed-Use Neighborhood

PRINCIPAL CLIENT: General Growth Properties
PRINCIPAL DESIGNERS: Duany Plater-Zyberk & Company, RTKL, SB Architects, Sasaki Associates, Torti-Gallas and Partners
LOCATION: Holladay, Utah

Retrofits have the potential to re-orient or replace generic, placeless suburban development with designs that distinguish that particular community's identity. Cottonwood is replacing a windowless mall with a mixed-use neighborhood of more than twice the density. Yet, because it is planned around very specific view corridors, uses the rural-to-urban transect, incorporates historical precedents and green design techniques, its placemaking fits it into its context at a variety of scales. This is a significant change for the second largest mall owner in the country. (See Chapter 7.)

▲ Color Plate 32: Rendering of the southern entry to the new Main Street as it crosses the to-be-daylit creek and focuses on a clocktower anchoring the central plaza.

◀ Color Plate 33: Proposed site plan in context.

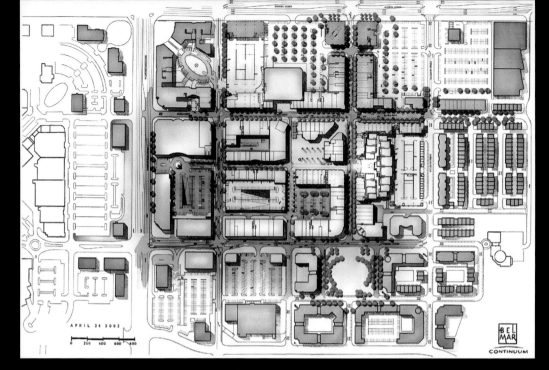

▶ Color Plate 34: "After" master plan rendering. Building locations and configurations have been altered slightly during the phased construction process.

▼ Color Plate 35: "Before" view of the Villa Italia. Only one building remains, the light gray anchor store on the upper left.

BELMAR: From Dead Mall to Green Downtown

PRINCIPAL CLIENT: Continuum Partners
PRINCIPAL DESIGNERS: Elkus/Manfredi Architects, Civitas, Inc.
LOCATION: Lakewood, Colorado

Suburban retrofits contribute to sustainability in a variety of ways, most of which are manifest at Belmar. It replaces an auto-dependent, private mall with an urban, walkable, and bus-served mix of uses and public spaces. It provides a range of housing types, diverse architectural styles, and variety of cultural activities, including but not limited to shopping, with the intention that it function as a downtown. It also uses green bonds to finance rooftop photovoltaics and a small wind farm. (See Chapter 8.)

▲ Color Plate 36: Belmar's "100% corner."

Color Plate 37: An ice rink animates the plaza in winter.

◄◄ Color Plate 38: Block 7 lines a parking garage with low-rent artists' studios at the ground-floor.

◄ Color Plate 39: A mews in a residential area at Belmar.

Color Plate 40: The lobby at The Laboratory of Arts and Ideas, a nonprofit gallery and "think tank" inserted in a typical retail building adjacent to the plaza.

◀ Color Plate 41: The green on a typical summer Sunday morning.

◣ Color Plate 42: Courtyard apartment and condominium projects frame the traffic circle from which the project takes its name and the iconic "Blueprints" sculpture.

ADDISON CIRCLE: Edge City Infill

PRINCIPAL CLIENTS: City of Addison, Columbus Realty/Post Properties
PRINCIPAL DESIGNER: RTKL
LOCATION: Addison, Texas

While the majority of suburban retrofits are on aging sites in first-ring suburbs, there are also several examples in more newly developed areas, including edge cities. Highly congested with workers and shoppers, edge cities are only now getting residents, walkable routes and public spaces. An edge city infill project, Addison Circle mitigates traffic congestion by providing both residents and workers in the nearby office complexes with a variety of pedestrian-oriented spaces, restaurants, and convenience shops, delaying or negating their need to drive. (See Chapter 9.)

Color Plate 43: An aerial view shows the edge-city context and the future light-rail tracks on the right.

DOWNTOWN KENDALL/DADELAND:
From Thriving Mall to New Downtown

PRINCIPAL CLIENT: ChamberSOUTH, Miami-Dade County Department of Planning & Zoning
PRINCIPAL DESIGNERS: Dover, Kohl & Partners, Duany Plater-Zyberk and Company
LOCATION: Kendall, Florida

Transit is a strong inducement for retrofitting. When high-rise zoning accompanied new stations at the Dadeland Mall and an office park, it provided the impetus for adoption of a new plan and code coordinating the redevelopment of the multiple-owner, low-density parcels in-between the stations. The former superblocks have been broken down by a new street grid that lines up with the mall's interior passages. It links with new public spaces formed by aggregating individual properties' open-space requirements around key anchor points. (See Chapter 10.)

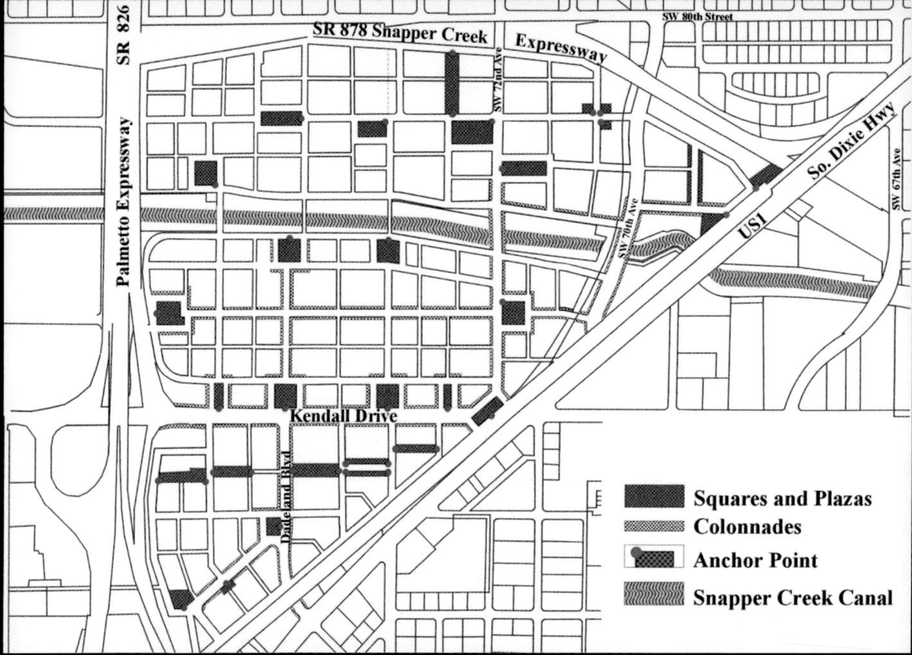

Squares and Plazas
Colonnades
Anchor Point
Snapper Creek Canal

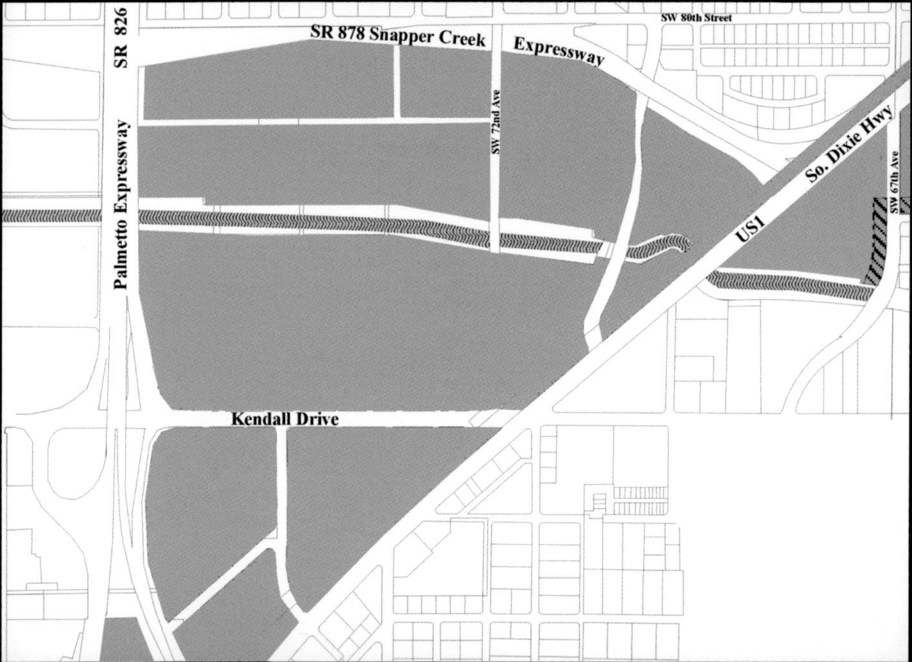

▶ Color Plate 44: The "after" plan (above) illustrates the new zoning, intended to trigger the creation of squares, colonnades, and new streets through an innovative application of setbacks and open space requirements. The "before" plan (below) illustrates the super-block condition.

▲ Color Plate 45: Panoramic view of new high- and mid-rise construction, mostly residential, at the southern end of the district, with the thriving Dadeland Mall in the right foreground.

▶ Color Plate 46: Mixed-use housing over retail replaced a car dealership and fronts a new street aligned with an entrance to the mall

WESTWOOD STATION: From Industrial Park to Live-Work-Shop-Play and Ride

PRINCIPAL CLIENT: City of Westwood, Cabot, Cabot & Forbes, and New England Development
PRINCIPAL DESIGNER: Elkus/Manfredi Architects
LOCATION: Westwood, Massachusetts

Suburbs have long relied upon industrial and office uses to augment their tax revenue while keeping them physically isolated from residents. The economy's post-industrial shift provides an opportunity to retrofit these sites into more integrated live-work-shop-play environments. Westwood Station's $1.5 billion retrofit of an industrial park is one of the most ambitious, taking advantage of its proximity to commuter and passenger rail, as well as the Route 128 corridor. (See Chapter 11.)

▲ Color Plate 47: "Before" view of the Westwood Industrial Park at the Route 128 Amtrak/commuter rail station.

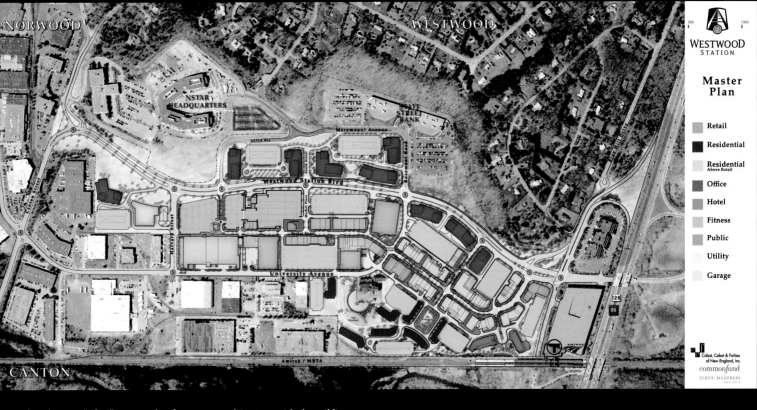

NORWOOD

WESTWOOD

CANTON

Color Plate 48: "After" master plan for Westwood Station, with the rail line along the bottom of the image and Route 128 to the right.

WESTWOOD
STATION

Master
Plan

Retail

Residential

Residential
Above Retail

Office

Hotel

Fitness

Public

Utility

Garage

Cabot, Cabot & Forbes
of New England, Inc.

commonfund

ELKUS | MANFREDI
ARCHITECTS

▶ Color Plate 49: "After" view of the new retail-lined street that cuts through former parking lots.

▼ Color Plate 50: "Before" aerial view shows three office buildings by Edward Durell Stone that were originally intended to be embedded in a high-density town center.

UNIVERSITY TOWN CENTER: Infilling an Office Park

PRINCIPAL CLIENT: Prince George's Metro Center, Inc.
PRINCIPAL DESIGNERS: Parker Rodriguez, RTKL, and WDG Architecture
LOCATION: Hyattsville, Maryland

There is great value, both environmental and cultural, to retaining existing buildings. However, today's "creative class" employees view yesterday's office parks as out-of-date and sterile. University Town Center is resolving this conflict by retaining its Edward Durell Stone-designed office buildings from the sixties and infilling their parking lots with a new Main Street, cinemaplex, grocery store, apartments and condominiums. The rather funky mix fulfills the original mixed-use intentions of the site and was triggered by the arrival of a nearby Metrorail station. (See Chapter 11.)

▲ Color Plate 51: The UTC plaza, with a new condominium building by WDG Architecture on the right and one of the E. D. Stone office buildings beyond.

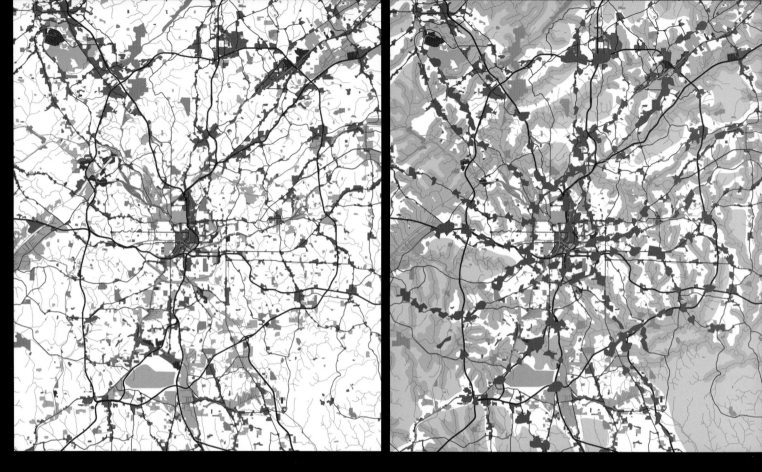

LWARPS – we can reverse sprawl

PRINCIPAL CLIENT: The City of the Future 2008 competition: Envision Atlanta in 100 Years
DESIGNERS: Georgia Tech Team; Ed Akins, Tristan Al-Haddad, Richard Dagenhart, Ellen Dunham-Jones, Janae Futrell, Michael Gamble, Ryan Gravel, David Green, Frances Hsu, Hanyun Huang, Allison Isaacs, Sarah Kiliniski, Swaleha Lalani, Jude LeBlanc, Tolek Lesniewski, Cassie Niemann, Miharu Morimoto, Brian Peterka, Gernot Riether, Ross Wallace, Jen Yoon.
LOCATION: Atlanta, Georgia

These plans from a more detailed proposal envision a condensed Atlanta whose outer subdivisions are regreened and whose corridors are densely retrofitted along the lines described in this book's Epilogue. The proposal requires: Green Infrastructure (biofuel farms/powerplants, stormwater harvesting, and intensive urban agriculture on 1000 stream buffers), Mobility Infrastructure (expanded transit modes on transit corridors), and Eco-Acre Transfers (development rights transfers from outer subdivisions to transit corridors).

▲ Color Plate 52: "Before" and "after" views of Metro Atlanta as sprawl is reversed.

Brooklyn Park's focus on new main streets off of, and perpendicular to, the arterial, the Temple Terrace plan lines the existing strips with new buildings and takes advantage of the intersection's inherently public visibility to create a new downtown that is highly integrated into its context.

In their "before" condition, two of the quadrants are dominated by aging 20-acre strip shopping centers. Only one, in the southeast quadrant, is owned by the city, so the plan calls for phasing, starting with the bulk of the public investment in that quadrant. A new street network is proposed on the superblock sites to increase walkability, better distribute traffic, and integrate the new mixed-use commercial buildings fronting the arterials with the residential development behind them. A new Main Street is proposed midblock in the southeast quadrant to connect an existing school, library, and fire department with a proposed new city hall and cultural center. New parking garages are proposed for three of the quadrants, with surface lots maintained in the middle of blocks. An existing garden apartment complex in the southeast quadrant is also proposed for redevelopment with a greater mix of housing types and a more interconnected road system. New parks, pathways, and streetscapes are proposed to tie into the city's signature golf course system of open space.

In addition to the improvements to the various parcels, the plan calls for 56th Street, the arterial running north-south, to be reconfigured into a multiway boulevard. Its frontage roads would better service the new retail and commercial buildings, while its tree-lined medians would buffer them from the higher-speed traffic in the middle lanes. This reshaping of commercial corridors into boulevards is becoming increasingly popular and is the next evolution in retrofitting commercial strips.

RETROFITTING THE CORRIDORS THEMSELVES: DESIGNING FOR MOBILITY OR ACCESS OR BOTH

In *The Boulevard Book,* authors Allan B. Jacobs, Elizabeth Macdonald, and Yodan Rofé illustrate numerous examples of grand urban multiway boulevards from Ocean Parkway in Brooklyn, New York, to Barcelona's Passeig de Garcia. (See Figure 4–19.) As the authors explain, "The multiway boulevard is unique because its parallel roadways serve distinctly different traffic functions. It directly addresses the functional problems posed by the coexistence of through movement and access to abutting land uses on major urban streets."[67] In addition to the two speeds of vehicular traffic, they also accommodate pedestrians, bicyclists, and buses graciously. The trees that generally line their medians as well as their sidewalks provide a range of environmental, aesthetic, and safety benefits to the neighborhoods and their residents—and not just the humans! The Champs-Elysées in Paris carries ten lanes of heavy traffic. However, as a multiway boulevard it manages to serve as one of the most memorable pedestrian experiences in the world. The cafés and pedestrians are buffered from the traffic by the boulevard's layered functions while they sit at the feet of the continuous streetwall of eight- to ten-story luxurious buildings that would never line up along a highway or commercial strip. And yet, most of the road surface of the Champs-Elysées, the middle part, is no different than an American commercial strip. The layers at the edges of the road, including the local lanes, medians, sidewalks, and trees, are what make it a multiway boulevard and add tremendous value to the adjacent real estate.

Figure 4–19 How do you design a nine-lane roadway to also serve as a social space? These men are playing dominoes in a median of Ocean Parkway in Brooklyn, New York, a grand multiway boulevard designed by Olmsted & Vaux in the 1860s. Ocean Parkway has seven central lanes, the middle lane being for left turns; two wide medians with trees, benches, and pedestrian paths; and two small parallel side streets. While the word *boulevard* generally refers to wide streets with planted medians, a multiway boulevard specifically incorporates the slower side streets. It is simultaneously a high-capacity thoroughfare, a linear park with popular gathering spaces, and an efficient access system for local streets.

Americans stopped building multiway boulevards in the 1930s. Traffic engineers feared that the complexity of the intersections would lead to high accident rates, and boulevards did not fit into the developed functional classification street system. This system classifies street design standards depending on whether the street's principal function is mobility or access, rather than both. Under the system, still in effect today, streets are either *arterials,* designed for the highest speeds and longest uninterrupted distances; *collectors,* considered a lower level of service because of the lower speeds for shorter distances as they collect traffic from local roads and connect them to the arterials; or *local roads,* whose primary purpose is to provide access to land with little or no through movement.[68] Much like the developments it accesses, the system is based on optimizing separated single uses accessed exclusively by automobiles. Pedestrians are not considered and trees are referred to in some of the design documents as fixed hazardous objects. The system bestows the highest level of service ranking for those streets that allow the most high-speed traffic flow.

So how does a high-speed suburban arterial become a clogged commercial strip? It usually begins with the transportation engineers laying out what they consider to be a rural road. To this day, the AASHTO "Green Book," which dictates design standards for all U.S. departments of transportation, bases level of service on a sliding scale between access (for urban conditions) and mobility (for rural conditions), with no consideration of suburban conditions. The assumption is that rural roads between urban centers should be designed to maximize traffic flow, so speeds are high and regulations limit intersection intervals and curb cuts. Walkability is not a factor to be considered in what is defined as a rural road. However, the new road's access to cheap land builds development pressures and the prospect of tax revenues. These in turn prompt local governments to grant commercial and subdivision rezoning requests along the length of the new road (usually resulting in far more land zoned for retail and commercial use than the community can support). The lack of interconnectivity between the newly developed parcels means that every trip into, out of, or between uses along that road now has to be made by car. Before long, the inherent contradiction of the commercial strip becomes evident. Designed for through traffic and mobility but zoned for uses requiring access, it no longer functions well for either.

The Transit Boulevard and the Urban Network

Many planners in recent decades have recognized the disconnection between transportation design and land use and have incorporated efforts at integration into ambitious regional plans. One of the earliest and most effective is the LUTRAQ plan for Portland, Oregon (Land Use Transportation Air Quality), begun in 1988 and led by Peter Calthorpe. His subsequent regional plans for Chicago, Salt Lake City, and Perth have informed his development of the Urban Network, an alternative to the functional street classification system.[69] It replaces the current system's dendritic pattern, which loads every trip onto the arterial, with a more interconnected network. By allowing local trips to rely more on what he calls connector streets, he is able to reduce the volume and number of lanes needed on primary roads, which he divides into avenues and transit boulevards. To further reduce road widths and therefore increase walkability, while at the same time clustering retail into walkable nodes, he proposes one-way couplets at the intersections of primary roads. His designs for San Elijo Hills and Issaquah Highlands insert village and town centers into the intersections made by overlapped one-way couplets. (See Figure 4–20.) Engineering analysis estimates that despite the dramatic reduction in road width and mix of uses, automobile travel time through the intersections should actually be reduced by 11%.[70]

Figure 4–20 The high widths and design speeds of contemporary arterial roads make them function as dividers between communities rather than serve the street's traditional role as a shared public space that seams both sides of the street together. Peter Calthorpe's design for San Elijo Hills uses a double couplet to narrow arterials into one-way halves that split around the town center, restoring the traditional role of the street to the arterial where it passes through a town.

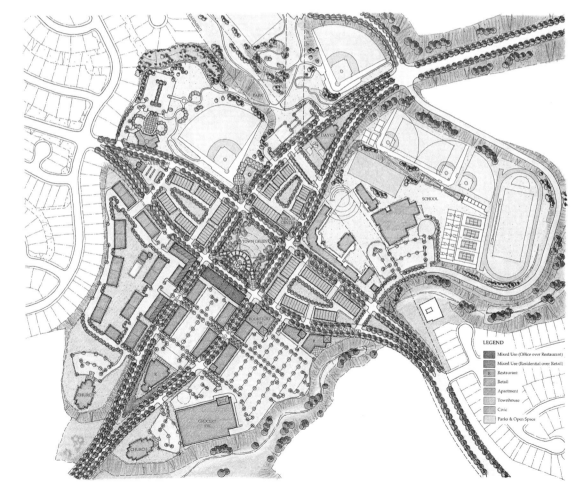

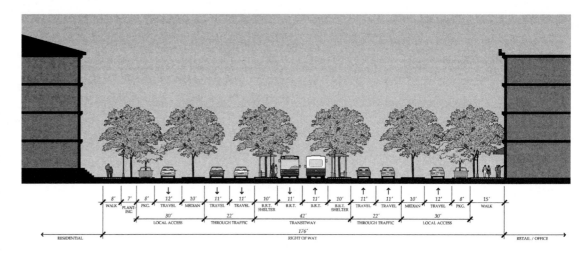

Figure 4–21 Mesa del Sol is an enormous twenty-square-mile mixed-use, high-tech, green community being planned by Peter Calthorpe outside of Albuquerque. It is also where he will test several of the ideas for the Urban Network, including the transit boulevard shown here. Lined with higher-density residential or commercial development, connecting town centers and incorporating a dedicated lane for transit, transit boulevards are designed to replace conventional arterial roads and commercial strips.

These are dramatic experiments in the integration of the design of the arterial road with its proposed land use and could have far-reaching implications for the future of commercial strips across the country.

However, the aspect of Calthorpe's Urban Network system that could have even greater ramifications on retrofitting commercial strips is the essential role played by the transit boulevards. (See Figure 4–21.) He describes these "multifunctional through-ways designed to match the mixed-use development they support" as the heart of the system.[71]

Gradually, the regulatory and market obstacles to multiway and transit boulevards are being removed. The Congress for the New Urbanism has worked with the Institute of Transportation Engineers toward updating the Green Book with context-sensitive design standards.[72] *The Boulevard Book* provided much-needed data refuting the perception that boulevard intersections are more accident-prone. In addition, retail has increasingly migrated from older commercial strip locations to more visible, more accessible, and larger sites at exits from the bypasses and ring roads of the now-completed interstate highway system.

Return of the Multiway Boulevard: Cathedral City

The first retrofit of a commercial strip corridor into a multiway boulevard in the United States opened in 1998 in Cathedral City, California. (See Color Plate 15.) Highway 111 is a state highway that links Cathedral City to the rest of the desert cities in the Coachella Valley, including Palm Springs to the east. In the early 1990s, the city leaders wanted to develop the city's reputation and a downtown. Realizing that most people's image of Cathedral City was the rundown and pedestrian-unfriendly area along the highway, they sought to redevelop it as a lively, pedestrian-friendly, mixed-use district with both civic, residential, and entertainment uses. In the face of Caltrans's desire to maintain the possibility of a seven-lane right-of-way, the city successfully obtained relinquishment from the state of ownership of that portion of Highway 111 that passes through the city.[73] Michael Freedman of Freedman, Tung & Bottomley Urban Design led the city and a resident/business design committee in the development of the plan to retrofit four blocks of what is

Figure 4–22 View of Palm Canyon Drive/Highway 111 where it passes through Cathedral City. California. Instead of a 45 mph four-to-six lane arterial abutted by typical commercial strip development. Cathedral City now has four lanes of 35 mph through traffic separated by a central planted median, as well as side landscaped medians separating a parking aisle with angled parking on the south and a bus lane on the north. Curb cuts are not allowed and buildings are required to have entrances onto the sidewalks. The design eliminated numerous angled driveways and streets that had previously compromised traffic flow, while it added new bus shelters and traffic signals.

now East Palm Canyon Drive as the Main Street of a new town center. Bruce Liedstrand, the city manager at the time, credits Freedman with helping the city council see how the retrofit could overcome the mismatch between the 40,000 cars a day passing through and the site's boarded-up buildings.[74] He has also said, "Had someone told us at the beginning of the project that we were going to attract $40 million in private investment into a part of town where no one wanted to be, and change California law so that we could redesign a state highway into a pedestrian- and transit-friendly grand boulevard, no one would have believed it."[75]

Jerry Jack, the traffic and development manager for the city, stated that "in terms of pedestrian safety, the redesign of the street has been an overwhelming success."[76] It is also an aesthetic success. The rows of palm trees, wide sidewalks, and welcoming street furnishings announce the city's presence to passersby with pride and create an attractive setting for the

stately new city hall, theater, town green, and fountain that dominate one block along the boulevard. However, it has been less successful at quickly attracting developers for the retail and residential. Starbucks arrived in 2005, a hotel has been in the works for several years, and residential development has been announced for one of the southern blocks. However, the pace has been slow and some streets reconfigured. As innovative as the city's transformation of the strip has been, its implementation of the associated built fabric has not followed through as planned. Liedstrand suggests that one of the lessons learned is the need to renew the vision as new city leaders come on board so they too fully understand and take ownership of its implementation.[77]

Michael Freedman argues that the boulevard configuration and streetscape improvements of projects like Cathedral City are essential strategies to restructuring aging commercial strips into a multinucleated pattern that enhances livability, mobility, and reinvestment opportunity.[78] Similar to Calthorpe, Jonathan Barnett, and others, Freedman proposes that the linear development patterns along commercial strips be reconfigured into a pattern of variously sized walkable centers at intersections and residential segments in between.[79] The Urban Land Institute similarly endorses this strategy of "pulsing" development along strips.[80] Like most of the large-parcel retrofits that have been discussed in previous chapters, Cathedral City is an example of a center or node. To improve mobility along the corridor, the development of such centers should be accompanied by downzoning or transfer of development rights in between the centers. What is particularly innovative about Freedman's argument is its emphasis on how the upgrading of the strip corridor to the more attractive and adaptable form of a boulevard can make it conducive to residential development in the in-between segments. He points to precedents

Figure 4–23 Exploring alternatives to conventional streetscapes, Darren Petrucci designed these canopies on 7th Avenue in Phoenix as part of a larger project entitled "Stripscape." Alternately providing shade during the day and security lighting at night, the canopies create small public spaces serving a variety of purposes. They provide seating areas at bus stops and incorporate public art panels into an "urban art gallery" while they serve as gateways to the neighborhood. These "amenity infrastructures" also serve as branding devices for the local business association of the neighborhood, the clients for the project.

such as Monument Avenue in Richmond, Virginia, or Commonwealth Avenue in Boston, where beautiful streetscapes accommodate both high-volume traffic and urban residences. While owners of property along strips currently zoned for commercial use may be understandably reluctant to accept what they perceive as downzoning, Freedman argues that the combination of retail's growing desire to locate in centers and the growing demand for affordable, urban housing in suburban locations means that "trading in" retail entitlements for residential entitlements can be more lucrative in the long run.[81]

Freedman's argument is bolstered by several studies. A study of Orange County, California, found more than 700 aging midsize strip centers along commercial corridors. The authors of the study, Richard Ramella and Randy Jackson of The Planning Center of Costa Mesa, estimate that retrofitting just a few hundred of these properties could accommodate the 600,000 new residents expected in what will be a built-out county over the next twenty years.[82] At a national scale, Arthur C. Nelson, a professor of planning and codirector of Virginia Tech's Metropolitan Institute, argues that 2.8 million acres of greyfields will become available and if only a quarter of them are

redeveloped, they could supply half of the housing demand by 2030.[83] With unmet demand for walkable urbanism already at 30%–40% of the market and demographic trends reinforcing this direction (see Chapter 2), the challenge is to redesign the corridors housing all of those greyfields into attractive, safe, walkable environments.

Various streetscaping strategies are possible, from multiway boulevards to simple tree-lined streets or more inventive designs that try to foster a unique identity. As part of a larger proposal for improving the public space along a high-volume corridor with struggling retail in Phoenix, Darren Petrucci designed a series of interventions, most notably light-box canopies. (See Figure 4–23.) Petrucci describes the project as a grassroots attempt by the sixty small local businesses to promote their identity as unique and distinct from the malls and shopping centers they compete with.[84]

The prospect of seeing commercial corridors converted into boulevards, whether canopy lined or multiway or transit boulevards, is indeed highly promising. The local benefits include relieving traffic congestion due to left turns, agglomerating retail into walkable centers more easily served by transit, and improving pedestrian safety with planted medians. At the regional scale, the provision of transit and access to jobs in suburban locations would be a major improvement for the poor—and for reducing VMT.[85] At the same time, the ability to accommodate new housing on greyfield properties where no one would otherwise desire to live promises to relieve expansion pressures for the region as a whole.

Experience suggests that this is best accomplished with transit incorporated along easily developable and redevelopable arterial corridors rather than in the rights-of-way of limited-access highways.[86] The replacement of limited-access urban highways with surface boulevards integrated into the rest of the street grid has many of the same benefits, as demonstrated by Octavia Boulevard in San Francisco and the teardown of the East Park Thruway in Milwaukee. Land that was undesirable because of its adjacency to an elevated highway is suddenly highly desirable when it has frontage on an attractive boulevard, especially if it is transit served. While the costs of retrofitting transportation infrastructure are prohibitive for many cities, more and more cities are committing to new transit systems extending into their suburban areas (Dallas, Denver, Los Angeles, etc.) and countless cities are considering boulevard conversions as investments they cannot afford not to make.

Rezoning Corridors: Three Examples in Atlanta

More common, more incremental approaches to retrofitting commercial corridors, either in tandem or alone, include rezoning, revising street standards, and streetscaping. Simply rezoning the commercial properties along strip corridors to allow for residential use can stimulate gradual transformation in a hot market area. This has been demonstrated by three very different strip corridors adapted to different kinds of communities in the Atlanta region: Memorial Drive, I-85 in Gwinnett County, and Buford Highway in Dekalb County.

With unrealized aspirations of grandeur, Memorial Drive links the downtown statehouse to the Civil War graves at the Oakland Cemetery and out to the monument to Confederate soldiers at Stone Mountain, fifteen miles east. Home to the nation's first Applebee's restaurant and first Home Depot, its aging commercial strips and gritty industrial properties have grown seedy. Approval in 2001 of HOPE VI funding for the redevelopment of Capitol Homes, a public housing project adjacent to downtown, into

a mixed-income neighborhood gave momentum to rezoning in accordance with Romm + Pearsall/Verge Studios' 2001 revitalization plan for the larger area. The city of Atlanta had already introduced a new neighborhood commercial zoning category specifically intended to discourage typical strip development. (See Figure 4–24.) In addition, the prospect of a new transit and park loop intersecting with the corridor further escalated prospects for change just as nearby neighborhoods began to attract more and more young professionals. Although new zoning specifically for this section of Memorial Drive was not adopted until 2006, property values were already exceeding the $2 million/acre price shortly before adoption as developers scrambled to assemble choice parcels. By November 2007, in addition to the Capitol Homes redevelopment and new urbanist brownfield retrofit at Glenwood Park, ten new projects had been built or planned along a 1.5-mile stretch of the corridor.[87] (See Figure 4–25.) Several of these are new five-story wrapped-deck condominiums over retail, although there are also some metal-clad townhouse projects and some loft renovations of industrial buildings. While Michael Freedman suggests the need to retrofit the strip in a grand manner in order to attract equally grand residences, these projects are tending to respond to their gritty context with an industrial aesthetic and form.[88] Over time, the new zoning's requirements for pedestrian-friendly building frontage, trees, and sidewalks will replace the asphalt curb cuts and alter the context—but one hopes the area will not entirely lose its unique blend of industrial character and historic monuments. The integration of new development into the existing neighborhoods is very much intended by the new zoning's attention to transitional heights to abutting residential neighborhoods. But the marketing's aim at a hip, young urban professional demographic reinforces the existing ten-

Figure 4–24 To replace commercial strip development with mixed-use, pedestrian-oriented development, the city of Atlanta adopted the Neighborhood Commercial District Ordinance in 2000. Its desired effect is illustrated in this before-and-after diagram produced by lead planners with the city. It was one of five new parallel ordinances that made up the city's Quality of Life Zoning Codes.

Figure 4–25 View on Memorial Drive in Atlanta showing older strip development set back from the road, adjacent to a new residential loft building with a restaurant at ground level, pulled right up to the street as a reflection of both the new zoning and the growing market for urban housing on corridors.

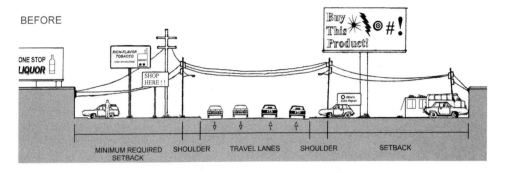

BEFORE

MINIMUM REQUIRED SETBACK   SHOULDER   TRAVEL LANES   SHOULDER   SETBACK

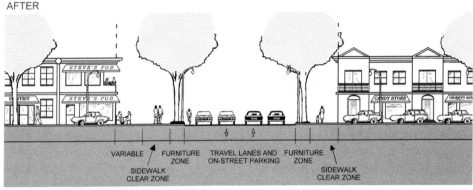

AFTER

VARIABLE   FURNITURE ZONE   TRAVEL LANES AND ON-STREET PARKING   FURNITURE ZONE   VARIABLE

SIDEWALK CLEAR ZONE   SIDEWALK CLEAR ZONE

City of Atlanta Neighborhood Commercial District Ordinance

sions between some of the older residents of those neighborhoods and those perceived as gentrifiers.

Tensions between new and old residents are often heightened by redevelopment. The demographic profile for Gwinnett County, to the northeast of Atlanta, has long been understood as overwhelmingly white, suburban, and middle class. However, rapid diversification of its population through immigration and a sudden change away from its progrowth leadership have positioned the county quite differently in recent years. In December 2005, the county approved rezoning to allow for 25-story high-rise residential towers along with other planned mixed-use developments within specified major activity centers along major thoroughfares, including Interstate 85. Unlike the City of Atlanta's Neighborhood Com-

Figure 4–26 This proposal to retrofit a shopping center reflects both the influx of prosperous Asians to suburban Gwinnett County and the county's new high-rise zoning along corridors. James Byun, an investor in the project called Global Station, described it as a minicity and as the epicenter for a new, upscale Asian community in Gwinnett, surpassing the older Asian community associated with strip shopping centers along Buford Highway.

mercial District Ordinance's efforts to integrate with existing neighborhoods, Gwinnett's zoning amendment establishes significant buffers (50–200 feet) and does not institute frontage requirements. Nonetheless, within six months of the rezoning, three developers proposed 25-story towers along Interstate 85 at sequential intersections.

One of the proposals, "Global Station," included ten high-rises on the site of two near-dead shopping centers on 38 acres adjacent to Gwinnett Place Mall, an aging superregional mall. The developer, former county chairman Wayne Mason, paid approximately $540,000/acre for the property and was betting $600 million that Gwinnett County also had pent-up demand for a mixed-use, urban-patterned, live-work-shop environment much like Atlantic Station in midtown Atlanta. His partner in the project, James Byun, believed that market would in fact reflect the ethnic changes in Gwinnett.[89] Asian buying power

in the county has risen nearly 1,000% in the past fifteen years and Gwinnett now has more than twice as many Asian-owned businesses as any other county in Georgia. While their parents may have worked in Asian restaurants or dry cleaners along Buford Highway, the current generation are young professionals attracted to Gwinnett for many of the same reasons that people first came to the county: dependable schools, roomy houses, and a probusiness environment that has also attracted Asian financiers, especially South Koreans looking for real estate investments in the United States. In July 2006, the *Atlanta Journal-Constitution* listed twelve new developments by Asian Americans in Gwinnett that revealed what it called "the Asian invasion."[90] In fact, one of the other high-rise proposals on I-85 is from Vietnamese-born developer Tina Dang, to redevelop one of the eight shopping centers she owns into a condo tower and retail complex. While the design proposed for Global Station suffered from a lack of integrated scales, especially between the ten identical, shiny glass towers and the neo-traditional set pieces at grade (see Figure 4–26), the project promised to establish a new social infrastructure specifically for the county's Asian population.[91]

Buford Highway, home to the extensive Asian— and Hispanic—population that Byun mentioned, provides an example of a third rezoning strategy along an Atlanta corridor. The portion of Buford Highway considered "in town" (just inside the border established by Atlanta's peripheral highway, Route 285) varies from five to seven lanes and is mostly lined with garden apartment complexes and strip malls from the 1970s. Originally oriented toward young single people (many of whom were leaving the central parts of the city as part of "white flight"), the apartment complexes have housed waves of different immigrant groups for the past two decades. The highway's well-worn dirt paths on the side of the road have only

Figure 4–27 These before-and-after views along Buford Highway, an aging commercial strip in Atlanta, illustrate how liner buildings placed within the front setback could urbanize the strip and improve pedestrian safety.

recently been replaced with streetlight-lined sidewalks along limited portions—despite the fact that it is home to Atlanta's largest percentage of non-car-owning inhabitants. Flanked by large superblocks, crosswalks are few and far between and the corridor has one of the highest rates of pedestrian fatalities in the state. The mismatch between the needs of the area's growing pedestrian population and the existing infrastructure, as well as the opportunities presented by the greyfield condition of the properties, led professors Michael Gamble and Jude LeBlanc at the Georgia Institute of Technology to propose a unique rezoning strategy to incrementally establish a healthier pedestrian network.[92]

The heart of Gamble and LeBlanc's fourfold proposal is a suggestion that Dekalb County allow property owners to build thin "liner" buildings within the front yard setback (currently sixty to seventy-five feet) of their property, in exchange for providing a public easement on their side yard setbacks (currently twenty feet). Over time, this trade-off would allow for the construction of new public rights-of-way through the superblocks, dramatically increasing interconnectivity, the pedestrian network, the opportunities for signalized crosswalks, and the public health of the corridor.[93]

Inducing Transit on a Corridor Through Form-Based Codes: Columbia Pike

Arlington County in northern Virginia has been one of the most proactive governments in retrofitting suburban corridors from low-scale to midrise. When the extension of the DC Metrorail system through Ballston to Rosslyn was announced forty years ago, the county developed transit-oriented guidelines that successfully accommodated massive residential and office growth while boosting transit ridership to record levels and winning the county numerous smart growth–related awards. Diana Sun, a county spokesperson, says, "It went from being a bit of a suburb into a real vibrant city. Arlington is cool now."[94]

Building on this success, in 1998 the county embarked on retrofitting another suburban arterial, but this time with transit as the goal rather than as the trigger. In order to encourage retrofitting along a 3.5-mile stretch of Columbia Pike at densities that would justify transit, the county is employing form-based codes that incentivize densification while exerting significant controls on form. Joe Kohl, an urban designer and partner in Dover Kohl & Partners, says that the Columbia Pike community saw the new buildings along the Ballston corridor as soulless and corporate.[95]

Figure 4–28 Before-and-after views of a single, multiparcel superblock along Buford Highway according to Michael Gamble and Jude LeBlanc's proposal. They illustrate how the permission to build within the front setback in exchange for a public easement for a road within side setbacks could incrementally lead to a more fine-grained, walkable road system.

Figure 4–29 View of construction of the retrofit of the Ballston-Rosslyn corridor with transit in 1989 and the dramatic change in scale from bungalows to ten-story buildings.

The goal of the form-based code is to add density without overwhelming the pedestrian Main Street. The code and plan dictate that the tallest buildings are located in the valleys and efforts are made to protect existing residences from gentrification.

Columbia Pike has remnants of its former Main Street character amidst the low-scale thrift stores, run-down retail, and stretches of single-family homes. In 2002 the county brought in Dover Kohl & Partners, working with Geoff Ferrell, to lead a community-based charrette. The resulting plan focuses redevelopment in four differentiated centers (referred to as districts) along the corridor. The resulting code was adopted in 2003 and consists of four documents intended to make the development approval process short and predictable. The first, the Regulating Plan, indicates what type of building can be built on any location within a district, its frontage type along a "required building line," tree and streetlight lines, as well as the minimum parking setback. The Building Envelope Standards govern height, fenestration, siting, and use, while the Architectural Standards are described as the dress code. They recommend materials and configurations of building walls, roofs, parapets, doors, and windows that are generally traditional but do not demand a particular architectural style. Streetscape standards similarly define required elements and preferred plant species.

Developers are not required to follow the form-based code. It is an optional overlay to the existing use-based zoning. However, the county incentivizes use of the code by allowing projects that follow the standards to build at greater density, to receive entitlement approvals within thirty days without public hearings for smaller projects and within sixty days for larger projects, and to be considered for county investments to bridge feasibility gaps.

Rather than simply prohibiting what is not allowed, form-based codes allow the community to voice its design preferences (to the extent that "the community" has expressed consensus about those preferences in the adoption of the code) and let developers know ahead of time what it is looking for. Subsequent amendments and updates have allowed the community to refine and modify the plans, including greater attention to historic preservation, affordable housing rehabilitation, and energy efficiency. In exchange for assuming this degree of control, the community allows the developer to build at densities (three to six stories, with one ten-story site) that are considerably higher than the surrounding neighborhoods but that will support transit and the county's long-term goals for accommodating growth with higher-capacity transit options. The county has already endorsed a five-mile streetcar transit system to augment bus service along the corridor, a system originally proposed in the charrette. The incentives are working—albeit more slowly than initially hoped. The first mixed-use development projects in the corridor in more than forty years are going forward on the sites of two older grocery stores.

RETROFITTING THE URBAN STRUCTURE OF COMMERCIAL STRIPS

Will Columbia Pike succeed in attracting enough density to convince the county to make the investment in the streetcar? The jury's still out, but it will establish an important precedent if it succeeds. It will demonstrate that it is possible to get the community to accept, and the private market to invest in, transit-supporting densities prior to requiring the public sector to invest in transit. This chicken-egg question of which needs to come first has perpetually dogged transit investments. If the transit goes in first, to induce development, it is unlikely to be able to generate enough early riders to pay its way, exacerbating such arguments against transit in the first place. Replacing lanes in existing corridors—as Columbia Pike is proposing—is an essential element of retrofitting suburban frameworks, but it is difficult to accomplish. Reserving a right-of-way for later transit is a good strategy, but it means that new development will have to be built with parking ratios that continue to support auto dependency. More often, the arrival of transit (or at least its promise) precedes development. Whether light or heavy rail, bus rapid transit, or streetcar, transit has been the trigger for higher-density zoning, transit-oriented development, and corridor retrofitting in examples such as Ballston, Virginia; Downtown Kendall/Dadeland in Kendall, Florida; and the planning for Denver's new light-rail system.

Figure 4–30 Sequence of simulations showing retrofitting along Columbia Pike, from commercial strip to urban building with street trees and transit once critical mass is achieved.

An alternative strategy to retrofitting existing vehicular corridors with transit is to seek out other kinds of corridors, such as the leftover spaces in between subdivisions and other uses. This is not the intention of an exciting new transit project in Atlanta, but it is one of its more important consequences. Called the Beltline, the project emerged out of Ryan Gravel's dual MArch and MCRP thesis at Georgia Tech. Gravel identified twenty-two miles of unused railroad lines that could be connected to form a new transit loop around the city. The loop more or less straddles the divide between the city's more compact streetcar suburbs and its more automobile-oriented subdivisions and strips. The project has since grown to also incorporate a system of parks. A tax allocation district has been approved for redevelopment of the approximately 6,000 acres of underdeveloped industrial land along the Beltline, and the city is actively planning the public rights-of-way and street networks prior to rezoning. Developers are already building mid-rise and planning high-rise projects along the Beltline—even though the transit may still be decades away. Ultimately, the Beltline is expected to generate at least 28,000 housing units

(a figure Gravel thinks is very low)[96] and as much as 1,400 acres of new parkland. (See Figure 4-31.)

But the lesson from the Beltline that may be more transferable is how it promises to improve the interconnectivity of the street system as well. Atlanta's "in-town" neighborhoods are notoriously fragmented from one another, forcing most through traffic onto arterial roads. The hilly terrain and the city's vast network of railroad lines exacerbate these divides. Much as contemporary subdivisions tend to turn their backyards toward the periphery of the property, Atlanta's older in-town neighborhoods tend to turn their backs to the railroad corridors. Now that the Beltline is turning those corridors into parks worth fronting on and establishing station stops where crossings never existed, there is a tremendous opportunity to not only retrofit the industrial properties *along* the Beltline, but also to retrofit and reconnect adjacent neighborhoods *across* the Beltline. The new crossing points promise to improve the efficiency of the overall street network enormously—for drivers, bicyclists, and pedestrians.

In essence, the Beltline is a reuse of a series of rail corridors. However, as a model, it could have

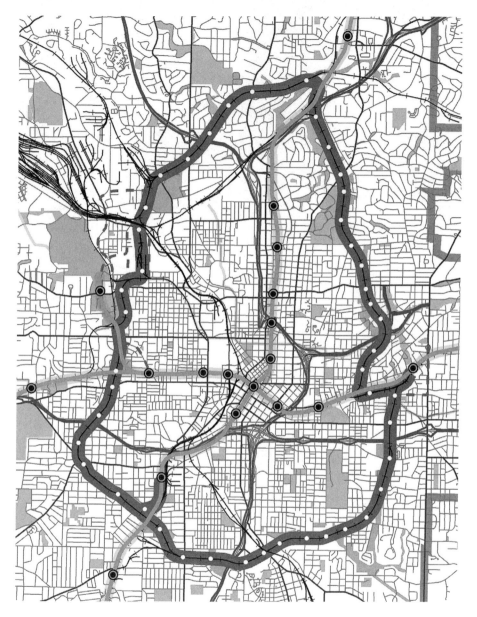

Figure 4–31   The plan for the Beltline in Atlanta, a 22-mile transit and park loop on little- or unused railroad lines that intersects with the city's north-south and east-west heavy rail transit system while providing access to approximately 6,000 acres of underdeveloped industrial land prime for retrofitting.

wider application inserted within the buffer spaces of conventional suburban pod planning, sometimes paralleling the arterials, and other times running between the cul-de-sac dead ends of subdivisions. While it may sound like pie in the sky, such visionary thinking is needed to go beyond simply retrofitting individual properties and to start retrofitting the systems as a whole.

Social Infrastructure

The physical form of the strip and its building types evolved over the twentieth century in ways that inhibited the development of locally owned third places and opportunities for building the kinds of networks that have traditionally been crucial to building collective social capital and civil society. The segregation of uses, increased auto dependency, standardization of development products, and dominance of chain retailers combined to produce a landscape that is neither physically nor socially well connected to the local community and environment.

Will the kind of retrofits this chapter has described reverse the decline in voluntary associations measured by Putnam in *Bowling Alone*? Will the clustering of synergistic activities in denser, more walkable environments foster greater levels of social interaction and build familiarity and trust? Will they result in safer streets and a more responsive democracy? These are very difficult qualities to measure, as the retrofits are highly varied and it is still too soon to attempt a verdict on any of them based on more than anecdotal evidence. Camino Nuevo's new schools, Santana Row's posh public space, and Cathedral City's new boulevard Main Street each contribute in different ways to enriching the social infrastructure of their communities. To look more closely at these questions, the next chapter focuses on the first retrofit of a shopping center, Mashpee Commons.

Chapter 5

Strips Case Study: Mashpee Commons, Cape Cod, Massachusetts

Attaching to a Well-Established Fragment of Urbanism

Name of project: Mashpee Commons (460,000 sq. ft. commercial and 482 residential units permitted as of 2007)

Location: Mashpee, Cape Cod, Massachusetts

Year constructed: 1986 to present, charrettes in 1988 and 2002

Master planners and primary building architects: Imai Keller Moore Architects

Charrette planner, code: Duany Plater-Zyberk & Company

Developer: Cornish Associates Limited Partnership

What it replaces: New Seabury Shopping Center (75,000 sq. ft.)

Size of site: 140 acres (60% preserved as open space)

Key features: new mixed-use downtown in a "no growth" region, an evolutionary development outward from a commercial core

Figure 5-1 One of the newest buildings at Mashpee Commons.

SUMMARY

Over the past two decades, the intersection of Routes 28 and 151 on Cape Cod in Massachusetts has evolved into a significant central place for the town of Mashpee and made history as the earliest retrofit of a suburban strip center. A humble neighborhood strip center has been transformed into Mashpee Commons, a lively commercial town center conscientiously tenanted with a mix of national and local retailers and enlivened with several important civic institutions. To realize this transformation, the developers have been tenacious in challenging local "no growth" sentiment and cumbersome local zoning in order to attain permits to build walkable streets and a later phase of attached neighborhoods with small-lot and attached housing types. Part of the challenge is environmental; Mashpee has no municipal sewer system and has experienced decades of rapid, haphazard growth, making residents and local government skittish about new development.

Because of the extended nature of the permitting process, the retrofitting of Mashpee Commons has been slow and evolutionary. With the recent celebration of a twenty-year anniversary, Mashpee Commons has now outlasted the 1960s strip center it replaced! There have been several incremental changes along the way: new liner buildings to screen parking areas, new mixed-use buildings with apartments above retail shops, the establishment of community events that have become traditions, the departure of some large tenants and the arrival of others. During this incremental process, the master plan for the attached neighborhoods has been substantially changed and adapted.

The primary retrofitting strategies at Mashpee Commons are as follows:

- Evolutionary demolition and rebuilding of a neighborhood strip center into a new mixed-use town center to comprise an "attachable fragment of urbanism." [1]
- Parallel planning of compact residential neighborhoods in adjacent areas that will plug into the commercial core to create a highly connected, walkable village center.
- Densification of a useful new node in an emerging transit network, a contribution to the retrofit of a region where seasonal traffic is heavy and many seniors become homebound when they can no longer drive.

Mashpee Commons is in the process of truly assuming the role of Mashpee's town center. (See Color Plates 16 to 19.) Massachusetts's Cape Cod, where the town of Mashpee is located, is a peninsula of 396 square miles jutting out into the Atlantic Ocean, historically comprised of small village communities dependent on farming, fishing, and whaling. Cape Cod today is perhaps best known as a place of summer homes for the wealthy, such as the Kennedy family. There is a sizable year-round population on Cape Cod as well, including many retirees, and the Cape's economy depends on servicing them as well as summer residents and tourists. The fast-growing town of Mashpee, with a year-round population of over 14,000, has a central, largely inland, location; the Commons is ideally sited near the center of this geographically central town, at the intersection of three busy roads—Route 28, Route 151, and Great Neck Road. (See Figure 5–2.)

All newly proposed development on Cape Cod is controversial. In his book *Place Making,* about developing new town centers, planner Charles C. Bohl asserts, "Mashpee Commons is an example of the sort of battle typically encountered when developers attempt to build town centers and other smart growth urban forms in what is essentially a no-growth environment."[2] Sprawl-form construction in recent decades, built in accord with antiquated and unsuitable suburban zoning protocols on a delicate coastal ecosystem, has unquestionably led to environmental damage and fueled intense antidevelopment sentiment. The challenge for the developers of Mashpee Commons, then, has been to argue that it is the building up of higher-density, mixed-use nodes in locations servable by transit and including affordable housing units that will do the most to relieve development pressure elsewhere and assist in efforts to preserve remaining open space on the Cape.

The Chace family's deep roots in Cape Cod and Doug Storr's background as an environmental planner meant that developers Buff Chace and Douglas Storrs, of Cornish Associates in Providence, Rhode Island, had more than a purely economic interest in the New Seabury Shopping Center. In the mid-1980s there was a plan in place to expand the existing center according to conventional retail development models to meet new demand. Rather than proceed with the plan, the owners conscientiously changed course and produced an alternate scheme to transform it from a small grocery-anchored strip into a walkable village-like shopping destination. Most of the original 75,000-square-foot center was retained, though several buildings were gut-renovated. (See Figure 5–3.) New shops with more traditional architectural detailing were added to form a small double-fronted outdoor mall surrounded by "streets" with sidewalks, transforming the center's focus from the car to the pedestrian. Inspired by the new

Figure 5-2
Location map.

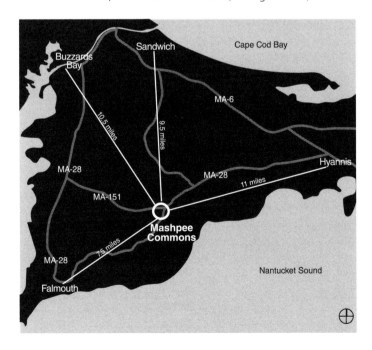

Figure 5-3 In the 1986 Chace and Storrs retrofitting plan, the Star Market supermarket building was retained. The tenant had a long-term lease, so the building was not altered. In 2007 the lease was up and the supermarket closed. As part of the evolutionary process, the building will soon be replaced with a two- to three-story mixed-use structure.

urbanist example of Seaside, Florida, the developers wanted to do more, to create a real village, like the older examples that existed elsewhere on Cape Cod. Thus began a long process, now over two decades in duration, of adding to that initial retrofit to establish a substantial town center.[3]

Master planning services were provided by Duany Plater-Zyberk & Company (DPZ), who led two charrettes for the site, one in 1988 and another follow-up in 2002, which resulted in a detailed implementation code. Other architects have contributed by designing various new buildings, additions, and tenant improvements over the years; Randall Imai of Imai Keller Moore Architects in Watertown, Massachusetts, designed many of the buildings and guides implementation of the master plan.

SITE HISTORY

Unlike other towns on Cape Cod, Mashpee does not have an established historical town center, healthy or otherwise. Its history was as an in-between place, comprised of Native Americans eking out a living by farming and fishing, and, later, a series of small oceanfront and lakefront residential areas. "Mash-

pee" is a Native American name, a reflection of the history of the town as the tribal home of the Wampanoag Indians, who met the Pilgrims at Plymouth. A sizable number of the remaining members of the tribe still live in the area.[4] The site of Mashpee Commons is at a crossroads of historic trails turned into major roads that connect the primary centers of the Upper Cape—Falmouth, Sandwich, Hyannis, and Buzzards Bay. The land around the crossroads was agricultural—cranberry bogs and other crops—as were much of the inland areas of the Cape. As the farms were abandoned in the late nineteenth century, land was reforested and then, since 1950, subdivided for new, large-lot housing (2-acre minimum). Nearby is the Massachusetts Military Reservation (formerly Otis Air Force Base), whose borders straddle Mashpee and neighboring towns.

In 1968 a modest shopping strip center was, logically, built at the rotary crossroads of Routes 151 and 28. (Atypical for the United States, there are a number of rotaries on the Cape dating from the 1950s.) The New Seabury Shopping Center met neighborhood needs with a supermarket, pharmacy, and other convenience businesses. In the 1980s Cape Cod was in the midst of a sustained residential building boom. By 1980, the number of housing units on the mainland Cape had more than tripled since 1950. By 2005, the number had grown an additional 54%, to over 150,000 units.[5] The town of Mashpee is leading the pack, growing from a mere 438 residents in 1950 to over 14,000 in 2007.

In 1986 the retrofitting plan, to reconfigure a strip center into streets and blocks to make the core of a "village center," was permitted and construction commenced. The new and improved center included the beginnings of two new primary cross streets, Market Street and Steeple Street. In order to avoid compliance with commercial zoning requirements for a minimum twenty-foot setback on each side of the street (a typical commercial zoning provision for new construction that in 1986 had not yet been widely challenged), the streets are actually defined as service alleys and driveways and remain privately owned. It is remarkable to compare the contortions required to build the rudimentary beginnings of a village center in the mid-1980s with the zoning and planning culture prevalent today, twenty years later, in which working around antiurban zoning with extensive overlays, or wholesale replacement of zoning codes, is becoming the norm.

The developers actively sought out civic uses: a post office was integrated into the core, and land was donated or deeded to the town for a public library, a church, subsidized senior housing, and a medical office building.

Chace and Storrs invited Andres Duany and Elizabeth Plater-Zyberk, already well known for their successes at Seaside, to conduct a charrette for the 40-acre commercial site, as well as 250 surrounding acres that they had acquired, to the north, east, and west of the original site. The charrette resulted in a master plan for the commercial center as well as a design for a series of interconnected surrounding residential neighborhoods.[6]

The first master plan included extensions of the street grid, established in the original retrofit, across Route 151 to the north and across Route 28 to the east. Compact residential neighborhoods of multifamily and single-family houses arranged around common greens were configured around the commercial village center. The remainder of the land would be conserved as open space. (See Figure 5–4.) The architectural idiom illustrated in the charrette renderings is a Cape Cod vernacular of wood shingles, simple boxy forms, small vertically proportioned windows and doors, and some colonial ornament.

The first phase of the North Market Street neighborhood, an extension of the primary Market Street

across Route 151, to the north, was permitted in 1993. The retail in the North Market Street neighborhood is of the "neighborhood" variety: another grocery store, a video store, a liquor store, a beauty parlor, a bank, and a dry cleaner. The "destination" retailers—boutiques and restaurants—remain in the village core. These two districts together were permitted for approximately 265,000 square feet of commercial use (retail, restaurants, and office), almost four times the area of the original shopping center, and for one hundred housing units, which would be "above the store" apartments and live/work units. The first thirteen housing units, "above the store" apartments, were not completed until 1998. They were the first new housing units of this type on Cape Cod in many years. The first three live/work housing units were completed in 2002, and another mixed-use building with twenty-four additional apartments was built the next year.

One of the sticking points in following through with the master plan, particularly the residential portions, was the question of wastewater. Cape Cod has no large-scale municipal sewer systems and there are none on the horizon. Towns on Cape Cod gave a pass to federal programs set up to fund such systems, instead opting for large-lot zoning and individual septic systems. This short-sighted policy has resulted in distressingly high nitrogen levels in aquifers, ponds, and coastal embayments that now must be redressed. A private facility, the first in Mashpee, was built to treat wastewater at Mashpee Commons, a significant upfront capital expenditure. There are now seven other such facilities in the town. The Mashpee Commons wastewater facility has to be expanded with each new development phase, incurring additional upfront expense.[7]

The battle for approval to build the adjacent residential neighborhoods began in earnest in 1998. Bohl describes "a dramatic, New England-style town meet-

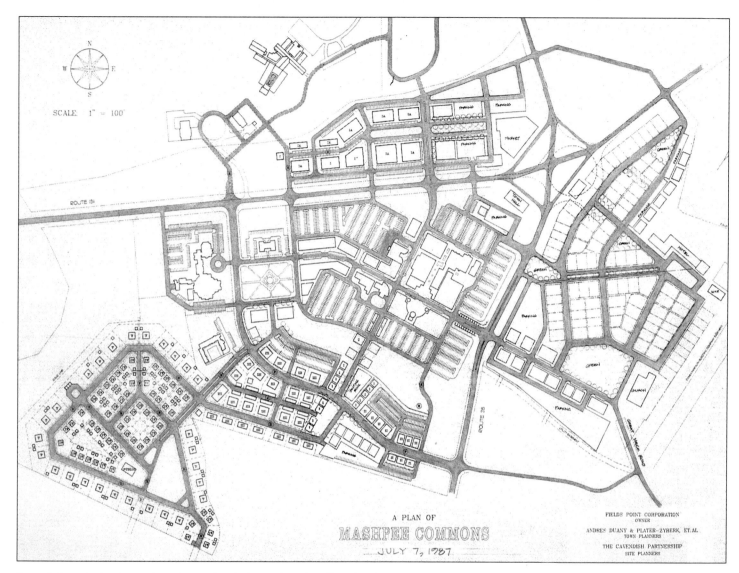

Figure 5-4 Early sketches, such as this one dated July 1987 from the office of Andres Duany and Elizabeth Plater-Zyberk, indicate an attempt to rethink the rotary to make it less of a car sorter and more of a connector, though in the end the rotary remained.

ing" in which the developers sought a two-thirds majority to approve four important amendments to the zoning code.[8] The amendments passed, but there were more roadblocks and delays. Storrs and Chace conducted a second charrette in 2002, again led by Duany Plater-Zyberk & Company, to directly address issues holding up the implementation of the residential portions of the overall master plan.

An outcome of the second charrette was a substantial reworking of the street network for the neighborhoods adjacent to the village core, and revisions to the mix of building types and their distribution in the neighborhoods. Other changes and adjustments resulting from the second charrette are as follows:

- Most of the proposed new housing is concentrated in the western neighborhoods of Jobs Fishing Road and Whitings Road.
- More typological specificity regarding the mix of housing types, including one hundred affordable units, to qualify for zoning waivers as allowed by Massachusetts inclusionary housing law.
- New locations and configurations of communal greens.
- Revised street network and intersections.
- Greater refinement of the civic armature.
- Drafting of the Mashpee Commons Code, a document reflecting the latest thinking of DPZ on form-based coding.

The Mashpee Commons Code (2002) consists of five documents to be used in conjunction: Regulating Plan, Urban Standards, Architectural Standards, Thoroughfare Standards, and Landscape Standards. The documents are based on the transect idea that DPZ has championed and codified (see Chapter 2). The Architectural Standards and Landscape Standards are simple, straightforward documents—one page each in length. The interpretation and application of the standards is left to the discretion of the town architect.[9]

In January 2007 the Mashpee Zoning Board granted approval for the neighborhoods of Jobs Fishing Road and Whitings Road. These two neighborhoods will include 382 dwelling units, of which 100 will be designated as affordable homes. There is a great variety of housing types: loft for-sale over commercial, apartments, townhouses, live/work units, duplexes, cottages, patio houses, and single-family houses, most with rear alley access. The affordable units are integrated throughout the neighborhoods, using the same architectural syntax as the market-rate units. This revised plan was the end result of an intensive two-year review period with the local zoning review board.

The Comprehensive Permit Law, known as Chapter 40B, was passed in Massachusetts in 1969 to promote the development of affordable housing in the face of local zoning codes that included provisions, such as minimum 2-acre lots, that made it virtually impossible to develop small, affordable housing units because the land costs would be too high. This type of "exclusionary" zoning had become commonplace in elite Massachusetts suburbs. To be in compliance with the statute, Chapter 40B requires all cities and towns to have 10% of their housing stock meet affordable standards (80% of area median income). In 2007, 300 of 351 Massachusetts cities and towns had not met this standard. Until they do, towns must permit qualified developers to submit proposals that may be out of compliance with local zoning but that include 25% of their housing as affordable units. The new housing neighborhoods in Mashpee Commons were approved through the Chapter 40B program and will make a significant contribution toward Mashpee meeting the 10% goal.[10]

It has been a long road for the developers of Mashpee Commons, but the realization of their original concept seems very close to fruition.

MORPHOLOGICAL ANALYSIS

Urban morphology is the study of the physical form of cities, concentrated on patterns of block, lot, and building aggregations. We use morphological analysis in our case study method to examine how the underlying morphological patterns have contributed to or impeded the effort to retrofit sprawl. To do this we have diagrammed the lots, streets, and buildings on and around each case study site at three points in time, ending with our projection for the near future (based on a number of inputs depending on the specifics of the case study).

The following series of figure-field diagrams illustrates the morphological transformations over time, from 1985 to projected conditions in 2025, on a square-mile area that includes Mashpee Commons. One can see both how the preurban fabric of farm roads, fields, and Native American trails conditioned the suburban road, lot, and building locations and how they in turn influenced the new street network of the village. In the diagrams, one may read three types of suburban tissue: *static tissues,* or planned subdivisions; *campus tissues,* such as apartment complexes and shopping centers; and *elastic tissues,* found on the arterial strips.[11]

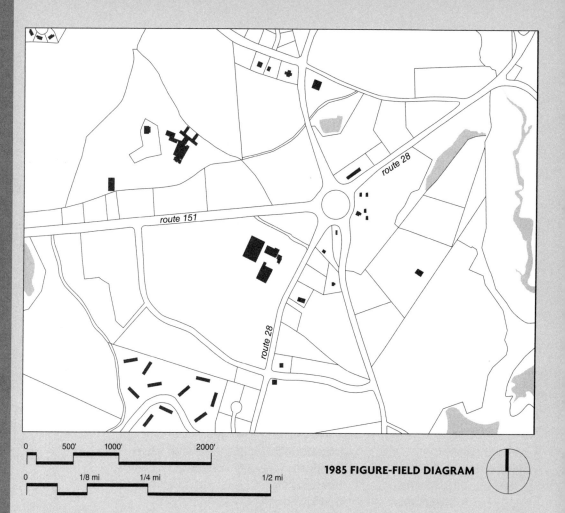

1985 FIGURE-FIELD DIAGRAM

Figure 5-5 1985 figure-field diagram. By the mid-1980s the town of Mashpee, the last to be incorporated on Cape Cod (in the 1880s), was growing rapidly. But not much of that growth had occurred as yet at the rotary crossroad, just some old farmhouses on the main roads and one new clustered apartment complex off Route 28. The forerunner to Mashpee Commons, the New Seabury Shopping Center, had been built in 1968 and served neighborhood retail needs. Customers arrived by car to the one-story, 75,000-square-foot center. Set back from Route 151, to the north, a municipal *campus* was forming—with a school, a boys and girls club, and the fire department—arranged in typical suburban form with curving, dead-end drives. Lots of varying sizes along the roads, comprising *elastic* tissue, are unbuilt, waiting in reserve for future commercial development. The owners of Mashpee Commons subsequently acquired many of these lots. Threaded through the area are traces of old Native American trails, indicated in the figure-ground diagram by narrow double lines. The demarcation of lots is heavily influenced by these ancient ways. Natural boundaries to the future Mashpee Commons area are formed by creeks and wetlands, on the eastern edge, and the Quashnet River to the west (just off the boundary of the diagram).

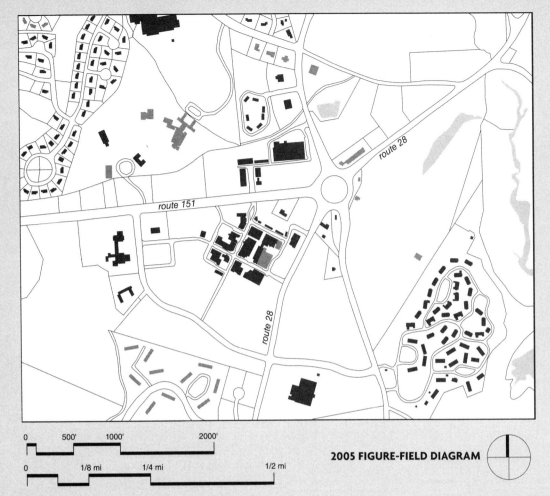

0   500'   1000'   2000'

0   1/8 mi   1/4 mi   1/2 mi

2005 FIGURE-FIELD DIAGRAM

Figure 5-6 2005 figure-field diagram. The two main cross streets of Mashpee Commons, Steeple and Main, are well established. Several new buildings have been built; some are mixed use, with offices or apartments above the stores (thirty-seven apartments by 2005). And there are three new live-work units. The buildings are one to three stories high. Steeple Street, which runs east to west, connects to Route 28 on the east and terminates at a Catholic church (hence "Steeple") on the west, forming an intersection with Job's Fishing Road. This bypasses the rotary, connecting Routes 151 and 28 and through to Great Neck Road, terminating in a large, new clustered condominium complex, a notable new *campus* tissue. Market Street runs north to south and connects on the south to Job's Fishing Road; on the north it crosses Route 151 to the North Market portion of the Commons. The large footprint of the supermarket pad, built in a location with excellent visibility and easy access

from the arterial roads, is easily discerned. The intersection crossing Route 151 is not particularly pedestrian friendly, although there is a crosswalk. The anomalous outparcel along Route 151, close to the rotary, contains a bank with drive-through lanes. Twenty-foot-deep liner buildings frame the edges of the parking lot where the stand-alone bank sits; there are thirteen small shops in the liners. A narrow liner is also included in the North Market Street area, adjacent to the supermarket. Just visible at the upper left corner of this diagram are the edges of a large-lot, single-family house subdivision configured around a golf course. Large lots on cul-de-sac streets predominate in static tissue subdivisions throughout Mashpee. To the south along busy Route 28, the Dartmouth Companies developed an as-of-right retail center called South Cape Village. The new center mimics Mashpee Commons a bit in form, with a pedestrian way, but it is not mixed use.

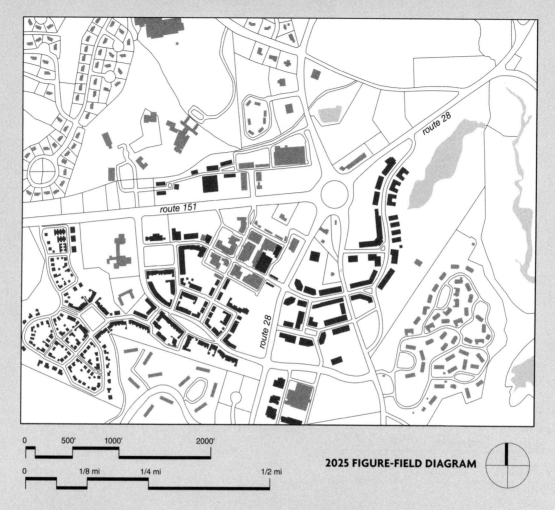

0   500'   1000'   2000'

0   1/8 mi   1/4 mi   1/2 mi

2025 FIGURE-FIELD DIAGRAM

Figure 5-7 2025 figure-field diagram (projected). After several revisions of the overall master plan, approvals were granted in 2007 and design commenced on two residential neighborhoods adjoining the town center to the south and west. The housing types in these neighborhoods vary widely. Subsequent phases to complete the master plan, consisting mostly of larger, mixed-use buildings, will be built in the North Market neighborhood and east of Route 28 (the final configuration of these buildings may differ from this projection). The new neighborhoods respect the pre-existing network of Native American walking trails. Sixty percent of the Mashpee Commons land has been preserved as open space—ponds, buffers, wetlands—and the trails permit access to some of these acres. By 2025, the interconnected street network, which connects with four-way intersections across the existing high-traffic arterials, will be well established. The interconnected nature of the street network will relieve pressure on the rotary by permitting local traffic to bypass it through a number of alternate routes.

FROM STRIP TO DOWNTOWN: MASHPEE'S THIRD PLACE

What has been accomplished to date, in terms of retrofitting, at Mashpee Commons? Chuck Bohl describes it in its current state as an "attachable fragment of urbanism."[12] Opportunities for attaching new compact neighborhoods to this now well-established fragment are on the verge of realization, the result of a persistent, committed developer. The project has taken its share of hits: dismissal as a mere "lifestyle center" despite the civic components and the intent to add substantial amounts of housing; copycat developments that invoke Mashpee Commons as a precedent but really are only lifestyle centers; critiques of the architecture as "nostalgic" although Cape Cod has a living vernacular to tap

into; and the recent collapse of the Boch Center for the Performing Arts, long expected to be a notable cultural anchor for Mashpee Commons, where a 900-seat theater was to be built.[13]

Despite these hits, we see many accomplishments that are excellent models for suburban retrofitting. First, and perhaps foremost, is the substantial network of civic infrastructure embedded in Mashpee Commons, and the developers' continued willingness to work with the town and other entities, such as the post office, to negotiate the necessary adjustments to keep those uses in the mix.[14] (See Figure 5–8.)

Also significant is the approach of building the commercial core first, the "attachable fragment," and then using its success to support adjacent, higher-density residential development. Conventional (and many new urbanist) greenfield developments often follow an opposite strategy: build the

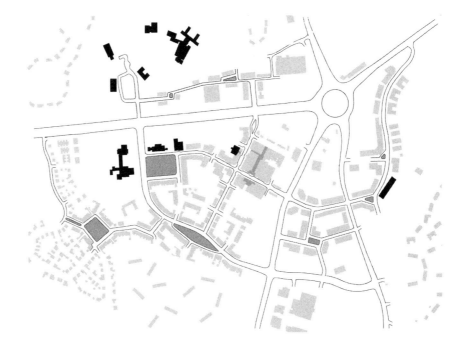

Figure 5-8 *Many public buildings and spaces—post office, public library, church, town green—have been successfully incorporated into Mashpee Commons. West of Job's Fishing Road, at the intersection with Route 151, is a Catholic church. To the south of it is Homeyer Village, subsidized senior housing, and across the street is the Mashpee Public Library. These civic institutions are grouped around the town common, all on land donated by the developers.*

housing first, then add commercial uses when a sufficient density has been achieved, or build small bits of neighborhood commercial use *solely* to meet the needs of the new residents. The conventional model works against sustainable urbanism goals of increasing housing densities and compact, walkable, transit-served locations. Mashpee Commons has created a sizable demand for compact housing types in adjacent locations, in a market that has long been dominated by large-lot, auto-dependent housing. This demand will undoubtedly improve the return on the market-rate housing that Mashpee Commons's owners will build, and is already being reflected in the rents and resale prices of other housing nearby.

Thirdly, we commend Mashpee Commons for the innovative (and counterintuitive, to many who practice retail architecture) use of small, shallow liner buildings. This unusual retail building type consists of 20- to 24-foot-deep liner buildings placed around the edges of parking fields to mask the parking from the view of pedestrians walking along the streets; conventional retail buildings are 70 to 100 feet deep. (See Figures 5–9 and 5–10.) They are shallow to not take away too many of the needed parking spaces. These liners also serve the function of completing two-sided retail streets in the village core. The small shops (350 to 425 square feet) are rented to local mom-and-pop stores, thus increasing the variety and uniqueness of retail offerings and providing opportunities for local businesses to become established. Because the floor area of the shops is small, but with adequate street frontage, the rents are lower than

Figure 5-9 Liner buildings at Mashpee Commons successfully house small, local businesses, like this flower shop, while completing the street.

Figure 5-10 The liner buildings' shallow footprint is only around twenty feet deep, equivalent to the depth of only one row of parking in the lot behind.

for other, deeper shops in the town center, which are more likely to be rented to national retailers.

The liners are extremely effective at achieving two goals: first, masking parking lots, and second, "incubating" local stores. While the shallow liner type goes against the grain of standard retail development practice, it may be argued that this is part of the point. Twenty feet is much too shallow for chain retailers' standard formats, not to mention the low ceiling heights. But these stores serve a valuable purpose as a vehicle for the developer to attract local businesses by offering small floor areas at low rents. The spaces remain available to rent to locals precisely because they are unappealing to the national chains. Mashpee Commons has become so popular (and profitable) that all of the shops could be leased at high rates to national chains, but this would undercut the leasing strategy of creating a unique, local place that could not be replicated anywhere else.

Less convincing are proposals, contained in the DPZ 2002 charrette report, to extend the narrow liner typology to other uses, such as senior housing. But we are not willing to dismiss entirely the possibilities of the type for other uses. The shallow liner has also been successfully incorporated at Belmar, used as subsidized artists' studios that enliven the ground floor of a parking garage (see Chapter 8), and, because of its versatility and relatively low cost, we expect to see the type used with increasing frequency in suburban retrofits.

Another piece of the puzzle to making Mashpee Commons not only a village center for Mashpee, but also a contributor to a more sustainable trajectory for the future of Cape Cod, would be to improve access to and use of mass transit. Census data from 2000 indicate that only 1.22% of Cape residents used transit to commute (and many of those who do are taking interregional buses to Boston). There

is, however, a local bus system on the peninsula that has seen gains in ridership over the past five years. The Hyannis-Falmouth Breeze, which has a fixed route but not fixed stops (residents may flag it down anywhere along its route), passes through Mashpee Commons.[15] It will be crucially important to improve transit to address the needs of increasing numbers of retirees, and to make it feasible for summer residents and tourists to leave their cars behind. The peninsula geography of Cape Cod is conducive to transit. The live/work residents at Mashpee Commons will, of course, have the easiest conceivable commute; they are, as Douglas Storrs says, "staircase commuters." The hope is that other small businesses that locate there will have workers who live very close by or who have the option of commuting by transit. The urban form patterns that are developing at Mashpee Commons, and its central location on the Upper Cape, suggest this outcome is feasible.

Is Mashpee Commons a successful "third place?" It has the particular challenge to address the needs of summer residents—shopping and movies as entertainment on nonbeach days—as well as to anchor a community of year-round residents, which includes many retirees. Mashpee Commons seems to be succeeding. The developers appear to take seriously their obligations toward community building in partnership with the Town of Mashpee. Mashpee Commons provides a refreshing alternative to the many other, more exclusively tourist-oriented businesses and developments on Cape Cod. In addition to sponsoring dozens of events, including a hugely popular August 4th Pops concert, the Commons publishes the Mashpee Commons *Courier*, which includes local news, book reviews, and profiles of town employees.

It will continue to be interesting to track the ongoing progress of Mashpee Commons over its next twenty years.

Chapter 6
From Regional Malls to New Downtowns Through Mixed-Use and Public Space

Figure 6–1 Originally built in 1964, the Avondale Mall in DeKalb County, Georgia, is typical of a growing number of dead malls nationwide. The debate over its future redevelopment as either a mixed-use town center or a Wal-Mart is typical of the discussion about such sites.

A mall is dead, its lifeblood of shoppers lured away by newer competition. The entrances are boarded up; the parking-lot asphalt is cracked and sprouting weeds; only memories remain. What will happen next with the large parcel of suburban land where the hulking building sits, on 40 or more acres? Most of the community members just want someone to come in and "fix" their mall and restore it to its pride-producing and tax-generating glory days. However, malls are dying faster than they are getting built. It is very unlikely that the structure will ever serve as a conventional shopping mall again. Will it become a blight-spreading white elephant or a form-shifting phoenix rising from the ashes?

One of the more promising reincarnations of dead malls is in the form of new downtowns and town centers. New town centers, in many cases the centers that suburban towns never had, are springing up around the United States, often replacing regional shopping malls.[1] The physical form of these centers resembles a traditional urban downtown more than a conventional suburban mall in two significant ways. First, they contain outdoor public space—plazas, greens, piazzas, and squares, as well as public streets and sidewalks. Second, the buildings contain a mix of uses—retail (of course), residential, office, recreational, and civic (post office, library, town hall). Unlike traditional downtowns, they tend to rely on public-private financing, are master planned to be built in coordinated phases, and are under single or very limited ownership. The owner then manages the mix of tenants, maintains the common spaces, and employs private security. These controlling techniques, borrowed from malls (and increasingly employed by business improvement districts, or BIDs, in older downtowns as well), enable town center retail to better compete in suburban markets. But they also limit the capacity of the place to generate the kind of cultural energy that results from chance juxtapositions in more traditional urban settings. The excitement and cultural identity associated with "downtown" becomes a significant part of the function of the public spaces and the mixed uses in these new centers.

The benefits of mixing uses are many, from increasing social diversity, safety, and a sense of community to reducing VMT and improving financial bottom-lines. By providing retail and office employees with housing, dining, and retail choices within walking distance of their jobs, mixed use can reduce automobile trips and parking spaces, spread peak traffic flow hours, improve the cost-effectiveness of mass transit, and in some cases facilitate carpooling commute trips. In a good mix, each use benefits from proximity to the other and they collectively generate a lively place.

To the degree that the mix of uses is configured in a way that is walkable and therefore convenient,

these new downtowns become increasingly attractive, especially as worsening traffic congestion makes driving around in suburbs less convenient. From 1982 to 2000 the U.S. population grew 19%, but the percent of time people spent stuck in traffic grew disproportionately, by 236%.[2] Other studies show that suburban traffic congestion has grown proportionately the most, causing the pronounced rise in the national average. As Al Gore has made clear, the issue here is not only the inconvenience this causes to drivers. John Norquist, president of the Congress for the New Urbanism, likes to refer to walkable urbanism as the convenient remedy to the inconvenient truth.

An additional benefit of mixed use is the economic advantage to municipalities and developers of being able to better ride out real estate market cycles by having a mixed portfolio, and being able to more flexibly respond to shifts in demand. However, the complexities of mixed use are demanding: retail developers need to partner with residential developers and vice versa or grow expertise in more uses; both still need to overcome financing resistance to mixed use even though it is getting much easier; and because suburbs have traditionally been zoned for single use and single lot size, mixed use often requires that developers seek zoning variances. And while there are many good smaller examples, the Urban Land Institute (ULI) recommends that the critical mass of mixed use needed in a suburban business district to establish and reinforce a sense of community is a minimum of 200,000 square feet of retail and 2,000 dwelling units within a ten-minute walk of each other.[3]

A key aspect of configuring a successful mix in a new downtown is to identify dynamic synergies between uses. One can identify a cycle of supporting uses: residential attracts retail, retail supports office, office supplies restaurants, and, coming full circle,

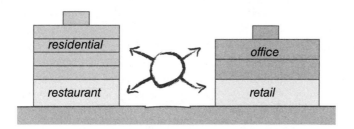

Figure 6–2 Synergy derives from uses that support one another and are located in close proximity.

SYNERGIES OF VERTICAL MIXED USE

restaurants attract residential use. These synergies are most effective when the uses are close together and it is convenient to easily move from one to the other. This is especially true of "vertical mixed use," where different activities are stacked within the same building and integrated into urban streets with ground-level retail and office and residential above. (See Figure 6–2.) The retail can typically only be supported on major streets and this works best for the most urban part of a new downtown (the T-6 and T-5 transect zones of the new urbanist SmartCode; see Chapter 2). "Horizontal mixed use" across a development is a useful strategy for integrating the various uses with compatible adjacencies. However, it should be distinguished from projects that merely set a hotel here and an office building there without establishing attractive, pedestrian spatial connections between them to increase connectivity. Similarly, a lifestyle center that integrates upper-level residences and existing neighborhoods into its Main Street should be distinguished from one that simply combines retail and restaurants without more synergistic variety. Zoning codes are increasingly recognizing the degree to which synergies between complementary uses allow the additional benefit of shared parking.

There is nothing new about mixed-use development. It has been the characteristic form of city making for centuries and has reappeared in both modern and traditional variations, in both urban and suburban locations, over the past forty years. The distinguishing factor of the more successful contemporary mixed-use developments is the walkable, fine grain of the integration of the uses and the quality of the public space that is established between them. Only by establishing a populated public realm can mixed-use developments live up to the social aspirations of a downtown.

THE SIGNIFICANCE OF PUBLIC SPACE

Public spaces are crucial for supporting the public life that binds a community. Throughout history, urban civilizations have engaged in the act of delimiting particular places as civic spaces distinct from their surroundings. Whether plazas, parks, or museums, investments in markers of their significance identify them as their community's shared forum. Colin Rowe's famous attention to figure-ground drawings of cities taught a generation of urbanists in the 1970s and 1980s to read these types of public spaces literally in black and white.[4] More recently, academic discussions of "the public" have expanded to recognize multiple publics and the more blurred distinctions between public and private space in ordinary life. Increased attention to the messy public space of the everyday street and the role of commerce in promoting social interaction has challenged public space to embrace multiplicity over unity at the same time that it has reinforced the key role of public space in community building.[5]

But does community building today rely on public space? Many critics and commentators contend that the political and cultural roles of physical public space have been replaced by the media, by shopping, and by the virtual world of cyberspace. The old distinctions between public and private space have been obliterated by television, cell phones, webcams, and blogs. Yet, rather than substitute for public space, they appear only to have fed a greater desire for direct experience of connectivity, especially in the suburbs. The provision of public places where people can congregate together freely and face-to-face remains essential to retrofitting suburbs into more urban places. In fact, the amenities of urban public life are precisely what compensate the residents of new downtowns for the loss of suburban private space. However, the ownership and accessibility of those amenities remains a controversial subject, with some arguing that the lack of contestation over public space in gentrified new downtowns limits their ability to serve as truly public spaces in which the entire community appears to itself.

Such places are lacking or neglected in many existing suburbs.[6] As sociologist David Brain asserts, "A case can be made that the erosion of meaningful public space by suburban development patterns (with their emphasis on parochial communities at the expense of what comes between) is part of what has become a kind of trained incapacity for public life."[7] *Community* emphasizes exclusivity and belongingness, and is abundant in suburbs. For many, it can also be found online where like-minded people easily find one another. Community is distinctly different from *civility,* which describes a set of behaviors and attitudes intended to support inclusion and opportunities for participation in public life, and is absolutely place based. The role of public space, then, is to cultivate civility, which in turn supports social interaction in a way that does not presuppose payment of fees or membership in a more limited community. Civility—or as described by Aristotle, the art of living together well—is the very purpose of the city. Brain argues that truly public spaces make visible the orders that signal societal stability, trust, and mutual respect in the shared common world—without requiring assimilation. Valued public

spaces with well-tended amenities, from public art to pleasant places to sit and hang out, send these signals.

Margaret Kohn, author of *Brave New Neighborhoods: The Privatization of Public Space,* similarly emphasizes the importance of intersubjectivity and opportunities for social interaction in distinguishing public space. However, she represents a not uncommon point of view that is critical of the attempts by new malls to recreate the atmosphere of old downtowns while restricting civic, political, and religious activity. The legal status of publicly accessible, privately owned spaces remains murky and continues to evolve; however, the courts have recognized that the physical form may ultimately be more important than ownership in determining the rights of users and owners.[8]

In an influential article from 1965, entitled "You Have to Pay for the Public Life," Charles Moore speculated about where in southern California one would go to stage a revolution given the dearth of densely populated public space. The question remains relevant and was most recently tested at Downtown Silver Spring, a retrofit in Maryland funded by a public-private partnership. The streets are owned by Montgomery County but leased to the Peterson Companies, the developer of the adjoining mix of uses, for one dollar. After the Peterson Companies' security stopped Chip Py, an amateur photographer, from taking pictures of the street and buildings, he wrote a letter to the County Executive and members of the county council asking where the public's civil rights end and the corporation's privacy rights begin. After considerable press, the company agreed to allow photography but did not slow the nascent "Free Our Streets" movement that the event precipitated. Over a hundred people gathered on July 4, 2007, at Downtown Silver Springs' Astroturf town green (a celebrated if unusual surface for public space) before marching through the streets, taking pictures, but more importantly demanding

Figure 6–3 Amateur photographers gathered on July 4, 2007, at the Downtown Silver Spring lifestyle center for a protest to assert their civil right to take photographs in the publicly owned but privately leased streets and Astroturf-covered green.

Figure 6–4 Aerial view of the Park Forest Plaza. Its distinguishing feature was a landscaped, pedestrian-only "mall" in the center of the complex, flanked by arcaded stores and surrounded by plentiful, free parking. The shopping center featured clean, modern forms and an overt reference to the Italian piazza in the form of an iconic campanile, or clock tower.

civil liberties in spaces that are developed with public assistance. (See Figure 6–3.)

The outcome of such demands will likely be debated for years to come; however, it is worth pointing out the importance of the inclusion of public space—even if privately owned—to the ability of a mixed-use new downtown to trigger just such public discourse and assembly for protest. Without it, a redeveloped mall site remains just that: a contained, concentrated circus of commerce and consumption.

A BRIEF HISTORY OF MALLS

Early suburban shopping centers sought to maintain the imagery of a traditional Main Street, with modifications to accommodate the newly popular contraption of the automobile. In the early 1940s, there was much speculation about the ways in which neighborhood shopping centers could be reconfigured to better accommodate automobiles. Then came the notion of providing a central space that would be free of automobiles. Four often cited precedents for what came to be known as "the mall" were the New England town green of the colonial period, the agora of ancient Athens, the piazzas of Renaissance Italy, and European boulevards.

In the immediate post–World War II period, large merchant builders began developing extensive planned communities of single-family houses and garden apartments in American suburban locations where land was plentiful, regulations were scant, and federal mortgage funding was readily available. The master plan for Park Forest, Illinois (1947–1951), included an open-air, pedestrian-only shopping center that was arguably the first built example of a suburban regional center. (See Figure 6–4.) In retrospect, Park Forest Plaza was notable for the way

Figure 6–5 The lush, mature landscaping of the open-air Cross County Mall in Yonkers, New York. Built in the mid-1950s, it escaped major expansion or enclosure over the decades and retains a neighborhood appeal. A major facelift, set to be complete in 2008, will upgrade building façades, add new retail area, and convert the office building into a boutique hotel (converting the mall into a lifestyle center), but the green mall spaces will remain.

the design integrated circulation to and through the plaza with the surrounding housing.[9]

Most of the mall developments that followed Park Forest Plaza, such as Victor Gruen's Northgate in Seattle (1950) and Southdale Center in Edina, Minnesota (1956), assumed that patrons would arrive by car and sought to maximize traffic circulation patterns on the mall periphery and parking lots, while focusing on the pedestrian shopper within. This, after all, was the supposed advantage of the "rational" separation of the two. In his classic book *Shopping Towns USA*, Gruen argued eloquently for the utility of shopping centers. He was motivated by a desire to prevent the destruction of community space by the intrusion of the automobile and unplanned, haphazard development. He sincerely wished to recreate an updated version of the pedestrian districts found in historic city

centers in Europe. However, he came to regret the monstrous malls his innovations spawned.[10]

The earliest shopping malls combined retail with civic uses like post offices, local government offices, and small offices for lawyers, accountants, and the like. Basically, the shopping mall was to have all the elements found on Main Street. But by the 1960s civic and small office uses were no longer welcome in new malls. An exception that in some ways proves the rule is the Cross County Mall in Yonkers, New York, designed by Lathrop Douglass in the mid-1950s, which features an eight-story office building and, surprisingly, has escaped receiving a major renovation or expansion through the years. (See Figure 6–5.) Many other malls were enclosed, expanded, and expanded again, such that the original construction is nearly impossible to discern and the resulting structures are difficult to appreciate as architecture.

By the 1980s, as suburban Americans were spending more and more leisure time in malls, a sophisticated critique of the shopping mall had emerged. Not only were malls and discount big-box retailers killing off Main Street's vestiges of public space, critics lamented that malls were substituting pure commerce and the spectacle of consumption for truly public space. Of course, in many suburban developments, there had never been a Main Street in the first place, just the local shopping plaza. And by the 1980s the demise of these early plazas had already begun while increasingly larger, more sprawling superregional malls were being constructed, such as the Mall of America in Bloomington, Minnesota (1992). But in retrospect, the construction of the bloated Mall of America, instead of setting a new benchmark for the mall as a souped-up entertainment theme park, marked the beginning of the end.

One of the counterpoint trends that emerged in this period, which plays a significant role in this story, is the revitalization of some urban Main Streets that had been written off for dead. Prominent examples are the Third Street Promenade (originally 1965, redesigned in 1989) in Santa Monica and One Colorado in Old Town Pasadena (1992; 120,000 square feet of retail space), both in greater Los Angeles. Older retail buildings on these streets were renovated, tenanted, and managed *as if* they were malls (the end result resembles a lifestyle center). A key component of the restructuring was the construction of peripheral parking garages, accessed from side streets and alleys, where the spaces are cheap, convenient, and plentiful. Restaurants and movie theaters make up a significant portion of the tenant portfolios of these two sites.

DEAD AND DYING MALLS

In *Greyfields into Goldfields,* a report by the Congress for New Urbanism (CNU), the authors identify a tremendous opportunity to "reclaim vast suburban swaths" by redeveloping so-called dead mall sites.[11] A February 2001 report by PricewaterhouseCoopers retail expert Steve Laposa that was commissioned by CNU concluded that 7% of regional malls were greyfield sites and effectively dead, and another 12% were vulnerable and would probably fail within the next five years.[12] The study also noted that smaller malls were more likely to be failing than larger malls. The average greyfield mall has 63 stores on 46 acres, while the average "healthy" mall offers 124 stores on 71 acres. While there are exceptions to this rule, such as the failed 106-acre Villa Italia mall that has become Belmar, in Lakewood, Colorado (see Chapter 8), it speaks to the trend in retail for ever-larger formats to establish critical mass. On the one hand, this is driving the outward expansion of large malls situated at highway exits into megamalls. On the other hand, it

is driving the redevelopment of smaller sites upward with multistory, mixed-use buildings that offer developers opportunity for a healthy return on their investment, while offering communities an opportunity for lasting regeneration.

The failure of shopping malls dotted throughout suburbia points at one of the primary dilemmas of American postwar suburbs: places seek to remain the same, yet by doing so they become subject to the sort of decline that can be countered only by change. As residents and especially homeowners struggle to maintain the status quo that signifies stability, suburban places are inevitably transforming. And in many instances, such as in the case of dead and dying malls, these transformations are beyond local control.

Dead mall sites are of great interest to developers, architects, and urban designers because they are generally located on large parcels of easily accessible land. They represent, as they did to the original designers of regional shopping malls, a tremendous opportunity to create something new with the potential to operate as a coherent whole. When regional shopping malls were first developed in already existing communities, they were often sited on wetlands, creek beds, or other areas of land that had been deemed unsuitable for residential subdivision and were therefore vacant and available. They were also typically located along major arterial roads, and later, highways, again sites not deemed appropriate for low-density residential use. Their apartness was part of the appeal. Later, large retail districts, surrounded by large parking fields, in turn surrounded by office and multifamily residential use districts, were designed into new master planned communities—as at Irvine in Orange County, California, and the Woodlands in Texas. There was no expectation that anyone would walk to the regional mall. Now that many have failed, and traffic congestion has made driving

Wall Street Players: Some of the Top Retail REITS

	2006 Revenue	Market Capitalization	Holdings
Simon Properties	$3,332.1 M	$20.9 B	280 properties in 38 states and worldwide comprising more than 200 million sq. ft.
Vornado Realty Trust	$2,712.1 M	$13.7 B	160 retail centers, many in cities; diversified with other building types
General Growth Properties	$3,256.3 M	$10.7 B	More than 200 malls comprising 200,000 million sq. ft.; purchased Rouse Corp. in 2004 and now holds several mixed-use properties
Macerich	$829.7 M	$5.5 B	90 malls and shopping centers
Weingarten Realty Investors	$561.4 M	$4.8 B	390 properties comprising 65 million sq. ft.; mostly big-box and neighborhood centers
CBL & Associates	$1,002.1 M	$1.6 B	110 properties, including 80 malls
Taubman	$579.3 M	$2.6 B	20 properties in 10 states, mostly high-end superregional malls
Pennsylvania REIT	$464.6 M	$1.1 B	50 malls

Source: National Association of Real Estate Investment Trusts (NAREIT), 2007

to them less convenient, they have terrific potential to be retrofitted into mixed-use places, knit back into their surroundings with a civic life that many suburbs are lacking.

The process of redeveloping existing urban and suburban sites is never simple. The history of urban renewal is a testament to the damage left in the wake of seemingly well-intentioned efforts gone awry. This difficulty is one of the main factors that encourages sprawl. In the absence of effective financial and political incentives, confronted by entrenched NIMBYism, and faced with the sheer complexity of small infill sites, developers seek profit in greener pastures.

Christopher Leinberger has described the role of real estate investment trusts (REITs) in recent years in perpetuating sprawl development patterns. Developers who rely on Wall Street investment must present their projects in the form of a tradable commodity or product of which Leinberger counts only nineteen types, all single use. The retail types are grocery-anchored neighborhood centers, big-box-anchored power centers, and lifestyle centers. While not currently being built as new "product" and therefore absent from this list, regional shopping malls are increasingly likely to be owned by one of a handful of powerful retail REITs (see table).

Leinberger has described some intriguing models for overcoming the financing handicap presented by REIT ownership by developing new, mixed-use REIT types. To a designer, the new types he proposes hardly seem revolutionary: for-sale housing or office over retail, burying the big box behind retail and office/housing, high-density rental housing surrounding parking structure with retail at grade, and retail with office or artists' lofts. But using current financial modeling tools, Wall Street analysts look at these propositions and see only confusion, risk, and ruin. But if complex, unique infill projects can be packaged *as if* they conform to a bounded, knowable, and repeatable prototype, they stand a much better chance of receiving a piece of the Wall Street pie.[13]

For the time being, Wall Street formulas remain relatively undifferentiated. The "vast suburban swath" of 40 or more open, developable acres that a dead mall generates is proving to be an appealing alternative to a greenfield site, even for conventional retail developers. But suitability for redevelopment also depends on location. The most advantageously located malls with respect to regional automobile transportation routes—highways—will be renovated and expanded in an effort to remain one of the 50 to 200 superregional malls that analysts at PricewaterhouseCoopers project will survive the current wave of consolidation. As Jonathan Miller writes, "The heyday of the great suburban mall is over. Regional shopping centers will live on. In fact, the larger so-called fortress malls, embedded on main drags near the most prosperous bedroom communities with the top tenant line-ups, should thrive. But in an over-retailed America, many tired, also-ran centers in secondary locations are doomed."[14] What is to become of these casualties?

The International Council of Shopping Centers (ICSC) and the Urban Land Institute (ULI), trade organizations for retail developers, are staking out new positions that could be termed proactive rather than defensive about the future of enclosed shopping malls, a building type and use that design professionals have become to loathe.[15] The Congress for the New Urbanism and smart growth advocates have become influential in shaping the new and evolving positions of the ULI and the ICSC.

Exact figures are hard to come by, but in 2007 the ICSC estimated that there are around 1,000 enclosed malls in the United States. These malls are grouped into two main categories of shopping centers: regional centers, of 400,000 to 800,000 square feet on 40 to 100 acres with a primary trade area of five to fifteen miles; and superregional centers, of more than 800,000 square feet on 60 to 120 acres and a primary trade area of five to twenty-five miles (where the primary trade area is defined as the area from which 60%–80% of the center's sales originate).[16] As the sun sets on the forty-year reign of new mall construction, new shopping center types—lifestyle centers, power centers—are on the rise.

Why are so many once-popular malls dying? One of the factors contributing to the precipitous decline of so many malls in recent years is the overabundance of retail square footage in the suburbs. Simply put, there are just too many stores and the "weak" do not survive. The amount of retail area per person in the United States grew from 15.2 square feet in 1986 to 20.2 in 2005, a 25% increase.[17] Much of this is accounted for by new locations for chain stores seeking blanket coverage of the marketplace. Because so much new retail "product" is being built each year, there is a tolerance, an expectation even, that some older same-store locations will be put out of business. Often, as in the case of Wal-Mart, the obsolescence of older stores is planned.

The U.S. rate of 20.2 retail square feet per person was *six times* the ratio for Sweden, the leading

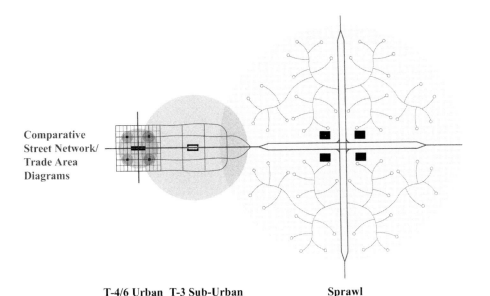

Comparative Street Network/ Trade Area Diagrams

	T-4/6 Urban	T-3 Sub-Urban	Sprawl
Square Footage/ Residential Unit	Same	Same	Same
Relative Scale	1.0	1.5	3.0 +
Average Distance To Daily Needs	1/2 mile	2 miles	3 - 5 miles or more

Figure 6–6 Regional retail scale comparative diagram by Seth Harry. A one-mile-diameter catchment area over a compact urban street grid with relatively high densities "catches" as many households as a fifteen-mile trade area centered on a mall at a suburban highway intersection surrounded by sprawling, low-density subdivisions.

country in Europe for retail square footage per person. And Sweden's rate is much higher than typical for Europe, probably skewed by the Swedish big-box retailer Ikea, which specializes in very large stores that also function as warehouses. Because there is so much retail space in the United States, filled with merchandise, not to mention plentiful online retailing options, the competition for customers is intense. Consequently, many stores, chains, and entire shopping centers are expected to fail. How did we reach this unsustainable state of affairs? It is a story of increasing market specialization, coupled with the abundant availability of relatively cheap, commercially zoned land.

The ICSC categories assume relatively constant suburban densities, a practice that has been challenged by new urbanists.[18] (See Figure 6–6.) As retail followed lower and lower net density development into the exurbs, the agglomerations of malls and other retailers had to get larger and larger. This phenomenon is driven by the fact that there is a relatively limited number of arterial roads upon which the dispersed exurban population must drive. If retailers hope to reach any shoppers at all, they must be in the few locations that reach *all* the shoppers and have the critical mass to justify the longer and longer drives. In contrast, an urbanizing context presents many more suitable locations for smaller chunks of retail. Higher net population densities mean that these chunks can be more closely spaced, which may lead to greater differentiation and specialization because a potential shopper can reach several locations within a reasonable travel distance. This means that there are more opportunities for urban retail formats to succeed in urbanizing suburbs with more compact street grids and increasing densities.

We contend that it will be vitally important to embrace a variety of uses in new and retrofitted downtowns and town centers. The ersatz urbanism of the newer lifestyle center format will only provide limited sustainability benefits and, if the uses remain limited to retail, will be vulnerable to the same sorts of forces that killed the mall. As shown in the Traffic Impact Analysis for the retrofit of Cottonwood Mall (see Chapter 7), by combining live-work-play, 25% of trips can be internally captured and made by foot rather than car. In addition, the presence of homeowners with a vested interest in the long-term value of the project bodes well for the longevity of a town center rather than a stand-alone lifestyle center that no one will care to preserve as it ages.

Hurdles to Redevelopment

THE BIG PICTURE

- Weak market demand: places with shrinking economies may not support new housing or employment uses. Redevelopment cannot proceed unless there is market demand for each component of the project.

THE SITE

- Encumbrances by department store leases: some mall tenants have leases or deeds that allow them to veto changes to the mall's layout even after they have shuttered their stores.

- Remote mall locations: far-flung locations where there is no surrounding community with which to connect are not the best sites for mixed-use retrofitting.

- Fragmented ownership with conditions, covenants, and restrictions: many malls are actually multiple ownerships joined together by contracts that require agreement for many types of changes. In such cases, the most recalcitrant owner can stop any redevelopment.

- Other uses might be easier; local governments that want mixed-use retrofitting need to take action to keep the land from getting tied up in big-box use.

THE PLAYERS

- Need for active civic leadership: the local government can be a hurdle or an ally. Many successful retrofits would not have been possible without support from public agencies.

- Lack of local capacity to accomplish complex projects: in some places the municipality or some entity with financial capacity must be willing and able to take on the risks of acting as a master developer and following through on plans.

- Risk-averse owners—the aggravation factor: redevelopment requires willing participants, so intransigence is a major barrier.

- The "do nothing" scenario: owners who have enjoyed decades of success beyond their original equity investment are less tolerant of the risks associated with undertaking a major redevelopment. Instead, they would rather wait for another investor (such as a big-box developer) to offer cash for the land value of the mall, garnering them a final payoff.

THE MONEY

- Overvalued land: once a mall begins to decline, its value falls, often precipitously. A mall's value is typically assessed at ten times the property's annual sales volume. Purchasers must anticipate a likely ongoing decline in sales volume when making an appraisal or risk spending too much on the property, thus severely limiting possibilities for redevelopment.

- Time and value gap: upfront costs for new utilities, roads, sidewalks, parks, and other streetscape amenities built in the first phase of a mixed-use retrofit usually cost more than the money brought in by the first buildings to come on line. The infrastructure costs may require atypical funding assumptions to make the numbers work during the early construction phases of the project.

(Adapted from Lee Sobel et al., *Greyfields into Goldfields*)

CHANGING USES TO MEET LOCAL NEEDS

How do you knit a dead mall site back into its context when the site is not on a highway or major arterial and will no longer support regional retail? One solution is to change the uses at the site to meet local needs—workplaces to provide jobs, classrooms for community colleges, public uses like a library or municipal offices, low-rent service retail, or parks and open space. The change-of-use approach often requires significant downsizing of the built area on the site. It also offers an opportunity to reclaim park and open space that may have been lost to commercial development in previous generations and to mitigate the environmental damage, especially to the local watershed, that the paved-over conditions of malls produced.

Examples of changing the use at mall sites to create needed local jobs in lower middle-class and blue-collar suburbs are Eastgate in Chattanooga, Tennessee; NetCenter in Hampton Roads, Virginia; and NetPark in Tampa, Florida. The big floor plates of department stores are ideal for a call center business. Adaptive reuse of these buildings usually involves adding windows and/or skylights to existing vacated department stores to bring in natural light. In some instances, the internal concourses of the mall remain intact but are unused.

In other examples, such as Downtown Park Forest and Willingboro Town Center, the local municipality has been forced to step in and assume ownership of the dead mall site in order to forestall the spread of blight. In these cases, outside forces have made the mall locations undesirable to national mall owners and retailers. Instead, the sites are remediated, downsized, partitioned, and repositioned for local uses. Asphalt is removed, some buildings torn down, and others adaptively reused, such as for a public library in Willingboro. It can be a struggle to attract a suitable new mix of local uses—neighborhood retail, small offices, arts organizations, senior housing. Another model, similar to the case of Phalen in St. Paul (discussed in Chapter 4) is to regreen a dead mall site, an approach that is particularly suited to sites that were once wetlands. "Pell Mall" is a hypothetical 2001 regreening proposal for a dying mall in Vallejo, California. (See Figure 6–7.) Instead, the mall was repositioned as an ethnic Filipino market.

Downsizing: Park Forest and Willingboro

As described in Chapter 3, when new, the planned community of Park Forest, Illinois, centered on a 48-acre outdoor pedestrian mall with a groundbreaking design from 1947 by Loebl, Schlossman, and Bennett. (See Figure 6–4.) The mix of shops, recreational activities, offices, and abundant free parking served as the principal gathering place for residents and hosted a range of popular community events. The primary anchors were Marshall Field, Goldblatt's, and Sears. In a now-familiar story, it proved a victim of its own success as locals chose to shop at newer, copycat malls, some built by the same developer who had built Park Forest. By 1995, the Park Forest Plaza, despite a mid-1980s overhaul, was dead. The real estate diagnosis was that it was poorly located. In particular, it defied conventional retail wisdom by being sited in the center of the community, too far from a highway and unable to benefit from a larger catchment area of potential shoppers.[19]

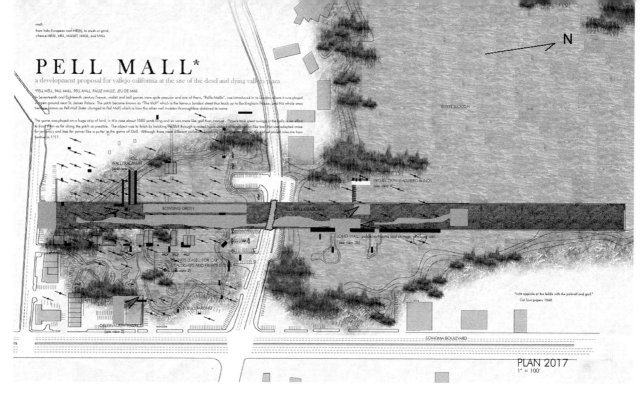

Figure 6–7 "Pell Mall" by Stoner Meek Architects, a finalist in the 2003 Dead Malls design competition sponsored by the Los Angeles Forum for Architecture and Urbanism. The provocative scheme proposes to gradually regreen the 40-acre Vallejo Plaza and adjacent Kmart ghost box in Vallejo, California, into a wetland habitat for the White Slough bird, along with other remedial uses. Above: Site plan showing gradual return of asphalt to wetlands. Left: Perspective view of recreational pier or "mall," featuring a wind farm for local energy production.

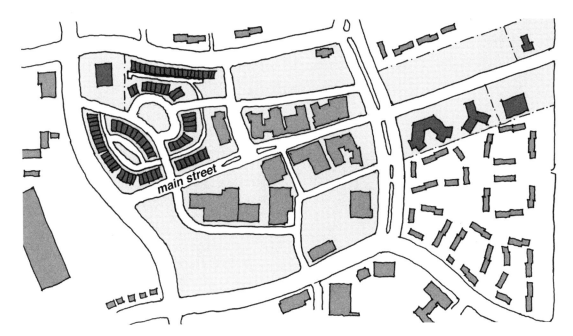

Figure 6–8 In Downtown Park Forest, the village took ownership of the dead plaza and cut streets through the central pedestrian mall. New housing—sixty-eight townhouses and senior housing—was built on parking lots.

Figure 6–9 Canopies along the storefronts in Downtown Park Forest are a vestige of an earlier, failed attempt to resuscitate the dying Park Forest Plaza.

Much effort has since gone into considering how this place might be retrofitted. Because of its poor location no outside developer was interested, so the Village of Park Forest stepped in, purchased it for a mere $100,000, and funded the redevelopment itself in the late 1990s. The plan, by the Lakota Group, which involved demolition of some buildings and the introduction of vehicular streets through the pedestrian mall, was heavily praised and won design awards. (See Figures 6–8 and 6–9.) But the resulting "Downtown Park Forest" is currently spottily tenanted. The tenants who are there—barber shops, resale clothing shops, piano teachers, etc.—are low-rent, neighborhood service businesses, although the village is having some success in reorienting the downtown toward cultural arts groups. No tenant has been found for the one large department store that was not demolished. Development of the residential pieces is progress-

Figure 6–10 Empty Sears store at Willingboro Town Center. While many of the buildings from the old Willingboro Plaza were torn down and the site has been admirably improved with drainage swales and rain gardens, some storefronts sit vacant, awaiting rehabilitation for new tenants that are yet to arrive.

ing; a senior apartment building and assisted-living facility was built on the Sears site and sixty-eight townhouses have recently been completed, selling for twice the median home price in town. With time it is expected to succeed. The Village, as the owner, is operating under a much different financing model and has different goals than is typical for mall retrofits.[20]

In Willingboro, a Levitt development in New Jersey begun in the late 1960s (initially white, now predominantly African American), the town has also committed significant resources to an attempt to renew a dead mall site. The Levitts had built a shopping mall called Willingboro Plaza modeled somewhat on the Park Forest Plaza, though with a location on an arterial road. It, however, suffered a similar fate when Interstate 295 was built in the 1970s and the traffic on Route 130 that the mall depended on for customers was diverted. The entire commercial corridor of Route 130 has declined and a major countywide initiative is under way to help revive it.

Frustrated by the inability of other developers to attract tenants to the mall, the township stepped in to broker a deal, providing $14 million in developer loans and financing for site remediation construction costs. A progressive developer, ReNewal Realty, is transforming the 56-acre site of Willingboro Plaza into a mixed-use "town center" that so far boasts a new, award-winning public library in an old Woolworth building (by Croxton Collaborative), classrooms for a local community college, and a new site design strategy to handle drainage and runoff. Also new to the site is a mail-order center for a pharmaceutical company, which added 850 new jobs, although the building is decidedly not urban or pedestrian in character. Townhouses were added at the rear of the site. The resultant project is a hybrid of conventional stand-alone suburban types combined on one site—office park, fast-food outlets, a supermarket, community college classrooms, public library, and multifamily housing.[21] As in Park Forest, the retrofit transformation has proceeded slowly. Much of the central portion of the property, such as the old Sears store, remains vacant. (See Figure 6–10.)

However, the committed involvement of town governments and the introduction of an unconventional mix of uses to meet local needs compose an important new model for transforming blighted retail properties that have proved no longer suited to the original use and form. But these projects face an uphill battle in the cutthroat atmosphere of retail real estate. As a result, reviews of such attempts to revive and diversify dead malls are generally mixed. Even though shopping areas were originally provided by merchant builders to boost residential sales, the differing rates of depreciation of the two land uses have led to a condition in which failed retail detracts from the value of houses in adjacent residential neighborhoods.

FROM ENCLOSED MALLS TO NEW DOWNTOWNS

The primary trend in mall retrofitting is the teardown of most or all of an aging enclosed mall and its replacement with a mixed-use town center development. There are also many, many examples of "mall-overs" that consist of remaking an enclosed mall into an open-air lifestyle center in which the land use remains exclusively retail; these are not our focus. We want to highlight a few major approaches toward retrofitting an enclosed mall into a new downtown.

First, malls that are no longer profitable but are in locations that would still support regional retail may be transformed into the center the suburb never had, as at Mizner Park in Boca Raton and Belmar in Lakewood, Colorado. Or a mall could be "turned inside out" in a process phased over several years, as planned at Winter Park Village, Florida. The risk in a phased process is that it will stall out before the complete transformation has been achieved, which seems to be the case in Winter Park. But when it is successful, the synergistic benefits can spread to neighboring areas and create a magnet in an area not long ago written off for dead.

Another popular approach is a hybrid one. Many dead mall properties are attractive for big-box development. Many moderate-income communities are attracted to discount retailers but also would like to have a walkable downtown. The solution is a hybrid development of mixed-use neighborhood retail, housing, and civic uses located adjacent to a big box or two. A key component of the hybrid approach is to negotiate big-box retailers into compromising their standard site plan and store formats. An example of a hybrid mall retrofit is CityCenter Englewood outside Denver.

Belmar and CityCenter Englewood, together with a cascade of other mall retrofits in the Denver metropolitan area, demonstrate how a series of new suburban downtowns can begin to remake a region into a pattern of polycentric urbanism, supported by mass transit. A process of full-circle urban renewal is illustrated by other examples, wherein older downtowns that experienced decline in the 1950s and 1960s, as new regional malls were constructed and sucked the life out of older Main Streets, were redeveloped through the urban renewal process into enclosed malls in order to compete. These malls subsequently failed and the properties are now being remade back into downtowns, such as in Rockville, Maryland, and Sunnyvale, California, where a 25-acre 1970s mall that had been built on the site of the old town center has itself been razed for a new, higher-density, mixed-use redevelopment.[22]

From Dead Mall to New Downtown: Mizner Park

A pioneering "greyfield to goldfield" project is Mizner Park in Boca Raton, Florida. Boca Raton is a small city (population 80,000) thirty-five miles north of Miami.[23] Although it is a city, it had grown in accord with suburban development patterns. Built on the 29-acre site of the failed Boca Raton Mall, constructed in 1972 and never successful, Mizner Park is now routinely referred to as Boca's downtown. It has already outlived the mall it replaced, but at the time it was opened, in 1990, it was a very risky proposition.[24] (See Color Plates 20 to 23.)

Mizner Park was the first successful replacement of an enclosed shopping mall with a new, mixed-use town center. Faced with the dying mall, the city government proactively invested $50 million in infrastructure improvements and created a community

Figure 6–11 The linear public green at Mizner Park.

Three- and five-story buildings with office space and apartments over ground floor retail flank the linear park. Four large parking structures are located in each quadrant of the plan. To the east, where the site abuts a residential neighborhood, the garages are lined with townhouses, masking the parking garages and making a graceful transition to the existing detached houses.

Later phases, realized because of the tremendous success of the first phase, added a nine-story residential building, a seven-story Class A office building, and a furniture store. In keeping with the city's requirements for a cultural component, the Boca Raton Museum, an International Museum of Cartoon Art (since closed and scheduled to be replaced with more retail), an 1,800-seat concert hall, and an outdoor amphitheater were built at the ends of the park. The latter two were fully programmed in 2007 and routinely attract significant audiences.

The master plan is rational and symmetric. In its organization, if not its architectural expression, it owes more to early shopping mall planning concepts than to traditional town planning. Mizner Park has been compared to the Piazza Navona in Rome;[25] in its dimensions and organization, however, it also recalls the now-demolished 1950s mall Shopper's World in Framingham, Massachusetts, designed by Ketchum, Gina & Sharp. (See Figure 6–12.) Differing from a mall, Mizner Park is flanked by parking garages rather than surface parking lots (allowing for greater urban connectivity). But like a traditional shopping mall or contemporary lifestyle center, it remains internally focused and object-like, presenting relatively blank walls to the arterial road. The architecture's basis on the regional aesthetic of Mizner makes contextual links that have been very popular, factoring into the community's strong embrace of the place.

Has it been successful? Eighteen years after the completion of the first phase, when a typical re-

redevelopment agency. The Boca Raton Community Redevelopment Agency (CRA) partnered with Crocker & Company, a private developer, and used a $68 million revenue and tax-increment bond to acquire the site. In terms of transforming the shopping mall into a downtown, it is particularly significant that, based on community input, the city charged CRA to keep two-thirds as public space and lease one-third for redevelopment as a mixed-use and cultural center.

In contrast to the demolished windowless, stand-alone mall, the new design, master planned by Cooper Carry Inc., followed city guidelines calling for use of famed local 1920s architect Addison Mizner's original colors and style. Mizner Park's arcades, balconies, terraced setbacks, and palm-lined sidewalks now center on the Plaza Real, a wide, lushly planted boulevard whose median also functions as a sizable linear public park.

In essence, Mizner Park replaced the concourse of the old enclosed mall with an expansive mall-type park ("mall" in the traditional sense of a large, linear green space), publicly owned and maintained. (See

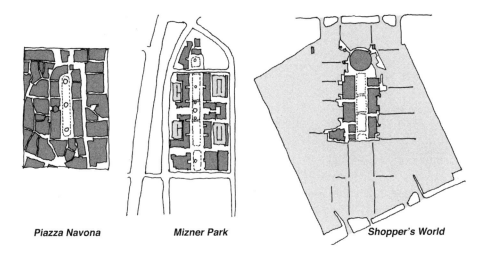

Piazza Navona   **Mizner Park**   **Shopper's World**

Figure 6–12 The "mall" space at Mizner Park is similar in scale and form to the Piazza Navona in Rome. But it also recalls the widely admired 1951 outdoor mall Shopper's World in Framingham, Massachusetts (the original buildings were torn down in 1994 and replaced with a power center, though the name remains).

gional mall would be undergoing a necessary major overhaul, it is still going strong and now is a significant source of tax revenue. The retail space is fully leased and profitable, the grouping of restaurants with outdoor seating continues to be a happening scene on weekend nights, and the residential units remain in high demand.

The project has deservedly been criticized for its lack of integration with its surroundings. The boulevard and park run parallel to an arterial road to the west, and are largely screened from view with vegetation and parking decks, and do not connect to local streets at either end. (See Figure 6–13.) Charles Bohl, in his book on developing new town centers, has characterized Mizner Park (like Mashpee Commons) as an "attachable fragment of urbanism," recognizing that when it was conceived there was not much for the project to attach to.[26] Nevertheless, the project has spurred redevelopment of adjacent blocks and inspired other communities and developers to emulate its success. Perhaps most importantly, Mizner Park proved the value of public investment in attractive urban public space conducive to communal events and socializing. As one of the first public-private partnerships involved in this kind of redevelopment, the CRA took its public responsibilities very seriously. The Boca Raton Community Redevelopment Agency is now undergoing a master plan update of the entire downtown area, led by Urban Design Associates. The intent is to extend the success of Mizner Park to other underutilized commercial properties to its south.

Figure 6–13 The edge condition where Mizner Park attaches to the arterial road.

Turning a Mall Inside Out: Winter Park Village

Winter Park Village is an example of a phased approach to retrofitting a mall. Winter Park is an old Florida railroad town of 24,000 inhabitants, built for wealthy summering Northerners, which now serves as a suburb of Orlando, six miles to the south. The intent of the master plan is to turn the mall "inside out" in gradual phases, in order to convert an inward-oriented mall structure, surrounded by parking, into a series of mixed-use blocks connected into the neighboring built fabric. The Winter Park Mall—400,000 square feet, enclosed, with two department store anchors—was built in 1962 on 32 acres. By the mid-1990s it was failing, victim to nearby newer malls and the successful revival of Park Avenue, Winter Park's original Main Street, which boasts a pedestrian-friendly, tree-shaded avenue of upscale boutiques, cafés, and restaurants, and a lively artisans' market.

When the stores closed, the property comprising the mall was largely consolidated into one parcel (a complicated process) and leased for redevelopment. In part to ensure that new development on the mall site would not threaten the success of Park Avenue, the municipality exerted influence on the mall's new owner, the Don M. Casto Organization, a suburban shopping center development group since the 1920s, to encourage a mixed-use redevelopment approach. The goal was to dovetail with the revitalization plans of the Winter Park Community Development Agency (CDA) for the adjacent Hannibal Square neighborhood, a historically African American "wrong side of the tracks" district dating back to the late nineteenth century. By the 1980s, buildings in the neighborhood were notably run down, especially when compared to other, predominantly white neighborhoods in generally affluent Winter Park.[27]

A public design charrette sponsored by the municipality was held in 1997; the design team was led by Dover, Kohl & Partners of Coral Gables, Florida. The charrette, which included open input from neighbors and other stakeholders, resulted in a phased redevelopment strategy. The strategy called for breaking the site up into blocks and the introduction of a gradual increase in density and new uses over time. Compelling diagrams by the design team illustrated how a mall could be redeveloped gradually, from the inside out. The concept was to concentrate new "seed" buildings with retail and office use in the center of the site, more or less on the footprint of the old mall, but with a street running along the path of the enclosed mall promenade. Interim parking lots would continue to surround the retail, but these would be gradually filled in over time with new housing of a scale compatible with neighboring areas, designed to wrap around and conceal parking areas, as at Mizner Park.

How is it working? Early phases resulted in the demolition of the mall, except for one of the anchor department store buildings. In the middle of the site a hybrid retail center was built with 350,000 square feet of retail and 140,000 square feet of office, featuring the national chains found in a typical lifestyle center (Regal Cinema, Cheesecake Factory, Ann Taylor Loft, Borders, Pier One) and an Albertson's supermarket. The central shopping street plan is organized as a T intersection. The small shops that line the trunk of the T have a second story of small offices. The large (twenty-screen) cinema is lined on the street-facing side with small eateries. (See Figure 6–14.) A small square with a fountain and benches anchors the street that forms the top bar of the tee, which terminates in front of the former department store building. The square provides a place for rest, but at 35 by 200 feet it is too small to support civic events. (See Figure 6–15.)

Figure 6–14 Winter Park Village was developed by the Don M. Casto Corporation on the site of a mall that was entirely demolished except for one anchor store building. The built plan partially fulfills the phased redevelopment strategy devised in 1997 for Winter Park by a team including Dover, Kohl & Partners and Glatting Jackson. Later phases, which at present seem unlikely to occur, call for infilling the parking lots with housing.

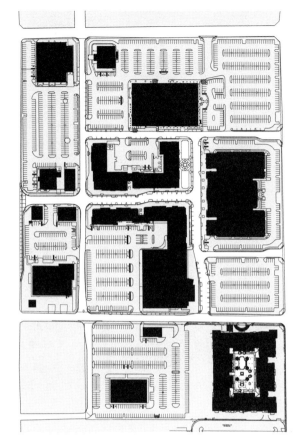

Figure 6–15 A fountain in the square at Winter Park Village in Winter Park, Florida. It is a pleasant place to relax while shopping.

As in most hybrid places, the transition from big stores with large parking fields, located at the perimeter of the site (Borders and Albertson's), to the pedestrian-oriented retail streets in the center is awkward, requiring patrons to cross through the parking lots, paved with a dark, highly absorptive asphalt. The heat reradiating from the asphalt creates very uncomfortable conditions on a typical Florida day. Other flaws in the project as built to date include multiple blank façades presenting toward surrounding residential neighborhoods and weak relationships to the primary arterial street. One of the authors drove right by it on a second site visit because with big boxes and stand-alone restaurant out-parcels on the arterials, it looked no different from the conventional strip retail around it. (See Figure 6–16.) A second phase in 2001 resulted in the conversion of the upper floors of the department store into fifty-eight loft housing units. It is a challenge to carve desirable unit plans out of the large floor plate of the store; interior units are lit only by skylights and light tubes. Many of the apartments are being leased as small office spaces rather than residences.[28]

As of late 2007, the phased redevelopment appears to have stalled out precisely at the point where additional density and new uses, especially at the periphery of the site, could truly transform it from a straightforward replacement of a mall by a lifestyle center—predominantly retail with only a

Figure 6–16 Winter Park Village still retains the inside versus outside distinction common to enclosed shopping malls; the architectural detailing and finishing budget is unevenly distributed. Clockwise from top left: Street view with cinema. No-frills approach from a parking lot toward arcaded entry to main shopping street. Emerging from the arcade into the project proper. Blank façade at rear of Albertson's supermarket, which abuts one of the primary pedestrian streets.

minimum amount of public space and *lots* of surface parking—into a walkable, low-rise, mixed-use district. Sadly, this is not yet happening. An additional disappointment is that the retail developer, the Don M. Casto Corporation, commissioned bland and cheaply detailed architecture for the new buildings.[29] The head developer, Brett Hutchens, who now runs the southeast division of Casto under the name Casto Lifestyle Properties, admitted recently that he hadn't wanted to "overspend" on architecture because he felt that the mixed-use lifestyle center was an "untested concept."[30] He was hedging his bets, and the resulting half-hearted implementation in the early phases may be having a negative impact on the forward momentum of the

entire redevelopment scheme. It appears that the present retail configuration is satisfactorily profitable to the owner and tenants, who therefore may not be that anxious for further redevelopment to occur within the boundaries of the project.

Hutchens lists other "lessons learned," which he is presumably applying on subsequent projects: he should have worked harder to establish a public-private partnership with the municipality in order to use redevelopment funds to finance structured parking and residential use in the first phase; he should have built three-story buildings, rather than two-story, on the main street; and he also wishes he had purchased more property around the site earlier, in order to have "more control over it."[31] Don Martin, the director of planning and community development in Winter Park, has a somewhat different view of the lessons learned. Recognizing that there were opportunities missed at Winter Park Village, he suggests that mixed-use, lifestyle retail developers note the following: make every attempt to execute their master plan without compromise (such as the concessions Casto made to Borders and Albertson's regarding store placement and parking); they should hire a number of architects to design the various buildings; close attention must be given to the public, civic spaces; and developers "need to loosen up and surrender some control."[32]

Another reason for the stalling out of the phased redevelopment master plan is community backlash to higher-density development elsewhere in town. When the West Winter Park redevelopment district was established in 1991, one developer, the Sydgan Group, bought up most of the vacant land in the area at bargain prices. While completing twenty-two new mixed-use buildings in the Hannibal Square neighborhood, the president of the group, Dan Bellows, stepped on more than a few toes. Long-time residents fear the effects of gentrification.[33] A scheme proposed by a local residential builder (who had partnered with Casto to construct the loft apartments in the department store) to build a 176-unit residential block with a 950-space parking structure has not been approved. The large complex, to be located at the southeast corner of the Village property, was deemed incompatible with the town-house-type residential units proposed in the 1997 charrette plan. The developers argued that parking needs dictated such a large structure to make the project feasible. Casto is trying again with a proposal to build 151 condominium units adjacent to a much scaled-down 314-space parking deck on an adjacent 4.8-acre site that had been publicly owned.

Winter Park Village is a cautionary tale about the challenges of implementing a phased, incremental "inside-out" redevelopment scheme. The charrette plan is elegant and exciting—its full implementation is seemingly out of reach.

Incremental Metropolitanism Around Denver: CityCenter Englewood

The Denver Metro region has experienced a cascade of first-generation regional mall failures in the past decade, resulting in a tremendous opportunity to reorganize the first-ring suburbs into a comprehensive multicentered metropolitan structure. The changes have been incremental, but profound. They have occurred in concert with the tremendous redevelopment efforts in the LoDo district of Denver, the redevelopment of the 4,700-acre Stapleton airport in east Denver, and the introduction of FasTrax, a plan to enhance bus service and add 119 miles of new light-rail to the region, funded to the tune of $4.7 billion by Colorado voters in 2005. Like other Western cities, Denver once had an extensive streetcar and suburban rail system that was completely abandoned in favor of the automobile. And because of a dependence on sales tax for government revenue in Colorado, the financial health of small municipalities is intimately tied to retail centers.

The transformation is astonishing. In a decade the number of regional malls in the Denver metro region has been halved, from fourteen to seven by our count. (See Figure 6–17.) Of the malls that remain, most are owned by large retail REITs. One independent mall that is still open, Westminster Mall, may not survive long. The city of Westminster, northwest of Denver on the route to Boulder, actually underwrote three-quarters of a $10 million mall facelift in 2000 in an attempt to shore up its primary cash cow. Other Denver suburbs have not followed suit.

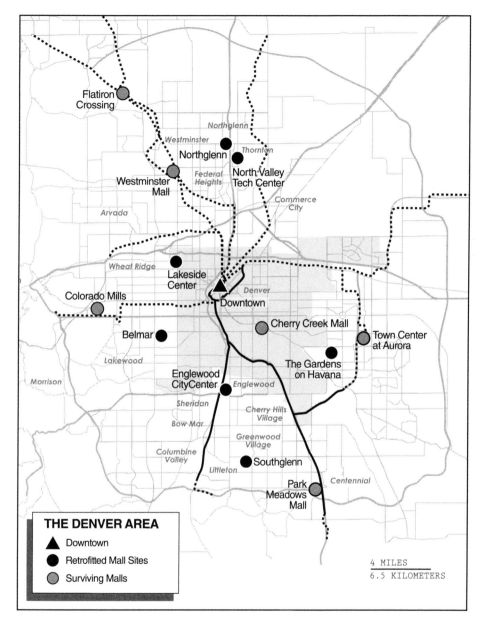

THE DENVER AREA

▲ Downtown

● Retrofitted Mall Sites

● Surviving Malls

4 MILES
6.5 KILOMETERS

Figure 6–17 A series of regional malls forming a ring around Denver have gone dark in the past decade: to the north, North Valley Mall and Northglenn Mall (Westminster Mall is still holding on); to the west, Villa Italia (now Belmar) and Lakeside Mall; to the south, Southglenn Mall and Cinderella City (CityCenter Englewood); and to the east, Buckingham Square Mall (The Gardens on Havana). North Valley Mall and Lakeside Mall were adaptively reused for low-rent office use. Northglenn was redeveloped into a power center, while Southglenn is being converted into a lifestyle center, renamed The Streets at Southglenn. Cinderella City and Villa Italia were heading toward the power center fate when local government intervened, foregoing short-term sales tax revenue in order to forge public-private partnerships with developers to shepherd the mall sites into new downtowns.

In 2001 the retrofit of the 1.3 million-square-foot Cinderella City Mall into CityCenter Englewood was completed. (See Color Plates 24 to 26.) The new development includes the adaptive reuse of a department store into City Hall; 440 apartments; 480,000 square feet of office and retail use, including Wal-Mart; and a new light-rail station. Cinderella City was built in 1968 in Englewood, a blue-collar, predominantly white suburb located just south of the city of Denver. Englewood has a sizable jobs base—23,500 work there full-time in manufacturing and in large medical centers. Like the "Levittowns" discussed in Chapter 3, the postwar housing stock—mostly two- and three-bedroom ranch houses—is in need of reinvestment.[34] In its day, the palatial Cinderella City had been a wonder to behold. It boasted extravagant fountains and three floors of stores packed onto a 55-acre site. When it finally turned back into a pumpkin in 1997, the local government stepped in to pick up the pieces. It purchased the land and formed a nonprofit corporation to broker redevelopment. Actually, they were buying *back* the land; it had been a public park with a creek running through it (and therefore land not suitable for residential subdivision) before it was developed into a mall.

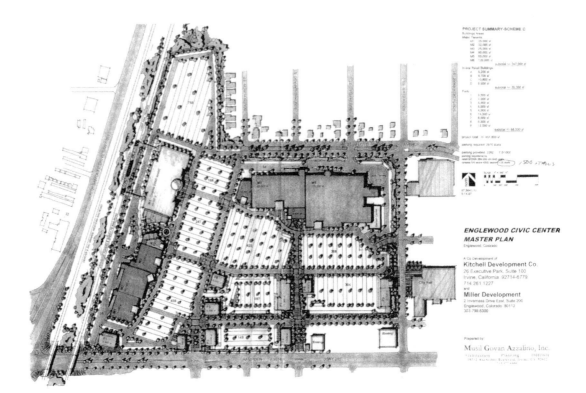

Figure 6–18 The first redevelopment site plan for Englewood for Miller Kitchell Development proposed a big-box power center, with its back to the light-rail station.

In taking over the site, the city was pioneering a challenging path. There were numerous challenges: a changing roster of developers; resistance to the mixed-use, town center concept; lukewarm cooperation from the transit authority in incorporating the adjacent light-rail station; and now, there is difficulty keeping the small retail shops filled, especially those located adjacent to the civic center where there is no street parking in front. The storefronts are now being rented for small service businesses, such as medical offices and accountants.

Their original expectation, in 1994, was for a big-box power center, as was developed at Northglenn. When a station on the new Denver light-rail line was located next door, plans for the site took a different direction. But as a result of a city-issued request for proposals (RFP), a retail developer specializing in entertainment/power centers, Miller Weingarten (then named Miller Kitchell), was already on board. The first Miller Kitchell site plan had a large multiplex cinema backing up to the transit station, ignoring the opportunity for a pedestrian connection. (See Figure 6–18.) The nonprofit Center for Regional and Neighborhood Action (CRNA) was helpful in educating officials about the potential to pursue transit-oriented development (TOD) at the site. As a result of a pilot study by the CRNA and the results of several public community forums, the Community Development Department hired Calthorpe Associates to develop a concept plan for mixed-use TOD.[35]

Market research and community polling indicated that discount retail was highly desired by Englewood

Figure 6–19 The built site plan by David Owen Tryba Architects is a hybrid, combining civic uses around the rail station, a substantial number of apartments, and, at the east end of the site, big-box uses.

Figure 6–20 The transit infrastructure at Englewood: Left: A bridge connects the station platforms to the city park. Right: The route from the park-and-ride lot to the platforms skips both the bridge and the retail.

Figure 6–21 Adaptive reuse of Foley's department store at Englewood and at Belmar. The same store prototype, built at two Denver malls in the 1980s, modified for different uses. The store in Englewood was only ten years old in 1994 when redevelopment planning began.

residents and workers. Therefore, a modified big-box scheme was pursued, incorporating new rental housing and a sizable city-financed civic center. (See Figure 6–19.) Englewood invested heavily in the project; one could say they were betting the farm. The fact that the local government was bearing most of the up-front development costs (and risk) made it easier to leverage concessions from Miller Weingarten and the national retailers they were bringing to the table, including discount giant Wal-Mart. (When an Englewood planner was giving a talk in 2007 about the project at a planning conference, the audience hissed audibly at the mention of Wal-Mart.)[36] The rental apartments, built by Trammel Crow, are arranged in a block form that integrates well with the existing street grid and the neighboring residential area. Renters of the units are thrilled with the direct access to downtown that the light-rail provides.

In examining the built result, the hybrid nature of the scheme is readily apparent; the redevelopment struggles can be read in the urban morphology. For example, the park-and-ride lot and bus transfer bays built by the transit authority are accessed directly from the platform, allowing hundreds of daily commuters to avoid crossing the ornamental bridge into the 2-acre park lined with small shops intended to serve the needs of those commuters. (See Figure 6–20.) Why this missed opportunity? At the time, the engineers and planners in charge of the transit piece wanted no part of TOD; their task was to build a station and parking lot on land to which they held a long-term lease. Another example is the awkward siting of the 135,000-square-foot civic building. The building is canted at an angle and wrapped by a parking deck that conceals it when approaching from the main arterial street to the south. But the building's footprint was fixed because it is an adaptive reuse of a Foley's department store building from the mall. (See Figure 6–21.) And what about the antiurban effects of a 60,000-square-foot Wal-Mart store? Well, the suburb was able to negotiate with the behemoth retailer to run tree-lined "streets" through its parking field, to use a custom-designed façade rather than its standard design, and to install large, arty murals on its façades. (See Figure 6–22.)

To counteract the fact that the big-box retailers at CityCenter threaten to make the project virtually indistinguishable from so many other power centers around the country, Englewood aggressively pursued an arts program to enhance the civic center. The civic

Figure 6–22 Englewood city officials negotiated with Wal-Mart for a nonstandard store façade as well as a tree-lined "street" through the parking lot to help make the big box a better neighbor.

building houses the Museum of Outdoor Art. Pieces of the museum's collection are installed throughout the adjacent park, which is large enough and suitably configured to host performances and other gatherings. Recently, the city started a free shuttle bus, called the ART, that travels directly from the front of the civic building, down Englewood Parkway (the central spine of CityCenter), and out a two-mile loop to other major retail and job centers in town.

Another notable attribute of the project is the reduction in parking spaces achieved by using a shared parking formula. Of the 2,810 parking spaces, approximately one-third are for commuters and the remaining two-thirds are for the 840,000 square feet of mixed-use space. That works out to an average of two spaces per 1,000 square feet, well below typical parking ratios of three to five spaces per 1,000 square feet.

As of 2008, the Buckingham Square Mall in Aurora, east of downtown, is dead and slated to be redeveloped into The Gardens on Havana. The primary developer, Miller Weingarten, initially re-

sistant to mixed-use development in Englewood, is applying at least some of the experience learned in Englewood to Aurora. Early redevelopment plans indicate a similar hybrid mixed-use scenario, including big-box retailers and one retail "street" terminating in an apartment block of approximately 300 units.

INFILLING AROUND A LIVE MALL

What about the 50 to 200 regional malls expected to survive the ongoing wave of consolidation? Can they be retrofitted? A promising strategy is to infill around a live mall. If transit arrives, reducing parking needs, or if structured parking is constructed, land may be freed up for new uses, as demonstrated in hypothetical diagrams by DPZ. (See Figure 6–23.) Or, as in the case of Surrey Central City near Vancouver, new uses can be built on top of a live mall. In Walnut Creek, California, new infill development between a live mall and the suburb's Main Street knit the two together into a whole that has proved greater than the sum of its parts.

You Can Save the Tree and Have Tiffany's Too: Walnut Creek

The highly successful infill development in downtown Walnut Creek, which has skillfully knit together a 1960s-era open-air mall and the old Main Street, is a story of careful municipal stewardship. Walnut Creek is an affluent suburb of 64,300 in Contra Costa County on the East Bay of San Francisco.[37] Planners admire Walnut Creek for making the most of a great location by creating a vision for its future, then sticking to the plan until it came to fruition. Decades ago officials in Walnut Creek decided to cluster offices

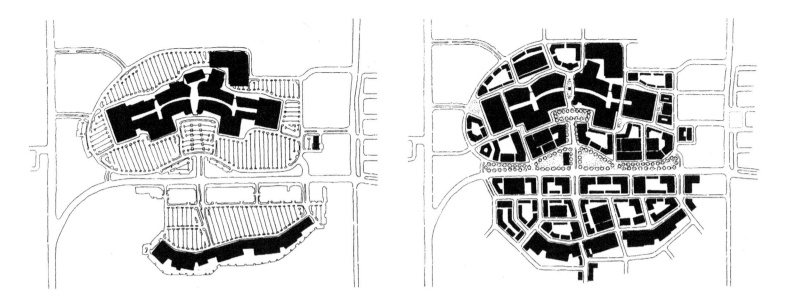

Figure 6–23 Diagrams by DPZ illustrating an "infill around a live mall" strategy.

and retail downtown, while providing a network of open spaces, parks, and trails throughout the predominantly residential suburb. "The decision was made not to sprawl out," says Bob Shroeder, a city councilman in the 1960s and 1970s.[38]

Broadway Plaza, an open-air mall anchored by Sears and JCPenney, was built adjacent to the historical downtown in 1951, capping over the creek that gave the suburb its name. The mall, which was never enclosed, was separated from the downtown by Mt. Diablo Boulevard, a busy arterial road. By the 1980s both retail areas were suffering. A BID was established around 1990 to try to breathe new life into the tired, sleepy downtown. Slowly, locally owned new businesses began to colonize the Main Street storefronts while national retailers decided to remain in the aging mall, which had been given a major boost when Nordstrom arrived in 1989. The planning department focused on producing a specific area plan intended to encourage new development that would knit the two areas together,

across the arterial, to form a hybrid downtown-mall plan. An old home improvement store building was demolished and Locust Street was extended another block to better knit together local streets. Traffic-calming measures, such as paved pedestrian crossings and intense yellow flashing lights, slowed and narrowed the arterial; another street was opened through the pedestrian promenade of the mall; and redevelopment of the properties forming the crucial connecting knuckle commenced. The public spaces in the connecting blocks were heavily landscaped and supplied with pedestrian-friendly amenities like benches, sculpture, fountains, and lighting. These improvements have made the downtown a desirable setting for civic events such as art festivals. Parking garages are hidden midblock in the Main Street area and in a two-story structure along the rear of the mall.[39]

One of the properties that proved key to making the connection scheme work is at the corner of Mt. Diablo Boulevard and North Main Street. Fittingly, the project there is called The Corner (The Corners was an early name for the nineteenth-century agricultural community that became Walnut Creek). The developers caused great consternation in 2000 when they requested permission to cut down a 200-year-old oak tree on the site, one of six mature oaks in the downtown. A critic for the *San Francisco Chronicle* wrote at the time, "The tree was a symbol, part of the terrain that had existed before suburbanization. Before BART and office towers. Before Broadway Shopping Center's Sears turned into Broadway Plaza's Nordstrom."[40]

A satisfactory compromise was reached. The building was reconfigured on the site, parking was located elsewhere, and the tree was saved, becoming the centerpiece of an unusual hidden oasis park off the increasingly busy shopping streets. And the developer landed a prized luxury-brand tenant, Tiffany & Co. You *can* save the tree and have Tiffany's, too. This sort of maneuver, requiring patience and finesse, is characteristic of the careful development guidance process that planners have undertaken in Walnut Creek, comparable to a long-running chess match.

New housing in the downtown area is also on the rise. The State of California required the suburb to build nearly 1,700 new housing units between 1999 and 2007 and, while the city has only met about 70% of this goal, most of the units that were built are in the downtown area. In 2004 an inclusionary housing ordinance was passed requiring 10% of new projects to be priced below market rate. Another ordinance was adopted requiring commercial developers to pay $5 per square foot into an affordable housing fund.

In 2006, in a sign of progress that goes along with success, Walnut Creek doubled on-street parking fees to $1 per hour. In late 2007, retail brokers were saying that the market in Walnut Creek was comparable with the ritziest areas of San Francisco and Palo Alto, and the rents being charged have followed suit. Where there had been Kentucky Fried Chicken, nail salons, and tire stores, there are now increasingly upscale stores, with projections that luxury brands Burberry and Gucci are on their way to join sister Tiffany.[41] Walnut Creek, once considered retail Siberia, is now characterized as the Beverly Hills of the East Bay.

From Mall to Transit-Served University and Office Tower: Surrey Central City

A forty-minute drive outside Vancouver, British Columbia, Surrey Central City has involved the retrofit of a dated-but-not-dead mall with the grafting on of a flashy new high-tech university campus. (See Color Plates 27 to 29.) A short walk from a stop on the regional light-rail SkyTrain system, the public-private development, planned and designed by Bing Thom Architects and completed in 2003, also includes a striking new 25-story office tower, the largest office building in the Vancouver region; it has been highly successful and a new master plan for additional development is under way. (See Figure 6–24.)

Construction involved some creative sequencing. While the 620,000-square-foot, two-level mall remained open, a three-story "galleria" was built over it, suspended seven feet above, and the office building was constructed next door. When the galleria was complete, the roof of the old enclosed mall was torn away, creating a soaring five-story space flooded with natural light. It is linked through a second atrium to the office tower by bridges; the result is a weave of vertical and horizontal circulation. (See Figure 6–25.) A former department store and the new floors of the galleria now house a new campus of Simon Fraser University, whose focus on emerging technologies is spinning off incubator business opportunities, supported in the office towers.

Figure 6–24 A master plan update by Bing Thom Architects for the city of Surrey's new development corporation is to be completed in 2008. The Insurance Company of BC that undertook the original development successfully sold the project in 2007 at a substantial profit. Simon Fraser University has exceeded their student enrollment projections for the campus and wants to expand.

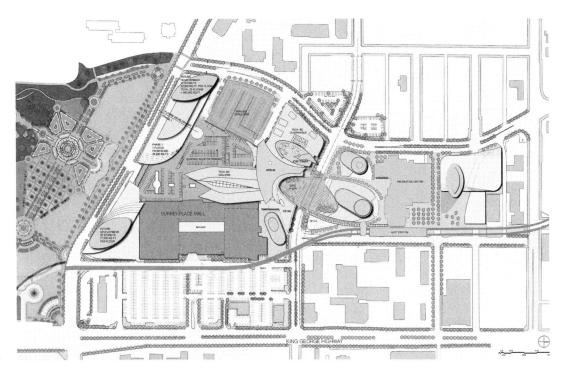

Figure 6–25 The dynamic atrium at Surrey Central City, where the shopping mall, university campus, and office building converge, is a centrifuge for shoppers, students, and office workers.

The tight grouping of the new buildings and the visibility of the high-rise (which stood in for LutherCorp's headquarters in the fictional city of Metropolis on the Superman television show *Smallville*) celebrate urban density and synergy between integrated uses. In contrast to the old, windowless mall, the new components make extensive use of structural glazing, intensifying the multiple opportunities for urban interaction between shoppers, office workers, and students. And in keeping with the recycling of the mall itself, fir peeler cores, a waste product of the local timber industry, were used by the architect to construct a dramatic wood tetrahedral space-frame over the atrium, providing a contemporary connection to the materials and building traditions of western Canada. (See Figure 6–26.)

Figure 6–26 The engineered wood roof, constructed from fir peeler cores, hovers over the expanded mall galleria at Surrey Central City.

THE ROLE AND FORM OF MIXED-USE AND PUBLIC SPACE IN RETROFITTED MALLS

Public space in these new downtowns takes many forms, some more truly public than others. Some projects incorporate open space that is publicly owned and maintained, as are the new through streets at Mizner Park. Others remain privately owned and operated, but include outdoor spaces that are aggressively programmed with activities in partnership with local community groups, such as Surrey Central City. Some contain an amazing variety of public spaces and activities, such as Belmar (see Chapter 8). Others fall short of the mark, despite the promise of their plans, such as Winter Park Village.

One significant factor that differentiates these dead mall retrofits is the capacity of the site to support new retail, based on location and demographics, and if so, what kind? The retail real estate industry seems to be getting the message that mixed-use can work for them, and that the provision of public space can also be beneficial to their health. But if the location isn't right, no amount of new benches and trees will attract the retailers. Then it is time to implement Plan B, and there really is no limit to the creative, useful new programs that could inhabit an appealingly large, contiguous dead mall site.

The case study chapters that follow describe in more detail aspects of mall retrofitting. Chapter 7 is an in-depth look at a charrette to design the retrofit of Cottonwood Mall in Holladay, Utah, owned by one of the largest retail REITs. Chapter 8 is an examination of Belmar, the ambitious and successful retrofit of the Villa Italia mall in Lakewood, Colorado.

The architecture, especially of the public spaces, is of the high quality we would like to see in all of these retrofitting projects, but too often do not. It is smart and spectacular. The mall has been thoroughly repositioned, from a stand-alone, auto-oriented, closed-in box to a fully engaged participant in a transit-oriented minicity, by the skillful grafting of new, high-density components in striking forms. The materiality of the architecture, which combines local wood with metal panel skins (a mix of zinc, titanium, and blackened stainless steel), echoes the laudable urbanizing agenda to create a hybrid typology of symbiosis. This project, in the skilled hands of Bing Thom Architects, illustrates the potential to approach suburban retrofitting not as a return to past forms but as a brave new synergistic world.

Summary of Techniques for Mall Retrofitting

- *Visioning sessions and design charrettes.* These are commissioned by a municipality to create a phased master plan. Envisioning a better, future state for a struggling area involves a leap of faith about the future that may or may not in the end prove realizable, but the very existence of an illustrated vision provides an important impetus for change. With a vision plan in place, municipalities can seek out amenable developers, either through an individual interview process or through an RFP process.

- *Scrape and rebuild, from the inside out.* Starting with a "fragment of attachable urbanism" at the center of the redevelopment site, with parking surrounding it, the intention is to fill in the parking lots with new construction over time, to be supported with structured parking at lower parking ratios as the site becomes more synergistically urban and walkable.

- *Planning from the outside in.* Wrapping an existing mall with street-facing liner buildings emphasizes uses the mall lacks, such as restaurants and housing, with the intention of eventually replacing the heart of the mall.

- *Creative public financing strategies.* Tax-increment financing (TIF) and sales tax breaks can be used to entice developers to take risks at a marginal site and to help them weather the hits if the retail portions of a project are not immediately successful. These enticements can be very important in coaxing a retail developer away from business-as-usual, auto-oriented design components, like supersized signage, in hybrid projects.

- *Establishing community redevelopment agencies.* These agencies, common in large cities but new to many suburbs, can guide the redevelopment process and act as a bridge between private developers and municipal officials.

- *Teaming developers with complementary areas of expertise.* The community redevelopment agency may have to play a "matchmaker" role in bringing the various developers together.

- *Tie-ins to regional mass transit initiatives.* Many regions around the country—Denver, Washington, DC, Salt Lake City, Los Angeles—are introducing or expanding transit systems, providing justification for increased density at retrofit sites adjacent to station stops. The difficulty is in successfully forming a partnership with the transit authority, which is tasked with efficiently engineering and constructing the system and may view redevelopment planning as an impediment to those goals.

- *Reusing some buildings, like department stores.* Many of the examples presented here made use, to varying degrees, of the built assets already on a dead mall site. Store buildings have been successfully reused as offices, apartments, and public libraries.

Chapter 7

Mall Case Study: Cottonwood, Holladay, Utah

From Concept to Press Release

Name of project: Cottonwood (650,000 sq. ft. retail and office; 500 dwelling units)

Location: near Salt Lake City in Holladay, Utah

Year constructed: 2010, Phase I (projected year of completion)

Planning: Duany Plater-Zyberk & Company

Architects: RTKL, SB Architects, Torti-Gallas and Partners, Sasaki Associates

Key consultants: Glatting Jackson Kercher Anglin, Sasaki Associates, Zimmerman Volk, Milesbrand

Lead developer: General Growth Properties (GGP)

What it replaces: Cottonwood Mall (760,000-sq.-ft. enclosed regional mall)

Size of site: 57 acres

Key features: first mall retrofit by GGP, one of the largest U.S. retail REITs

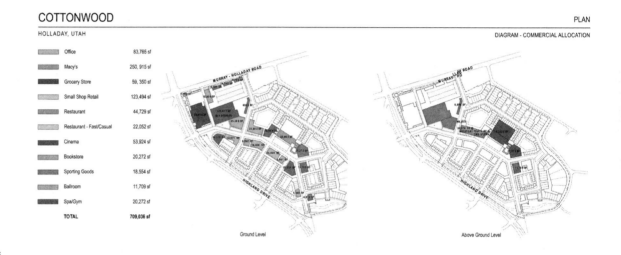

COTTONWOOD   PLAN

HOLLADAY, UTAH   DIAGRAM - COMMERCIAL ALLOCATION

	Office	83,765 sf
	Macy's	250, 915 sf
	Grocery Store	59, 350 sf
	Small Shop Retail	123,494 sf
	Restaurant	44,729 sf
	Restaurant - Fast/Casual	22,052 sf
	Cinema	53,924 sf
	Bookstore	20,272 sf
	Sporting Goods	18,554 sf
	Ballroom	11,709 sf
	Spa/Gym	20,272 sf
	TOTAL	**709,036 sf**

Ground Level   Above Ground Level

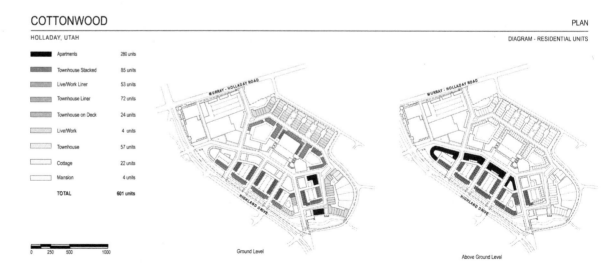

COTTONWOOD   PLAN

HOLLADAY, UTAH   DIAGRAM - RESIDENTIAL UNITS

	Apartments	280 units
	Townhouse Stacked	85 units
	Live/Work Liner	53 units
	Townhouse Liner	72 units
	Townhouse on Deck	24 units
	Live/Work	4 units
	Townhouse	57 units
	Cottage	22 units
	Mansion	4 units
	TOTAL	**601 units**

0 250 500 1000

Ground Level   Above Ground Level

SUMMARY

How do the necessary parties get together to make a retrofit happen? And when they do, what is the process by which the retrofit master plan is developed? This case study is a record of this process for a project that is in many ways typical and in other ways distinct. It is typical in that the 1960s regional mall on the retrofitting site, Cottonwood Mall, is dying. The only buildings deemed worth salvaging are anchor stores; the rest may be demolished. Market analysis indicates that a mixed-use town center, combining retail, office, and residences, could work in the relatively affluent area, spreading financial risk and capturing the synergies of diverse users. It is atypical in that it is owned by one of the largest retail real estate investment trusts (REITs) in the United States, a company that until now has shied away from mixing uses on its properties. The "patient capital" required for mixed-use retrofitting is a considerable risk for a Wall Street–traded firm with impatient investors.

This retrofit is in its early stages and, if other retrofits are a guide, the exact mix of uses and site plan will undergo considerable revision before completion. Our focus here is on the process of the design charrette, during which key design and market direction decisions were made. For Cottonwood, a pair of condensed design workshops were held, one in Miami and one in Utah, at which a collection of stakeholders, designers, and expert consultants were convened, including author Ellen Dunham-Jones.

The planning behind the retrofitting of the Cottonwood Mall in Holladay, Utah, just outside Salt Lake City, by General Growth Properties (GGP) of Chicago provides a revealing illustration of one project's process of marshalling the complexity of a mall retrofit from the concept stage to the final plan.

The redevelopment plan to convert the 57-acre mall into a mixed-use town center was officially announced July 5, 2007, with estimated completion of Phase I construction by 2010. (See Color Plates 30 to 33.) However, the backstory leading up to this event concerns the trend toward consolidation within the retail and mall industries.

Figure 7–1 The new Cottonwood will incorporate a wide range of retail uses and housing types on multiple floor levels. The first set of diagrams shows the uses at ground and above ground and includes the following: office, Macy's, grocery store, small shops, restaurant, fast/casual restaurant, cinema, bookstore, sporting goods, ballroom, and spa/gym. The second pair of diagrams shows the various housing types on the ground and above ground levels. These include 280 apartments, 85 stacked townhouses, 53 live-work liners, 72 liner townhouses, 24 townhouses on deck, 4 live-works, 57 townhouses, 22 cottages, and 4 mansions.

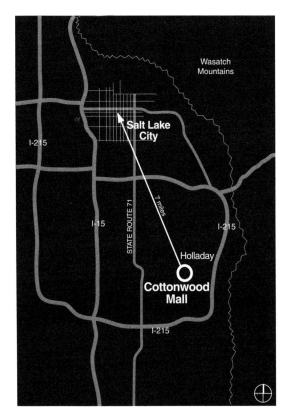

Figure 7–2 Location map.

REPOSITIONING MALL PROPERTIES

Because likely sites for mall construction have become increasingly difficult to find, one way for mall companies to grow and offer one-stop shopping for retail chains seeking multiple new store openings is through acquisition of other mall companies and their properties. In 2004, GGP bought the Rouse Corporation and the $7.2 billion cash purchase expanded GGP's reach from forty-one to forty-four states and their portfolio from 178 to 215 regional malls, making them the second-largest owner of shopping centers and malls in the country, as well as the second-largest U.S.-based publicly traded REIT. Financial analysts expected GGP to keep to its specialization in retail and sell off the mixed-use projects and planned communities that had come with the deal (including Rouse's flagship, Columbia, Maryland). Instead, recognizing the high sales per square foot in Rouse's mixed-use retail, GGP chose to capitalize on the mixed-use expertise of the Rouse people and properties to reposition weaker malls in competing markets or less visible locations.

To do just that, in 2005 GGP appointed Thomas D'Alesandro IV to serve as senior vice president and co-head of development. He was charged with overseeing the company's master-planned community portfolio, and evaluating the "redevelopment potential when there is capacity and/or opportunity to transform a General Growth retail center into a mixed-use property."[1] D'Alesandro brought experience developing the award-winning mixed-use town center at Reston, Virginia, where 3.2 million square feet of retail and office, a hotel, and 2,000 residences were integrated onto 85 acres. In a conventional mall format, the retail alone would have required a 100-acre site. From the developer's perspective, high density allows a far greater return on the cost of the land, and at Reston the synergies between the uses has resulted in

each of the categories outperforming its peers across the state. D'Alesandro had similar results retrofitting the 1970s mall at The Woodlands outside Houston into Woodlands Town Center. An innovative "Main Stream" waterway connects the residential neighborhoods to a new town square that anchors the mall to new office and hotel development, both of which are the best performing in Houston. Eager to build on this success, D'Alesandro has initiated numerous mixed-use projects at GGP. One of the first to get built is Nouvelle at Natick. (See Figure 7–3.)

GGP's first test case of a fully integrated, vertical mixed-use town center with civic aspirations on the site of an existing mall is the retrofit of the Cottonwood Mall in Holladay, Utah. A prime candidate for retrofitting, Cottonwood was built in 1962[2] and was last renovated in 1984. Although its high tax revenues were a big factor in the City of Holladay's decision to secede from the county and incorporate in 1999, competition from newer malls began to impede Cottonwood Mall's performance. By 2001 local newspapers described its condition as "trying" and by 2003 described its future as "a mystery." In 2004 it had a 25% vacancy rate and only three businesses left in operation on the second level. By the time of the design charrette in July 2006 it was only 40% occupied and tenants were not willing to enter into long-term leases. Nonetheless, the property was located in a relatively affluent trade area with growth potential, and, despite a complex lease agreement with Macy's and JCPenney, the site was completely under GGP's ownership.

In addition, the project had strong local support. Kris Longson, a vice president of development with GGP, believed that mixed use would provide not only the highest and best economic return for GGP, but also the greatest contribution to the community. A lifelong resident of Holladay, Longson lives a quarter mile from the site and is a local leader in the area's

Figure 7–3 Nouvelle at Natick consists of 215 luxury condominiums in eight- to twelve-story liner buildings in between Neiman Marcus and Macy's at The Natick Collection, an upscale enclosed mall outside of Boston. Although the residential liner fronts onto a wetland with little possibility of establishing future connectivity to adjacent neighborhoods, it is a forward-thinking example of both enlivening the blank façades of a shopping mall with residences and of greening its roof, at least in part, so as to provide residents with a more attractive view and outdoor amenity space. With construction nearing completion, the units, priced from $460,000 to $1.2 million, were selling well in October 2007 despite the flat residential market. This view shows the upper floors of the buildings designed by Add Inc. overlooking the Martha Schwartz–designed garden adjacent to the mall's atrium skylights.

very influential Church of Jesus Christ of Latter-Day Saints. As a person of high standing in both GGP and in the community, he is vested both personally and professionally in the project and has been highly motivated to seek a redevelopment plan that serves both. As the lead developer of the mall before it was acquired by GGP, Longson had been planning for the mall's makeover one way or another for ten years.[3] From GGP's perspective, the redevelopment of the site with big-box retail was a viable option, despite its distance from a major highway. The mayor, city council, and city planner were well aware of this scenario and expressed a preference for a mixed-use town center on the site to help strengthen their still newly incorporated city.

MARKET STUDY AND MINI-CHARRETTE

With these conditions in place, GGP conducted an in-house market study of the existing mall in 2005. The study documented average household income, daytime population, and population within three,

five, and ten miles.[4] The study further documented the population's demographic characteristics, demographic and population trends, employment and education characteristics, and the age and tenure of the housing stock.[5] The study reinforced the general strengths of the market and belief that an upgrading of the property would better capture the upscale households that compose 37% of the primary trade households. To do so, GGP envisioned enhancing the retail experience and market by adding uses: a cinema, office space, and residences.

With this general mixed-use program in mind, GGP engaged Duany Plater-Zyberk & Company (DPZ) to produce a master plan. Two of the founders of the Congress for the New Urbanism, Andres Duany and Elizabeth Plater-Zyberk have earned a seminal reputation for leading efforts to replace suburban development patterns with more traditional and more urban typologies (including Downtown Kendall, Upper Rock, and Mashpee Commons, illustrated elsewhere in this book). Although architects by training, DPZ typically produce urban master plans and graphic form-based codes to direct the design of the architecture rather than design individual buildings. DPZ typically produce their master plans onsite and in public, working with allied experts and local citizens during a seven- to ten-day consensus-building charrette.

Although DPZ have planned over 300 communities, they had never worked with GGP and recognized the potential impact of a client with such large holdings to advance new urbanist goals.[6] However, since their schedule was already booked when GGP called, the best they could accommodate was a four-day private mini-charrette in a storefront in the Village of Merrick Park, a GGP-owned lifestyle center in Coral Gables, Florida. The site was not far from DPZ's office and allowed participants to walk around and learn from successful new and old examples of two- to seven-story mixed-use buildings and urban fabric. Elizabeth Plater-Zyberk, the design partner in charge of the project, visited the Cottonwood Mall site prior to the arrival of GGP and city officials in Miami in March 2006.[7]

Existing site conditions significantly determined the retrofit's layout. Holladay is a predominantly residential community of single-family houses located in the Great Salt Lake Valley, with prominent mountain views to the east and hot summers and snowy winters. The site occupies the southeast quadrant of the intersection of two bus-served arterial streets. (See Color Plate 33.) Murray-Holladay Road, oriented east-west, connects the site to Holladay's historic village center less than a mile away. Highland Drive, the north-south route, is bordered by a creek that contributes to seasonal flooding and places much of the western side of the site in a FEMA floodplain. The designers faced constraints on the more residential eastern and southern edges of the site.[8]

Plater-Zyberk kicked off the mini-charrette with a slide show of great public places, many of them in Europe and well liked by Longson. In subsequent correspondence with Ellen Dunham-Jones, Plater-Zyberk recalled the design process:

> As is our custom at the outset of a charrette, each person on our team produced a design proposal for the site. This is one way to ensure the broadest sweep of ideas: iterative design and critique then reduces the schemes until there is one inevitable solution to all the given challenges. However, in this case, Kris [Longson] looked at one of the first-generation plans and said, "This is it." I proposed that he should allow our method to play out. He insisted that we focus on the one, which evolved into the Cottonwood plan. Kris's longtime involvement with the site and with the community gave me confidence that his reaction was informed and rational.[9]

According to Patrick Peterman, then development director with GGP, many of the other schemes more or less followed conventional wisdom for laying out a lifestyle center with retail as the main driver. Instead, Longson encouraged DPZ to do what they do best and focus on urban placemaking and the integration of uses.[10] The resulting scheme is driven largely by the site's natural features and view corridors within the Great Salt Lake Valley. (See Figure 7–4.)

The mini-charrette platted master plan is color coded to indicate uses and building types, parking counts, approximate square footages of the varied uses, and three detailed renderings expressing the proposed character of the buildings and open spaces and one bird's-eye rendering showing the project in context. Compiled into a book, it provided a clear vision for the project, enough with which to solicit buy-in by GGP, its major retailers, and community representatives. It did not include specific information about building layouts or street widths. It demonstrated the general capacity of the site to be developed as a mixed-use town center, but not the impacts of the project on either GGP or the community in terms of costs and revenues, traffic, zoning, or environmental performance. After internal review by GGP, those would become the goals of the follow-up interdisciplinary full charrette.

To gain greater insights into the viability of residential development within a mixed-use redevelopment of the site, GGP retained Zimmerman/Volk Associates (ZVA) to identify the extent and characteristics of the potential market, and to determine the optimum market position for new housing units that would reflect market preferences. The ZVA target market analysis is a proprietary methodology, refined over nearly two decades, that reveals market preferences for housing types that are not discernible through conventional supply-and-demand analysis.

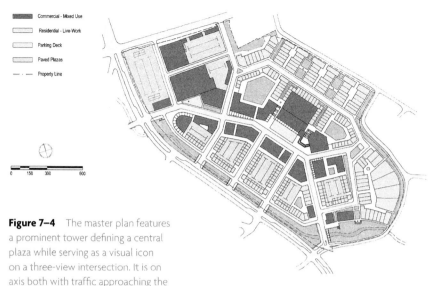

Commercial - Mixed Use
Residential - Live-Work
Parking Deck
Paved Plazas
— · — Property Line

0   150   300   600

Figure 7–4 The master plan features a prominent tower defining a central plaza while serving as a visual icon on a three-view intersection. It is on axis both with traffic approaching the project from the south and on the new Main Street traveling east, where it aligns with views of Twin Peaks and Mount Olympus. In general, the project employs the rural-to-urban transect tapering from T-5 through the center to T-3, the general density of Holladay, at the residential edges. Arcades are proposed along strategic portions of the main street as protection from both sun and snow. The upper floors of the mixed-use buildings on the main street with mountain views are predominantly given over to residential, while those without mountain views are planned for commercial leases. The existing Macy's structure remains intact. The long frontage along Highland Drive, to the south, is proposed to become a tree-lined linear park centering on the to-be-restored creek. Restaurants will overlook the ends of the creek with three- to four-story residences in between.

Conventional supply-and-demand analysis establishes "demand" by subtracting current "supply" (the number and type of housing units being leased or sold) from projections of household change in a specified market area. If a particular housing type has not been built in that market area—for example, bungalows on small lots—there is currently no supply-demand methodology that can quantify a market for that housing type; therefore, since no units of that housing type have been built and sold in the past, it is simply assumed that there is no "demand" for that housing type.

In contrast, ZVA's methodology determines market "potential" for an array of housing types. Their analysis is based on the premise that, since every year between 15% and 18% of American households move from one dwelling unit to another, an in-depth understanding of the lifestyle and housing preferences, and the financial capacities of those households that are moving in a specified market area can reveal the market "potential" for a variety of housing types, whether or not they have been

previously produced in that area. The methodology integrates household migration and mobility data from the Internal Revenue Service with household segmentation analysis[11] to quantify that market potential through a matrix of housing types and tenure that reflect market preferences.

The flexibility of the methodology—which has been equally successful in positioning HOPE VI public housing redevelopments and very high-end vacation resorts—has made ZVA's services highly sought after for both urban revitalization efforts and new urban developments in greenfield locations. When applied to a development site—and adjusted for nonmarket factors such as, in the case of Cottonwood, density objectives—the ZVA findings provide a developer with the housing revenue assumptions for the development pro forma.[12]

The mini-charrette master plan developed by DPZ incorporated 310 residential units without specifying tenure. ZVA's analysis established that an optimum mix derived from market preferences, with increased ratio of more land-efficient multifamily housing types, smaller average unit sizes, and reduced parking ratio for the rental units, yielded a larger number of units. Factoring in nonmarket issues, such as construction costs and parking configurations, led to a new target number of 534 units, with the difference largely made up of high-end condominiums. As at many suburban retrofits, the target market analysis also showed that the largest potential market for the property, at over 60%, would be younger singles and couples.[13] ZVA estimated that 83% of these younger, childless households would move to the site from outside the city of Holladay, mostly from Salt Lake City and California.

With improved expectations on the residential market bolstering GGP's interest in the redevelopment, the only hindrance to advancing the project further was the need to avoid upsetting the mall's relatively few current tenants and triggering a stampede before final decisions had been made and a calendar for demolition established. As a mall company, GGP's relationship with its tenants is both paramount and, in the case of retrofitting, extremely delicate. Until negotiations with the major new and existing tenants were secure, GGP was compelled to insist upon absolute confidentiality by all participants about the project. This would not have been necessary had the mall been completely shuttered but was deemed the most responsible way to work with and protect the still-active leases in the underperforming mall. The secrecy did not stop GGP from showing the mini-charrette master plan to local community leaders and seeking their input, but all such meetings were kept private and each person signed a confidentiality and nondisclosure agreement.

CHARRETTE

The word *charrette* has an interesting history and several connotations.[14] As a general term, charrette is commonly used by architects to refer to the intense production of design documentation during the week or days prior to a deadline. In urban design, it refers more specifically to a gathering of people (usually a combination of local stakeholders and multi-disciplinary professionals) working collectively to produce consensus on a design direction. The more or less simultaneous input from community members, local historians, environmental consultants, clients for each of the uses, code officials, fire and safety officials, traffic engineers, contractors, and cost estimators allows complex considerations to be factored into the design process in a condensed time period. Charrettes are an efficient means of accelerating design decisions, a valuable tool for educating all involved about the trade-offs required to meet multiple objectives, and a useful means for integrating a project into the community and building local support.[15]

In various guises and durations—from a single afternoon to a week or more—charrettes have become relatively common practice in urban design. New urbanists, in particular, employ them as a way to engage stakeholders and build public consensus. Charrettes have also proved to be an effective way to bring specialized consultants together to share nonstandard and unconventional methods with clients and to prepare for local resistance to these new ideas, not only from the public but also from local experts and officials. GGP's desire for secrecy ruled out such a public charrette, and they had never used one before. However, GGP agreed that because this was such a new direction for the company it was important that everyone, including the contractors, understand the big picture and the charrette would serve that purpose well. In addition, the efficiencies of gathering so many consultants together at once were not lost on Longson. Even though the charrette cost over $500,000, he estimated that he would have spent 30% to 40% more in both time and reimbursables to schedule separate coordination meetings. Plus, he had a dying asset and was interested in how the charrette would accelerate decision making. A charrette would provide GGP with a very precise deliverable in a short amount of time.

GGP convened a private charrette in one of Cottonwood's vacant shops for a full nine days in July 2006. (See Figure 7–5.) Over forty professionals were involved. In addition to the DPZ team (ten architects, planners, an IT specialist, and a charrette coordinator), nine architects, urban designers, and an environmental graphics designer from the Dallas office of RTKL and two architects from SB Architects in San Francisco were brought in for their particular ex-

Figure 7–5 The design charrette was held in a former Gap store at the mall. It was transformed into an impressive temporary studio with a small theater space for presentations; a less formal pinup area with conference table; a large workspace with approximately twenty tables and power outlets; a command center with copy machine, printer, plotter, reference books on new urbanism and Salt Lake City, and a multitude of drawing supplies; and a well-stocked snacks and drinks table and area for serving catered lunches and dinners

pertise in the retail and residential mixed-use buildings. Additional consultants included two landscape architects from the San Francisco office of Sasaki Associates, David Carrico for illustrations, and Billy Hattaway for transportation engineering and analysis.[16] Todd Zimmerman of ZVA was unable to attend. Brad Reynolds, a local residential developer, and Ted Didas, a local civil engineer, as well as the mayor, city manager, and several members of the city staff and city planning commission attended. Ellen Dunham-Jones attended as an observer and everyone signed confidentiality agreements.

On the client side, GGP manned the charrette with several senior people from the Chicago headquarters as well as several from the Salt Lake City regional office in development, planning, construction management, asset management, and leasing. They also brought in four contractor/cost estimators from the Chicago-based firm of Walsh Construction and three from the Salt Lake City–based firm of Camco Construction.

In addition, members of the Holladay City Council were invited to participate at all stages but staggered their visits so as to avoid establishing a quorum, which would have necessitated calling a public meeting. Their opinions, ideas, and knowledge of the area's history, resources, values, and decision making were actively sought and used by the charrette team. Because it was not a public forum and the majority of the city council members were never all present at once, individual members were able to speak candidly about communal desires and fears, especially concerning traffic and low-quality construction. They were generally enthusiastic about the potential of the project to improve their town and as such respected the mall owner's need for secrecy at this stage of design.

Would the project have benefited from a more open public process with more communal input, as is more typical of urban design charrettes? It is certainly possible that more concerns and ideas about particularizing the design to engage the specifics of this place might have been voiced and incorporated. Plater-Zyberk speculates that had it been a public charrette, the designers would likely have looked beyond the site boundaries more, examined a coordinated transformation of all four quadrants of the arterial intersection and proposed a design for that portion of Murray-Holladay Road that connects Cottonwood with the old village center. It would likely have allowed the citizens of Holladay to be engaged in the process of placemaking, begin early discussion of other future scenarios for their city, and become more vested in the future public life of their newly incorporated city's new Main Street.

These are important issues, and most retrofits involve some form of public-private partnership as well as community involvement.[17] However, democratic and community-building ideals do not always match the real needs of the owners of private property, even when they are involved in the production of seemingly public spaces such as streets and squares and expenditures on public improvements. In the case of Cottonwood Mall, GGP is committed to retaining private ownership of the streets and open spaces (so as to control their maintenance) while making them open for public use. Like most retrofit developers, GGP asked the city to contribute to the cost of infrastructure improvements to the site, including raising much of the site six feet above the floodplain. This was granted, but not without considerable debate over whether or not the developer was being given a free ride. It is likely that a public charrette would have helped build greater support for the project's various contributions to the community.

Longson and Plater-Zyberk led the charrette and made everyone's roles clear at the outset. Although the outlines of the master plan had already been established during the mini-charrette, there remained much reworking and refinement to be done. The goals of the charrette were to advance the dimensions and building typologies of the design enough so as to allow more detailed testing of its costs and impacts on the company and the community. How might the housing type and quantity targets be met and work with the varied retail depths required along the main street? The parking configurations had to be tested and traffic generation compared for the mixed-use design versus big box on the same site. How should construction be phased? Could flooding issues and seasonal variation in water quality and volume be addressed while making the creek into an attractive feature? What kind of architectural languages would connect the buildings, signage, and street furnishings to the region's building traditions and climate? Would green roofs and other environmental strategies make it worth going for Leadership in Energy and Environmental Design (LEED) certification? A well-known specialty market had expressed interest in a location at the prime northwest

corner; would they be willing to forego a surface parking lot in front of the store? What hopes and concerns did neighbors have for the site and how might the project better fit into local and regional redevelopment plans? What implementation strategies would work best with the city of Holladay—overlay zoning or rezoning—and give GGP both the control and the flexibility that they were looking for? And how much was all of this going to cost?

After introductions and orientation to the project, the entire team spent the first afternoon and next morning touring both new and old buildings, neighborhoods, and thoroughfares in Holladay, Salt Lake City, and nearby Park City to seek out and document good examples of a range of traditional housing types and their styles, colors, materials, and construction. The team also toured recently completed projects to better understand the local market's standards and expectations on everything from curb details and signage to shared parking and pricing strategies.

The rest of the schedule was arranged to allow individuals and small groups to work steadily and simultaneously on various assigned tasks while Longson and Plater-Zyberk pulled whoever was necessary into scheduled coordination meetings. These meetings were on specific topics: public officials/city, engineering/environmental, residential, commercial/retail, village center/town, landscape/site improvements, Macy's, and the specialty market. These meetings were less about immediate problem solving and more about educating the consultants through dialogue about the design's intentions, gathering information, airing questions, and determining directions and responsibilities for their resolution. Opening and closing presentations bracketed the week, while pinup reviews were scheduled at the close of each day. The pinups were the time for the small teams of designers to present their proposed solutions or refinements to their assigned

Figure 7–6 This rendering of the view on the main street toward the cinema and plaza shows some of the attempts to connect with the particular patterns of the place, including modeling the cinema's windows on the Salt Lake City train station, the use of deep overhanging cornices, and providing snow-shielding arcades on some, but not all, of the south-facing retail exposure.

tasks. After group discussion of the options presented, Longson and Plater-Zyberk would narrow the choices and give further instructions. On those occasions when the discussions were raising more questions than answers, Plater-Zyberk would identify "a drawing that needs to happen" as a way of advancing resolution and keeping up the pace of productivity (i.e., rather than engage the entire group in discussing minutiae, we need a snow removal diagram, a trash collection diagram, etc.).

The group typically assembled at 9:00 a.m., ate lunch in the studio, and went out for a large group dinner at 7:00 p.m. Most of the out-of-staters took advantage of a hiking trip into the extraordinary mountain terrain on Sunday morning, but otherwise worked straight through, including through most of the night before the final presentation.

Gathered into a digital slide show, the final presentation to two groups of city council members integrated the multiplicity of detailed concerns and proposals into the bigger context of designing for a healthy, sustainable future while building on the physical and communal traditions of the past. The general organization of the master plan was little

changed from the mini-charrette, but it was now much further developed and incorporated stories, building traditions, and particularities of the place.

Plater-Zyberk emphasized the historic context photographs in describing Holladay's inaugural condition as a setting for gatherings oriented to mountain views with mixed-use buildings and aspirations of a graceful life reflected in simple buildings with fine porches and balconies. She suggested that these would inspire the new Cottonwood's declension of urban, outdoor spaces at the center of the site toward its less dense, open spaces and greens at the edges and distinguished between how the city's historic places were enlivened by people rather than by a dozen paving materials and McMansion gables—common contemporary means of evoking tradition. Longson reiterated how this particular site's history as a place of gathering and dining would be amplified by the new plan to better serve today's community.

Landscape architect Alan Ward of Sasaki Associates described the visual and ecological qualities of the open spaces. Water is particularly precious in the West and the design incorporates strategies to ensure both that the surface of the creek is within the sightlines of passersby even during the dry months and that drainage from the project's green roofs feeds the creek.

Transportation engineer Billy Hattaway further enlarged the scope of the discussion and explained the rationale behind the new urbanist approach to street layout and trip generation. He presented a brief history of how the federal and states' classification of streets into arterial, local, and collector streets established the DNA of sprawl development patterns accompanied by high-speed roadways that create a more hostile and less safe environment for pedestrians and bicyclists. He contrasted this to the statistics of the healthier and safer alternative provided by traditional neighborhood development patterns before

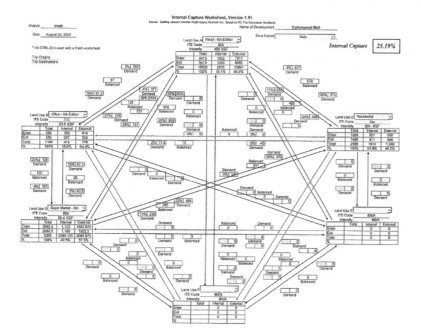

Figure 7–7 The Internal Trip Capture Worksheet for Cottonwood's retrofit produced by Billy Hattaway demonstrates how the complex interactions between the mix of uses result in capturing trips on-site. Even though this scenario accommodates 90% of the retail of the base case of the existing mall and increases density through additional residential and office space, the mix of uses enables an additional 7,234 daily trips to be "captured" internally, reducing the net external trip ends by approximately 25%.

showing the city of Holladay's traffic and accident statistics. Hattaway proposed that instead of following the regional tradition of extremely wide urban streets, Holladay should create a slower, more pedestrian-supportive street system by designing a network of narrower travel lanes, especially in the Cottonwood redevelopment.[18] He also proposed the addition of medians, possibly tree lined, onto Highland Drive to ease flow in and out of and adjacent to the project and presented diagrams of truck turns on the project's proposed streets to demonstrate that delivery of goods into the project can be accomplished.

The community's concerns about traffic were addressed in the 115-page traffic impact analysis that Hattaway completed after the charrette. Detailed analysis of existing demographics, traffic patterns, roadway segments, area intersections, and neighborhood traffic intrusion were provided along with projected impacts. Relying on industry-standard

methods to calculate new trips and to calculate pass-by trips and internal capture, the report compared trip rates for three development scenarios.[19] The base case of the existing mall at full capacity of its 735,000 square feet was found to generate 24,826 daily trip ends. Redevelopment of the site as a power center with 970,000 square feet (to which the site was already entitled by right) was found to raise the trip ends to 60,199. However, the third scenario, redevelopment according to the charrette master plan, yielded a reduction in net external trip ends to 21,206. Hattaway says, "Conventional traffic studies often inadequately account for the benefits of mixed-use development in reducing the generation of external trips. In projects like that proposed for Cottonwood, the mixing of retail, office, and housing uses provides for a balancing of trips generated and attracted which results in the 'internal capture' of trips. In addition, we found that the project, due to the specific mix of uses, should result in a decrease in traffic during peak flows compared with the other options considered for the site."[20]

By the end of the charrette week, the largest unresolved questions concerned the exact mix of housing types, the precise arrangement of the specialty market and parking, the precise nature of the rezoning of the property, and the cost of the project in relation to expected revenues. Longson was optimistic on all counts and expected to have signed agreements in place with his current tenants within a month and to announce the project to the public shortly thereafter.

Contrary to expectations, almost a year elapsed before the press release. Peterman estimates that half of the time between the charrette and the press release went to working out the construction budget and pro forma so as to present a convincing case to the GGP Executive Capital Committee and get approval to move forward.[21] The other half of the time went to back-and-forth negotiations between Macy's and the specialty market, complications arising from the specialty market's acquisition of another specialty market, and agreement with JCPenney on termination of their lease.

In the meantime, the public permitting process moved forward. First, the city adopted language to amend their general plan to allow for mixed-use development. Second, Francisco Garcia of DPZ helped the city write a "regional mixed-use" zoning category to apply to developments over 30 acres in size and requiring submittal of a detailed site development master plan. Third, the city changed the zoning for the Cottonwood Mall site from C-2 to the new regional mixed-use category. Finally, the site development master plan was submitted to the city council for approval as an amendment to the city's General Plan in November 2007. Despite the nearly year-and-a-half delay and ongoing development, the plans announced in July 2007 were little changed from those produced during the charrette (except for the location and treatment of the parking for the specialty grocer).

BENEFITS OF THE CHARRETTE

Besides the charrette's quantifiable benefits to GGP in time and billable hours, the charrette process also provided substantial qualitative improvements to the design, enhancing the expected experiential, social, environmental, and financial performance of the place. While many of these aspects might have evolved through more conventional means of project design and development, their integration in the design was significantly improved by the literal integration and immersion of so many diverse forms of knowledge and expertise in the same room for a focused period of time. Specific examples of these enhancements include the following:

The modification of generic conventions into place-specific, climate-appropriate, and community-oriented design

By meeting onsite and going out to different neighborhoods for dinner each evening, the charrette encouraged participants to be inspired by local patterns. Terri Powers and Mark Thorsen, the GGP leasing experts, suggested locating the coffee shop with an eastern exposure, the exit from the cinema toward the sunset, and shaded patios with mountain views for the dinner crowd. Instead of trying to keep consumers on their feet, as in a conventional mall, they encouraged the provision of plenty of places to explore or to sit and enjoy the views. In addition, after discussions with the city's community development director, DPZ developed a rezoning proposal keying the master plan to versions of the SmartCode's T-3, T-4, and T-5 zones customized to promote local building character.[22]

Learning from community leaders and building consensus

Although the secrecy limited community participation, there were various city council members present throughout the charrette eager to represent their constituents' concerns and aspirations. The team found potential ways to build on meaningful local traditions. The plaza stairs will be planted with plum trees to recall the original orchard on the site and to provide a setting for the annual "singing Christmas tree," one of the mall's fondly remembered events.

Innovative, integrated ideas arising out of interdisciplinary collaboration

The combination of contractors, leasing agents, architects, landscape architects, planners, and residential builders working together resulted in everyone having to consider more variables than usual, and a considerable amount of cross-education for all involved. This allowed for thoughtful integration of the work in several ways. The new zoning codes will incorporate GGP's tenant criteria on elements like awnings and signage. The mixed-use building designers learned from the leasing agents to use the lobbies, rather than the stores, as grade breaks and to stagger the locations of lobbies and paseos from the mid-block parking garages so the views from these spaces were of storefronts. Discussion of green roofs on the parking decks allowed for double- rather than single-loaded residential liners at the top. The detailed studies of various orientations of the theaters within the multiplex, location of the lobby, and a balcony/gallery overlooking the plaza were analyzed both in terms of enhancing the theater's civic function and in relation to parking garage access. The various designs for housing revealed occasional conflicts between those that were driven principally by concern for internal operation and the desire to use conventional layouts and those that were driven from the outside in and were more concerned with the view of the building from the public space than with the view from the units. The multiplicity of perspectives resulted in collaborative solutions that more effectively addressed both internal and external function.

Speed of troubleshooting and decision making

The charrette not only sped up the design process, but it also sped up the identification of potential problems. Getting input at the start about the site's geology and variable soils immediately limited the amount and location of concrete construction and meant the designers knew they would be limited to stick construction. Seasonal variations in water volume challenged the landscape architects to design an aesthetically pleasing linear park under both dry creek beds and flood control conditions. The local fire marshal's concerns about narrow streets and driveway courts inhibiting the access and operation of emergency vehicles, especially large fire trucks with cranes, were resolved through a combination of trade-offs between the street pattern, sidewalk widths, block depths, the building construction types, and the use of sprinklers. Although the adjustments were quite minor, they affected dimensions at every scale and their early coordination saved countless hours in the long run. Even when resolution was not completely achieved, as in agreement between Macy's, the specialty market, and GGP on the relationship of the market to the main street and to Murray-Holladay Drive, the assessment of the options by multiple perspectives clarified the issues.[23]

Coordination and design development without uniformity

While the existing Cottonwood Mall employs uniform materials, signage, and enclosure to clearly brand itself as a private, commercial environment, the retrofit of the mall into a more urban place, a town center with multiple uses and owners, demands a more public identity with more diverse—but coordinated—expression. The charrette format similarly balanced acceptance of the basic organization of the mini-charrette master plan with an openness to new ideas and an expansion of spatial differences. RTKL's improved design for the southern entry onto Main Street, anchored by a restaurant overlooking the water, was quickly incorporated. So were the refinements by GGP's leasing and marketing people to the retail spaces. To attract a mix of approximately 60% nationals and 40% local retailers, they varied store depths, introduced more exposed corners, and rearranged the ballroom and introduced an upper-level spa with mountain views. The number of housing types was expanded from three at the mini-charrette (wrapped deck, live-work, and stand-alone townhouse and cottage) to include western wrapped deck with courtyard, double-loaded stacked townhouse, and wrapped flats with embedded parking on flat garage deck. Within what is intended to be a relatively diverse set of buildings, with individual store awnings and signage, the branding of the environment will operate principally in terms of infrastructure—manhole covers, lampposts, and tree grilles, signifiers of a privately owned but shared public realm.

There is an old quote attributed to Otto von Bismarck that laws, like sausages, are better not seen being made. The retrofitting of a suburban single-use property into a more sustainable mixed-use, urban environment is a similarly complex process, parts of which are necessarily done behind closed doors. That does not mean that the end results are necessarily any less satisfying. In mixed use, a single crucial tenant can wield enormous bargaining power and delay what is already a slower and more costly process. The need to create a new zoning category for the city for "regional mixed-use" similarly took additional time. At the time of this writing, the project has gone public and has been subjected to the kind of questions and scrutiny that are both deserved and to be expected. GGP asked for, and after some debate received, public investment in a TIF to cover infrastructure improvements, mostly for flood control. GGP expects to benefit from its investment in this property, but the city of Holladay and the Great Salt Lake Valley stand to benefit as well. Understandably, the discussions with local residents, much like the discussions among the professionals during the charrette, tend to focus on immediate costs and benefits. However, the larger contributions of the project to a more sustainable future should also be recognized. The project fits in well with the goals of Envision Utah, a forward-looking regional plan for the Great Salt Lake Valley that built consensus for accommodating more of the region's exceptionally high expected growth

in compact, transit-served development on existing and infill sites.[24] Although Plater-Zyberk asked about connecting the project to Envision Utah at the start of both charrettes and one of the city council members recalled participating in the regional planning effort, there was little discussion during the charrette of the ways in which the project contributes to these regional goals. As designed, the new Cottonwood promises to accommodate over 500 households in a live-work-shop environment, convert approximately 17 of its 57 currently paved acres to permeable open space, and validate the attractiveness of more compact, urban living in an area whose zoning has not previously allowed that option.

On the one hand, it is possible to give the credit for this transformation to timing. Open-air lifestyle centers are currently more fashionable than enclosed malls and GGP is simply making a good business decision to reposition the property, especially given the circumstances of owning competing malls in the same market. On the other hand, GGP also deserves credit for persevering through the delays and complexities of shifting their model. They could have simply put a big-box lifestyle center in place and reaped the kind of short-term gains that fuel higher REIT valuations on Wall Street. But the CEO, John Bucksbaum, is committed to steering his company toward more environmental stewardship and hired D'Alesandro to advance mixed-use retail instead.[25]

Will Wall Street punish GGP for investing $550 million in a project that will take longer than usual to provide dividends? Will the project endure longer and perform more sustainably than the dead mall that it is replacing? Obviously it is too soon to tell, but the potential for GGP to scale up Cottonwood's lessons in place-specific design to retrofit its hundreds of stand-alone shopping malls into sustainable, mixed-use centers is extremely promising.

Chapter 8

Mall Case Study: Belmar, Lakewood, Colorado

"Enrich Your Life, Not Your Lawn" in Lakewood's New Downtown

Name of project: Belmar (3.3 million sq. ft.)

Location: near Denver in Lakewood, Colorado

Year constructed: 2001 to 2012 (projected year of completion)

Planning and urban design: Elkus Manfredi Architects, Ltd., and Civitas, Inc.

Architects: Elkus Manfredi Architects, Van Meter Williams Pollack, and others

Lead developer: Continuum Partners, LLC

Residential developers: McStain Neighborhoods, Trammell Crow, Sunburst Design LLC, and Harvard Communities

What it replaces: Villa Italia (1.2 million-sq.-ft. enclosed regional mall)

Size of site: 104 acres

Key features: twenty-three walkable urban blocks, publicly owned streets, LEED-certified buildings, and sustainable site design

Figure 8–1   Teller Street in the commercial core of Belmar.

SUMMARY

Belmar is an example of exemplary sustainable urbanism, having overcome many of the inherent limitations and challenges in retrofitting regional malls. It is providing a dense, varied urban place that is beginning to function as a downtown for a large, sprawling suburb that never had one. Lakewood, Colorado, a collection of residential subdivisions just to the west of Denver, has grown into the state's fourth-largest municipality with over 140,000 residents. Working closely with the city, the developers of Belmar converted a 104-acre site that formerly held an enclosed mall in a sea of parking, accessible only by car, into a mixed-use, walkable destination with nearly triple the built area, which combines shopping, residences, and office and civic uses on twenty-three urban-scaled streets and blocks. It contains a richly programmed, interconnected series of public spaces for civic uses. Also significant is the project's commitment to sustainable development and green building. New buildings are LEED certified, site drainage is carefully handled, demolition materials were recycled, one building was adaptively reused, a 1.8-megawatt rooftop solar array is in construction, and there is even a wind farm in one parking lot.

A diverse range of household types and tastes are accommodated in the project's 1,300 housing units in the form of rentals over retail, townhouses, loft condominiums, and zero-lot-line houses. The architecture avoids "cutesy" gingerbread in favor of durable materials and simple detailing. Designed by several architects, the mixed-use buildings at the core of the project are mostly built with masonry cladding in a style dubbed "American Mercantile."[1] The purely residential buildings at the edge are wood construction and employ more color. The variations read as authentic to the history and climate of Denver.

The privately held development company plans long-term ownership of the highly complex project, employing carefully controlled, but flexible, oversight. Both the city and the developer were willing to forego short-term income for long-term value. The positive effects of the retrofit are extending into the neighboring blocks and corridors, bolstered by Lakewood's commitment to infilling and urbanizing.

The primary retrofitting strategies are as follows:

- Scraping and rebuilding of a dead mall greyfield superblock into a new mixed-use downtown by dividing the site with public streets that connect with adjacent streets to form discrete urban blocks.
- Blocks developed in phases where the mix of uses on each is subject to adjustment over time, while the street matrix is fixed.
- A continuous network of streets and open spaces within which avant-garde arts programming occurs to enliven the atmosphere and enrich the experience of going "downtown."

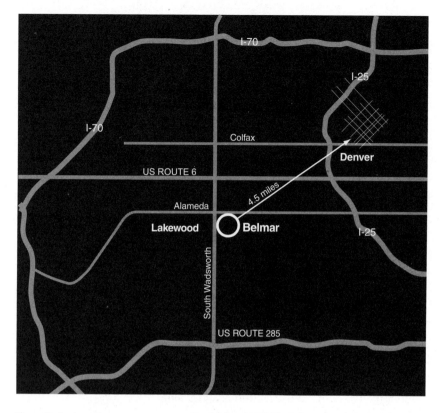

Figure 8–2 Location map.

diversity and change. Since 1969 the demographics have diversified somewhat as the suburb has grown and attracted younger Hispanic residents to its east side, while many white residents have aged in place. Lakewood is hoping to attract new residents to span the gap. City Manager Mike Rock says, "We're heavy on the over-sixty and the under-six and we're light in the middle, and we want to change that."[2]

The developer, Continuum Partners, is a relatively small, local, privately held development company run by Mark Falcone. Continuum had ambitious plans for the project from its inception. As Continuum Principal and Chief Development Officer Tom Gougeon insists, "It's *not* a shopping center imitating the form of a downtown."[3] It is a new downtown that, once seeded and nurtured, will have the necessary urban structure in place to grow and change over time. Continuum cut its teeth on 16 Market Square, an adaptive reuse project in the now-popular LoDo warehouse district of Denver and was recently tapped to develop the new transit district around Denver's historic Union Station.

The master plan for Belmar is a joint effort by Civitas and Elkus Manfredi Architects. Civitas is a Denver-based landscape architecture and urban design firm and Elkus Manfredi is a Boston-based firm that has developed considerable expertise and clout in the retail and mixed-use redevelopment market through their involvement in the planning and design of several recent successful projects, including CityPlace in West Palm Beach, Florida; The Grove in Los Angeles; and Americana at Brand in Glendale, California. In construction is Westwood Station in Westwood, Massachusetts (see Chapter 11).

When build-out is complete around 2012, the 1.2 million-square-foot mall will ultimately be replaced by 3.3 million square feet of new construction. Almost half of the new building area is reserved for residential use: 1,300 apartments, condominiums, townhouses,

Beginning in 2001, Belmar has been under construction on a 104-acre site in the spread-out suburb of Lakewood (population in 2000: 144,000; area: 42.9 square miles), in Jefferson County, directly to the southwest of downtown Denver. (See Figure 8–2 and Color Plates 34 to 40.) The name derives from the 750-acre Belmar Estate, which the land was part of before the construction of the Villa Italia mall in 1966. The thirteen separate subdivisions that joined to form Lakewood were incorporated into a city in 1969, in a defensive maneuver to avoid annexation into the city of Denver, then under a school busing order. As this history suggests, Lakewood had a fairly homogenous demographic profile of primarily white, middle- and working-class residents, fearful of

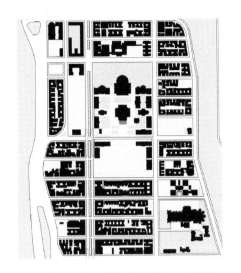

Morningside Heights, 1915

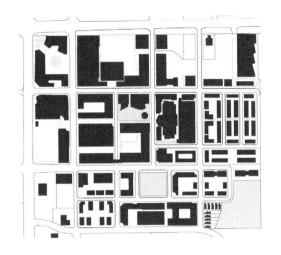

Belmar, 2015

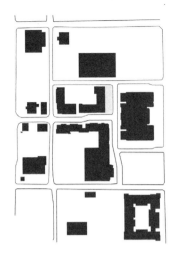

Winter Park Village, 2015

Figure 8–3 Comparison of rapidly built districts, spaced a century apart: Morningside Heights in New York City, Belmar, and Winter Park Village in Florida. To accommodate large floor plates, such as for a grocery store, parking decks, and a multiplex cinema, the building footprints at Belmar are larger than in Morningside Heights; however, the scale of blocks and streets and the degree of enclosure and definition of open spaces is similar. In contrast, the mall retrofit at Winter Park Village near Orlando, sited on a similarly sized parcel, is ringed with fields of parking, disappointingly similar to the mall condition that preceded it and eroding the integrity of the new blocks and streets.

and zero-lot-line homes. The remaining half is split 55/45 between retail and office use. The site plan of the new Belmar includes 9 acres of open space, including a 2.2-acre park occupying a central block in the southern residential area and a 1.2-acre public plaza in the heart of the commercial district. One hundred four acres is a large piece of land to redevelop all at once into an urban district. In comparison, Battery Park City in New York, a huge undertaking, is 92 acres. As the diagram illustrates, Morningside Heights in Manhattan between 110th Street and 125th Street is roughly the same size as Belmar, and was initially built out in about the same amount of time—a rapid fifteen-year process from pastures to densely built city blocks. (See Figure 8–3.)

The area of Jefferson County that is now Lakewood was once rural farmland, subdivided into the quarter-section (160-acre) homesteads bounded with arterial roads that shape so much of the built landscape of the American West. The first residential subdivision in the area, called "Lakewood," was platted

in 1889. On the large parcel at the increasingly busy corner of South Wadsworth and West Alameda—a broad arterial that at one time was a formal City Beautiful boulevard connecting Denver to scenic Red Rocks—the Villa Italia was constructed and opened in 1966. (See Figure 8–4.) In researching dead and dying malls, we have found that each mall had a superlative statistic attached to it: the first/largest open-air/enclosed/two-story mall built west/east of the Mississippi/Rockies/Chicago. Villa Italia is no exception. Upon opening, it was advertised as "the largest enclosed mall west of Chicago," a title it did not hold for long.

Villa Italia was fabulously successful and much beloved, a setting for high school proms and civic events such as the yearly Italian Festival. In the 1970s, the mall was a key component in the economic viability of the newly formed city of Lakewood. In the early 1990s it was still going strong, in revenue if not in reputation. It had become a teen hangout, purportedly drawing in a rough crowd from outside Lakewood while providing as much as 50% of the city's

Figure 8–4 Villa Italia, an enclosed regional mall, was built on a superblock at the busy corner of South Wadsworth and West Alameda in 1966. The 104-acre site has been retrofitted into Belmar, comprised of twenty-three urban blocks and 3.3 million square feet of new, mixed-use construction—shops, offices, and 1,300 residential units of varied types.

tax base.[4] But just a few short years later the economic engine had broken down. Promised improvements such as a multiscreen cinema were not materializing, while in the retail industry department stores were being consolidated and anchors closed.

In the vicious do-or-die cycle of keeping a regional mall viable, it was time for a substantial makeover or the introduction of a new paradigm. Which would it be: renovated mall, power center, lifestyle mall, or new downtown? A 1998 article in the *Denver Business Journal* quoted a retail broker saying the site would "be a good community center or power center site."[5] Similar sentiments had been expressed about another failed mall site in the Denver suburbs, which became CityCenter Englewood—part big box, part civic center, part TOD at a new light-rail station (see Chapter 6). The mayor, Steve Burkholder, appointed a citizens' advisory committee to strategize improvements to the mall. In an article in *Governing* magazine, Christopher Swope describes the process by which the committee gradually—and with much reluctance—came to the

conclusion that what they really cared about were the social and civic activities more than the mall itself.[6] Municipal officials in Lakewood decided to forego the lure of quick revenue returns and rejected the big-box power center option (after all, in a suburban city of over 42 square miles there are numerous other suitable sites for big-box retailers). Instead, the mayor and chief planner, Frank Lane, working with the highly active and informed citizens' advisory committee, actively searched for a redevelopment partner interested in pursuing a longer-term strategy of creating a downtown for a suburban city that had never had one. The recognition that they now wanted a downtown not unlike the LoDo district in Denver or downtown Boulder was quite a shock to those for whom the mall had been an inoculation against having to go into the city. The extent of the shift in their thinking about both their own identity and the form of a downtown is revealed by the suburban layout and background position given to the 1998 Lakewood Town Center, including a city hall, library, and cultural center, built across Wadsworth Boulevard from Belmar. The public buildings sit behind a new strip mall facing vast parking lots.

Gougeon says that although Lakewood had recently made these investments in civic buildings next door, "They weren't organized in any fashion that creates a sense of community or identity."[7] The Villa Italia site offered Lakewood the chance to make up for that lost opportunity and Continuum was selected as the developer. Market research demonstrated that the site was still viable for regional retail, possessing a large, relatively affluent, underserved population nearby and excellent visibility from still-busy arterial roads. Initial plans to phase demolition and keep viable parts of the mall in operation were nixed when the mall lost three of four department store anchors in quick succession. The fourth anchor, owned by the May

Company, proved uncooperative with the redevelopment plans and unwilling to give up its lease on a building less than fifteen years old. In the end a negotiated settlement was reached when the city initiated eminent domain proceedings. Continuum was forced into an accelerated building schedule, though still phased over ten years.

In retrospect, Continuum feels that the accelerated schedule was a blessing in disguise. The need to demolish and build lent tremendous momentum to the process and seems to have fueled its success. We agree. There is a substantial risk that too much of a piecemeal, incremental approach to such a major restructuring of the fabric will stall out at a "good enough" stage, as at Winter Park Village, before sufficient transformation to create real urbanism and long-term value has been achieved.

Even so, because the first phase's buildings lacked visibility from Wadsworth Boulevard, it was difficult to establish an identity for the site and interest in sales and leasing when it opened in 2004. The new mixed-use buildings were on centrally located blocks, not on the periphery. Instead of seeing the new streetscapes, passersby saw mounds of raw aggregate, recycled from demolition materials and waiting for reuse.

Despite the initial inauspicious views of the project, it is selling well. Just as the city hoped, the success of Belmar is lifting neighboring boats: surrounding property values are up and reinvestment is occurring. The city is proactively preparing to accommodate the new growth with corridor vision plans and rezoning in place for Alameda Avenue, where Belmar sits, and along Colfax to the north where an old rail corridor is being rejuvenated for transit.[8] At the terminus of the rail corridor is the Denver Federal Center, which was the largest federal employment center outside Washington, DC (and the place of employment of many Lakewood residents). It is now closing down and Lakewood has annexed all 700 acres.

"GREENING": FINDING THE FUNDING FOR SUSTAINABLE URBANISM

The total development costs for Belmar are expected to be $750 million—a very large sum of money for a small, private development company to manage. How did they do it? In fact, Continuum is part of the Pioneer Companies, a group of development partnerships run by Falcone's family from a base in New York State, who provided internal equity for much of the project. However, Continuum was able to raise $320 million in funding through two innovative sources: a public improvement fee (PIF) negotiated with the city of Lakewood and green bonds awarded by a federal government program.

About $165 million, or more than one-fifth of the total development costs, was spent on public improvements to the greyfield site before redevelopment: property acquisitions, environmental cleanup, asbestos removal, utilities installations, and drainage control. Continuum paid 25% of these up-front costs and financed the rest through bonds. Lakewood's city council and redevelopment authority then passed a resolution in 2001 permitting Continuum to charge a 2.5-cent public improvement fee or PIF—a sales tax that remits to the developer rather than to public coffers—to pay off the bonds. The city also waived one cent of its two-cent sales tax at Belmar to provide additional aid in paying off the debt and reduce the burden on customers. The discount will continue for twenty-five years or until the debt is paid off. This arrangement put the sales tax at Belmar on a par with most city sales taxes in the area.[9] At existing sales figures, city officials expect payoff to occur ten years early.

Finding funding for predevelopment costs is crucial because these costs are the burden of redeveloping greyfield and brownfield sites, versus building in exurban greenfield conditions. As Gougeon admits,

Figure 8–5 A small urban wind farm, funded with national green bonds, graces one of the few surface parking lots at Belmar.

Figure 8–6 Street parking meters were installed at Belmar from the beginning, and parking in the garages is free, to encourage higher turnover of on-street spaces for those running short errands. Belmar's meters were Lakewood's first.

"It was certainly different from buying 100 acres of cornfield."[10] Sustainable urbanism is dependent upon building on these types of sites but finding the funding can still be very difficult.

Continuum was at the right place at the right time when it secured its green bonds. Belmar was one of four developments nationwide to qualify for these bonds under the American Jobs Creation Act of 2004. Under the program, selected developers who demonstrate energy-efficient construction were allowed to borrow money and not have to pay taxes on the interest. Belmar received $200 million to fund the installation of a 1.8-megawatt rooftop photovoltaic system on the roofs of parking decks and lots, to harvest solar energy with the intention of providing up to 20% of the power supplied to the project, as well as for other energy-efficient improvements. Colorado senators and representatives are credited with helping Belmar qualify as one of the four chosen projects.[11]

The green bonds have been used, as mandated, to add sustainable design features to the project specifically intended to increase energy efficiency, such as a parking lot wind farm, photovoltaics, and evaporative cooling systems. (See Figure 8–5.) Belmar has also become a demonstration site for the Colorado Public Utilities' legislated mandate to increase renewable energy use statewide and is benefiting from generous rebates. Many of the buildings have been designed to meet LEED certification criteria; some of the buildings were entered in the program and achieved a LEED Silver rating. Passive sustainable site design strategies are also included in the project, like using high-albedo paving materials and harvesting and replanting vegetation from the site, including several large ponderosa pine trees in the plaza. Gougeon believes that LEED standards will become the standard building codes of the future, while an amalgam of LEED for Neighborhood Design and form-based codes will comprise zoning in the future. David Manfredi, principal of Elkus Manfredi and the lead designer of the master plan, credited some of the developer's and the city's commitment to green design to geography and the outdoor lifestyle of the West. "The commitment to green at Belmar when we were planning it ten years ago was greater than we see today at most of our projects on the East Coast."[12]

A third route to sustainable urbanism is via reduction in car trips and vehicle miles traveled. The mix of uses and tripled density at Belmar address this goal, as well as eight regional bus routes that now thread through Belmar's streets. In addition, Continuum built structured parking in the first phase (probably too much as it turns out, according to a parking audit performed by Continuum). In a reversal of conventional thinking, and in line with the theories of Donald Shoup, structured parking is free while on-street parking is metered as a short-term parking management tool, not a revenue source.[13] (See Figure 8–6.)

Q. What do you think of the suburbs?

A. Suburbs are uniformly boring.

Q. So how did you go about making the Villa Italia Mall retrofit *not* boring?

A. There was a joke going around about Lakewood, "Ten minutes from downtown, but why bother?" Things aren't easy to do, politically, in Lakewood. Even though we have done many cutting-edge things, we have to work very hard to convince a conservative, cautious community with some libertarian elements in it to let us do our job. The main thing we did with Belmar is we gave the community a place to brag about and a place to go. A place to take their friends on Friday night. We created a sense of pride for people to walk around and say, "Yeah, this is cool!"

Q. Do you think you achieved good public space at Belmar?

A. One of the things that will make Belmar age well is that there's always something new to look at, either because one business left and another came in or because something new just got built. Certainly The Lab is a very creative activity, but really one of the best public spaces is that plaza. Kids pushing the round ball that sits on the water, all the young people there on a Friday night sitting outside the pub, 'cause you can smoke outside. In the winter you have people skating. That's real— it's not an artificial dynamic like going to strictly a museum or a library.

Q. What role did the fine citizens of Lakewood play in the redevelopment process?

A. I think it's unfair and an abdication of responsibility when local governments simply turn to a citizens' group and say, "What do you want? What should we do?" Representative government says that at the end of the day it's really those elected officials and their staff who need to take that responsibility with appropriate participation. But you need to create venues for participation that are meaningful. It's not meaningful to ask a group of civilians to come up with the final determination of what the reuse of a mall is. But what it is appropriate to do is to use an iterative process to talk about the components that make a place interesting and livable. What do you want to preserve? What do you want to change?

Q. How did the public-private partnership with Continuum Partners come about?

A. City officials in Lakewood had a very broad concept. We wanted a more interesting urban space. And we were willing to forego revenue in order to create long-term value. We didn't issue a formal RFP [request for proposals]. Through a mutual friend, I had an informal lunch with Mark Falcone, of Continuum. The relationship evolved from there. Continuum was far in before there were any formal agreements with the city.

Q. How has the partnership worked out?

A. We feel lucky, but lucky by design.

Mike Rock was interviewed by June Williamson on August 7, 2007. He has lived in Belmar since the first apartments were completed, and he recently purchased a zero-lot-line townhouse there. He walks to work.

MORPHOLOGICAL ANALYSIS

Urban morphology is the study of the physical form of cities. The following series of figure-field diagrams illustrate the morphological transformations over time, from 1975 to projected conditions in 2015, on a square-mile area that includes Belmar. One can see both how the preurban grid of the quarter-section (160-acre) divisions of the historic Public Land Survey System conditioned the suburban road and lot locations, and how buildings are sited in response to this grid. The new block structure of Belmar knits into the historic morphology, but is unable to challenge the dominance of the arterial road network. In the diagrams, one may read three types of suburban tissue: *static tissues,* or planned subdivisions (comprising much of Lakewood); *campus tissues,* such as apartment complexes and, of course, the shopping mall; and *elastic tissues,* the most transformable type, found on the arterial strips of Alameda and Wadsworth Boulevards.[14]

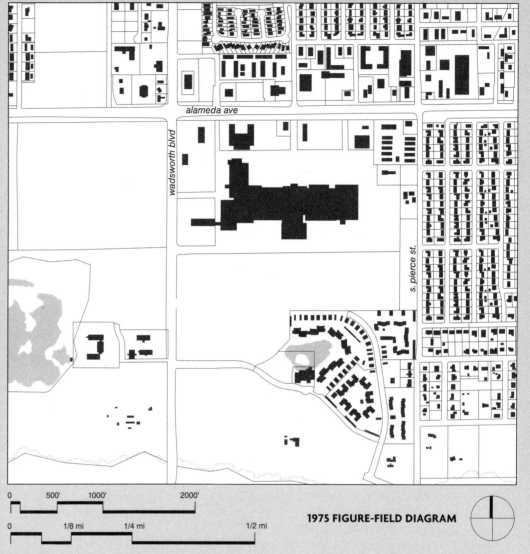

1975 FIGURE-FIELD DIAGRAM

Figure 8–7 1975 figure-field diagram. Villa Italia had been open and operating for nearly a decade. The outlines of the 750-acre private estate from which the mall site was carved can be clearly discerned, bounded on the northeast corner by Alameda Avenue and South Pierce Street. Also clearly readable are the quarter-section (160-acre) divisions of the historic Public Land Survey System. Portions of the estate had been developed already as clustered apartments, on sites south of Villa Italia, while an office complex was built west of Wadsworth on the site of the estate's original mansion, facing a man-made lake. In tune with zoning and planning practice of the time, these three new uses—residential, office, and retail—were segregated from one another. If the original estate was one large *campus,* it now had several smaller campuses embedded within it. To the north and east of Villa Italia are small-lot, single-family residential subdivisions. These constitute the *static* tissue of Lakewood. Along Alameda, a number of large to medium parcels were developed for commercial use and constitute *elastic* tissues. Historically, the main east-west strip in Lakewood is Colfax, a couple of miles north, with Wadsworth as a primary north-south connector. With the construction of Villa Italia, the action migrated south.

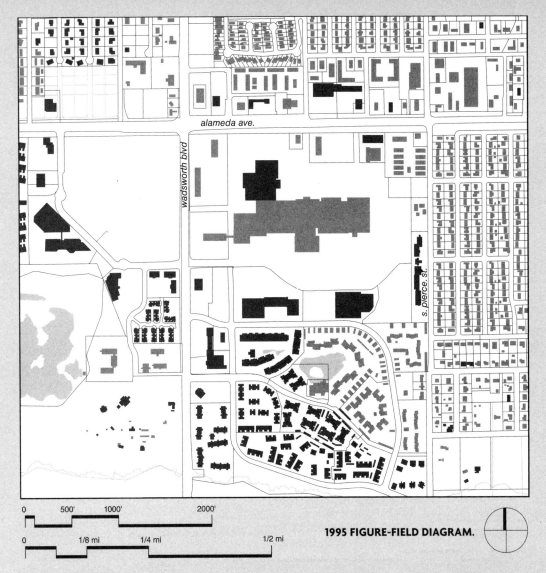

alameda ave.

wadsworth blvd

s. pierce. st.

0	500'	1000'		2000'

0	1/8 mi	1/4 mi	1/2 mi

1995 FIGURE-FIELD DIAGRAM.

Figure 8–8   1995 figure-field diagram. By 1995, a municipal office building had been built in Lakewood's planned civic campus (east of Wadsworth and north of the lake), and the city was far along in planning for the rest of the complex. Additional clustered apartment complexes were built, filling in the *campus tissue* to the south of Belmar. The roads in the new development form a winding, internalized loop, only minimally connected to the framing arterial roads, with no discernable block structure. The residential fabric remained almost wholly static and unchanged. The mall had grown a bit, with the addition of a new anchor and some big-box retailers on outparcels to the south. By this time there was an understanding that the mall might be entering a period of decline, although sales tax revenue was still strong.

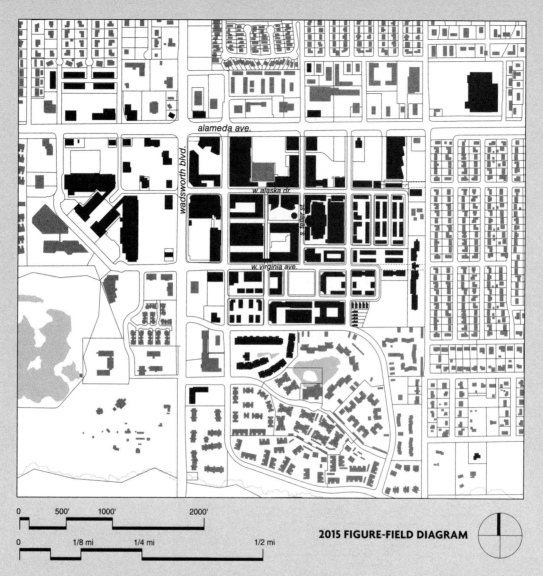

alameda ave.

wadsworth blvd.

w. alaska dr.

s. teller st.

w. virginia ave.

0   500'   1000'   2000'

0   1/8 mi   1/4 mi   1/2 mi

2015 FIGURE-FIELD DIAGRAM

Figure 8–9 2015 figure-field diagram (projected). In 1998, the $62 million Lakewood Town Center civic and commercial project was completed. The project includes a cultural arts center with a theater, a new public library, and city offices, as well as office space and nearly 300,000 square feet of grocery-anchored retail space, originally intended to complement the now-demolished mall. The civic center, while fairly dense, remains auto oriented in design, with service loop roads designed to efficiently deposit cars into parking garages rather than streets and blocks.

Across Wadsworth, the mall site has been almost completely transformed. The only building remaining housed one of the anchor stores, located such that West Alaska Drive could comfortably pass in front of it. The street grid from surrounding blocks has been extended through the site to form twenty-three new urban-scaled blocks. The majority of the streets were deeded to the city as public ways. Continuum does not own the buffer parcels along South Pierce Street and was not able to continue the street grid all the way through, but this remains a possibility for the future.

Figure 8–10 The Belmar Urban Apartments, designed by Van Meter Williams Pollack Architects, comprise sixty-six affordable family rental apartments, flats, and townhouses organized along a central pedestrian walk. A total of 1,300 new dwelling units, half for sale and half for rent, are planned for Belmar.

Figure 8–11 Wrapped blocks: (a) in the "full wrap" the bulk of a multiplex cinema is concealed in the center of the block; (b) a "partial detached wrap" of retail liners embed a reused former department store building into the block.

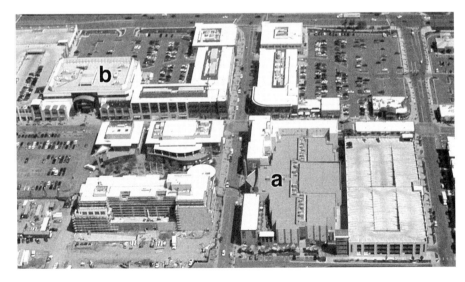

Alaska Drive and Teller Street form the main retail intersection, the "100% corner" in retail-speak, of the new Belmar district. (See Color Plate 36.) Townhouses and zero-lot-line houses are located on the blocks closest to preexisting single-family homes. (See Figure 8–10.) Mid-rise apartments wrapped around parking decks—Texas donuts—are located to the south, adjacent to preexisting apartment blocks, whose tenants can now fairly easily reach the center of Belmar on foot. There are additional apartments, loft units, and condominiums above retail on the blocks closest to Teller and Alaska.

Uses with larger footprints—a Whole Foods grocery store and "mini boxes" of 10,000 to 40,000 square feet—are located on blocks adjacent to Wadsworth and Alameda. A hotel is planned for the Wadsworth and Alameda corner. Larger uses on more central blocks are wrapped, using various design strategies. There is the "full wrap," seen on the theater block, where a sixteen-screen multiplex is completely concealed in the center of the block and lined with three mixed-use buildings and a parking garage. The wrappers are detached from the cinema, creating alleys for service, loading, and emergency egress. The garage itself has a liner strategy: the street-facing edge of the ground floor contains artists' studios with plate glass windows. Then there is the "partial wrap, attached or detached." The Whole Foods store, built to the standard of the chain's "urban" format, has a partial attached wrap on the nonarterial sides, containing retail and office use. The reused department store building has a partial detached wrap, composed of adjacent buildings that meet the street, with a gap at the recessed entry to the store building, which has been opened up with new windows and a skylight.[15] (See Figure 8–11.)

In addition, there has been some new construction on Alameda. A Home Depot was built on Alameda one block east, which does not represent a change in typical suburban development practice, but more high-density mixed-use infill is expected at major intersections along the avenue, as encouraged by the Alameda Corridor Overlay District initiated by Lakewood, based on a vision plan by Dover Kohl & Partners.

FROM BUNKERS TO STREETSCAPES: PUBLIC SPACE

A few miles from Belmar, going west on Alameda, is the Denver Federal Center. It is a forbidding place, with high security fences, guards, and, quite literally, bunkers; it is a place where a well-intentioned citizen cannot take a photograph without risk of being questioned and possibly detained by the federal police. In contrast, Belmar really is a public place. All of the buildings are owned and managed by Continuum or its associated entities, but the streets, sidewalks, and parks are owned by the city of Lakewood and are considered public space, with all the civil protections that status affords.

Retail tenants are a mix of national chains and locally owned stores and restaurants. Tom Gougeon says, "What we do is borrow the strength of those national retailers because we need them, because that's who dominates the U.S. retail world today. But we consciously make the decision that we're going to forgo some income and make a commitment to having a mix out there."[16] The need to have a strategy that purposely passes up revenue can be a hard pill for developers, property managers, and city officials to swallow. But it is the local shops that distinguish a new downtown (and old ones, for that matter) and make it a destination. While critics decry the "mallification" of the city, we can be thankful for conscientious developers who strive to enliven the suburban mix.

In the classic gentrification cycle observed in older urban districts, low rents attract hip local boutiques and cafés to an area, and the independent building owners are happy to have them. At some point, if the businesses are successful and the area becomes popular, the owners, each seeking to cash in, are likely to independently decide to raise rents. This move often ends up displacing the local merchants that made the area hip and viable—thus undermining the factors that led to the increase in the properties' value in the first place. This cyclical process is happening in Walnut Creek, California, to the dismay of many of the funky retailers who helped lead the revival of the old Main Street and can no longer afford rising rents. A large single owner, however, can make the longer-term decision to subsidize local businesses for the good of the whole district, as has happened at Belmar (and Mashpee Commons; see Chapter 5).

The leasing group at Belmar came up with a strategic plan for enlivening the mix; they identified and targeted successful independent businesses in the Denver area that they would like to have at Belmar and devised attractive leasing agreements to entice them to come. For example, Falcone invited the chef of a popular local Mexican restaurant to relocate to Belmar. When the chef demurred because he couldn't afford it, Continuum invested in the restaurant in order to make it possible. In addition, Continuum created Block 7, a row of 500- to 1,000-square-foot studios and galleries on Saulsbury Street that rent for a discounted rate of $350 to $400 a month. The small studios function as a ground-level liner, activating the façade of the structured parking deck for the sixteen-screen cinema located on the opposite side of the block. Block 7, combined with The Lab, has made Belmar a must-visit stop on the Colorado contemporary art circuit. (See Figure 8–12 and Color Plates 38 and 40.)

The Laboratory of Arts and Ideas opened in a storefront in 2004. It was originally intended to be an outpost of the Denver Art Museum, run by a museum curator, but it soon took on independent status (subsidized by Continuum) with an ambitious mission to fertilize avant-garde art and culture in the suburbs. (See Figure 8–13.) Director Adam Lerner organized The Lab as a kind of think tank, where discussions, lectures, and publications are as important as exhibitions, to make a "kind of public forum to create an intellectual and cultural community" in, and on, the suburbs.[17]

How "public" are Belmar's open spaces? Are they providing Lakewood's inhabitants with the variety of social and civic functions that they hoped for in their downtown? We believe so and credit the design of the streets as well as programming and design of the skating rink/plaza and town green. The new public streets at Belmar have a right-of-way of seventy-five feet with generously wide sidewalks, leaving only thirty-four feet for the roadway, too narrow by Lakewood street standards. Lakewood worked hard with the local fire district to change the standards for Belmar. The skinny streets slow traffic, improving safety for pedestrians. They allow good visibility across streets, aiding the retail's viability. And, perhaps most importantly to the project's long-term sustainability, in conjunction with the three- to five-story buildings, they create the

Figure 8–12 In Block 7, working artists occupy small studios with glazed storefront, lining a parking garage. At eight o'clock on a Monday evening in summer, many of the artists can be seen at work in their studios, visible to passersby. A style article in the *Denver Post* weighed in on Belmar a few years after completion of the first phase, proclaiming, "The food is getting tastier, the art is getting artsy-er."

Figure 8–13 In 2006, The Laboratory of Arts and Ideas at Belmar, a nonprofit contemporary art space, inaugurated an 11,500-square-foot facility. The interior space, designed by Belzberg Architects, contrasts with its host building, with a protruding, amoeba-like canopy, part of the "Aurae Wall," a precision-milled parametric form that twists through the space.

Figure 8–14 Belmar hosts the annual Italian Festival, a tradition retained and expanded from Villa Italia days, which draws huge crowds to the streets.

sense of a beautifully outfitted outdoor public room with the kind of spatial intimacy that is conducive to social interaction and community building. These well-proportioned streets were rigorously detailed. Says Gougeon, "A great deal of thought went into the relationship between the street and the sidewalk. No detail was too small, from custom designed light fixtures to tree grates to manhole covers."[18]

One memorable design feature that makes Belmar streets distinctive is a custom-fabricated stainless steel cable over-the-road lighting system reminiscent of those often found in narrow European streets, where buildings are tall in proportion to the street width. These systems are relatively rare, except on festival occasions, in the United States. "If you see a photo with that lighting system, people will say, 'Oh, that's Belmar, that's Lakewood,'" Gougeon says.[19] The fire marshal was not very happy about the overhead lighting and we found it bordering on making the streetscape overly busy. At night it compresses the space of the street, increasing its

sense of intimacy and centrality. But by day we felt its vertical subdivision of the space interfered with the well-established spatial dialogue between buildings facing each other. However, it is expressive of the high level of care given to the design of the public realm at Belmar. We were glad not to find the mistakes so common in poorly planned lifestyle centers, where sidewalks often incorporate inappropriate steps and ramps because the streets have been improperly graded and coordinated with retail pad elevations. The streetscape at Belmar is both welcoming and intelligently, thoroughly designed.

The programming of the public spaces by Continuum and Lakewood is multilayered, complex, and expensive. It is a far cry from the feel-good mall programming of the past—runway "fashion" shows and Santas at Christmas—conceived with the single-minded purpose of drumming up sales. Belmar has a yearly Italian Festival that draws crowds of up to 10,000 (see Figure 8–14), a weekly farmer's market, and contemporary art lectures

Figure 8–15   The 2.2-acre green at Belmar, occupying a full block and located on axis with Teller, the main north-south street, is a quiet place.

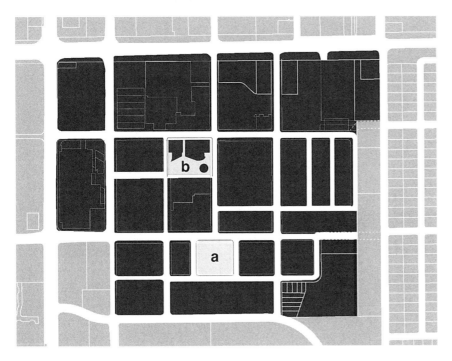

Figure 8–16   The 23-block structure of Belmar. The green (a) and plaza (b) occupy central locations around which buildings are organized.

and events at The Lab, which regularly attract weeknight audiences of more than one hundred, many traveling out from Denver into the 'burbs. And then there is "Lakewood on Parade," a yearly event that used to take place in a high school parking lot and now travels proudly down Teller Street to the green. As for street and sidewalk maintenance, city funds for streets are transferred to Continuum for higher-than-typical service. For example, snow at Belmar is removed rather than plowed to the curb.

The bocce courts provide an example of how all of this effort is encouraging the formation of community bonds. They were temporarily located on a not-yet-built lot as part of the Italian Festival celebrations. Belmar residents enjoyed them and formed a "Save the Bocce Courts" group. Continuum now plans to find a new location for the courts when the time comes to build on that space.[20]

The two most explicitly public spaces are the plaza and the green. Manfredi describes them as the anchors of the project, serving an analogous, if counter, role to those of the department store anchors of a conventional shopping mall. Together with the streets they define the open space system around which the entire precinct is planned. The plaza is located just off the intersection of the two main streets, Alaska and Teller, very much in the center of the downtown. The green culminates the axis of Teller Street and serves as a gateway to the project for those arriving by bus. A quiet and leafy park, it provides a local focal place for passive recreation by the immediate residents. (See Figures 8–15 and 8–16.)

The plaza, on the other hand, is intended to attract a larger public and, according to Manfredi, provide opportunities for informal gathering absent the desire or need to shop.[21] The design brings together several elements in an attempt to populate the place with multiple audiences. The building to the north of the site was deliberately programmed with social activities to reinforce the plaza, including a bowling alley and bar. There is outdoor restaurant seating and a water feature with a huge, 15,000-pound granite ball suspended on a thin film of water that is especially compelling to children eager to engage with it. Clusters of mature pine trees were replanted here from elsewhere in the site. Civitas landscape architect Craig Vickers talks of how they were composed spatially, along with other features of the plaza, for a fluid, laid-back effect.[22] The dominant feature is an oval plaza surrounded by sculptural poles suspending strings of lights over the space. In the winter, the oval converts to an ice-skating rink. (See Color Plate 37.)

The designers and developer all say they agonized over the location, program, and configuration of the 1.2-acre plaza and continue to brainstorm about programming options and other adjustments. Manfredi worked on the renovation of Rockefeller Center's iconic (and profitable) ice rink but worried about repeating what could be considered a cliché. After consideration of a variety of alternatives, the team was not convinced that any other use would keep the plaza lively and welcoming through the winter months and focused on making it work. Rather than throw up an oppressive canopy, the designers adjusted the height of the building to the south so that it would provide adequate winter shade to keep the ice from melting in Colorado's bright winter sun. The rink has indeed proved immensely popular and worthy of the care brought to its design.

NEW USES/NEW USERS

The advertising tagline for Belmar residential real estate reads, "Enrich your life, not your lawn." According to landscape architect Vickers, "Belmar is full of ideas intended to almost *train* suburban people in urban thinking . . . how to understand it and how to look for what to enjoy here." For additional training, Lakewood offers a Civics 101 class at city hall across the way. So what exactly might it mean to train suburbanites in urban thinking? Gougeon is explicit about one possible meaning. Belmar is the one place in Lakewood where two vastly different demographic groups—Spanish speakers in the transitional east side neighborhoods and more Anglo and educated residents from the west side—can come together. These groups go to different churches, and their children attend different schools, but Gougeon believes that Belmar is a place where they "actually do have something in common." He feels a social obligation, as well as a commercial imperative, to make it so.

And what about the new residents who are actually living at Belmar? One new townhouse condo resident, Susan Mann, is an enthusiastic convert to the neighborhood. She "rarely needs a car except when she's doing business outside the area. And she recently got herself a Vespa scooter so she can tool around the neighborhood if she feels like it."[23] Tom and Janis Keating also live in a Belmar townhouse, which they love. But their grown son, Andrew, who lives with them and works in a Belmar restaurant, shrugs when asked whether Belmar is sufficiently cool. He says it is much better than the suburb they lived in before and it is great to be able to walk to work, but it doesn't really compare with LoDo in Denver.[24] (See Figure 8–17.)

Figure 8–17 The Keatings hang out at The Oven, a highly regarded (nonchain) restaurant and wine bar on Teller Street where their son, Andrew, is a pizza cook. They are eager to talk about how thrilled they are with their new urban/suburban life and quickly list the reasons why: first, the urban experience; second, the proximity to Denver; third, the neighborhood (the fact that there is a neighborhood); fourth, they can park the car on Friday night and not touch it until Monday morning; and fifth, all the amenities are within walking distance.

There are some populations who are marginalized and unwelcome, such as the rowdy teenagers who used to have free rein in the mall; the public plaza at Belmar was purposely designed to be skateboard unfriendly. And the elderly "mall walkers" were none too happy to lose their 72-degree year-round exercise route. Another group that is discouraged from hanging out in the new downtown is panhandlers. In 2004, Lakewood launched a preemptive strike against them by passing a city ordinance against "aggressive panhandling" of the sort often found in areas dominated by suburban form, where panhandlers approach drivers at red lights or in parking lots.[25] Of course, the need to address the issue of panhandling and street

vendors at all through public ordinances can be read as a sign of increased urbanity: the owners of malls, where all space is privately owned, have a right to prohibit a much larger range of undesirable behaviors.

Belmar is well on its way to becoming a real, adaptable, changing-over-time downtown for Lakewood. The blocks that were completed at the time of this writing, in 2008, comprise one of the most impressive examples of instant urbanism we have seen. However, like most of the larger retrofits, the edges are still either unresolved or less successful. We are eager to follow progress there over the next several years (and decades) to observe the ongoing process of transformation.

Chapter 9

Edge-City Infill: Improving Walkability and Interconnectivity

Joel Garreau's 1991 book, *Edge City: Life on the New Frontier,* gave a high-profile name to a new development pattern indicative of the radical shift of wealth production out of cities and to their peripheries. Building on Robert Fishman's seminal writings on "technoburbs" as a new kind of postsuburban urbanism for polycentric metropolises,[1] Garreau used the term *edge cities* to describe the agglomerations of recently constructed office towers, malls, hotels, and highways in suburban locations.[2] Despite their mix of uses and incorporation of relatively tall buildings, planners have derided them for epitomizing the worst attributes of sprawl: luring investment and jobs away from the city, inducing clogged traffic on arterials designed for through traffic, and forcing auto dependency even for internal trips due to the spread-out locations of buildings.

Figure 9–1 Tysons Corner, Virginia, shown here in 2007, exemplifies the development patterns associated with edge cities: superblocks dominated by vast surface parking lots surrounding large commercial buildings and shopping malls. The fringes of the blocks have smaller convenience retail and service uses lining the wide arterial roads.

However, Garreau declared their proliferation evidence of a revolution against conventional planning wisdom, in favor of a new generation of populist city making. He celebrated developers' abilities to come up with new market-driven configurations reflecting American values and preferences for suburban locations. With great wit, historical reference, wonder, and hyperbole, Garreau explained the inexorable forces and rational logic underlying this historic boom in building new urban cores outside of cities. The only reservations he expressed about edge cities concerned the quality of the places themselves. In fact, he admitted that they were rough around the edges and still lacking in many fundamental urban and communal qualities. However, he assured readers that Americans are smart cookies and would no doubt tinker with and improve them over time.

REDIRECTING EDGE CITIES

Indeed, much to the chagrin of the designers and planners that he angered, time is proving Garreau correct. Many of the 171 edge cities that he listed at the time are now over twenty years old. Some are thriving, such as Tysons Corner outside Washington and Perimeter Center outside Atlanta, and are engaging in retrofits in order to better accommodate continued growth while improving how people get around. (See Figure 9–1.) Others, like Sherman Oaks in Los Angeles and White Plains, New York, have been leapfrogged and are becoming more walkable and more urban in order to reposition themselves. Like the examples throughout this book, in both cases, the interventions are transforming entirely auto-dependent commercial and retail areas into more urban, more mixed-use, and more sustainable places.

What Garreau did not get right was his assumption that the traditional placemaking characteristics of the nineteenth-century city—such as pedestrian-friendly interconnected streets—had been superseded forever by edge cities' acceptance of auto dependence and dominance. In a cheeky piece for the *New Republic,* Garreau argued that Americans are much too practical and time pressed to walk when they can ride. "What purpose do sidewalks serve, after all, but to attract the dreaded skateboarder?"[3] However, the initial convenience of driving to a confluence of malls, office parks, and highways was short-lived and the jokes about having to sprint across a dozen or more lanes of traffic to get from work to lunch wore thin in the face of just that reality. Traffic congestion, impossible left turns, and parking lots at capacity have combined to diminish the convenience and speed of automobile travel in these environments.

It is perhaps the developers who most recognize the need for improvements to edge cities. Jonathan Barnett observed in 2002, "The Galleria District in Houston, one of the nation's oldest edge cities, has recently become a tax increment reinvestment zone. Property owners are taxing themselves to construct, retroactively, the streets and parking systems needed to support high-density development. The decision to take action was caused by competition from newer developments on the rapidly expanding edge of the Houston metropolitan area."[4] The Urban Land Institute published *Ten Principles for Reinventing America's Suburban Business Districts* in 2002. Its recommendations include "creating interconnected, pedestrian-friendly, mixed-use districts from existing isolated superblocks" and "creating pedestrian-friendly places that encourage interaction."[5]

These strategies are recommended both as a means to protect the value of current properties and as recognition of latent underused value. Large surface parking lots between buildings are increasingly being eyed as potential public green space (as at Century City, outside Los Angeles) or infill building sites (as at Cumberland Galleria, outside Atlanta). High-density residential has begun to balance the mix of uses and interweave the existing complexes, as at Addison Circle (outside Dallas) and Perimeter Place, a retrofit within Perimeter Center. New mixed-use town centers are providing pockets of walkability within larger edge cities like Legacy at Plano, while new rail stations are attracting high-density transit-oriented development into edge cities, as at Downtown Kendall/Dadeland (outside Miami) and the plans for Tysons Corner (outside Washington).

What is the competition that is driving gleaming, speedy edge cities to reposition themselves with more mixed-use and pedestrian infrastructure? It may be the 157 examples of walkable urbanism that Christopher Leinberger identified as hot real estate markets in a 2007 Brookings Institution study. To arrive at his parallel but qualitatively reversed list, Leinberger surveyed the top thirty U.S. metropolitan areas for places with floor-area ratios above 0.8 and up to 40.0 that are mixed use, compact, and regional-serving; generally between 100 and 500 acres in size; generally accessible by multiple transportation means; and walkable to nearly every destination once in the place.[6] In his new book, *The Option of Urbanism,* Leinberger echoes Garreau sixteen years earlier in saying that "the United States is on the verge of a new phase in constructing its built environment."[7] Contrasting "walkable urbanism" to what he calls "drivable sub-urban" development, Leinberger argues that the former commands a 40%

to 200% price premium for adjacent and otherwise competitive projects and represents 30% to 40% of the current market and considerably more in the future.[8]

Even Garreau's thinking has evolved along similar lines. In a 2006 article he predicted the "Santa Fe-ing of the World," or the rise of places of which the entire point is face-to-face contact.[9] He argues that shoe leather and donkeys gave us cities like Jerusalem. Railroads gave us cities like Chicago. Passenger jets gave rise to edge cities in otherwise inconvenient locations like Dallas, Seattle, and Atlanta. But today, the networked computer is enabling us to completely avoid going to workplaces, stores, schools, entertainment venues, etc., let alone to cities—except in order to interact with others face-to-face. He cites William Mitchell's observations on the hybridizations of book stores and coffee shops into Wi-Fi lounges as accommodation of the human desire for both individuation and association.

Now that digital technology has overcome Sante Fe's relative remoteness, the city's vibrant natural and urban setting has attracted significant numbers of the digitally savvy and mobile entrepreneurs who can choose to live wherever they want.[10] They have elected to locate in a place that affords them both high-speed digital connections and low-speed public and private hangouts along engaging, walkable streets with a strong local identity and highly civilized culture. They have not, by and large, chosen to live in anything remotely like an edge city. This is why even Garreau now recognizes the emergence of what he calls "Edge City 3.0." He writes, "The boom market in Edge City is going to be for retrofitting large pockets of civilization into what is now usually an auto-oriented monoculture."[11]

Designing Walkable Places

Many factors influence the degree to which people walk or drive.[12] In general, walkable places are convenient, safe, and interesting.[13] How do designers promote these characteristics in ways that support urban form?

- Block size is probably the most important factor in determining walkability because it also indicates interconnectivity. Block sizes and patterns vary considerably across the country. Not counting the streets, Portland, Oregon's 200' x 200' blocks are among the smallest and make for very convenient pedestrian routes. Many of Chicago's blocks are 330' x 660' and stretch the rule of thumb to avoid blocks whose perimeter length exceeds 1,800 feet. Larger blocks—unless they contain pedestrian cut-throughs—significantly inhibit walkability.

- The distances people will walk vary. They will walk further for their commute trip to work or school than they will to a restaurant during their lunch hour. By drawing quarter-mile and half-mile radius circles around activity centers, designers can get a good indication of what is within a five- to ten-minute walking distance. Most Americans will not choose to walk further than ten minutes except for recreation or their work commute.

- Density and mixed use also increase walking while reducing driving. At thirteen people per acre there is an increase in walking for shopping and a decline in automobile use. Eight dwelling units per acre is considered the minimum to support transit. Greenhouse gas emissions decrease as household density increases, and at an accelerated rate as workplace density increases, especially from thirty-five to seventy-five people per acre and sharply more so beyond that.

- Streets with people on them and with people overlooking them through windows promote safety. Buildings should front streets with windows and doors that put "eyes on the street." Designers can also increase density and transit in proximity to major pedestrian routes as ways of increasing the number of people on the street.

- Narrow streets or streets with medians are safer to cross than wide streets and are one of several traffic-calming techniques designers can use to slow traffic.

- Sidewalks, especially if they are tree lined or otherwise buffered from traffic, also increase pedestrian safety and comfort. Street furnishings with places to sit welcome pedestrians and enhance walkability, as does the sense of place conveyed by streets that are spatially bounded with enough symmetry in the pedestrian's cone of vision to feel like an "outdoor room."

- People are more likely to walk when they find the sights along the way of interest. Routes should afford pleasure both in their distant views, perhaps aligning with terminal vistas, as well as with details that reward close looking, as in textures, plantings, or shop windows.

- Attractive environments attract more people and more opportunities for building social capital. Designers should provide opportunities for pedestrians to greet and observe other people and their activities. Avoid monotonous or blank building façades, oversupplying parking, or spatially separating pedestrians, buildings, and cars from each other.

Figure 9–2 These views of the rapid development of Las Colinas, Texas, in the 1980s display the logic behind edge cities' auto-dependent form. Tall urban office buildings seemingly transplanted from downtown to "nowhere," they in fact cluster around the intersections of hub-and-spoke suburban highways with access to a significant airport. Reliant upon both roadways and electronic networks, their lack of need for proximity to other buildings is reflected in their autonomy from one another and lack of interconnectedness with each other, the street, or the neighboring shopping malls.

It's not only market-savvy coolhunters like Garreau and Leinberger who are advocating walkability. Environmentalists have long pointed out the degradation to air and water quality caused by our ever-increasing auto dependency.[14] More recently, public health researchers have recognized the negative impact this has on human health. Dr. Howard Frumkin and Dr. Richard Jackson, the current and former directors of the National Center for Environmental Health at the Centers for Disease Control, joined with Dr. Lawrence Frank, a chaired professor at the University of British Columbia, to document the wide range of health effects related to living in sprawl, including the impact of car emissions, accident rates, social isolation, and, in particular, reduced levels of physical activity. Recognizing the growing correlation between urban sprawl and human sprawl, they note that the percentage of obese Americans more than doubled, from 15% to 31%, between 1980 and 2000. What also more than doubled over the same time period is the number of hours the average American spent driving.[15] While there are plenty of other factors at work, subsequent research has shown that people who live in walkable neighborhoods have lower body mass indices on average than those in nonwalkable neighborhoods.[16] The collective implication of these studies is that suburbs are not quite the healthy places in which to raise a family as has commonly been perceived, nor are cities as unhealthy.[17] The implications for policy makers to change development regulations are profound—as are the obstacles.

Edge cities are not about to become handcrafted adobe villages anytime soon. As in Las Colinas, Texas, edge cities are predominantly built of glittering glass and polished stone office buildings designed in the 1980s. (See Figure 9–2.) Transforming them into walkable urbanism conducive to social and physical activity is a significant challenge, and over the years many experts have expressed skepticism.[18] Edge cities' auto-dependent infrastructure, their relative lack of strong political leadership, the rise of neighborhood resistance to change and slow-growth zoning efforts, and the demographically homogenous population that contrasts significantly with its urban core counterpart are the reasons most often cited for low expectations of edge-city urbanization.[19] As several researchers have noted, the residents of edge cities are even more wedded to their automobiles than suburbanites in general and other than being highly concerned about traffic congestion, draw "enormous equity from the high quality property and community they live in."[20] They see little benefit to change, and the authors of one study state, "This presents a picture of caution for planners and elected officials from Edge Cities. Edge Cities are a myth; better to think of them as Edge Suburbs. Tread carefully in propounding or even in relying upon the values of urban America to effect policy and programs."[21]

Additional challenges to retrofitting edge cities include both their dearth of public spaces and pedestrian-scaled infrastructure as well as the need to operate across multiple parcels. The high quality of place in Santa Fe is not a consequence of any single building. Rather, it is the result of the collective shaping of spatial and tactile experiences by multiple buildings in concert with the public realm. This kind of placemaking across multiple parcels necessitates public leadership and public-private partnerships—a return to exactly the kind of coordinated master planning, establishment of design codes, and infrastructure for walkability and interconnectivity that is anathema to the ad hoc, market-driven processes that gave rise to edge cities in the first place.

Can the benefits of walkability overcome these challenges? Can they make enough of a difference to make edge cities more sustainable? We document

several places that are trying. Addison Circle, Legacy Town Center, and Perimeter Place are introducing pockets of walkable urbanism on large infill parcels within edge cities. Although they are not retrofitting already developed property in the same way as the rest of the examples studied throughout this book, they are arguably indirectly retrofitting the edge cities themselves by altering behavior and reducing the VMT associated with them. Tysons Corner, Hacienda Business Park, Coliseum Central, Tukwila, and Downtown Kendall/Dadeland (discussed in detail in Chapter 10) are edge cities that are exploring various strategies to more directly and systemically promote retrofitting across multiple parcels.

THE EVOLUTION OF EDGE AND EDGELESS CITIES

So what exactly is an edge city? Some of the best-known examples are Tysons Corner, Virginia, outside Washington, DC; White Plains, outside New York City; Chicago's Schaumburg area; Costa Mesa in Orange County, California; and the aptly named Perimeter Center outside Atlanta. In 1991 Garreau identified 123 mature edge cities in the United States. In conjunction with those he identified as emerging edge cities, they accommodated two-thirds of all American office facilities and 80% of them only materialized since 1970.[22] To make his list, an area had to be perceived by the population as one place, have more jobs than people, and contain a minimum of 5 million square feet of office space and 600,000 square feet of retail space in an area that was not characterized as urban thirty years earlier.[23]

Some of the individual complexes in edge cities are ambitious, mixed-use designs that incorporated the progressive techniques of the day. Irvine, the

Figure 9–3 The 127-acre Greenway Plaza in Houston is an unusual edge city in that it is also a retrofit of sorts, having replaced 300 homes (see Chapter 2). Highly auto dependent, it was one of the nation's first large-scale, planned urban developments to emphasize greenbelts and extensive landscaping. By the early 1980s it had a 400-room hotel, an underground shopping mall, and a sports arena home to professional teams; it also housed over 12,000 employees in ten office towers. Its developer, Kenneth Schnitzer, was convicted then exonerated of fraud in the S&L scandal.

Houston Galleria, and Greenway Plaza adapted several of the popular strategies of modern urbanism then popular in downtown revitalization. (See Figure 9–3.) Well intended to separate people from fast-moving cars, this is an urbanism of superblocks with separated uses, separated transportation systems, and buildings separated from streets. A mix of mostly horizontal pedestrian linkages are then employed to connect the parts back together, including megastructures, pedestrian malls, raised walkways, plinths, plazas, and public art pieces.[24] Housing was rarely integrated into the mix, especially in the edge-city examples, and the pedestrian infrastructure generally stopped at the ring of surface or structured parking, discouraging connection to future or existing adjacent development except by car. In most edge cities, either the planned linkages were never built or they were never planned for in the first place. While there is often a planned regional mall or office complex that gives the area its identity, the development of nearby properties is generally ad hoc.

Century City, a forerunner of edge cities, was planned in the 1960s as a sleek second downtown for Los Angeles. However, overpasses that were supposed to connect the high-rise business district to new residential communities were never completed; the communities have become private, gated enclaves; and the council member for the area says, "Right now, Century City is a rabbit warren. . . . [To walk between uses] you have to know the secret path and follow a trail of bread crumbs."[25] However, the current condominium boom has spurred a greening task force of property owners, developers, and planners to look into how to integrate condominium towers into the office high-rises while adding the open space, trees, and pedestrian connections that residents will require. Instead of separating pedestrians from cars, residences from workplaces, and buildings from streets, the new plans call for tree-lined medians in pedestrian-friendly boulevards and sidewalk-fronted pocket parks between buildings. It has been called "one of the most ambitious attempts to remake a section of Los Angeles into a place where people could get to shops, restaurants and even offices on foot."[26]

Universally described as market-driven, there are nonetheless numerous policy decisions that, often inadvertently, significantly contributed to the development of edge cities. In some cases, they evolved from deliberate metropolitan planning attempts to decentralize development away from the core city, as in the Greater Toronto area suburban mixed-use centers policy of 1980. In more cases, edge cities resulted from the kind of less considered planning processes that Jonathan Barnett has aptly described. These range from federal decisions regarding the location of peripheral intercity highway intersections to local municipalities' tendency to overzone commercial land along such highways.[27] In addition to these factors providing ample developable cheap land with minimal regulation, the combination of the Tax Reform Act of 1981 and the gradual deregulation of the savings and loans institutions (S&Ls) resulted in unprecedented availability of cheap money in 1980s capital markets targeted for real estate investment.[28]

However, by the late 1980s overbuilding produced a glut of "see-through" office buildings in the sunbelt and insolvency for hundreds of S&Ls. Upon their collapse, the Resolution Trust Corporation (RTC) was charged in 1989 to "dispose of massive quantities of troubled real estate" and held the equivalent of fire sales on thousands of properties in the recession of the early 1990s.[29] For a period in the 1990s, the loss of Fortune 500 companies left White Plains, New York, with the highest office vacancy rate in the Northeast. Since then, the RTC's bargain prices have enabled some of the well-heeled new owners to make further, mostly mixed-use, investments in the properties and position them well for the market's later recovery.

Nonetheless, the point is worth reiterating that, despite Garreau's boosterish and well-informed depiction, the development logic that produced edge cities was not based on insatiable market demand. Although it has become standard practice to describe their popularity in terms of providing workspace that was newer, less expensive, safer, closer to executive housing, and closer to many workers' homes than that located in traditional downtowns, examination of their history suggests there was nothing inevitable about the form of the edge cities that the market delivered.[30]

Edgeless Cities

In fact, there are new studies refuting the dominance of edge cities in suburban office markets. Urban researchers Robert E. Lang and Jennifer LeFurgy argue

that edge cities have been leapfrogged by even less compact office complexes that they have dubbed "edgeless cities." Because office spaces do not require specialized infrastructure and many see little benefit from an upscale, higher-cost, edge-city location, large numbers of suburban office buildings have been built in low-density strips of commercially zoned property along highways or in other highly dispersed locations. Lang and Lefurgy argue that the quantity of suburban office space in these difficult-to-quantify edgeless cities nearly doubles that in edge cities.[31] The landscapes of Route 400 north of Atlanta or various routes surrounding Princeton, New Jersey, are prime examples of edgeless cities. These borderless swaths dotted with unconnected office complexes are continuing to grow and are even harder to retrofit.[32] Although the bulk of edge-city office space serves firms requiring some degree of proximity, it may be that edgeless cities reveal the flip side of Santa Fe: commercial enterprises that can locate wherever they want (especially because of the Internet) and that are choosing the least expensive places.

In general, edge cities have competed with edgeless cities by becoming more, not less, urban. In 1996, researcher William Fulton observed, "The easy money of the '80s is long gone. The financial and professional firms that filled the edge city office buildings are downsizing fast. Most significantly, the edge cities are becoming increasingly landlocked. They're no longer land-rich, emerging districts where office buildings or shopping centers can be built more quickly and cheaply than elsewhere. Competitively speaking, they're becoming more like downtowns."[33] This is also reflected in their governance structure. While most edge cities began in unincorporated municipalities, growing problems with traffic and inadequate infrastructure and services have necessitated the formation of various governmental and civic authorities—from transportation

Figure 9–4 The circular intersection that gives Addison Circle its name can be seen in the center of this aerial view of the project under construction. The diagonal railroad tracks divide the project from the pre-existing office park to the south. Mid-rise corporate buildings for larger tenant offices will line the tollway to the east, while well-detailed, brick, four- to ten- story, mixed-use, street-facing courtyard buildings frame the two main axes. "Texas donuts" (see Chapter 2) will fill out the urban residential neighborhoods behind them. At build-out, 28 of the public-private project's 124 acres will be for public use and another 25 acres for public right-of-way. It will house 4,800 units and 6 million square feet of mixed commercial space.

management authorities to business improvement districts and public-private partnerships. The physical manifestations of this process of urbanization have taken several forms, starting with the introduction of residences and walkable, mixed-use neighborhoods or town centers.

INFILLING EDGE CITIES

The insertion of urban residential and retail formats into edge cities has numerous benefits, particularly, and perhaps counterintuitively, in terms of mitigating traffic and reducing VMT. As already pointed out in the discussion of Cottonwood (Chapter 7), the addition of density and mixed use to areas of high trip attraction can actually reduce traffic congestion. The keys to making internal trip capture work are making sure the new uses substitute for what would have otherwise been external trips—and making sure the new trips are pedestrian friendly. This is particularly

true in suburban employment centers. Studies have shown that giving employees the opportunity to replace after-work shopping trips with pedestrian-based midday trips led to a doubling of transit use and increases in ride-sharing trips.[34] Also, by providing office workers with places to shop or socialize after work, the retail helps to stretch and thin out the evening rush hour. At the same time, the residential infill in edge cities reduces commuting lengths for those residents employed nearby and reverses the commute direction for those employed outside the edge city.

Addison Circle

Addison Circle and, later, Legacy Town Center, are prime examples of just such walkable, mixed-use infill in edge-city contexts. They are also significant steps in the refinement of a new urban development pattern for suburbia. Both are part of a series of projects in the Dallas area designed by RTKL Architects and developed by Robert Shaw and Art Lomenick.[35] In both

Figure 9–5 Addison Circle is designed to take advantage of the planned extension of the Dallas Area Rapid Transit system along the tracks that in this 2007 view separate the project, shown on the left, from the existing office park on the right.

Figure 9–6 For the most part, Addison Circle's public streetscape is successfully urban and highly pedestrian oriented. However, this view shows the lack of coordination between the designers' urban spatial definition and the traffic engineers' treatment of staggered signage as if drivers were covering long distances at a high speed on a suburban arterial

cases, the team was sought out based on the success of their redevelopment of the largely run-down and vacant State/Thomas area, a part of the Uptown Dallas neighborhood just north of downtown.[36] Applying the same new urbanist codes, public-private investment agreements, and transit-ready approach to the unwalkable edge-city environments of Addison and Plano was more of a challenge, but both projects have been equally embraced by the market and introduced further refinements to the pattern.

Fourteen miles north of Dallas, Addison is a first-ring suburb that became home to the largest concentration of business and retail activity in the Dallas area. With a daytime population of 160,000 that dropped to 14,000 at night, Addison in the early 1990s typified edge-city, auto-dependent, disconnected development patterns. Introducing a more urban pattern constituted a significant risk and was Post Properties' largest investment in a mixed-use environment and a significant shift for a company primarily known for garden apartment complexes.

City leaders in Addison agreed with Post that the success of Uptown Dallas could work further out of town. Their 1991 comprehensive plan called for a new center of town where residents could "live, work, play, and stay." When the Dallas Area Rapid Transit agency (DART) announced plans for light-rail to reach Addison adjacent to the last large undeveloped land parcel in the city and the North Dallas Tollway, city leaders seized the opportunity to give their city a town center and attract more residents. They established a public-private partnership with Shaw's Columbus Realty Trust and the site's landowner, Gaylord Trust. They did extensive visioning exercises, an economic impact study, and a market study, and adopted a new zoning code and development standards for what has become a multiphase 124-acre project. (See Figures 9–4 to 9–6.) The first two phases provided 1,300 apartments and were fully leased

street system signal the shift in the primary purpose of the street from providing high-speed mobility to cars, to providing high-quality access to shops and green space for pedestrians. (See Color Plates 41 to 43.) The result is a high-quality public realm that both the city and residents are very proud of.[39] The project received a CNU Charter Award in 2002. The public spaces have been well used during festivals, and pedestrian activity is only likely to increase when the DART station opens in 2010.

Legacy Town Center

Further up the North Dallas Tollway, the affluent, family-oriented town of Plano is home to one of the largest master-planned office parks in the world. Legacy Park is also the first office park to incorporate an infilled, mixed-use town center. (See Figure 9–7.) Its owners, Electronic Data Systems (EDS), liked what they saw happening in Addison Circle and reassembled the team along with the addition of Duany Plater-Zyberk & Company. The park's numerous corporate campuses provide jobs to over 45,000 people in a completely auto-dependent suburban setting. A study done prior to the completion of the town center showed that half the workers in Legacy would leave the office park at lunch to run errands, driving between two and five miles.[40] EDS recognized that providing an attractive and convenient onsite environment for these trips, along with a hotel and restaurants, would improve the value of its in-park locations and met with Art Lomenick, then of Post Properties, in 1997. He suggested that providing integrated housing would make it feel like a real place.[41]

Stephen Scott, manager of EDS Real Estate Asset, was quoted in 2004 as saying that workers' morale is "a huge issue" for employers and that "the

Figure 9–7 Legacy Town Center, shown under construction just to the right of the tollway, is a 150-acre insertion into Legacy Park, a 2,600-acre master planned office park in Plano, Texas, characterized by islands of geometrically organized office buildings and parking lots. The central axis through Electronic Data Systems' complex aligns with the lake that forms the centerpiece of Legacy Town Center.

within six months. In 2005, David Ward, executive vice president for Post Properties' southwest region, said they only had about a 4% vacancy rate and "The rent is well above the market because of the place we created there. It has stayed full through some tough market times."[37] Condominiums and townhouses added in later phases also sold very quickly, often before completion of construction.

Of particular significance, the city of Addison invested $9 million in high-quality infrastructure, three times the normal streetscape allocation,[38] to produce a pedestrian-friendly street grid and linear park system. Twelve- to fourteen-foot sidewalks, trees at 25-foot intervals, extensive brick paving, and the integration of public parks and public art into the

Figure 9–8 Unlike Addison Circle's focus on attracting more residents, the principal driver behind Legacy Town Center was the provision of 600,000 square feet of retail to serve the office park's 45,000 employees. Like Addison Circle, nightlife has grown, especially on Bishop Road (shown).

challenge of the suburbs is that they're dull. [Legacy Town Center] is the anti-dull."[42] However, it took some trial and error to figure that out. The retail developer, Fehmi Karahan, initially tried to lure national retailers with an upscale version of a strip mall, The Shops at Legacy, facing the six-lane Legacy Drive with surface parking in front. However, in 2006 the *Wall Street Journal* reported, "Retailers that pushed for surface parking turned out to be wrong. Today the hottest location isn't Legacy Drive but the narrow Bishop Road, where the stores are a sidewalk's width from the curb."[43] (See Figure 9–8.) In later phases, instead of providing mall shops and appealing to families, Karahan focused on providing an environment more like Addison Circle, with places for young professionals to socialize. He brought in Starbucks, trendy local and regional retail and restaurants, and an Angelika theater for art films. For the most part they were built in an open-air, two- to five-story urban environment linked to a 400-room hotel and focused on a man-made lake and town square directly opposite the gate to EDS's corporate campus.

The 2,700 apartments were principally built as a means to bolster the customer base for the shops and make the restaurants viable after hours. At first, Karahan Companies had trouble filling the 375,000 square feet of retail. The gradual construction of 1,600 apartments and townhomes and 550,000 square feet of office space in the project's first 75 acres achieved the critical mass needed to make it highly successful. The apartments and townhouses have proved very popular, especially with the younger, single, "new economy" workers and their preference for more urban lifestyles. A 2004 *USA Today* article cites several residents in their twenties happy with their walkable commutes and nightlife. Certainly the interest Legacy Town Center has spawned in numerous blogs and discussions of the bar scene in local papers testifies to its popularity. Plans were announced in 2005 to slightly more than double each of the uses by crossing Legacy Drive and developing the remaining 75 acres. Completion of the whole is expected by 2009 and includes a few eight- to nine-story buildings, a bus station, and a $3 million "dancing" fountain by the designer of the Bellagio fountain in Las Vegas.

Perimeter Center

In other edge cities, residential infill has occurred simply by adding either self-contained garden apartment complexes, or more recently, high-rise condominium towers in with the office towers. In Atlanta alone, as of November 2007 twelve new condominium towers were planned by various developers on

Figure 9–9 Perimeter Place's main street has four lanes of angled parking and feels more like a parking lot than a public street. It leads to The Manhattan, a luxury condominium tower, shown here under construction in 2006. A Super-Target big-box store with a surface parking lot sits immediately behind the retail shown on the right. Behind the camera's frame, a six-story perimeter block apartment building with retail on the ground floor continues the street wall of the main street. Each of these parts is a familiar development type; however, their juxtaposition is unusual and makes for a particularly hybrid form of urbanism.

Figure 9–10 Home to a superregional shopping mall (shown in part at the bottom of the image), several large strip shopping centers, and office parks, Perimeter Center Parkway Northeast just west of the mall extends uphill to become Perimeter Center's main street, running north-south and terminated by a high-rise, The Manhattan. A MARTA transit station surrounded by parking sits across the east-west parkway just west of the lower end of the main street. The project's high-albedo white roofs on 42 acres can be seen flanking both the main street and a secondary road that crosses at a planted traffic circle (the project's only prominent unasphalted open space). The retail buildings front onto the streets and back onto surface parking lots, except for the SuperTarget, immediately east of the high-rise, which fronts onto the equally supersized parking lot. The large building southeast of the traffic circle is a wrapped deck apartment building.

Figure 9–11 The on-street parking and street trees that buffer pedestrians from traffic, generous sidewalks, human scale, material variations, lighting, street furnishings, building street fronts, and attractive shade from the tree canopy make Legacy Town Center's streets very pedestrian friendly. But are they succeeding in getting the edge city's workers to substitute walk or bike trips for car trips?

parking lots or older office building sites in the Perimeter Center area and nine 40-story towers were to be developed by The Related Group in the edge city surrounding Lenox Mall. Much of this interest was spurred by the sell-out success in 2006 of the first condo tower at Perimeter Center, The Manhattan, a 27-story luxury tower at the apex of Perimeter Place, the area's first mixed-use infill project.[44] (See Figure 9–9.) Surprisingly, developers were initially resistant to the community's requests for more residential development within Perimeter Place.

With a name equally as incongruous as the term *edge city,* Perimeter Center made Joel Garreau's original list. Named for its location on Atlanta's perimeter highway, Route 285, the Perimeter Business District has 26 million square feet of office space,

4,000 businesses, 6 million square feet of retail space, three rail stations, more than 30,000 households and 40,000 residents, and 115,000 employees as of 2006 with expectations of 213,000 by 2013. On the site of two former three-story BellSouth office buildings, Perimeter Place has built a town center with four miles of sidewalks, 325 apartments, 227 high-rise condos, 500,000 square feet of retail space (much of it big box), and 14 restaurants. (See Figure 9–10.)

Like Legacy Town Center, the development of Perimeter Place between Atlanta's Perimeter Center mall and office park was originally driven by retail and restaurants. The developer, the Sembler Company, primarily develops shopping centers in Florida. Perimeter Place is one of a growing number of mixed-use retrofit projects that the company's satellite office in Atlanta has developed, gaining experience with urbanism each time. The Sembler Company's initial proposal in 2002 called for big-box stores on the 42-acre site in the landlocked edge city.[45] However, the Perimeter Community Improvement District undertook a Livable Centers Initiative study in 2001 as a means to reduce congestion and improve walkability in the area. The public input and plans by Urban Collage identified the site's potential for mixed use; Sembler agreed to reconfigure their plan and tenant mix and, after considerable pressure from the Dunwoody Homeowners Association, to incorporate housing. Jeff Fuqua, the company's president of development, had difficulty at first finding a subdeveloper for the tower. However, by 2004, as construction started, he predicted, "In five years, many more people will live in the area. It will feel much more like a city as the years go by, as opposed to what it is today—a large office submarket with a retail component and very little housing. People want to live in a pedestrian-oriented, retail environment."[46]

How Effective Are the Infill Strategies?

The Shaw/Lomenick/RTKL team's successful creation of popular walkable, mixed-use urban neighborhoods within unwalkable contexts has spurred more such projects in the Dallas area, including the transit village in downtown Plano, Village on the Green at the Galleria, and more. In each case, they have proven the existence of a strong market for urban housing and retail that targets young professionals and provides them with the urban public spaces and nightlife that allow for easy socializing and networking. Uptown Dallas proved there was a market for housing at urban densities with proximity to downtown and transit. Addison Circle proved that one developer could provide both the residential and the retail and that the market also existed adjacent to a planned light-rail stop in an edge-city environment. Legacy Town Center doubled the size and proved that it also exists within a planned and extremely spread-out edge-city office park even further from downtown. However, they also proved just how specific that market is and are often chided as examples of "Starbucks urbanism" or yuppie playgrounds. Instead of the suburban glorification of family life centered around a home that is completely segregated from the workplace, mixed-use suburban retrofits expand suburban choices by physically integrating workplace and lifestyle.

But are they integrated enough with their larger context to promote walkability outside of their boundaries? The spaces between Legacy Park's various campuses are so wide open that they are home to grazing bison. Knowing that it would be impossible to connect in all directions, RTKL and DPZ established buffer zones on three sides of Legacy Town Center and concentrated the development's massing on the front edge opposite the EDS headquarters.

Perimeter Center is much denser but remains highly fragmented. Even the transit station is disconnected from the Main Street/Parkway by a grove of trees. While The Manhattan's placement is prominent, it dead-ends the main street and limits interconnectivity. The east-west street is equally limited, with little in the context to connect to.

Bounded by an airport, a rail line, and the North Dallas Tollway on three sides, Addison Circle's interconnectivity is also limited. But the plan's location of public spaces as hinges and nodes along major existing routes increases its visibility and connection to the larger context. It also uses a traffic circle as a public green, but at a much larger scale that functions as a gathering space and with an iconic artwork that identifies arrival at Addison Circle. (See Color Plate 42.)

Employees in Addison, Legacy Park, and Perimeter Center are using their new town centers, but are they walking there? Sometimes. According to a study published in 2000 of three edge cities around Toronto that were deliberately planned with restaurants and shops to reduce car trips and increase walkability, only slightly more than half of the office workers walked when reaching an intracenter destination from their workplace. However, the authors concluded that insufficient compactness and a sterile street-level environment may have contributed to the aversions of office workers to walking.[47] It would also seem that the type of retail and parking available makes a difference. Sembler's hybrid combination at Perimeter Place and other projects of big box, restaurant, and residential takes advantage of current internal trip capture methodologies to show reduced external trips, but is this realistic with retail formats and parking ratios that are so clearly oriented to the automobile? Will Perimeter Place's ultimate contribution be its demonstration of the market for residential within Perimeter Center such that when more of the area infills with housing, the internal trip capture rate for the whole area will in fact be significant and both promote more walking and less driving?

EDGE-CITY RETROFITS ACROSS MULTIPLE PARCELS

Research suggests that Addison Circle and Legacy Town Center's inclusion of retail should be resulting in increased carpooling for the area as a whole. Similarly, the inclusion of housing in all three examples should be reducing VMT and congestion in the larger region. These are great subjects for future research. At present, all we can say for certain is that while edge-city infill projects expand housing choices and create walkable places, questions about their effectiveness at changing larger patterns have prompted exploration of alternative strategies for more systemic edge-city retrofits across multiple parcels.

The most extensive built example is Downtown Kendall/Dadeland, the subject of Chapter 10. (See Color Plates 44 to 46.) The edge city of Dadeland-Datran in Miami-Dade County, rechristened "Downtown Kendall," became an Urban Center District in 1999, with a new form-based regulating plan that has successfully encouraged private developers to interconnect adjacent parcels with through-streets, open paseos, and new squares and plazas, formed by grouping together required open space areas on contiguous parcels. Thirteen separate large projects have been proposed under the new regulations and the new urban street framework is emerging.

Other would-be centers have been harder to get off the ground, despite great promise. One such example is the Nassau Hub, the centerpiece of Nassau County Executive Tom Suozzi's vision for "New Suburbia," a hybrid smart growth strategy of "preserving those things that we love about the suburban life" while addressing the need to increase the tax base through growth, to curtail property tax hikes and the exodus of young people, and to combat traffic congestion.

It sits a few miles from Levittown, an open void of highway interchanges and parking lots, around the decrepit Veterans Memorial Coliseum, and flanked by other important Long Island institutions such as Hofstra University and the Roosevelt Field Mall. A 2005 planning study by FXFowle Architects suggested strategies for interconnecting the existing anchors and for filling in the voids. (See Figure 9–12.) Specific dire needs on Long Island are multi-family housing (85% of Long Islanders live in single-family houses, according to the 2007 Long Island Index) and intra-island transit that can connect locations *within* Long Island, rather than simply connect to New York City.

Planning is rare on Long Island, a region that is passionately attached to the idea of *not* being urban. A case in point is the town of Hempstead, where the Nassau Hub is located. With 760,000 residents spread over 142 square miles, it is the largest "town" in the United States. Perhaps in response to the lack of planning capacity, hopes for the Hub plan seem to have been reduced to a single $2 billion megaproject called The Lighthouse. The owner of the Islanders hockey team and a major real estate player, Charles Wang, proposes to build a new stadium and surround it with 5.5 million square feet of mixed-use development on a large 150-acre parcel formed by combining his land with 77 acres to be leased from Nassau County. At the time of this writing, it is unclear how the regional needs for better transit and affordable housing will be addressed by the scheme.

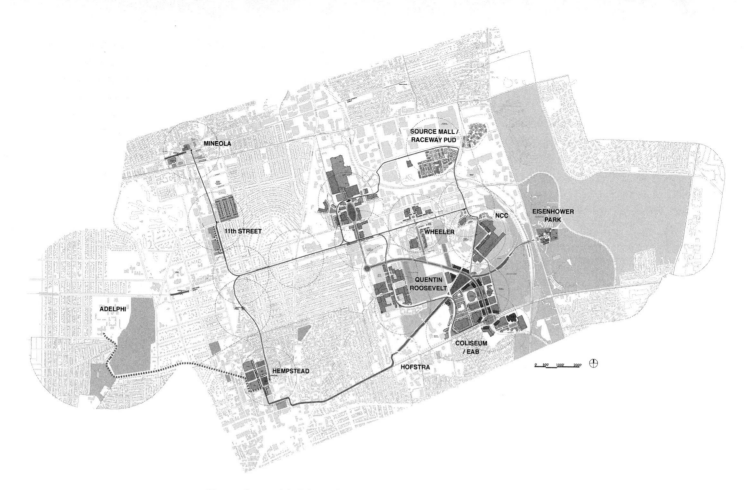

Figure 9–12 A 2005 planning study of the Nassau Hub in the Long Island town of Hempstead by FXFowle Architects identified numerous important institutions that are now isolated from one another, but have the potential to be interconnected by mass transit while the parking lot voids are infilled with new development.

Tysons Corner, Virginia, is the site of another proposed major edge-city retrofit based on mass transit. Very similar in size to Perimeter Center, Tysons Corner is bigger than the central business district of Miami and San Diego. It is also landlocked but in a corridor whose employment is expected to increase 63% over the next twenty years. It can only grow up rather than out and will require massive infrastructure improvements to do so. After many years of study and strong governmental support, a new 23-mile extension to Washington, DC's Metrorail to Dulles Airport was planned with four of the eleven stations at Tysons

Corner. Despite debates over tunnels versus elevated rails, the expectation had been to use new transit-oriented developments at the stations to introduce residents, walkability, and interconnectivity to the area.

State leaders were shocked when the rail line was denied funding in January 2008. Should it eventually go forward, it will be an important example of suburban density preceding transit rather than the other way around. If it has indeed been completely killed, it is a lesson in the high costs of acquiring land and threading rail through already well-developed locations.

Mass transit figures into all edge-city retrofits one way or another, but several additional strategies have also emerged for urbanizing the built fabric internal to these areas. Freedman Tung and Bottomley, urban planners and designers in San Francisco, proposed focusing new mixed-use development in the Tukwila Urban Center in Tukwila, Washington, around a new street to connect the existing mall with a planned transit station.[48] (See Figure 9–13.)

The Hacienda Business Park in Pleasonton, California, has 7.2 million square feet of office space, even larger than Tysons Corner and Perimeter Center. It also has a BART station at one end but remains frustratingly auto dependent due to the large distances between buildings. Less than a third of the park can be reached from the station in a ten-minute walk. The Environmental Protection Agency (EPA) has funded a study of extending access through the park with personal rapid transit. An alternative proposal accepts the inevitability of some degree of automobile commuting but tries to increase walkability and density through infill between the office buildings.[49] (See Figure 9–14.)

Figure 9–13 The Tukwila Urban Center is a 1,000-acre regional center located in a booming region with aging properties. The promise of a new rail corridor adjacent to the edge city prompted this proposal by Freedman Tung and Bottomley to insert a new mile-long walkable street lined with a lifestyle center, housing. and office to connect the mall, in the foreground, to the new station across the river.

Figure 9–14 Fifty-five percent of the vast acreage of Hacienda Business Park outside Oakland is taken up by surface parking lots. This set of diagrams from 2003 by John Ellis of Solomon E.T.C., a WRT Company, explores the possibility of freeing up that land for infill development by consolidating parking into new parking garages. The sequence shows existing building footprints, existing surface parking, potential parking garage sites, and potential parcels thus made available for development.

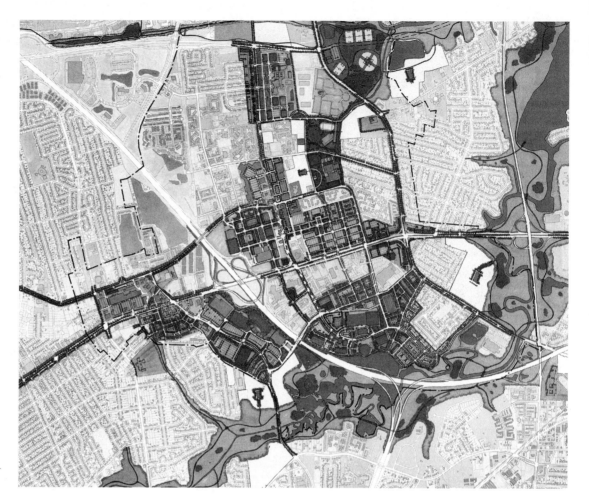

Figure 9–15 Urban Design Associates proposed both a series of walkable nodes on mostly greyfield sites and the improvement of two commercial strips, one into a boulevard and the other with streetscaping to seed further retrofitting of the 1,900-acre Coliseum Central area.

Retrofitting on this scale takes time, and although the Coliseum Central Master plan for Hampton, Virginia, by Urban Design Associates (UDA) was adopted by the city council in 2004, construction on the first phase did not begin until 2007.[50] The Coliseum area has more of the characteristics of a large fragmented collection of aging greyfield sites than of a posh edge city. While it is not booming as much as the other examples, it still has significant retrofit opportunities. Zimmerman/Volk Associates

found evidence of a market for approximately 287 new residential units per year while Economic Research Associates saw a market for redeveloping the three most vulnerable retail greyfield sites, plus an additional 82,000 square feet of retail, as well as between 91,000 and 148,000 square feet of small-scale office space.

UDA approached the area as a series of separate but related sites with different constraints and opportunities. (See Figure 9–15.) They recommended the construction of six new neighborhoods in various site-specific pockets, including several greyfield sites poised for immediate redevelopment to be retrofitted into walkable nodes with new, tighter street grids and smaller block sizes. The first of these, the Coliseum Mall, has since been demolished and is being retrofitted by Steiner + Associates into the Peninsula Town Center.

In addition, they made recommendations for minor improvements to the still-viable properties, such as the hotel district adjacent to the Coliseum, to both upgrade them and anticipate their eventual redevelopment. These include the following:

- Develop driveways as if they were streets lined with sidewalks and street trees.
- Terminate driveways with landmark façade elements.
- Convert parking lots into smaller, landscaped parking rooms.
- Locate parallel parking in front of stores.

THE FUTURE OF EDGE CITIES

Of all of the types of retrofits we have studied, the prospect of retrofitting edge cities is perhaps the most daunting. The DNA of the context is so utterly auto dependent. There is so little urban structure to connect to. In Scheer's terms, they are collections of campus tissues and should lend themselves to the kind of infill or redevelopment we have seen in the examples throughout this book. However, their enormous size so inflates the scale of the investment needed to effect change that it is tempting to write them off as future antiques destined to a certain kind of obsolescence once oil prices escalate or popular expectations for authentic urban environments pass them by. Urbanists have derided the artifice of edge cities ever since Garreau coined the term. The retrofits earnestly attempt to instill urban qualities and behaviors while simultaneously accepting, by necessity, suburban parking ratios in the form of "Texas donuts" and tidy new landscapes that lack the messiness of older urban places. Are these hybrid places hopelessly kitsch poseurs—or are they the seeds of a new incremental metropolitanism?

Within the increasingly polynucleated metropolis, edge cities already function as regional retail and office nodes. Do we need to reimagine what cities are so as to include these hubs of high-rises out on the highway? More importantly perhaps, we need to reimagine how to evolve edge cities into more self-sustaining centers and contributors to more sustainable regional networks.

This is where walkability and interconnectivity come back into play. While not a panacea, walkability contributes significantly to economic, social, and environmental sustainability. While walking is not absent from the suburbs, it does not serve the same social role it does in cities. Whether the model is Santa Fe or Rockefeller Center, walkable urbanism that builds social capital through compelling placemaking has both an intrinsic value and a particularly significant potential role in retrofitting the antiurban aspects of edge cities. One example of this in action is Downtown Kendall/Dadeland, discussed in the next chapter.

Chapter 10

Edge City Case Study: Downtown Kendall/ Dadeland, Miami-Dade County, Florida

Zoning the Creation of New Blocks and Squares over Multiple Parcels

Name of project: Downtown Kendall Urban Center District (more than 3,000 residential units, 350,000 sq. ft. of retail/commercial, 110,000 sq. ft. office, and a hotel)

Location: Kendall area of unincorporated Miami-Dade County, along U.S. Route 1 corridor

Year adopted: 1999

Planning consultants: Dover, Kohl & Partners, Duany Plater-Zyberk & Company

Street design: Hall Planning & Engineering

Client: Chamber South, Miami-Dade County Department of Planning & Zoning

What it replaces: automobile dealerships, parking lots, and low-rise apartment complexes around the Dadeland Mall

Size of district: 324 acres

Key features: use of form-based zoning to encourage the subdivision of large parcels and the creation of a network of pedestrian-serving streets and squares

SUMMARY

The retrofitted Downtown Kendall/Dadeland is emerging as a significant center as the Miami metropolitan area slowly evolves into a polycentric region. Transit is a strong inducement. When high-rise zoning accompanied new stations at the Dadeland Mall and an office park, it provided the impetus for adoption of a new plan and code coordinating the redevelopment of the multiple-owner, low-density parcels in between the stations. The special district zoning ordinance passed in 1999 by Miami-Dade County requires developers to build for pedestrians with regulations shaped to explicitly address street frontage conditions, the placement of through streets and paseos, and the configuration of open space. The zoning bulk allowances were not altered; instead, specific direction was provided to encourage the breaking up of the existing superblock platting and to provide shaded colonnades along the major streets. The regulating plans link new public spaces formed by aggregating individual properties' open-space requirements around key anchor points.

The ordinance, drafted by Victor Dover, Joseph Kohl, and Elizabeth Plater-Zyberk following a successful community visioning charrette led by their respective firms, resulted in a flood of developer applications. By 2004, more than 3,000 residential units and half a million square feet of commercial space had been permitted or built in the district, making the new urban block form discernable. Downtown Kendall demonstrates how an edge city can be infilled to improve walkability and interconnectivity between and through multiple parcels.

The primary retrofitting strategies at Downtown Kendall are as follows:

- Conducting a community visioning charrette, a model that has since become a standard tool in the county's planning department.
- Drafting a model form-based zoning ordinance for an urban district, in a location well served by transit.
- Establishing an innovative regulatory method for creating an interconnected network of pedestrian streets and squares over multiple parcels.

Figure 10-1 Street view in the Downtown Kendall special zoning district. Two new projects, the high-rise condos at Metropolis and the mid-rise mixed-use Downtown Dadeland, bracket a preexisting office building to form an aligned urban streetscape.

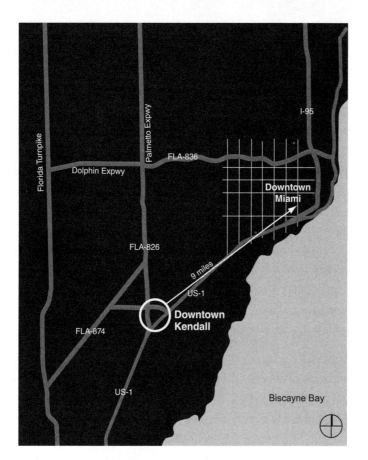

Figure 10-2
Location map.

In 2001, town planner Victor Dover began a presentation of his firm's work on the Downtown Kendall master plan by saying, "If you know this area, downtown Kendall sounds like an oxymoron. Its technical name is the Greater Dadeland Regional Activity Center."[1] At the end of the twentieth century, Dadeland was a typical edge city in an unincorporated part of Miami-Dade County, comprised of a 1.4 million-square-foot regional mall, strip retail, and scattered office buildings, surrounded by low-rise apartment complexes. It is located along the U.S. Route 1 corridor, about nine miles south of downtown Miami. (See Figure 10–2.) An elevated Metrorail line runs along the highway, with two stations bracketing the district.

The retrofitting process began in the mid-1990s when the local chamber of commerce deduced that redevelopment plans were brewing for a car dealership site across from the mall. The group, called Chamber South, realized there was a window of opportunity to build consensus on a more urban future for the area; they contacted the Miami new urbanist town planners Dover, Kohl & Partners to assist in envisioning that future. The area, also known as Dadeland-Datran because of the Dadeland Mall and Datran office complex there, had already been designated a "regional activity center" in the county's Comprehensive Plan. (In Miami-Dade County, the Comp Plan takes precedence over zoning.) The arrival of mass transit had the potential to trigger redevelopment at a much higher density and the zoning rights were already in place, but what form would it take?

After about three years of preparation and legwork, the group sponsored a charrette in June 1998, run by Dover, Kohl & Partners with Duany Plater-Zyberk & Company. It was funded by a consortium of stakeholders, including the Florida Department of Community Affairs' *Eastward Ho!* Initiative, Florida Power & Light, Miami-Dade Transit, South Florida Water Management District, and local property owners (including the mega-REIT Simon Properties, owner of the mall) in order to examine ways to improve mobility and to enhance use of the two new transit stations.

The boundary of the 324-acre charrette area was defined by three roads: U.S. Route 1, the Snapper Creek Expressway, and the Palmetto Expressway. In retrospect it would have made sense to include both sides of the Route 1 strip, but to do so was politically difficult because of NIMBY sentiment in Pinecrest, the newly incorporated, highly affluent district to the east of the strip highway. The master plan that resulted was designed to achieve three basic goals: (1) to transform the strips into arcaded boulevards; (2) to direct new development into perimeter block buildings; and (3) to combine 15% open space areas required for each parcel into shared, publicly

Figure 10-3 Before-and-after urban simulations produced by Urban Advantage for the 1998 charrette, showing how the harsh south Florida sun could be mitigated by arcaded streetwalls along Dadeland Boulevard. Note the figure on the far left, hot and sweaty on the edge-city sidewalk, brisk and cool under the shady arcade. Simulated images like these are highly effective in communicating the intent of form-based code provisions.

Figure 10-4 An evocative rendering from the 1998 charrette illustrating the potential to transform Snapper Creek, an engineered drainage canal, into an urban river. The waterway is one of several dug during the early twentieth century to drain parts of the Everglades and control flooding to assist agriculture in south Florida. A result like this is difficult to code and would require coordination from the local water district that, in the case of Downtown Kendall, did not ultimately materialize.

accessible squares. The challenge was how to achieve these goals across multiple parcels with myriad owners without curtailing as-of-right zoning or triggering Florida's strict antitakings laws.

The new name given to the district, Downtown Kendall, signaled the intention to create a recognizable, pedestrian-oriented downtown in the place of the amorphous edge city known as Dadeland-Datran. For the time being, both names are in use. (The confusion is exacerbated by the name given to one of the first postcharrette redevelopments: the seven-block project, built on the car dealership site, is called "Downtown Dadeland.")

The charrette team produced a master plan and illustrative drawings that suggested an urban character for a future downtown at Kendall—graceful, shady, colonnaded streets and squares and mid-rise perimeter blocks with red tile roofs. (See Figure 10–3.) The images, however, are illustrative only. As Victor Dover has pointed out, "As long as the urbanism is right…it does not much matter what the architectural vocabulary turns out to be."[2] The compelling graphics of the charrette certainly helped to build public support for the important steps that followed: giving the master plan some teeth in the form of a regulating plan and an ordinance to create a special district. Most evocative of all were images suggesting the transformation of the Snapper Creek drainage waterway into an urban canal. (See Figure 10–4.)

REGULATING AN URBANIZING FRAMEWORK

As Jonathan Barnett has argued, the dispersed nature of edge-city development is a direct response to zoning, and therefore the solution also lies with government action.[3] Joseph Kohl and Elizabeth Plater-Zyberk labored to innovate new regulatory language for the ordinance that could encourage the rebuilding of the district in forms that would fulfill the master plan vision. Several redevelopment projects were already in the works, and the consultants worked with the developers to make alterations that would permit the projects to conform to the intent of the ordinance, in the process helping to improve the efficacy of the ordinance itself.

Kohl and Plater-Zyberk purposefully avoided regulating through conventional zoning tools like FAR (floor-area ratio) and height limits, instead defining bulk in terms of number of stories. They produced three interrelated regulating plans. One plan defines subdistricts, with tapered story limitations to ease transitions to adjacent residential zones. A second regulating plan locates new "streets" of varied types. Rather than using setbacks, they introduced the tool of street types to require larger parcels to be "broken up" into smaller blocks by through-ways—some pedestrian, some for vehicle traffic as well—in locations that were roughly designated in the plan. The locations could not be precisely mapped, as that would constitute a "taking" by Florida law. The new streets and passages would remain privately owned, but with public right-of-way.

A third regulating plan addressed open space. (See Color Plate 44.) The strategy was to coerce developers regarding how and where they placed the 15% open space per parcel (already required as part of the Comprehensive Plan). The regulating plan aggregates chunks of open space from adjacent parcels in order to form larger, shared spaces. This last goal was encouraged by mandating the open space on each parcel to be attached to a defined "anchor point." The open spaces of multiple adjacent parcels, all attached to the same abstract anchor point, combine to create a larger square or plaza, although owners are responsible only for the design and construction of their portion of the whole. The area beneath the two-story colonnades required on main boulevards also counts toward the open space requirement.[4]

The effort of developing the ordinance for the Downtown Kendall Urban Center District, officially adopted in December 1999, was a radical departure for zoning and planning in south Florida. For the consultants it was instrumental in laying the intellectual framework for the SmartCode and other variations on form-based coding now being adopted by municipalities across the country. These new codes are replacing Euclidian zoning laws that have, in many jurisdictions, remained in place and largely unchallenged since the 1920s. The main innovation in the regulating plans, which differentiates them from conventional zoning and has become a hallmark of form-based codes, is that they work not by use and lot, but by the intersection of lot (which subdistrict it is in) and the type of street each side of the lot faces (street frontage).

This first experience was an extremely positive one for the planners of Miami-Dade County. In 2002, the county formed an in-house Urban Design Center to implement the charrette method. The planners hope to get ahead of the redevelopment curve by creating area plans and special district zoning ordinances for a series of other locations throughout the county. As of 2008, there have been more than a dozen subsequent charrettes. Some, like Downtown Kendall, are in designated "activity centers"; others were conducted in response to requests from communities for better local planning. (See Figure 10–6.) The overarching planning goal is to encourage higher-density development, both in terms of population and built

Figure 10-5 Snapper Creek in 2006 as higher-density retrofits replace low-density garden apartments on the north side of the canal. The new buildings developed thus far do acknowledge the water's edge more actively than their predecessors. "Back of the house" parking decks and service areas for Dadeland Mall, however, continue to define the southern edge.

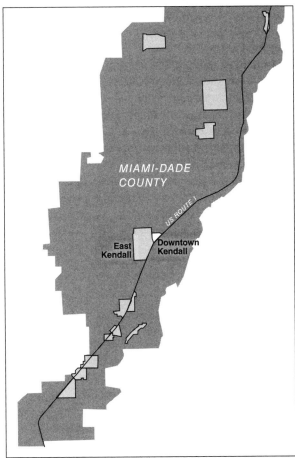

Figure 10-6 Since 1998 a dozen similar charrettes have taken place in the region, many along the north-south U.S. Route 1 corridor. They have been led by the Miami-Dade County Urban Design Center, following the methodology pioneered at Downtown Kendall. One of the most recent area plan charrettes was for East Kendall, the largely residential neighborhood to the east and south of Downtown Kendall. (Source: Miami-Dade County Urban Design Center.)

area, at these centers or nodes, many of which are transit-served, in order to defuse pressure to expand the boundaries of the county's urbanized areas.[5]

The response from the development community to the new code was astonishing, even for condo-crazed Miami. At the end of 2006, county planners had processed applications for thirteen substantial projects within the Downtown Kendall Urban Center District.[6] Two of the largest—and a study in contrast—are Downtown Dadeland and Metropolis at Dadeland. Downtown Dadeland hews closely to the intent of the code; it is comprised of 416 condos and 125,000 square feet of retail in seven blocks on a 7.5-acre parcel that used to be the Williamson Cadillac dealership. The perimeter block buildings are seven stories high, over two levels of underground parking (a high water table made construction a challenge). Metropolis at Dadeland, on the other hand, is a pair of glitzy, vaguely art deco towers, comprised of 267 condominiums with twenty-five different floor plans wrapped around and piled on top of large parking decks. The 25-story towers are built to the maximum number of levels the code allows. But although the form and style of the two projects differ sharply, they are aligned on the newly emergent street grid. (See Color Plates 45 and 46 and Figure 10–1.) Another grouping of new urban blocks has emerged north of Snapper Creek, formed by new mid- to high-rise apartment and condominium buildings. (See Figure 10–5.)

MORPHOLOGICAL ANALYSIS

The following series of figure-field diagrams illustrates the morphological transformations over a fifty-year period, from 1975 to projected conditions in 2025, on the square-mile area of the Downtown Kendall district. The preurban condition of large farm fields, irrigated by Snapper Creek and crossed diagonally by U.S. Route 1, strongly influenced the pattern of suburban growth. In the diagrams, one may read three types of suburban tissue: *static tissues,* or planned subdivisions; *campus tissues,* such as apartment complexes, office groupings, and shopping centers, including the Dadeland Mall; and *elastic tissues,* the most transformable type, found along U.S. Route 1 and, to a lesser extent, along Kendall Drive.[7]

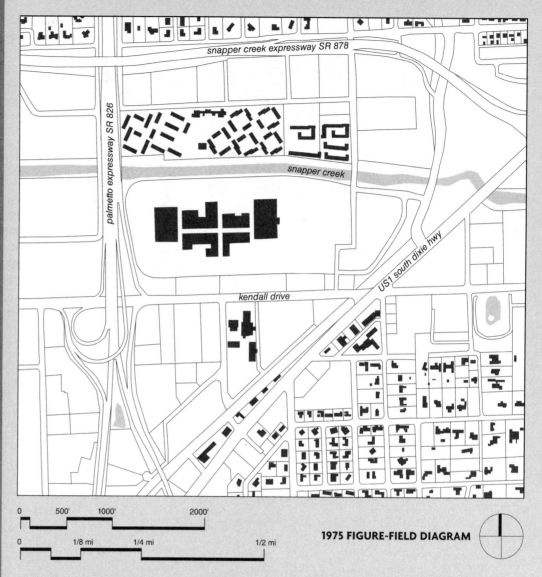

1975 FIGURE-FIELD DIAGRAM

Figure 10-7 1975 figure-field diagram. The Dadeland Mall was built in 1962 on a triangle of land formed by U.S. Route 1 and two newer state roads: Snapper Creek Expressway and the Palmetto Expressway. To the south of U.S. Route 1 the affluent community of Pinecrest, with a *static tissue* of large houses on minimum one-acre lots, was well established. *Campus tissues* of low-rise apartment complexes had been built across Snapper Creek, to the north of the mall, and more would come as remaining parcels of agricultural land were subdivided for residential and commercial development.

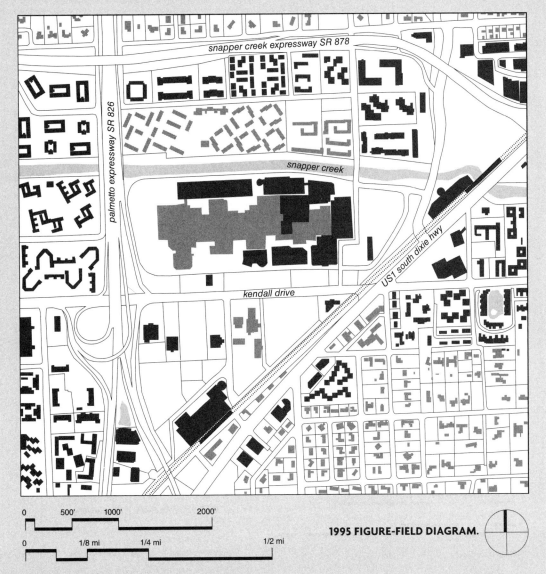

1995 FIGURE-FIELD DIAGRAM.

Figure 10-8 1995 figure-field diagram. By 1995, just before the Downtown Kendall charrette, the area had filled in haphazardly, as an edge-city node, with new apartment complexes and freestanding office buildings but with no new streets. The Metrorail transit line was constructed along a preexisting rail corridor that shadowed U.S. Route 1. Two stations were built in close proximity, bracketing the area, each with a substantial, multistory parking garage. The northern station services the mall, and the southern station links to the Datran office complex. It was at this point that Chamber South began to realize the potential for future growth in the area, and the necessity of planning for it.

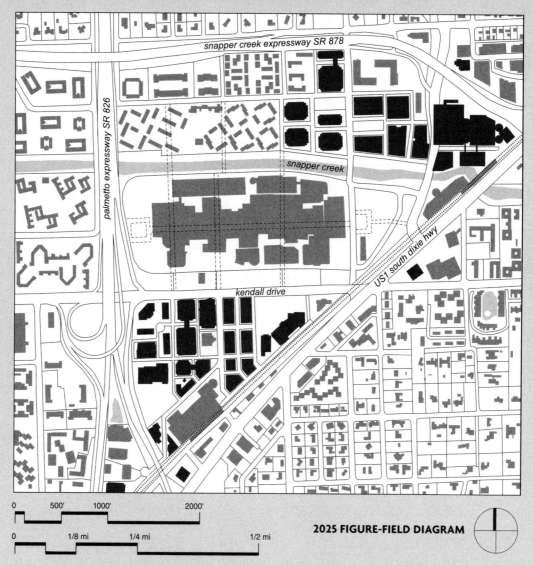

snapper creek expressway SR 878

palmetto expressway SR 826

snapper creek

US1 south dixie hwy

kendall drive

| 0 | 500' | 1000' | | 2000' |

| 0 | 1/8 mi | 1/4 mi | 1/2 mi |

2025 FIGURE-FIELD DIAGRAM

Figure 10-9 2025 figure-field diagram (projected). Since the Downtown Kendall Ordinance was adopted in 1999, the area has experienced phenomenal redevelopment growth as a participant in the massive wave of condominium development throughout Miami. Over 3,000 new housing units had been added by 2007, and, gradually, more will come despite a slowdown. This astonishing rate has permitted the rapid emergence of a new street framework in Downtown Kendall despite the nonparticipation of the mall property. Larger parcels (*campus tissue*) have been cut through with streets in the locations dictated by the ordinance so that a coordinated set of urban-scaled blocks is emerging. The new streets remain privately owned, but the public right-of-way is assured. Many of the new buildings are tall towers, rather than the mid-rise perimeter blocks that the original master plan envisioned, but they are placed on blocks with arcades along the streets. It remains a possibility (a probability, even?) that sometime in the future the mall property will undergo a major redevelopment, at which time the provisions of the ordinance will be triggered and through streets will be cut through, as has occurred at so many other regional mall sites.

DEMOGRAPHIC ANALYSIS: REAPING THE BENEFITS OF INTERCONNECTIVITY

By 2004, just five years after the ordinance, more than 3,000 residential units, 350,000 square feet of retail/commercial, 110,000 square feet of office space, and a hotel were in permitting or construction. The many private developers involved adjusted quickly to the new code. As Miami-Dade planner Subrata Basu asserts, "Developers can deal with anything you tell them as long as it is predictable…as long as it gives them what they need to make money."[8] So the planners are satisfied and the private developers, so far, are profiting comfortably. How about other stakeholders and users?

Many of the condominiums in the Metropolis towers were purchased by wealthy Latin Americans to use as second homes; their habit of visiting Miami for shopping sprees has made the Dadeland Mall extremely profitable.[9] Now they can walk to shop. Also, about 15% of the units were sold to people who work in the Datran office complex, so they too can now walk.[10] These "captured" trips are essential to realizing the benefits of urbanism, benefits that edge-city conglomerations do not provide. Another piece will be adding bus rapid transit along Kendall Drive. As it is, the Metrorail stations were developed to a suburban prototype, with large park-and-ride structures and weak pedestrian connections. The required colonnades are facilitating interconnections by providing continuous shaded zones for walking, although we found that some colonnades as built are awkwardly linked to the streetscape. (See Figure 10–10.)

Simon Properties, the mall's owner, participated in the initial charrette, but had a change of heart when the ordinance was adopted. They sued. As a reporter wrote at the time, "Both sides broke bread during a county-funded planning workshop in 1998. But a schism formed after zoning changes became official, prompting Dadeland to file a formal claim of property-rights violation. In taking that action, the mall opposed the Kendall master plan after the County Commission had approved it."[11] In essence, the owner was worried that the fortunes of the Dadeland Mall could turn and that it might once again become known by the zombie moniker "Deadland." County planners, on the other hand, feared that the lawsuit would doom the entire ordinance, but that didn't happen.[12] The mall's owner won a right of exemption from having to introduce through streets, as long as the property is rebuilt within a year of sustaining substantial damage (as in a hurricane). Otherwise, the ordinance would apply.

Figure 10-10 While the evidence at Downtown Kendall suggests that private developers welcome the types of restrictions included in form-based codes because the specificity can speed up the design process while lowering the risk due to the knowledge that neighboring properties will be built similarly, significant kinks remain in implementation. At the Downtown Dadeland project, the required arcades at the perimeter streets are elevated and interrupted by large ventilation shafts for the parking levels below. As a result, they function poorly as covered extensions of the public sidewalk. So while they meet the letter of the code, they do not fully succeed in meeting the spirit.

The coincidence of the plan and the housing boom of the mid-2000s contributed to the project developing faster and at higher density than expected. As a result, neighbors outside of the district, who supported the plan with the expectation that it would operate as a containment vessel for redevelopment pressure, came to fear that their homes would become targets anyway and that the affordability of the area would be diminished.[13] There was also concern about increased pressure on area schools, as the school district had not been part of the planning process (although, given the types of units that have been built, not many of the new residents are school-age children). The area of Kendall to the east and south became the site of a 2006 area plan charrette in part to address these not unreasonable NIMBY-like concerns.

The rapid pace of redevelopment has allowed Downtown Kendall to function as a vivid case study of the power of new codes to radically change the morphology of an edge city.

Chapter 11

Suburban Office and Industrial Park Retrofits to Recruit the Creative Class

Suburbs have a long history of accommodating the workplace. From manufacturing facilities to office parks to distribution warehouses, the forms of suburban workplaces have reflected the larger economy's shifts from a basis in agriculture to manufacturing to ideas and services. Today, the form of the suburban workplace is changing again. Developers and municipalities are converting outdated suburban office and industrial parks into walkable, mixed-use business districts that reflect both the changing nature of work in today's postindustrial economy and the habitat preferences of its leading workers, the "creative class."

Instead of physically, functionally, and stylistically separating the place of work from that of the home in strictly defined single-use areas, today's retrofits are designed to offer the wired, overworked knowledge worker the multitasking convenience of interconnected mixed use as well as its creativity-enhancing spaces for social networking and recreation. The incorporation of relatively dense urban housing, public spaces, and abundant retail and restaurants into suburban areas formerly limited solely to commercial or industrial activity deliberately blurs the physical boundaries between living, working, and playing. Instead of the compartmentalized worlds of the corporate Organization Man, today's mix of uses supports the fluid, hybrid work styles of the growing creative class. Live-work lofts, Wi-Fi networks in coffee shops, and spaces for casual and formal networking, from dog runs to power lunches, accommodate this class's redefinition of work as the exchange and creation of ideas and its permeation into all the hours and spaces of the day. In the process, the relatively generic, uniform, and auto-dependent spaces of the suburban office park are being retrofitted into unique, synergistic, and walkable urban places.

How deep is the trend? There are not nearly as many retrofits of industrial and office parks yet as there are of shopping centers and malls. In part this is due to the longer life span of office and industrial enterprises, the generally more durable buildings constructed for them, and municipal desires to maintain industrially zoned land. Generally, the sites that are being redeveloped are those with great accessibility: industrial zones on rail lines and office parks on major arterials with transit access. Although most of these sites were originally cheap land at the outer edges of development, away from residential neighborhoods, today much of their value stems from their altered position in the region. As growth has expanded outward, and residential has infilled closer to the arterials, these sites now occupy relatively central locations with desirably shorter commutes. In 2004, Steve Crosby, chairman of the National Association of Industrial and Office Properties, felt there was still more interest in redeveloping old warehouses and factories in cities' industrial districts than in suburban office parks, but said, "It's clearly come onto our radar screen."[1]

SUBURBAN INDUSTRIAL PARKS, OFFICE PARKS, AND CORPORATE CAMPUSES

In part, the low profile of these retrofits has to do with the overshadowed history of suburban workplaces.[2] The dominant narrative of suburbia has focused on its role as an escape from the places of work. The nineteenth-century beginnings of suburban development as we know it today—the leafy, patrician enclaves—were explicitly marketed as healthy, familial retreats away from the sooty, crowded conditions of industrialized cities. Yet throughout the twentieth century, most cities and many suburbs included a minimally serviced industrial district for heavy industry along a waterfront or a rail line on land deemed relatively undesirable for other uses. Already in 1915, Thomas R. Graham's book *Satellite Cities: A Study of Industrial Suburbs* documented how the availability of electrical power and trucking allowed manufacturers to build single-story factories with assembly lines on remote sites out of the cramped and more vertical cities.[3]

In the 1950s American residential and commercial developers began building 50- to 200-acre suburban "industrial parks" for light industry. Subdivided with provisions for streets, utilities, and building design guidelines, industrial parks were often incorporated into the edges of planned communities adjacent to highway interchanges. A 1957 bulletin by the U.S. Department of Commerce recommended layouts with forty-foot-wide culs-de-sac, fifty-foot setbacks, fifty-three-foot rail easements, and off-street parking to service the 1- to 5-acre lots within the superblocks.[4] Suburban communities eager to secure tax ratables (to assist with the costs of baby boom–related growth) welcomed industrial parks with tax breaks. By 1963, the lure of these amenities and, in many cases, nonunionized labor succeeded in drawing more than half of all industrial employment to suburban locations. By 1981 approximately two-thirds of all manufacturing activity took place in the "industrial parks" and new physical plants of the suburbs.[5]

In the 1970s as American manufacturing was on the wane, many industrial parks evolved into research parks and office parks. The most revered of these, and the first so-called "technology office park," was the Stanford Industrial Park, built in 1951 in Palo Alto, California, and later renamed the Stanford Research Park. It was designed like a university campus with parking behind the buildings and requirements for tenants for 60% of the lot to be open space.[6] While technology and research use grew significantly, parks for generic office use were more the norm and their evolution brought significant numbers of white-collar jobs out of central cities and into the periphery.

There are many factors that contributed to the high demand for suburban office space, including the tremendous expansion in office services jobs as American companies differentiated their products and expanded overseas. Advances in telecommunications, from fax machines to computing, enabled corporations to spin off back office work to cheaper space in the suburbs. Civil rights conflicts and reduced federal spending for inner-city social programs precipitated "white flight" from both central business districts and city neighborhoods. Corporate personnel departments at the time reported that they considered the workforce in the suburbs to be more educated and more reliable at lower wages. Increased suburban populations, high levels of automobile ownership, and the new interstate highway system all facilitated suburban commuting.

These forces spurred the creation of two new development types: the corporate campus for a single company and the 10- to 200-acre suburban office park for multiple tenants. Corporate campuses, like the 1954 General Foods complex in White Plains, New York, incorporated cafeterias, health clubs, gift stores, and walking trails to enable employees to remain on the grounds all day and presumably work longer hours; the clusters of signature mid-rise buildings around pristine greens conveyed a sense of privacy and privilege, akin to attending an elite private school. By the 1990s, several observers of development patterns noted that the locations of suburban headquarters were typically within a twenty-minute drive of the CEO's home and country club.[7] The convergence of executive-priced residential neighborhoods and high-end office space resulted in what real estate analyst Christopher Leinberger dubbed "the favored quarter," a pie-shaped wedge heading out from downtown that garnered the successive waves of suburban office development.[8]

The dot-com boom of the 1980s spawned a new generation of corporate campuses along beltways, especially in Silicon Valley and along Boston's Route 128. However, the combination of the tech bust in 2001 and the increasing use of overseas outsourcing contributed to the decline of many of these properties. After significantly downsizing, Texas Instruments, Hewlett-Packard, and Lucent have all recently sold corporate campuses to developers who expect to redevelop them as mixed-use neighborhoods. Not only is the land deemed more valuable for housing, but there is also increasing skepticism about the viability

of corporate campuses in today's more globally competitive technology market. Instead, leaner, "restructured" companies are looking more toward flexible, "plug and play" space adaptable to changing needs.

Older corporate campuses are also being retrofitted. One of the most notable is the 1957 headquarters for Connecticut General Life Insurance on 600 acres in Bloomfield, Connecticut. The Wilde and Emhart Manufacturing Research buildings were designed by Gordon Bunshaft of Skidmore Owings and Merrill. The former features courtyards and sculptures by Isamu Noguchi and furnishings by Florence Knoll. Widely published in architectural histories, the low-rise glass and steel building with sylvan views became an iconic symbol of the world of work inserted into a garden. However, employees in the nearly fifty-year-old, mostly glass building complained about its monotonous layout and uncomfortable thermal qualities. Slated for demolition in a redevelopment plan, its companion, the Emhart Manufacturing Research Building, was torn down in 2003 to make way for a golf course, 150 houses, 200 luxury apartments, 60 more residential units, and a 275-room hotel and conference center. Joe Mondy, a spokesperson for Cigna, the current owner, stated, "The property is evolving. It's going from simply a place to do business to a place where people can work, live and play."[9] However, after several years of campaigning that the modernist office park was on a par with older, historic structures in need of legal protection, preservationists succeeded in getting Cigna to agree to restore the Wilde Building and preserve much of the grounds. While office park retrofits are often welcomed for the same reasons as retail retrofits, their greater likelihood of having high-quality architecture raises the stakes for choosing preservation instead. Indicative of resistance to demolition of buildings like the Wilde Building, Yale University held a symposium in 2002

Figure 11-1 Office park development exhibiting typical characteristics: wide streets bereft of pedestrians, isolated office buildings, acres of parking lots, and few complementary uses. Hacienda Business Park, Pleasanton, California.

on "Saving Corporate Modernism." The retrofit of University Town Center in Prince George's County, Maryland, described in detail in Chapter 12, includes office buildings by Edward Durell Stone that were preserved while infill occurred around them.

Generic office parks are less likely to have employed signature architects and are often prime candidates for retrofits. The 31-building Koger Center in Jacksonville, Florida, was hailed as the first suburban office park in the country when it was built in 1957. With ample ground-level parking and easy highway access from its then-rural location, it is now known as Midtown Centre and was the subject of a redevelopment charrette with community members in early 2006.

Office parks and corporate campuses continue to be designed very similarly to industrial parks even though they no longer contain the dangerous uses that legitimately need to be kept at a distance from residences. They are typically limited access, single-use superblocks with elaborately landscaped setbacks and vast parking lots, equal in square footage

to the interior space of the buildings. The architecturally uniform buildings are typically distinguished simply by names like "Building 1," "Building 2," etc. In general, the older office parks are more likely to be retrofitted, because of their layout, age, and closer-in location; however, the extremely large setbacks of newer office parks have triggered infill proposals such as those for Hacienda in Pleasanton, outside San Francisco. (See Figures 11–1 and 9–14.)

By the late 1980s new suburban office space was increasingly concentrated in the edge cities and edgeless cities discussed in Chapter 9. Although they are difficult to systematically retrofit and offer poor to nonexistent pedestrian and transit choice, the Urban Land Institute argues that dispersed suburban business districts offer great flexibility for modest interventions that can improve interconnectivity and encourage pedestrian-friendly environments to develop.[10]

NONCONCENTRIC PATTERNS OF COMMUTING

In combination, industrial parks, office parks, corporate campuses, edge cities, and edgeless cities have contributed to a radical shift in where Americans work. By 1999, one-third of the top twenty-five U.S. central cities had less office space than their suburbs and the suburbs' share of office space had grown to 42%, up from 26% in 1979.[11] Are the available choices in suburban office space serving contemporary needs and are they sustainable?

The impacts of this shift on the environment and on various measures of quality of life have been profound. The typical twentieth-century model of urban development as a job-filled central core surrounded by rings of lower-density, mostly residential suburbs has been transformed into a more irregular pattern typified by Los Angeles and Atlanta, cities with multiple business districts and every variety of suburban office park, industrial park, corporate campus, edge city, and edgeless city. Supported by changes in transportation and telecommunications, the polycentric model has the capacity to provide a wider range of choices in formats, costs, and locations to both employers and employees, while reducing the length of suburban commutes. However, the one choice it does not grant—independence from the automobile—is becoming increasingly problematic for both employers and employees. The speed, convenience, and glamour initially associated with commuting by car have been replaced by frustration with congestion and unpredictable trip times. As congestion on suburban arterials increases, going out to lunch or out to a business meeting takes considerably longer than it used to.

In growing regions, tenants recognize that concerns about traffic's impact on productivity and quality of life cannot simply be outrun by moving to ever further out locations. The increasing cost of land and difficulty of finding unbuilt sites with good accessibility are driving many developers to look at the outdated condition of many closer-in suburban workplaces as prime opportunities for retrofitting and redevelopment. Similarly, suburban municipalities blessed with commercial tax revenues but burdened with clogged arterials are increasingly trying to encourage more mixed-use nodes, including the incorporation of residences into commercial areas as a way of reducing commute lengths and overall VMT. These driving forces are significant, but another factor that is assisting the reversal of the outward expansion of office space is the growing appreciation of the need for companies, especially in globally competitive fields such as information technology, to provide workplaces that are more attractive to the younger, skilled workers they need to recruit than they are convenient to senior management.

Advantages of Office and Industrial Park Sites for Retrofitting

- Locations on highways
- Locations on rail lines that may also include commuter lines
- Extensive infrastructure in place
- Generally flat and well-drained
- Extensive surface parking lots that provide infill sites and opportunities to improve water quality
- Aging buildings, especially industrial uses, that are likely to be outmoded
- Office parks likely to have mature landscaping
- Opportunities for "hip" loft conversions

Polycentric Atlanta: BellSouth in Lenox Park, Midtown, and Lindbergh City Center

In 1998, BellSouth, Atlanta's second-largest employer and a $23-billion-a-year telecommunications powerhouse, had 18,000 employees in 75 buildings scattered throughout the greater metro area. As Herschel Abbott, the company's vice president of governmental affairs, described it, "Like the city, we not only grew, we spread out."[12] In an ambitious reversal of these trends, in early 1999 the company announced the Atlanta Metro Plan, a consolidation of almost 60% of those employees from 25 buildings into three new, in-town, transit-served business centers on redevelopment sites. Citing the need for flexibility to shrink or expand, the company rejected ideas to build a suburban corporate campus or a ninety-story urban high-rise, opting instead for two eight- to sixteen-story towers at each of the three business centers, each with nearly identical—and easily leasable—large floor plates. In addition to building limited parking on-site, the company would build four parking garages dedicated to BellSouth employees at outlying stations of the MARTA rail system and increase access to transit from 30% to 85% of its workforce.[13] This commitment to transit was driven by the growing costs and frustrations over the region's traffic situation. Unpredictable travel times to and between the company's scattered sites were a problem and the lack of foreseeable solutions was a real concern. Metropolitan Atlanta had just become the first city in the United States to lose the right to spend federal transportation money on new road expansion projects due to its lack of compliance with clean air standards and failure to come up with an acceptable transportation plan to meet emissions limits. In addition, Hewlett-Packard had just canceled expansion plans in the region, explicitly citing traffic congestion and long commutes. In the context of the bad national press Atlanta received at the time, BellSouth's plan was celebrated as a triumph of smart growth and corporate leadership.

However, BellSouth's CEO, Duane Ackerman, insisted that the company was in fact acting in its own self-interest. Many of the company's space leases were due to expire shortly anyway and the company bet that owning rather than leasing made better business sense. Furthermore, the company expected to increase productivity both by consolidating workers and easing collaboration, and by the increased access to transit both for commute trips and trips between its business centers. However, perhaps most significantly, the company recognized that by focusing on improving the quality of life for its employees and providing the best-designed

telecom workplace of the future, they could improve recruitment and retention, critically important goals for high-tech businesses.

After mapping employees' home addresses, they discovered that workers were commuting from all directions but that the geographic center of the highest concentrations was to the north of downtown Atlanta, within Atlanta's "favored quarter" or most desirable commercial district. In a report on the Metro Plan commissioned by BellSouth, local newspaper editorial board member David Goldberg wrote, "The temptation to go farther north was tempered by two factors: the tenuousness of highway capacity and lack of rail service much beyond I-295, and the knowledge that many of the young, highly-skilled knowledge workers they hoped to attract from around the country preferred an urban environment to suburban living."[14]

After considerable NIMBY opposition, including several lawsuits from neighbors over parking and tree removal, the three business centers in Lenox Park, Midtown, and Lindbergh City Center were completed in 2004. The project is a retrofit at the large scale, consolidating dispersed suburban activities into more compact, more urban conditions. It is also a retrofit at the local scale of the centers, as each involved redevelopment and the provision of varying degrees of mixed use, urban amenities, and housing and transportation choices for employees. Lenox Park was built on the site of a former golf course and incorporated some of its open spaces as gardens. Lindbergh City Center redeveloped MARTA park-and-ride lots with structured parking and the first phase of a multiple parcel transit-oriented development. The Midtown center replaced an urban church with new buildings, a public park, and a commercial center. All of the building interiors feature state-of-the-art open offices and furnishings intended to foster flexibility, teamwork, and creativity. Two of the sites are immediately adjacent to MARTA rail stations, and the third is within a fifteen-minute walk of a station and is served by a BellSouth shuttle. Despite this proximity, BellSouth received criticism for incorporating large parking garages into the centers.

The significance of a high-tech company like BellSouth forgoing the administrator-driven logic of the favored quarter and instead privileging the preferences of its younger employees is extremely telling about the ways that large companies are now seeing urbanism rather than suburbanism as a way of improving the quality of life for their employees.

RECRUITING THE CREATIVE CLASS

The recognition that suburban office parks are no longer as competitive as mixed-use environments for attracting and retaining employees is in keeping with Richard Florida's theories about the rise of "the creative class."[15] A professor of economic development and public policy at George Mason University, Florida builds on the arguments of Daniel Bell and others about the significance of ideas and innovation in a postindustrial economy. He theorizes that human creativity has replaced raw materials, physical labor, and even flows of capital as the primary generator of economic value. As a result, a new class structure is emerging with profound impacts on communities and the value of places.[16] Unlike Bell, he sees its leaders not as technocratic managers, but as highly creative thinkers who fuel innovation, urban development, and American competitiveness. Florida argues that the creative class constitutes a distinct segment of society: the one-third of American workers whose jobs require them to creatively solve problems and advance new thinking. In his words, the members of the creative class are paid

not to execute a plan, but to tune it. However, given current and projected labor shortages of highly educated, digitally savvy "knowledge workers," the most sought-after members of this creative class can afford to be choosy about where they want to work. The crux of Florida's thesis is that the members of this class are increasingly selecting the area in which they want to live *before* finding a job—reversing the pattern of many of their parents and grandparents. As a consequence, companies that want to recruit them, especially those in high-tech fields, need to locate in places that appeal to the creative class. More to the point, Florida emphasizes that cities that want to recruit leading companies need to focus their economic development activities more on improving their quality of life and sense of place than on the more conventional strategies of offering companies tax breaks or investing in silver bullets like stadiums. Even in New York City, Mayor Michael Bloomberg established a permanent "desk for creative industries" within the office of economic development. Places provide the ecosystems that harness human creativity and turn it into economic value.[17]

Florida's extensive study of the early success of Silicon Valley and Boston's Route 128 in attracting investment, followed by that of places like Austin, Texas, and Dublin, Ireland, convinced him that the critical factors for attracting the creative class to a particular place are technology, talent, and tolerance—"the three Ts." In assessing places to live, he proposes that members of the creative class know they may not stay with one company for very long and therefore look for "thick" markets in technology. As creative thinkers, in many cases accustomed to the ambiance of the university research lab, they also strongly value networking and seek out places with deep talent pools. Finally, and perhaps most controversially, Florida found a significant statistical correlation between cities that attracted the creative

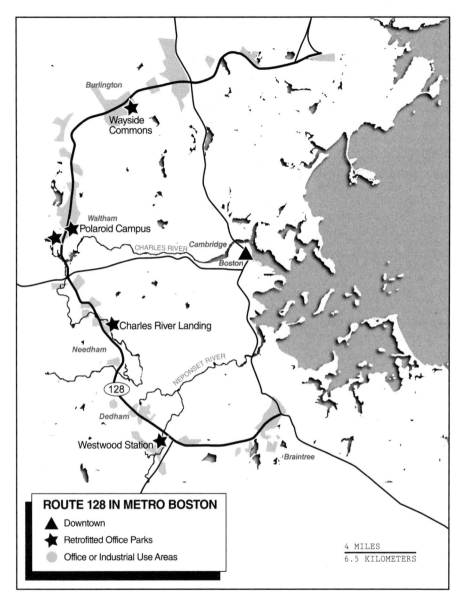

Figure 11-2 Numerous redevelopment sites can be found along Boston's Route 128, "America's Technology Highway." Many of the sites, such as Westwood Station, are along commuter rail lines that provide convenient, direct links to downtown Boston, creating a tremendous opportunity to mitigate decades of dispersed development patterns.

class and cities that ranked highly on both a gay index and a bohemian index. He explains this interest in places that not only tolerate diversity, but also celebrate it, in terms of the desire, if not need, for creative people to be able to comfortably fit in without conforming to conventions. The success of Silicon Valley owes a great deal to the openness of its bankers and venture capitalists to comfortably discuss loans with tieless nerds and tattooed entrepreneurs in a way that is unthinkable in more conservative and established financial environments. As he put it in a 2002 interview, "You cannot get a technologically innovative place unless it's open to weirdness, eccentricity and difference."[18] The implications of such statements for the physical environment extend from furnishing offices with foosball tables to locating the workspace in communities where employees can easily plug into a range of activities that provide them with the opportunity to validate their identities as creative people.[19] He argues that the creative class looks for places with a vibrant street life, diverse kinds of people, openness to newcomers, café culture, arts, music, outdoor recreation, and an inspiring natural setting.[20] In other words, they're seeking the kind of mixed-use, mixed-income, 24-hour, pedestrian-oriented, public space–focused environments in which cities have long nourished cultural creativity and which suburban retrofits are beginning to provide.

Critics have dismissed Florida's "creative class" arguments as a now-faded fad like the dot-com boom to which they were allied. However, the collapse of technology firms in places like Boston's Route 128 is spurring retrofits that buy into his arguments.[21] When combined with both the cost-driven aspects of retrofitting, blighted properties, dearth of cheap land, underperforming asphalt, and the smart growth incentives, the creative-class argument provides cities, developers, and designers with another persuasive rationale for retrofitting the suburbs. It shows up both in projects that are bringing residential and retail to suburban office and industrial parks as well as in projects that are bringing office space to sites that were exclusively residential or retail. (See Figure 11–2.)

Creative Campus: SkySong

An example of the latter is SkySong, under construction on the site of a dead mall at the intersection of two commercial corridors in Scottsdale, Arizona. Its promotional material draws heavily on creative-class arguments. According to the project's website, "It is a place where the architecture, lifestyle and amenities in and around the center stimulate and encourage creativity and new ideas.... SkySong will attract knowledge workers and corporations from around the world.... Oriented around shaded and landscaped pedestrian scale boulevards with street-level retail, public gathering places and open spaces, water features and bike paths, SkySong will serve the needs of businesses, research and technology industry and academia while building vital networks between university innovations, regional progress and the global technology industry."[22]

The Arizona State University Foundation and others are developing the mixed-use project on land leased from the city. It will house the ASU Scottsdale Innovation Center, one of ASU president Michael Crow's many initiatives to lead the growth of both the university and metropolitan Phoenix.[23] Envisioned as a next-generation technology park with incubator office space for university-based start-ups and others, the site is equidistant from downtown Scottsdale and the main campus. It is expected to accommodate 1.2 million square feet of office, research, retail, and hotel/conference center space, in addition to residential use, in several four-story buildings in a four-block

urban configuration with alley-served parking decks. The central intersection and plaza are anchored by an iconic shade structure that gives the project its name. Three hundred twenty-five one-, two-, and three-bedroom wrapped parking deck apartments occupy the block furthest from the intersection and adjacent to single-story courtyard apartment buildings in a residential neighborhood.

The incorporation of residential into spaces for retail and working is relatively new. The residents should play a vital role in supporting the retail and enlivening the development after hours. Shuttle bus service will connect the site to ASU and to downtown Scottsdale, and there are plans for light-rail on Scottsdale Boulevard, but it lacks greater connectivity to adjacent sites. It will be interesting to see whether its impact remains largely at the regional scale or whether this predominantly commercial retrofit will trigger further redevelopment along the busy corridor.

RETROFITTING SUBURBAN WORKPLACES

The desire to recruit the creative class and the companies that seek them is the catalyst behind many retrofits of suburban workplaces, and it highlights the contrast between conventional suburban development's segregation of living, working, and recreation from the new developments' efforts to mix them. Florida views the contrast in terms of the differences between the stereotypical corporate team player chronicled by William Whyte in the 1950s as the Organization Man versus the creative class's networking entrepreneur. The Organization Man grew up in the Depression and placed a high value on the security of his nine-to-five job and the thirty-year mortgage on a piece of private property that it allowed. Whether caught in "the rat race" or pleased with his contribution to the collective work of the organization, suburbia provided him with a home as his castle: private, separate, and family centered.[24]

Contrast this to members of the baby boom generation who believe that work should be a means to personal fulfillment. The networking entrepreneur's personal identity is likely to be integrally tied to his or her "work"—but not to the specific series of jobs and project-based contracts. Enjoying the creative aspects of work, he or she is more likely to blur the old boundaries and play games at the office, network at the café, and telework at home. (See Figure 11–3.) "Casual Fridays," geeks as pop culture heroes, and the adoption of counterculture marketing slogans are further examples of what Florida calls "the Big Morph" whereby the creative class is "drawing the spheres of innovation (technological creativity), business (economic creativity) and culture (artistic and cultural creativity) into one another in more intimate and powerful combinations than ever."[25]

Figure 11-3 The work-to-home commuting pattern of the corporate Organization Man of the 1950s differs significantly from the fast-paced, fluid, technology-enabled work styles of today's creative-class knowledge worker.

The market has responded to the need for environments that are conducive to flattened social hierarchies, temporary teamwork, and multitasking with both mixed-use urban places as well as new hybridized combinations of uses from office lifestyle centers, residential lofts, and "spadominiums" (luxury residential condominiums incorporating spa services).[26] Municipalities are also increasingly recognizing the need to shift from focusing solely on making themselves kid-friendly or business-friendly, and instead encouraging the construction of these talent-friendly environments.

While SkySong is relying principally on new office space to create a talent-friendly environment, several other retrofits are introducing residential uses to existing suburban office space. At one end of the spectrum are projects like the Upper Rock District, Westwood Station, and University Town Center, which are radically urbanizing suburban office parks with predominantly residential, mixed-use infill. At the other end are less integrated insertions of single residential buildings into suburban office parks, revealing the trend to elide the distinctions between domestic and commercial space.[27]

Glass Box Lofts: Cloud 9 Sky Flats

One of the more unique examples of this is Cloud 9 Sky Flats in Minnetonka, Minnesota. It is a retrofit of a mid-1980s, shiny glass and concrete ten-story class-A suburban spec office building into residential lofts. (See Figure 11–4.) Facing townhouses and mid-rise office buildings with vast surface parking lots on three sides while overlooking a landscaped pond and freeway on the other, the site was not particularly conducive to attracting creative residents. However, its location on the freeway within Minneapolis's "favored quarter" gave the developer

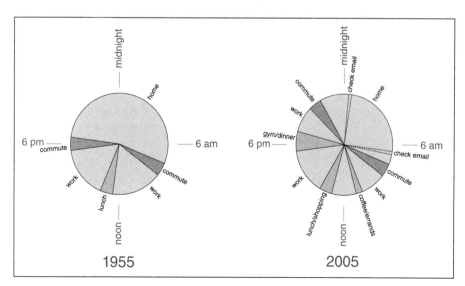

1955   2005

Figure 11-4 Julie Snow Architects and decorator Linda Miller converted Opus Corporation's 1985 spec office building into the stylish residential lofts of Cloud 9 Sky Flats in Minnetonka, Minnesota

hope when a major tenant pulled out in the midst of a depressed office market in 2004. Jerry Trooien of the JLT Group recognized that the space was worth more as housing. He hired Julie Snow Architects and decorator Linda Miller to design chic, minimalist, urban lofts with ten-foot ceilings, exposed concrete columns, open floor plans, flat-screen televisions, and wireless Internet and phone.

Targeted to entry-level home buyers, the decidedly hip and stylish units appeal to those who may live in the suburbs but do not necessarily associate themselves with conventional family-centered lifestyles. Although the conversion of older brick or cast iron warehouses and factory buildings into residential lofts has been going on in cities for decades—with tremendous appeal for creative people—Cloud 9 is one of the first conversions of a suburban workplace. The large, deep floor plates long favored for office buildings do not lend themselves easily to residential requirements. Cloud 9's long and relatively narrow floor plate easily accommodated units along a double-loaded corridor, but its post-tensioned concrete construction required that floors be x-rayed for cables before holes could be punched to accommodate plumbing chases. Sections of the

mirrored glass façade were replaced to provide each unit with at least some clear-glazed operable windows. And the 45-degree-angle facets in the plan, originally designed to increase the number of corner offices, provide great views out of those units—but also views into them from neighboring units. Despite these difficulties and the building's unusual history and location, nearly half of the 162 units were reserved in less than a month.[28]

Since then, the market has slowed and Kurt Williamson of the JLT Group says that if they were to do it over again, they would probably incorporate more mixed use, with a restaurant on the ground floor overlooking the lake, and leave the first few floors as office, only converting the upper floors to residential. As it is, the building is not mixed use nor does architect Julie Snow foresee the building inspiring further retrofits in the current market. Nonetheless, the project has demonstrated a market not only for urban housing in the suburbs, but in office buildings in the suburbs. Julie Snow says its most visible impact at present is in the view of the building at night where instead of parallel fluorescent fixtures, the varied residential lighting reveals its new inhabitants.[29]

Figure 11-5 Rendering of Upper Rock, a 2004 proposal for infill development around two existing office buildings in Rockland County, Maryland, following the principles of sustainable urbanism and including a prominent, vegetated sound wall along the highway. Proposed new uses include converting the office building to lofts, adding senior housing, and building a telework center and incubator space. The design was developed during a 2004 charrette run by Duany Plater-Zyberk & Company for The JBG Companies.

Lofts on the Interstate: Upper Rock

Like Cloud 9, the Upper Rock District, a 20-acre retrofit under construction in Rockville, Maryland, is also converting a suburban office building to trendy, "urban" lofts intended to appeal to the creative class's "worker-as-artist" persona. Again, the three-story building's long, rectangular floor plate lends itself to a double-loaded corridor layout. In this case, the ground floor is given over to live-work units. The live-work units are expected to further broaden the appeal of the project to the entrepreneurial members of the creative class—and, perhaps more importantly,

engage the building with the lively streetscape proposed to replace the current surface parking lot. Unlike Cloud 9, the lofts at Upper Rock are part of an ambitious and comprehensive office park retrofit.

Master planned by Duany Plater-Zyberk & Company (DPZ) for The JBG Companies, Upper Rock aspires to model a much-needed upgrade for everything that is "outta-date" about the thriving but congested and largely built-out I-270 "Tech Corridor" (also called "Rockville Pike"). The project's website describes Upper Rock as Montgomery County's first "post-suburban" community. Instead of long commutes to disconnected mid-rise office buildings,

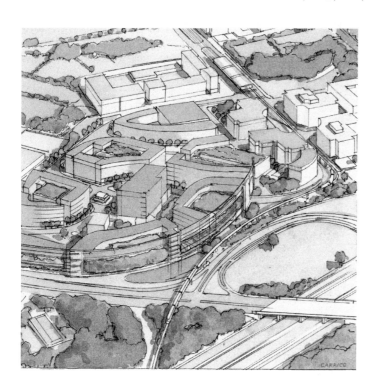

Figure 11-6 Simulations of the proposed conversion of a low-rise office building at Upper Rock into residential lofts, followed by the introduction of new infill buildings and streets.

Why So Many Retrofits in Rockville, Maryland?

In addition to the Upper Rock District, Rockville is also home to Twinbrook Commons (a dramatic retrofit of a park-and-ride into a TOD) and Rockville Town Center (a redevelopment of its failed downtown mall, several adjacent parking lots, and stand-alone buildings into mixed-use urbanism). Is the confluence of so many retrofits a consequence of both Rockville's and Montgomery County's long-standing reputations for socially progressive policies and development, including requirements for inclusionary zoning and significant commitments to mass transit? The state's pioneering smart growth policies that redirect growth to existing infrastructure? The county's desire to reduce commute lengths that are exacerbated by its having more jobs than housing? The high cost and scarcity of developable land in both the booming metropolitan DC market and the corridor that houses Rockville's flourishing biotechnology industries? All of the above contribute to the "three Ts" that Richard Florida credits with attracting the creative class: technology, talent, and tolerance. These projects may be tapping into, rather than attracting, a creative class that's already in place.

Upper Rock proposes to build a walkable, transit-related, mixed-use, mixed-age neighborhood heavily employing green technologies and creative-class arguments. (See Figures 11–5 and 11–6.)

Located at the east corner of the I-270 interchange with Shady Grove Road, the site was agricultural until developed as the Danac Technology Park in 1970. Soon surrounded by office parks and strip malls, the eastern edge of the site borders King Farm, a successful and award-winning 430-acre new urbanist community founded in 1997. The site is less than a mile from the Shady Grove stop on the Washington, DC, Metro and will be within a ten-minute walk of a light-rail stop when the planned Corridor Cities Transitway is completed.

In 2004, JBG had already received permits to build two new office buildings and a parking garage but were eager to try for zoning approval to extend mixed-use development to the site. When they hired DPZ to run a charrette with community members in May of that year, a Kodak photo-processing plant had already been torn down; the older three-story office building remained and a new eight-story LEED-Silver office building for the federal General Services Administration had been built. Community participants' desires for green construction, non-chain-store retail, extensive public art, and affordable senior housing led to several innovative elements in the plan: a 1,500-foot-long, 50-foot-tall public art screen wall along the interchange intended to function as a solar collector, wind harvester, and gateway to Rockville; green roofs for most of the buildings and permeable pavers in the public spaces; and the development of a market building for inexpensive "incubator" local retail (perhaps modeled on those at Mashpee Commons and Seaside, Florida), as well as inclusion of a large restaurant near the project's entrance. The project will provide approximately 850 condominiums and apartments, plus 106 moderately priced units reserved for seniors in five wrapped parking deck residential buildings organized around a series of walkable streets, art-filled public spaces, and courtyards designed for social interaction. While the innovative elements promise to give the project a unique and intriguing identity, much of the success of the placemaking is riding on the ability of the five wrapped-deck residential buildings to produce a convincing urbanism and pedestrian scale.

Unlike many retrofits of comparable complexity, Upper Rock is not a public-private partnership. Although the city and county have been supportive and come through with the necessary permits, the costs are being handled entirely by The JBG Companies. Focused solely on the DC area and with extensive experience in owning and managing their properties, JBG views Upper Rock as a long-term investment and has been willing to accommodate the community's requests and address their concerns. As is typical of many retrofits, the principal fears are that the project will generate increased traffic and increase enrollment in schools. The developer hired consultants to analyze both concerns and determined that largely due to the anticipated creative-class market, fewer than forty school-age children are expected to live in the development. The traffic study compared the expected impact from the already-approved office buildings and from the proposed mixed-use project on a notorious nearby intersection and concluded, "Because the proposed Upper Rock District project is virtually all residential in an overwhelmingly commercial area, the rush hour traffic will flow against the prevailing traffic.... The projected traffic at Rte. 355/Shady Grove Rd. at the peak hour would be virtually unchanged with or without the project."[30]

As an example of redevelopment that accommodates sustainable growth without consuming undeveloped land, the project won two smart growth awards before a single spade of greyfield asphalt was turned. It's too soon to tell whether the project will live up to its promises, but explicit attempts to attract the creative class should provide great opportunities to test Florida's theses. Will the incubator retail succeed at particularly capturing women-owned small

businesses—as expected given the fact that most small businesses are women owned and the expectation that like the creative class, women prefer urban experiences with "eyes on the street"? Will the creative class use transit and work at home in accordance with the projections? Will the creative class accept retrofitted office parks and suburban commercial districts as viable settings for their lives?

RETROFITTING INDUSTRIAL PARKS

Developers retrofitting suburban industrial parks are asking the same questions. Industrial parks tend to offer more advantages for redevelopment than office parks. They are often on existing rail corridors with transit opportunities and the buildings are likely to be outmoded or abandoned and available relatively cheaply. On the other hand, municipalities are often reluctant to lose whatever industrially zoned space they have and developers may not be eager to contend with brownfield contamination issues.

Two industrial parks in Massachusetts were recently bought for redevelopment and illustrate very different approaches. Preferred Real Estate Investments (PREI) bought a 260-acre industrial park in Attleboro, near Providence, that had been a Texas Instruments (TI) manufacturing campus before the company contracted its operations. TI will continue to maintain operations in one building but left six vacant buildings on the site with direct access to a freight and commuter rail line and Route I-95, as well as easy drives to two airports. PREI specializes in the redevelopment of industrial sites and in addition to leasing the vacant buildings (including a wastewater treatment plant and a railyard building) is constructing additional commercial buildings intended to position the property as a mixed-use corporate campus. At the same time, they are infilling the site with upscale residential. They have contracted with Toll Brothers, the national homebuilder, to build luxury homes and condominiums on the wooded parts of the site. The residential and commercial uses are not integrated into a walkable, urban neighborhood, but the project does demonstrate the private sector's interest in accommodating growth in underused suburban industrial properties that no longer contain hazardous uses.

Instant Urbanism: Westwood Station

The public sector shares this interest and the large-scale retrofitting of the 141-acre University Avenue Industrial Park in Westwood, a suburb eleven miles south of Boston, into the "instant city" of Westwood Station is largely a result of proactive efforts

Figure 11-7 Out with the old and in with the new: removal of signage from the closing industrial park in Westwood, Massachusetts, soon to be replaced with the 4.5 million-square-foot TOD Westwood Station, master planned by Elkus Manfredi Architects for Cabot, Cabot & Forbes.

by the town. (See Color Plates 47 and 48.) The affluent town of Westwood, population 14,000, is known for its good schools, neighborhoods of single-family homes, and long-standing ban on alcohol sales ("dry towns" are not unusual in Massachusetts, where the bans have been used as a means to limit commercial development rather than behavior). The town's active promotion of a high-density, mixed-use center with approximately 1,000 condominiums and apartments and numerous liquor-serving restaurants, promising nightlife, is a radical change in direction for the elite suburb. It has been fueled by the desire to generate tax revenue by building a new transit-oriented neighborhood that will help the town meet the state's affordable housing laws while also improving both the water supply and connections to the I-93/I-95 interchange.

The park's 1.3 million square feet of industrial and warehouse space was built in the 1960s and 1970s and provided the vast majority of the town's commercial tax base. However, since the late 1980s, that base has fallen considerably. During the 1990s the town tried to revitalize the park with the ad hoc introduction of new corporate buildings, with some success. However, with vacancy rates in the park nearing 30%, in 2004 the town established an Economic Development Advisory Board. The town then approved three Mixed Use Overlay Districts (MUODs) created by the board to formalize a series of master plan, site plan, and building design review processes while stimulating a more coordinated approach to redeveloping the park as a transit-oriented, mixed-use development. (In Massachusetts, zoning decisions are made at the local town government level rather than at the county level.) The MUODs encourage new commercial, retail, and residential uses, but require that all new residences be located within a ten-minute walk of the existing combined commuter rail/Amtrak station.

In 2006, Cabot, Cabot & Forbes, the original developers of the park, after reacquiring most of the site, combined their expertise in commercial real estate with the retail expertise of New England Development and announced redevelopment plans for the site in accordance with the rezoning. The $1.6 million in tax revenue that the site currently generates is expected to multiply several times over when the site is redeveloped as the 4.5 million-square-foot Westwood Station, the largest (in square footage) retrofit by a single development entity we encountered in our research. In fact, it is being touted as the largest suburban development project *ever* in Massachusetts.[31]

The Elkus Manfredi Architects–designed plan, only slightly modifying the original street grid, establishes a Main Street leading from the station through a lifestyle center with approximately 300 residences above more than 60 one- and two-story specialty shops, leading restaurants, and cafés. It then transitions into an open-air mall with familiar, more family-centered retail, including a department store, two junior anchors, and more family-oriented restaurants for a significant total of 1.2 million square feet of retail. An additional 700 apartments and condominiums are placed a few blocks to the south of this street. As required by the MUOD, 12% of the units will be reserved as affordable units and another 5% will be for moderate-income buyers. A parallel street from the station will be lined with 1.75 million square feet of commercial office, lab and research, and development space. One or more hotels are also expected to join the mix, indicating the degree to which Westwood Station is being considered a destination, a significant node in the region, rather than a locally serving mixed-use neighborhood.

In fact, the topography as well as the resistance from neighboring areas to connected streets mean that Westwood Station may operate more as a regional than a local destination. On the surface, the decision to locate all of the new residences within a ten-minute walk of the transit station is a commendable idea. However, it also means that the new residents will be isolated from the rest of the town. Westwood appears to be treating the project like something to be kept at a distance rather than a welcomed new member of the family. David Manfredi, principal with Elkus Manfredi Architects, said that in addition to the limited physical connections to Westwood, some people are critical of the project's lack of cultural connections. This is a project that is approximately the same size as Belmar but with more office space and no attempts to bring in art or civic organizations. "The city could bring in a library, but it would have to evolve in its thinking first."[32]

The project is designed well with respect to natural systems. Looking out for the long term, Cabot, Cabot & Forbes are investing in a more sustainable central energy plant and initiated the project's inclusion in the LEED for Neighborhood Design pilot program. The project will replace sewered hardscape parking lots with more permeable surfaces and redirect storm water to recharge into local wells and the Neponset River, improving the town's water quality. In addition Elkus Manfredi brings a strong commitment to the design of walkable public spaces. David Manfredi says, "You design these precincts around open space. They are the anchors."[33]

Westwood Station is an example of the sort of "instant cities" we contend are necessary for the low-density suburban realm to be systemically retrofitted into a sustainable, polycentric metropolitan region. It will be a multimodal transit-served, walkable, dense destination neighborhood with a critical mass of housing, retail, and jobs. It will infuse Westwood with a new mix of youthful residents. Similarly, University Town Center in Prince George's County, Maryland, examined in depth in the next chapter, is a vivid example of infilling an office park to become a more vibrant, transit-served, mixed-use community.

Chapter 12

Office Park Case Study: University Town Center, Prince George's County, Maryland

Finishing a Job Started Almost Half a Century Ago

Name of project: University Town Center (240,000 sq. ft. retail and 610 residential units added to 1.3 million sq. ft. office)

Location: Hyattsville, Maryland, in Prince George's County

Year constructed: 1963–1971 (office park); 2003–2008 (retrofit)

Land planner: Parker Rodriguez

Urban design and streetscape design: RTKL Associates, Inc.

Architects: WDG Architecture (condos), RTKL Associates, Inc. (student apartments), and MV+A Architects (retail)

Developer: Prince George's Metro Center, Inc.

What it replaces: parking lots around three existing Edward Durell Stone office buildings

Size of site: Phase I—56 acres, Phase II—100 acres

Key features: transit-oriented infill redevelopment within an existing office park in an affluent black suburb

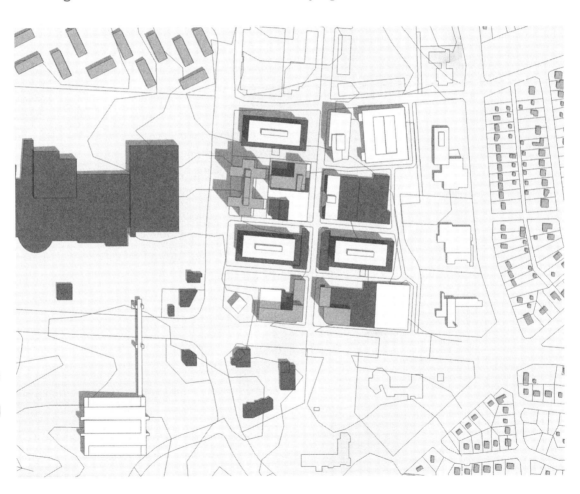

Figure 12-1 A mix of new uses infilled around three older mid-rise office buildings at University Town Center.

SUMMARY

University Town Center is the realization of a half-century-old dream to counter the patterns of suburban sprawl by building a high-density, mixed-use complex in a transit-served location near Washington, DC. In the early 1960s, developer Herschel Blumberg and his brother Marvin, just beginning their careers, asked renowned modernist architect Edward Durell Stone to develop a master plan for 140 farmland acres in Prince George's County, on the outskirts of the town of Hyattsville. With a deal in place to include a station stop on a planned Metro line on their property, they envisioned a program of high-rise apartment towers interspersed with office blocks set on a plinth containing amenity-rich plazas with escalators leading to a full retail concourse below. But in the end all that was built were three mid-rise office buildings tenanted with federal agencies, surrounded by parking lots. New Town Center had become an auto-oriented government office park.

In the ensuing decades, Prince George's County transitioned from blue-collar white to a majority black, affluent population, ready for new choices. When the Metro finally arrived in 1993 and the area around it was designated a Transit District Overlay Zone, Herschel Blumberg decided the time was ripe to revisit his earlier ambitions. He began a new master planning process that has resulted, in a first phase, in the refurbishing of the office buildings and the infilling of parking lots with a pedestrian-oriented street network linking an eclectic collection of new uses: shops, restaurants, a cinema, a supermarket, student apartments, and high-end condominiums. The resulting design aesthetic is haphazard, a far cry from the unified campus that Stone's office proposed in 1963, but the messiness is in itself revitalizing. It is a unique and authentic place, with a specific history that evokes a narrative of reinvention—qualities that appeal to Richard Florida's creative class.

The primary retrofitting strategies at University Town Center are as follows:

- Including a wide mix of uses, distributed both horizontally (new buildings filling in between the old) and vertically (such as apartments stacked above a supermarket).

- Capitalizing on the arrival of mass transit and new zoning encouraging higher-density development.

- Using shared parking strategies and new parking decks to create sites for infill buildings without demolishing the existing office buildings or losing any primary tenants.

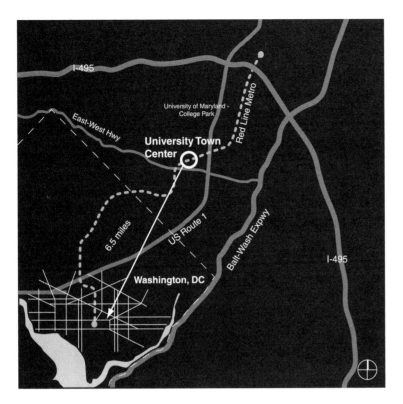

Figure 12-2
Location map.

After decades of obstacles, the owner of University Town Center is now realizing a long-standing vision for a new type of suburban center. Phase I occupies a 56-acre parcel along East-West Highway, near the Prince George's Center Metro stop in the Washington, DC, suburb of Hyattsville, Maryland. (See Figure 12–2.) The developer, Herschel Blumberg, of Prince George's Metro Center, Inc., has owned the tract since it was cut from a large country estate in the 1950s. In 1959 Prince George's Plaza, the county's first regional shopping mall (designed by Lathrop Douglas), opened to great fanfare on the neighboring parcel. Blumberg and his brother Marvin hired the prominent architect Edward Durell Stone to design a new suburban town center on their property. They were young, inexperienced, and extremely ambitious. As Marvin Blumberg

told the *Washington Post* in 1963, "We walked into Mr. Stone's office with our hats in our hands and our ideas spilling over. He listened to us and became our mentor for what we hope will be an answer to the critics of suburban sprawl."[1]

The brothers had originally hoped to hire Mies van der Rohe, but they found Mies's preliminary scheme problematic. He had proposed floor-to-ceiling plate glass windows for the apartment towers and Blumberg, the father of young children at the time, had the temerity to question the design as potentially dangerous. Herschel Blumberg says Mies haughtily replied, "That's the mother's problem."[2] So Blumberg turned to the less orthodox Stone, a highly regarded modernist and the designer of the Kennedy Center and New York's Museum of Modern Art, to design a high-density, modern, mixed-use complex. Stone's scheme was in keeping with the Urban Land Institute's progressive recommendations from that era that encouraged the latent urban ambitions originally accompanying many suburban formats.

Stone's 1963 master plan for "Prince George's Town" was a direct response to the problems of suburban sprawl as perceived at the time. The architects wrote, "The short-sighted exploitation of land around many of our cities has produced chaotic results. On the one hand is the proliferation of single family homes on small plots of ground development en masse....On the other are decaying clusters of small commercial centers. A recent innovation in suburbia, the shopping center, has added new problems with its emphasis on the automobile and the resultant proliferation of traffic and road building."[3] Their solution? A scheme with mid-rise office buildings, high-rise apartment towers, townhouses, a ground-level retail concourse, an extensive network of public pedestrian-only plazas over two to three levels of parking tucked into sloping ground, and an on-site rapid transit station. Amenities on the plazas were

Figure 12-3 Metro One and Metro Two in 2005, before completion of retrofit.

to include putting greens, playgrounds, sculpture gardens, and an ice-skating rink.[4] Reminiscent of the program for Rockefeller Center, its amenities would have likely attracted the creative-class members of its day.

In retrospect, however, the modernist urban design concept—of shunning streets and handling traffic underground coupled with the expectation of creating a highly activated, pedestrian-only series of elevated public plazas—was doomed to likely failure, in terms of both pedestrian activation and traffic management. Other examples from the era that were more fully built out, such as Greenway Plaza in Houston and Century City in Los Angeles, did not achieve expected results.

Three mid-rise Class A office buildings designed by Stone were built at Prince George's Town: in 1963, 1968, and 1971 (now called Metro One, Two, and Three). Though built in accordance with the master plan, the buildings ended up surrounded by surface parking lots instead of the intended urban bounty of plazas, sculpture gardens, shops, apartments, and towers. (See Figure 12–3.)

What went wrong? Additional development was stalled for decades due to changes in the marketplace, the rerouting of I-95 away from an anticipated location directly adjacent to the site, and a delay of several decades in the opening of the rapid transit line.

TRANSIT PROVIDES OPPORTUNITY FOR INFILLING WITH MIXED USE

When the Washington Metro stop finally opened in late 1993, Blumberg initiated plans to retrofit the office park, by then considered Class C space, and finally bring the mixed-use vision to fruition. A key government tenant was considering relocation to a new office park with better amenities for its employees. Blumberg engaged planner Jay Parker of Parker Rodriguez to develop a scheme to create a Main Street through the central north-south axis of the site and obtain the necessary rezoning approvals. Planning officials were eager to further the goals of the transit-oriented development overlay zoning district that had been established around the new Metro stop. When master planning was underway, the tenant not only agreed to remain at the site, but also funded a new office building, Metro Four, to house the National Center for Health Statistics. That building, designed by WDG Architecture, was completed in 2003.[5]

Also completed were numerous site and infrastructural improvements, such as new sidewalks, crosswalks, and a shuttle bus to the University of Maryland in nearby College Park. One major impediment to creating a pedestrian-friendly environment remains: East-West Highway. A little-used pedestrian bridge that links the Metro stop to the mall highlights the problem. Pedestrians routinely jump the fences on both sides of the highway and in the median and dodge high-speed traffic to avoid the inconvenience of using the bridge. Parker, who is also master planning the Belcrest Center mixed-use complex directly adjacent to the Metro station, hopes that traffic-calming measures will eventually be implemented to transform the highway into a multiway boulevard. Meanwhile, the Department of Transportation has responded to the dangerous

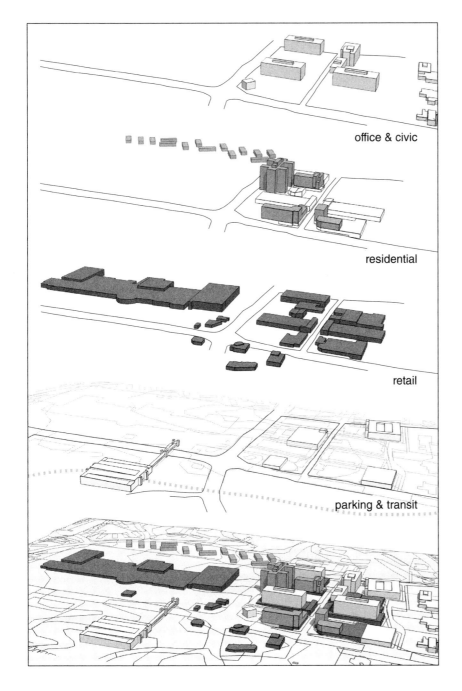

office & civic

residential

retail

parking & transit

jaywalking by raising the median barrier from four to eight feet high—a move that is more "pedestrian-defensive" than pedestrian-friendly.[6]

Echoing the 1960s concept, the current master plan calls for a mix of uses infilled around the renovated office buildings. The precast concrete cladding on the older buildings has proved durable and provided a significant reduction in heating and cooling loads when compared to glass curtain wall construction.[7] Office tenants housed in the older buildings include a wide range of government agencies, a post office, the local police department, a day care center, medical and dental offices, a music school, and a satellite campus of Prince George's Community College. A significant redevelopment challenge was keeping the 6,000 office workers in the existing buildings happy during the construction period, most critically by providing interim parking and also by mitigating the impact of construction dust and noise.[8] Considerable design coordination was required to integrate the below-grade parking decks and service routes around the site.

One new use is a sixteen-story apartment building called The Towers, marketed to college students. The Towers contains more than 900 bedrooms in a combination of two-, three-, and four-bedroom apartments. This innovative residential building type has been a resounding hit and was filled immediately with students from several nearby universities, including the University of Maryland, Howard University, and the Catholic University of America. When it opened, the lease rate for the apartments was phenomenal, indicating a sizable pent-up demand. The Towers had a 90% close ratio, "meaning pretty much everyone who comes through the door leases," according to leasing manager Stacey Lecocke.[9]

Figure 12-4 Exploded perspective diagram of the mix of uses at University Town Center and neighboring sites.

Also included are a fourteen-screen cinema topped with additional office space, three condominium buildings over street retail and restaurants, a hotel, a supermarket, and a below-grade parking structure topped with a public plaza. Different architects—RTKL, WDG Architecture, and MV+A Architects—were engaged to design the buildings. (See Figure 12–4 and Color Plates 49 to 51.) The strategy of using a variety of architects and styles allows for a more eclectic, and more urban, architectural expression of inclusivity rather than the conformity of suburban sameness or the exclusivity of the unified historicist styling of many mixed-use developments. We should note, however, that the eclecticism is paired with some disappointing lapses in construction quality.

Also unique is the public art program at the site. (See Figures 12–5 and 12–6.) The developer has chosen the patriotic theme of American history, manifested in a series of quirky public art pieces by Phillip Ratner and in the selection of new street names: Freedom Way, America Boulevard, Liberty Land, and Independence Plaza.

Figure 12-5   The new public plaza at UTC, above a parking deck built into the slope of the site, surrounded by an eclectic set of new and old buildings.

Figure 12-6   A sample of the patriotic public art by Phillip Ratner. His pieces are dotted throughout UTC.

MORPHOLOGICAL ANALYSIS

The following series of figure-field diagrams illustrate the morphological transformations over an eighty-year period, from 1940 to projected conditions in 2020, on a square-mile area that includes University Town Center. Over this long time period, one may discern how the area's growth was conditioned by the preurban fabric of large agricultural estates and dense village centers, crossed by country roads. In the diagrams one may read three types of suburban tissue: *static tissues,* or residential subdivisions (the oldest blocks, already built by 1940, have rear alleys); *campus tissues,* such as the apartment complexes, office park, and shopping mall built on farmland; and *elastic tissues,* found along parts of East-West Highway.[10]

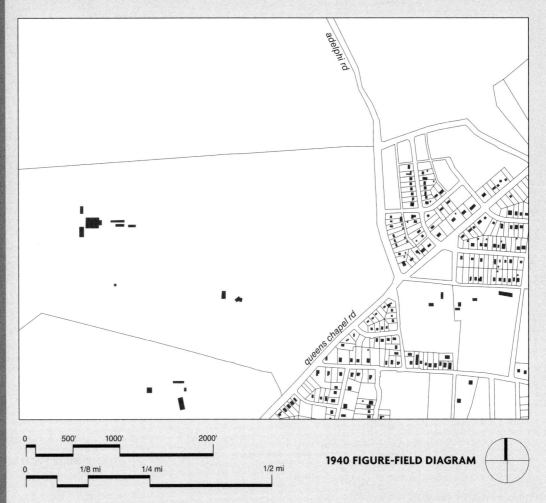

1940 FIGURE-FIELD DIAGRAM

| 0 | 500' | 1000' | | 2000' | |
| 0 | | 1/8 mi | 1/4 mi | | 1/2 mi |

Figure 12-7 1940 figure-field diagram. Farmland and large estates dominated the area north of the small town of Hyattsville. The largest was the Heurich tract, owned by a prominent brewer who was the second-largest landowner in Washington, DC, in the early twentieth century. U.S. Route 1, the primary road connecting the major cities on the eastern seaboard, was a few miles to the east. Some tracts around the estate already had been subdivided into compact single-family house neighborhoods. Narrow lots and back alleys characterize the static tissue of these prewar blocks.

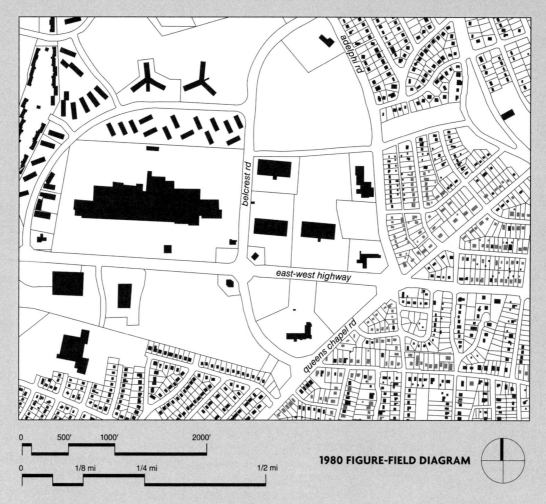

1980 FIGURE-FIELD DIAGRAM

Figure 12-8 1980 figure-field diagram. In the 1950s, a road was widened and extended into East-West Highway, which forms the southern border of the University Town Center site. The Heurich tract became *campus tissue*. A large portion was developed in 1959 as Prince George's Plaza, originally open-air but later enclosed. Surrounding the mall was a series of 1960s mid- and high-rise apartment complexes containing over 2,000 units. On the UTC site, to the east of the mall, three office buildings from E. D. Stone's master plan had been developed. The rest of the site was used for surface parking. To buffer the office use from the neighboring single-family house neighborhood, and to honor commitments from the developer to the community, a series of low-rise buildings for civic and religious uses were built—a public library, churches, a community center, and a synagogue. These buildings line the eastern edge of the property, forming a buffer and a barrier. The high density assumed in the 1960s master plan was predicated on two conditions that by 1980 had not been met: the routing of Interstate 95 along an adjacent wetlands corridor and the construction of a Metro station.

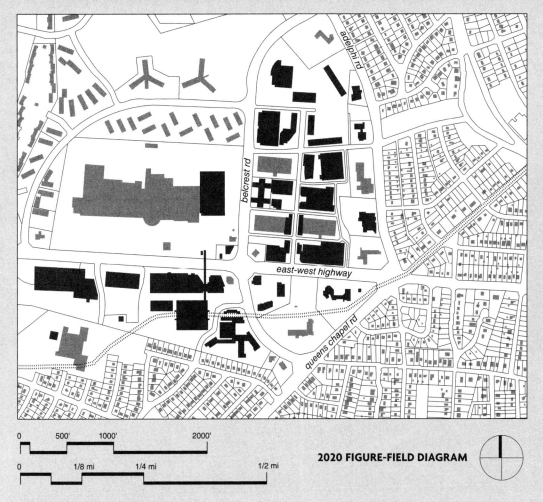

0   500'   1000'   2000'

0   1/8 mi   1/4 mi   1/2 mi

2020 FIGURE-FIELD DIAGRAM

Figure 12-9   2020 figure-field diagram (projected). The density of development in the district around the Metro station, completed in 1993 and finally fully integrated into the system in 1999, will have increased substantially. At full build-out, 600 residential units will have been added at University Town Center Phase I and another 260 units in Mosaic at Metro, a HUD-funded multifamily development with retail across the highway. The new streets crossing through University Town Center support pedestrian activity but do not connect through on the east and are not public ways (there are parking decks below). And so the site remains essentially a campus tissue. Through traffic remains on Belcrest Road, which was widened and upgraded with sidewalks. The link to the Metro stop is awkward, requiring a bridge crossing and passage through the mall parking lot. Nevertheless, a significant infilling agenda has been achieved. Blumberg has been guarded about plans for Phase II, to be able to respond to the market, so the diagram illustrates only one possible option. It is possible that some of the older, low-rise neighboring apartment complexes will be razed and the sites rebuilt at higher densities, should there be sufficient market demand. A newly created arts district along historic Route 1 nearby is expected to thrive.

Morphological analysis clearly shows how the series of "buffers"—churches, a public library, a community center—built on land donated by the developer in the 1960s to separate his project from the single-family house neighborhoods to the east is now an impediment to extending the street network effectively through the retrofitted site. Instead, the new "streets" remain just internal ways, although they are a tremendous improvement. (See Figure 12–10.)

DEMOGRAPHIC ANALYSIS: APPEAL TO THE CREATIVE CLASS?

Between 1940 and the present, the demographics of Prince George's County shifted from working-class white to majority black. Many of these residents are affluent (in 2000 the county was ranked 120th in the country in income), although there are poor neighborhoods as well. The middle-class residents have been underserved until recently, invisible to higher-end national retailers. Jay Parker describes Prince George's as "the ugly step child" of the region, ignored while development dollars flooded into adjacent counties. Most commentators agree that racism, "the big 'r' word," played a role, although county officials have avoided publicly saying so.[11] Blumberg, as a long-term local developer with intimate knowledge of the community, judged it a good time to attract upscale restaurants.

With the residential buildings he hedged his bets. A twenty-two-unit luxury condominium building sits next to the amenity-rich student apartment building, The Towers; each appeals to a different demographic group. (See Figure 12–11.) The Towers is seeding the area for future college-educated "creative-class" residents who are thrilled to be living off-campus in dormlike accommodations. Resident Stephanie Enaje enthused to the University

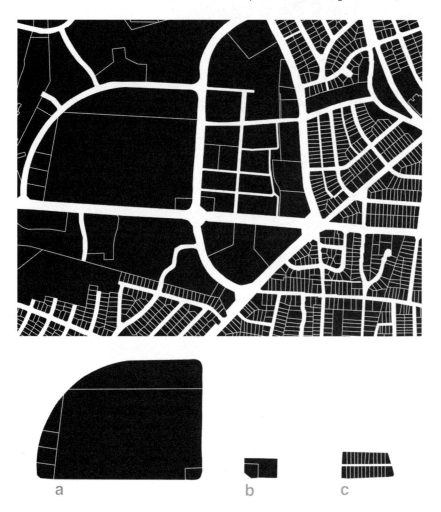

a   b   c

Figure 12-10   Diagram of block structure at UTC. The campus tissue of the office park, once similar to the mall next door, (a) has been broken up into smaller blocks (b) that more closely resemble the static tissue of the residential blocks (c). The fairly steep change in grade across the site, sloping down from the southwest corner to the northeast, and the string of buffer sites makes some connections difficult if not impossible to achieve.

Figure 12-11 The Towers at UTC, a 900-bed private "dorm" designed by RTKL housing students from several area universities, is just visible behind the zinc-clad Plaza Lofts' twenty-two condominiums, designed by WDG Architecture. Residents in both types of housing have ready access to the Metro and to nearby stores and restaurants.

of Maryland student paper, "It's weird that I live here...it's too nice. It's cool—the movie theaters and restaurants—because of jobs. I can just walk across the street."[12]

A creative culture is emerging throughout Hyattsville, not just at UTC. Older sections of town have attracted a significant number of working artists who have moved into prewar houses and have built studios in vacant buildings and storefronts along the Route 1 strip. Recognizing this phenomenon the Maryland-National Capital Park and Planning Commission (M-NCPPC) created an arts district in 2004, intended to keep the working artists in place in affordable studios rather than to create a gentrified gallery district. In other words, the district is for producers, not consumers, of art. These "creatives" also add to the allure of University Town Center. UTC isn't trying directly to recruit the creative class, but may in the end be more successful than many of the other retrofits we studied. It will be interesting to compare Westwood Station's relatively formulaic creation of place against UTC's relatively unique elaboration of place and see which accrues more appreciation over time. Florida would no doubt agree that in the end it's all about making successful places.

Epilogue

The Landscape of Incremental Metropolitanism in 2050

This book has introduced readers to a wide range of suburban property types that are conducive to retrofitting into more urban, more sustainable places. We have tried to impress upon readers the possibilities for positive change and regeneration of suburban areas and regions. Our enthusiasm is based on recognition of the changes that are already transforming the role and identity of many suburbs. Postwar suburbs that developed as "bedroom communities" at the outer ring of the metropolis now hold relatively central positions and have a new potential to attract a wider mix of uses and households. This is important not only as jobs continue to decentralize but also as households continue to shrink. Suburbs built for families with lots of kids face a future where 85% of new households are expected to be without children. Even more recently developed edge cities have tapped into this market for urban housing in suburban locations as they have begun repositioning in response to growing frustrations with traffic congestion. This frustration has led numerous communities to vote in support of funding extensions of mass transit systems into suburban areas.

But are current suburbs and metropolitan regions adequately prepared for the further changes to come? The U.S. population is expected to increase in 2050 by half again what it was in 2000. The question confronting suburban communities is whether to build on the systemic changes just identified and accommodate growth where it helps the region perform more sustainably; or to limit growth and risk economic decline as well as legal challenge; or to continue current expansion with sprawling development patterns that further stretch commutes, social segregation, and land consumption.

It will be a challenge for many communities to recognize just how intertwined their economic, social, and environmental well-being is with that of the larger region. We believe that instead of continuing to expand the edges of our metropolises, it is far more sustainable to redirect growth inward where it can help redevelop existing—but poorly performing—areas into more sustainable places. While our urban centers would all continue to benefit from revitalization, the fact is that from an environmental perspective, their inhabitants already enjoy the lowest-impact lifestyles per capita in the region. Instead, the focus for redevelopment should be those parts of the metropolis with the highest auto dependency and VMT, highest per capita greenhouse gas emissions and per capita runoff, and least diverse social, housing, and transportation choices. By retrofitting unsustainable suburban properties into networks of more urban, compact, and connected places we can incrementally retrofit the sprawling region into a greener polycentric metropolis.

Our enthusiasm for this vision is tempered by concern over how the hybrid character of most retrofits will affect their long-term performance. How great will reductions in VMT or possible future transit ridership be if retrofits continue to provide standard suburban parking ratios? What will happen to the "public" streets and squares controlled by private developers over time, especially as the retail ages and/or faces competition from additional retrofits? Will retrofits' populations and price points diversify over time? Obviously, it is too soon to tell and there is still much work to be done to advance redevelopment strategies. At present, we can only imagine what future generations of retrofits will be like and how they might overcome these questions.

As a complement to the book's documentation of existing suburban retrofits, we close with a speculative and hopeful vision of how these future generations might overcome the limitations of their hybridity and incrementally produce a more sustainable metropolis. As in Chapter 4, we will borrow Chester Liebs's device of describing a trip through time and space along a typical, though hypothetical, route out of town—only this time we will imagine that our journey takes place in 2050.

We start by returning to the sites of the first generation of retrofits, the earliest dating from the end of the twentieth century. As has already been explained, these retrofits were typically located on the sites of dead malls at major arterial intersections. Visiting in 2050 we can still see how they are generally organized around a reestablished street grid and tend to concentrate density and urban placemaking more or less at the center of the site, tapering down to lower-scale buildings and/or parking at the edges of the property so as to better fit into the context at the time. This is the case with Mizner Park, Belmar, and Santana Row, where the urban experience of the Main Street was originally in strong contrast to the surroundings, but also relatively isolated from them in order to establish the communal sense of an outdoor public room.

The frontage along the arterials was particularly difficult to "urbanize" at that time, with no residents willing to live along the strip and few retailers willing to locate at the sidewalk with a dual entrance to the parking behind. However, the success of the retrofits over time triggered further retrofitting of adjacent properties. Streetscape upgrades and rising land prices combined to transform the remaining surface lots along the arterial into parking garages wrapped with retail and residential above. Once more of the context had developed an urban character, the relative interiority of the central urban spaces became a liability and the retrofits engaged in some further retrofitting themselves to improve the connectivity and visibility of their Main Streets to the arterials. Nonetheless, many of the original national chain stores have moved on to newer developments. Local shops have replaced them and are able to do well providing neighborhood services to what is now an established and expanded community. Their "instant city" status long forgotten, the original residential units are now seen as authentic precursors to the rest of the area's retrofits. Despite their age, they are well maintained, and historic preservationists have vowed to resist any further modifications.

We soon come upon the second generation of retrofits lining the arterials in between the major intersections. Dating from the first decades of the twenty-first century, these are the other varieties of "underperforming asphalt" properties. More architecturally varied than the single-owner retrofitted mall sites, they include the former office parks, industrial parks, strip malls, big-box stores, garden apartment complexes, and residential subdivisions. Not only are their former identities all but obliterated, but also it is no longer easy to pick out the borders between them. The Surgeon General's 2020 warning that superblocks are dangerous to communities' public health led to the establishment of new roads in between parcels, providing far more interconnectivity and walkability between retrofits. The local municipalities have gained experience with taking ownership over streets developed privately and now the entire interconnecting street grid is publicly owned and maintained. Citizens recall with pride the marches through the streets in 2040 against privatization of the transit system.

The connection from the walkable retail streets to the transit station in these early retrofits is still relatively awkward. Sometimes it appears as if the engineers were more concerned with getting people from the train to the parking garage than with getting them to the surrounding development. Other times, it appears as if the developers were more interested in the density that proximity to the stations allowed than in investing in well-designed connections that would better encourage use of the transit. Nonetheless, even if we do have to hike across a bridge, it is not difficult to find our way and we hop on the transit boulevard's new express line.

While a few cities pioneered the return of the streetcar or light-rail to the arterial in the early twenty-first century, the momentum for mass transit in the suburbs accelerated sharply in 2015 after gasoline prices topped $10 a gallon. Increasingly, as the first-generation retrofits' TIF bonds were

paid off, cities were able to invest in new transit technologies. The new lines were routed with an eye toward retrofitting lower-density, closer-in locations—especially so as to affordably accommodate both employers and middle-to-lower-income households eager to trade in the pricey commutes from their "edgeless city" office buildings or starter homes on the suburban periphery. Stations were located at intersection nodes to maximize accessibility, and transfers of development rights were used extensively to build up dense, mixed-use job centers at the station nodes. Transit-led, this third generation features far better integrated transit stations, considerably higher-density development, location-efficient mortgages (for housing and office), and significantly reduced parking ratios. These features along with highly energy-efficient construction and renewable energy systems led to the surprising claims by formerly sprawling cities like Atlanta and Washington to have met both the 2030 Architecture Challenge for carbon-neutral buildings and the Congress for the New Urbanism's 2030 Community Challenge to reduce VMT by 50%.

Over time, the retrofits' popularity relaxed suburban residents' initial fears of the encroachment of "the city" into their midst. Form-based codes continued to encourage urban qualities but eased up on trying to limit stylistic expression. Passing these retrofits now, we can see how many of them compete to distinguish themselves as unapologetically urban, diverse, and modern, with architecture that looks forward more than it looks back.

In between stops we pass rows of urban housing fronting the boulevard while their backs taper down in density to meet the twentieth-century neighborhoods behind them. While some of these neighborhoods succeeded in their bids for historic preservation, many of them have also retrofitted in various ways. Some neighborhoods have sold out to denser redevelopment. Others have allowed granny flats, shared neighborhood business centers, and other modest changes to respond to the less family-centered population. The joint campaign by the secretaries of Energy and Environment to "connect up the culs-de-sac" failed to significantly expand road networks but led to more interconnected pathways for bicyclists and pedestrians.

Further out, the distance between nodes increases and the dramatic impact of the fourth generation of retrofits becomes evident to us as we remember the late twentieth-century landscape. Out here, the transit primarily serves existing towns rather than retrofits, often running on the old nineteenth- and twentieth-century rail lines. Instead of fostering densification, this generation of retrofits is engaged in radical regreening. Where cheaply constructed subdivisions and strip malls used to sprawl, we now pass intensive agriculture, tree farms for cellulosic biofuel production, wind farms, constructed wetlands harvesting storm water, new reservoirs, community allotment gardens, public parks, and nature preserves. The changes were initiated by the severe water shortages experienced in the West and South. Many metropolitan regions enacted sweeping changes in water management, the first of which was the condemnation of all buildings within 1,000 feet of streambeds. Property owners were allowed to transfer their development rights to the transit nodes, a system that expanded over time to allow entire subdivisions that remained either too close to wetlands, too dependent on aging septic systems, or too far from transit to sell out and be regreened. A few off-the-grid digital homesteaders remain on the larger lots and squabble periodically with the Corps of Green Infrastructure Engineers. But overall the mass movement to reverse sprawl has gone surprisingly well.[1] (See Color Plate 52 of the "LWARPS—we can reverse sprawl" plans for Atlanta to get a taste of what such a scenario might mean for a region.)

Even though the metropolis as a whole in 2050 is more populous than it was in 2000, it has cleaner air and water and is also far more self-sufficient. The retrofits have amplified both the urban and the green aspects of the metropolis, adding a greater variety of living and working choices at a variety of price points for the diversifying citizenry. Individual suburbs constructed on the premise of ample family households and supplies of cheap oil, cheap water, and cheap land have adapted well to the demographic, environmental, and energy challenges of the twenty-first century by incorporating retrofits. At the regional scale, the retrofits have improved the sustainability of the system as a whole by incrementally redirecting growth from the periphery inward and redeveloping underperforming suburban areas. Overlaying the region's more or less continuous sprawl, the retrofits have introduced a healthier and more integrated network of polycentric development and green infrastructure. No one can predict what this landscape of incremental metropolitanism will look like in yet another fifty years, but we remain optimistic.

ENDNOTES

Introduction

1 In our research we examined over eighty examples of retrofits and case studies. Samples were limited to projects that were redevelopments of existing greyfield properties or, in the case of edge-city infill projects, were within the boundaries of an existing edge-city office park. Aspects of this work have been published in Ellen Dunham-Jones and June Williamson, eds., "Retrofitting Suburbia," *Places* 17:2 (Summer 2005).

2 For a complementary development of this argument see Douglas Farr, *Sustainable Urbanism: Urban Design with Nature* (New York: John Wiley & Sons, 2008). For more details on the benefits of VMT reduction see "The 2030 Communities Campaign: Planning to Drive Less," http://www.cnu.org/sites/files/2030CommunitiesCampaign.pdf.

3 See Robert Fishman on "technoburbs" in *Bourgeois Utopias* (New York: Basic Books, 1987). See also Frank Hobbs and Nicole Stoops, U.S. Census Bureau, Census 2000 Special Reports, Series CENSR-4, *Demographic Trends in the 20th Century* (Washington, DC: U.S. Government Printing Office, 2002).

4 See Brenda Case Scheer, "The Anatomy of Sprawl," *Places* 14:2 (Fall 2001): 28–37.

Chapter 1

1 Sociologist Jean Baudrillard's theorization of simulacra proposes that the contemporary world is dominated by copies for which there are no originals, an observation that several authors have related to the architecture of suburbia. See in particular, Jean Baudrillard, *America*, trans. Chris Turner (London: Verso, 1988).

2 Examples from the popular press include the following: Karrie Jacobs, "The Manchurian Main Street," *Metropolis*, June 2005, 110, 112, 114; Thaddeus Herrick, "Fake Suburban Towns Offer Urban Life Without the Grit," *Wall Street Journal online*, June 1, 2006; John King, "Instant Urbanism, Citified Suburbs Becoming New Model for the Bay Area," *San Francisco Chronicle*, April 8, 2007.

3 Although on a per acre basis cities look like big polluters and energy users compared to suburbs, the story is reversed in a per capita view. See J. Holtzclaw, T. Clear, H. Dittmar, D. Goldstein, and P. Haas, "Location Efficiency: Neighborhood and Socio-Economic Characteristics Determine Auto Ownership and Use: Studies in Chicago, Los Angeles and San Francisco," *Transportation Planning and Technology* 25:1 (2002): 1–27. Although the building sector in the United States (as defined by Ed Mazria's *2030 Architecture Challenge*) emits 48% of greenhouse gases while transportation accounts for 25%, it is the interaction between the two that exacerbates consumption. A recent study by *Environmental Building News* found that for an average office building in the United States, 30% more energy is expended by office workers commuting to and from the building than is consumed by the building itself for heating, cooling, lighting, and other energy uses. For an office building built to modern energy codes (ASHRAE 90.1-2004), more than twice as much energy is used by commuting than by building use. See Alex Wilson with Rachel Navaro, "Driving to Green Buildings: The Transportation Energy Intensity of Buildings," *Environmental Building News,* September 2007.

4 Greyfield sites, known for their abundance of surface parking lots and aging suburban buildings, are commonly distinguished from greenfield sites (undeveloped land) and brownfield sites (former industrial sites, often with contaminated soil).

5 As Jane Jacobs pointed out in *The Death and Life of American Cities*, one of the benefits of older buildings is that they provide space for activities that cannot be afforded with the high rents of new buildings and therefore are often missing from new developments.

6 Reid Ewing, Keith Batholomew, Steve Winckelman, Jerry Walters, and Don Chen with Barbara McCann and David Goldberg, *Growing Cooler: The Evidence on Urban Development and Climate Change* (Washington, DC: Urban Land Institute, 2008).

7 Center for Transportation and the Environment (Atlanta, GA) and Lanier Parking Systems, Inc. (Atlanta, GA), "Atlantic Station Monitoring and Evaluation Update: Year Two Assessment," Draft, November 2006.

8 The rise in single households, the decrease in households with children, and the rise in aging and minority households in the suburbs are all well-documented trends contributing to increased demand for more urban housing options in the suburbs. See Ellen Dunham-Jones, "Suburban Retrofits, Demographics, and Sustainability," *Places* 17:2 (Summer 2005): 8–19, and Martha Farnsworth Riche, "How Changes in the Nation's Age and Household Structure Will Reshape Housing Demand in the 21st Century" (U.S. Department of Housing and Urban Development, 2003).

9 The master plan and replacement zoning for Downtown Kendall/Dadeland, in Southern Florida, was designed through a collaboration between Miami-Dade County's Urban Design Department, Dover Kohl & Partners, and Duany Plater-Zyberk & Co.

10 Questions of size and density are closely related to land prices. The higher the land value, the higher the density needed to pay for it and the greater the need to pay for structured parking. Fitting dense development and structured parking onto smaller parcels in suburban areas with zoning restrictions can be difficult. Andrés Duany estimates that it takes a minimum of 15 acres to establish a synergistic mix of uses and sense of place in a context without much to build on.

11 Similarly, Lee Sobel of EPA's Office of Policy, Economics, and Innovation studied seventy-three smart-growth projects under construction between 2000 and 2004 and found that twenty-two involved high-production builders (defined as producing more than 4,000 dwellings/year). See Philip Langdon, "EPA Presents Smart-Growth Ideas to Big Builders," *New Urban News*, June 2007.

12 In an article where the CEO of Toll Brothers ranked the economic performance of most of his projects F's, F-minuses, or F-minus minuses, "The best grade, B-plus, went to Toll's 'city living' apartment projects in the New Jersey suburbs of New York, while similar projects in the city received a B, as did Princeton, N.J., and the states of Delaware and Connecticut." Floyd Norris, "Blame for Poor Home Sales? It's the Press, a Builder Says," *New York Times*, November 9, 2007.

13 In addition, Steven McLinden argues, "For years large retailers have been downsizing a store here and there when necessary to fit inside a small urban site. Now, though, they are shrinking across the board to control costs and cope with Wall Street's relentless demand for growth and efficiency." See McLinden's "Big Boxes Shrinking in Order to Grow," *Shopping Centers Today*, August 2007.

14 See Richard Plunz, *A History of Housing in New York City* (New York: Columbia University Press, 1990), 56–57, and Charles Lockwood, *Manhattan Moves Uptown* (New York: Barnes & Noble Books, 1976), 313–320. Lockwood relates the anecdote of how the famed Dakota apartment building on 72nd Street got its name: it was considered so far out in the boondocks when designed in 1880 that people joked it might as well have been in the Dakotas!

15 But then for the most successful neighborhoods there is the phenomenon of historic districts, created specifically to preserve the coherence of building fabric all dating to the same time period by preventing incremental redevelopment or rehabilitation of individual buildings with "incompatible" architecture.

16 In a prescient article from 1995, Joel Garreau predicts the conversion of Kmart stores by artists into lofts and the coveting of relics of the suburban past, such as dry cleaners' revolving racks, as high status symbols. He further predicts that, as in SoHo, lawyers will follow artists, gentrify them out, and convert the lofts into gated communities called "The Estates at Place K." "Edgier Cities," *Wired*, December 1995, 158–164.

17 Tim Love has articulated the problems with block-sized buildings in new development in "Urban Design after *Battery Park City*: Opportunities for Variety and Vitality in Large-Scale Urban Real-Estate Development," *Harvard Design Magazine* 25 (Fall 2006/Winter 2007): 60–70. Neal Payton and Brian O'Looney, from Torti Gallas & Partners, have described the taxonomy of "Texas donuts," parking decks wrapped with housing, in "Seeking Urbane Parking Solutions," *Places* 18:1 (2006): 40–45.

18 This claim is made by Alan Berube, a Fellow at the Brookings Institution, based on 2000 census data and the 2005 American Community Survey, published in "Two Steps Back: City and Suburban Poverty Trends, 1999–2005" (Washington, DC: Brookings Institution, 2006), http://www.brookings.edu/reports/2006/12poverty_berube.aspx.

19 We are using the term *metropolitanism* in much the same way as many new urbanists and smart growth advocates use *regionalism* to refer to a metropolitan area as an integrated network of developed and undeveloped places. While *regionalism* focuses on targeting areas of conservation to balance targeted growth areas, *metropolitanism* focuses on the polycentric networks that have superseded older city-versus-suburb dichotomies.

20 Publicized examples include Boston's Westwood Station, Dallas's Mockingbird Station, Los Angeles's Del Mar Station and Mission Meridian, and Phoenix's Century Plaza (conversion and expansion of a high-rise office building into residential lofts).

21 In addition to reconstructing suburban commercial strips as boulevards, Milwaukee, Boston, Portland, and San Francisco have replaced elevated urban highways with surface boulevards that stimulate new development.

22 Even Ernest Burgess, who gave us the now very outdated Chicago School's concentric zone theory of urban development, recognized in the 1920s the presence of what he called "satellite loops." He characterized these suburban business and entertainment centers as being in the ring of "better houses" by their "bright lights" and "equalitarian" family structures (as opposed to the patriarchal structures of European immigrant households in the inner city and mother-centered households in the commuter zone). Ernest Burgess, "Urban Areas," in *Chicago: An Experiment in Social Science Research*, ed. T. V. Smith and Leonard D. White (Chicago: University of Chicago Press, 1929).

23 Robert E. Lang, "Office Sprawl: The Evolving Geography of Business" (Washington, DC: Brookings Institution, 2000), http://www.brookings.edu/reports/2000/10metropolitanpolicy_lang.aspx. For a more nuanced description of office development patterns and locations, see also Robert E. Lang, Thomas Sanchez, and Jennifer LeFurgy, "Beyond Edgeless Cities: Office Geography in the New Metropolis" (2006) for the National Center for Real Estate Research, http://www.realtor.org.ncrer.nsf/files/LangEdgelesses.pdf/$FILE/LangEdgelesses.pdf.

24 "Cities are growing again after decades of decline. Atlanta, Chicago, Denver, and Memphis literally 'turned around' by converting a 1980s population loss into a 1990s population gain." Bruce Katz and Andy Altman, "An Urban Renaissance in a Suburban Nation," *Ford Foundation Report,* Spring–Summer 2005.

25 Michael Sorkin, "The End(s) of Urbanism," *Harvard Design Magazine* 25 (Fall 2006/Winter 2007): 18.

Chapter 2

1 He acknowledged that there were many "other" suburbanites. Kenneth T. Jackson, *Crabgrass Frontier: The Suburbanization of the United States* (New York: Oxford University Press, 1985), 6.

2 Becky Nicolaides, "How Hell Moved from the City to the Suburbs" in *The New Suburban History,* ed. Kevin M. Kruse and Thomas J. Sugrue (Chicago: University of Chicago Press, 2006), 80–98.

3 Robert Fishman, *Bourgeois Utopias* (New York: Basic Books, 1987), 206.

4 Historian Paul Mattingly seconded Fishman's point: "Suburbia has become more than a convenient foil to explain urban decay and a culture of narcissism; it has become a cultural canon that often resists contextual data supporting a different perspective and a different landscape." Paul H. Mattingly, "The Suburban Canon over Time," in *Suburban Discipline,* ed. Peter Lang and Tam Miller (New York: Princeton Architectural Press, 1997), 38–51.

5 Sam Bass Warner Jr., *Streetcar Suburbs: The Process of Growth in Boston (1870–1900)* (Cambridge, MA: Harvard University Press, 1962, 1978).

6 Barry Checkoway, "Large Builders, Federal Housing Programmes, and Postwar Suburbanization," *International Journal of Urban and Regional Research* 4:1 (March 1980): 21–44. The home-building industry is even more consolidated today. Todd Zimmerman of ZVA estimates that because 75,000 homebuilders watch the same presentations at their annual convention on what houseplans sold best that year, 30% of the new product in any given year across the country will be more or less identical.

7 Kevin M. Kruse and Thomas J. Sugrue, ed., *The New Suburban History* (Chicago: University of Chicago Press, 2006), 6.

8 Frank Hobbs and Nicole Stoops, U.S. Census Bureau, Census 2000 Special Reports, Series CENSR-4, *Demographic Trends in the 20th Century* (Washington, DC: U.S. Government Printing Office, 2002).

9 Arthur C. Nelson, "Leadership in a New Era," *Journal of the American Planning Association* 72:4 (Autumn 2006): 393–407.

10 James Hughes and Joseph Seneca, Rutgers Regional Report, *The Beginning of the End of Sprawl?* Issue Paper No. 21, May 2004.

11 This high-rise housing boom is being driven by the city's top net gains in 25- to 35-year-olds, a group that prefers to live in the city rather than the suburbs by a two-to-one margin. Christine Van Dusen, "Atlanta: City Migration Fuels Condo Building Boom," *The Real Deal*, September 1, 2007.

12 William H. Frey, "Metropolitan America in the New Century: Metropolitan and Central City Demographic Shifts since 2000" (Washington, DC: Brookings Institution, 2005).

13 See RCLCO, "Generation Y in the Marketplace" at http://www.rclco.com/generalpdf/general_Aug2720081149_ULI-_08-27-08.pdf and Ellen Newborne and Kathleen Kerwin, "Generation Y," *Business Week*, February 15, 1999.

14 Roper Starch Worldwide, prepared for AARP, "The Baby Boomers Envision Their Retirement: A Segmentation Analysis" (February 1999), http:// www.aarp.org.

15 Linda Bailey, "Aging Americans Stranded without Options," *Surface Transportation Policy Project* (April 2004), http://www.transect.org; and Jennifer Dorn, Administrator, Federal Transit Administration, presentation at Rail-Volution Conference (September 22, 2004), citing an AARP report from 1999, http://www.reconnectingamerica.org/pdfs/DornSpeech.pdf.

16 Linda Saslow, "Nation's 'First Suburb' Aims to Be Most 'Green,'" *New York Times*, December 16, 2007.

17 Recognizing that this population corresponds more to the urban and Democratic profile of the 2004 presidential election than to that of the exurban suburbanites who voted overwhelmingly Republican, it is perhaps not surprising that politicians are paying attention to the political impacts of urbanization in the suburbs.

18 Robert Puentes, "The Evolution and Current State of First Suburbs: An Agenda for Action," paper presented at the Center for Suburban Studies, Hofstra University, March 18, 2005, http://www.brook.edu/metro/speeches/20050318_firstsuburbs.pdf.

19 Long Island Index, *Long Island Index 2007*, http://www.longislandindex.org (accessed April 4, 2007).

20 Long Island Index, "A Tale of Two Suburbs," *New York Times*, Op-Ed, April 1, 2007.

21 Lance Jay Brown, presentation at an affordable housing workshop sponsored by the Institute for Urban Design, New York City, May 17, 2007.

22 Dean Katerndahl, phone interview by June Williamson, December 18, 2007. The *Idea Book* and further information about the First Suburbs Coalition is available at http://www.marc.org/firstsuburbs/.

23 The city of Seattle allows the development of accessory dwelling units in Section 23.44.041 of the Land Use Code. In August 2006, Mayor Greg Nickels signed Ordinance 122190, which allows detached accessory dwelling units (DADUs) in single-family zones in Southeast Seattle (south of I-90 and east of I-5). The ordinance became effective on September 14, 2006. http://www.seattle.gov/dpd/Planning/Alternative_Housing_Choices/Overview/default.asp (accessed December 18, 2007).

24 Cynthia Daniels, "Talk about Buying in Bulk! Entire Subdivision for Sale," *Atlanta Journal Constitution*, March 8, 2007. There are two other subdivision retrofits underway in Atlanta at the time of this writing: CitySide at Town Center by Marthasville Development LLC and a retail project in Gwinnett County on the site of Essex Drive.

25 Ralph Bivins, "Outdoor Plaza at Greenway Will Be Named for Schnitzer," *Houston Chronicle*, December 12, 1999. Bill Schadewald, "Smooth and Stormy Memories of Schnitzer," *Houston Business Journal*, November 5, 1999.

26 Louis G. Redstone, *The New Downtowns: Rebuilding Business Districts* (Malabar, FL: R. E. Krieger, 1976), 142–143. See also the Greenway Plaza website, http://www.greenwayplaza.com/home/about.asp (accessed April 17, 2007). The business park core of the property, the 60-acre Phase I, has been owned since 1996 by Crescent Real Estate Equities.

27 Lisa Rein, "MetroWest Point Man in Fight of His Life; Developer Surprised to Be Locking Horns with Rep. Davis over Sale of Fairfax Parcel," *Washington Post*, September 12, 2005, Metro B03.

28 See MetroWest project website, http://metrowestva.com/about/index.html.

29 Quoted in Carl Levesque, "Station Master," *Big Builder*, February 1, 2005.

30 Rein, "MetroWest Point Man in Fight of His Life; Developer Surprised to Be Locking Horns with Rep. Davis over Sale of Fairfax Parcel."

31 Lisa Rein, "Metrorail Opts to Sell Parcel in Vienna; Density of Development around Station a Point of Contention That Threatened Project," *Washington Post*, November 18, 2005, Metro B01.

32 Pulte Homes Corporation, "Metro West Proffers: Pulte Homes Corporation," http://metrowestva.com/about/index.html (accessed April 16, 2007).

33 Paul Mitchell Hess, "Rediscovering the Logic of Garden Apartments," *Places* 17:2 (Summer 2005): 30–35.

34 Anne Vernez Moudon and Paul Hess, "Suburban Clusters: The Nucleation of Multifamily Housing in the Suburban Areas of the Central Puget Sound," *Journal of the American Planning Association* 66:3 (2000): 243–264.

35 Quoted in Kenna Simmons, "The Home Front," *Georgia Trend* (June 2006).

36 Susan Rogers, "Superneighborhood 27: A Brief History of Change," *Places* 17:2 (Summer 2005): 36–41.

37 There are numerous examples of this phenomenon, often impacting both garden apartment complexes and their neighboring strip malls, as in Arlington, Virginia, and Buford and Memorial Highways in Atlanta. Buford Highway's garden apartments were largely built to accommodate white flight in the 1970s. Since then they have accommodated several waves of new immigrants: eastern Europeans in the 1980s, followed by Asians in the 1990s, and Mexicans in the past decade. Although the apartment complexes tend to be differentiated and dominated by a single ethnic group (where they can build on communal networks), the strip malls are heavily mixed, with Korean, Vietnamese, Mexican, and other small shops constituting a globally diverse public realm.

38 William H. Whyte, *The Organization Man* (New York: Simon and Schuster, 1956), quotes from Chapter 22, "The New Roots."

39 Village of Park Forest, Illinois, "Request for Proposals for a Strategic Planning Study," issued August 3, 2006. The study was funded by a grant from the Illinois Department of Commerce and Economic Opportunity. HNTB and Economic Research Associates,

"Village of Park Forest Strategic Planning Study,"
May 2007.

40 Tania E. Lopez, "1 Less Low-Rent Option," *Indianapolis Star,* December 25, 2006, A01.

41 See, for example, Peter Rowe, *Making a Middle Landscape* (Cambridge, MA: MIT Press, 1991), especially Chapter 3, "Houses in Gardens," 67–95.

42 For a thorough introduction to the rural-to-urban transect, see the themed issue of *Places* 18:1 (Spring 2006), especially Charles C. Bohl with Elizabeth Plater-Zyberk, "Building Community across the Rural-to-Urban Transect," 4–17, and Brian O'Looney and Neal Payton, "Seeking Urbane Parking Solutions," 40–45, from which the diagrams are borrowed.

43 O'Looney and Payton, "Seeking Urbane Parking Solutions."

Chapter 3

1 A version of this case study was published as June Williamson, "Revisiting Levittown," *Places* 17:2 (Summer 2005): 46–51.

2 Marc Weiss, *The Rise of the Community Builders* (New York: Columbia University Press, 1987), 2.

3 William H. Whyte, *The Organization Man* (New York: Simon and Schuster, 1956); Herbert Gans, *The Levittowners: Ways of Life and Politics in a New Suburban Community* (New York: Vintage Books, 1967).

4 Richard Sherman, "Park Forest: A Model for U.S. Planned Towns," *Star Newspapers,* September 11, 1988.

5 Corey Kilgannon, "Change Blurs Memories in a Famous Suburb," *New York Times,* October 13, 2007.

6 The Plaza was designed by architect Richard Bennett, who gave up a tenured position at Yale to be part of the Park Forest design team. For more on the Park Forest Plaza and other early shopping mall designs, see David Smiley, "History of the Victor: Constructing Shopping," *Lotus International* 118 (2003): 4–25.

7 Gregory Randall, *America's Original GI Town: Park Forest, Illinois* (Baltimore: Johns Hopkins University Press, 2000), 73.

8 For comparative statistics on Park Forest and other suburbs, see William H. Hudnut III, *Halfway to Everywhere: A Portrait of America's First-Tier Suburbs* (Washington, DC: The Urban Land Institute, 2003).

9 HNTB with Economic Research Associates, "Village of Park Forest Strategy Planning Study: Inventory and Existing Conditions Background Report," May 2007, http://www.villageofparkforest.com (accessed February 1, 2008).

10 Gans, 5–12; supported by personal observations on a visit to Willingboro by June Williamson, January 18, 2005.

11 Jack H. Morris, "Living Together: How One Suburb Acted to Integrate Smoothly, Avoid Major Incidents," *Wall Street Journal,* December 28, 1970; Gans, 375–380.

12 J. R. Reid, Burlington County Planner, interview by June Williamson, Mount Holly, New Jersey, January 18, 2005; Denise Rose, Willingboro Township Manager, interview by June Williamson, Willingboro, New Jersey, January 18, 2005.

13 David Rusk, "The 'Segregation Tax': The Cost of Racial Segregation to Black Homeowners," (Washington, DC: The Brookings Institution, 2001). He asserts that on average black homeowners receive 18% less value for their homes than white homeowners. This is exactly the difference in value between Levitt-built houses in Levittown, Pennsylvania, and those in Willingboro.

14 Karen Beck Pooley, "The Other Levittown: Race and Place in Willingboro, NJ," *The Next American City* 1:2 (June 2003), http://americancity.org/magazine/article/the-other-levittown-pooley/.

15 Center for Transit-Oriented Development, "Hidden in Plain Sight: Capturing the Demand for Housing near Transit" (Oakland, CA: Reconnecting America, September 2004, revised April 2005), http://www.reconnectingamerica.org/public/reports.

16 The apartment courts that remain rentals are in poor condition and are considered by the village to be a troubling source of crime. Village of Park Forest, Illinois, "Request for Proposals for a Strategic Planning Study," issued August 3, 2006, http://www.villageofparkforest.com (accessed February 1, 2008).

17 Barbara M. Kelly, *Expanding the American Dream: Building and Rebuilding Levittown* (Albany: State University of New York Press, 1993), 104–118.

18 See Renee Chow, *Suburban Space: The Fabric of Dwelling* (Berkeley and Los Angeles: University of California Press, 2002).

19 Brenda Case Scheer, "The Anatomy of Sprawl," *Places* 14:2 (Fall 2001): 28–37.

20 HNTB with Economic Research Associates.

21 Denise Rose, interview.

22 Anne Moudon and Paul Hess, "Suburban Clusters: The Nucleation of Multifamily Housing in Suburban Areas of the Central Puget Sound," *Journal of the American Planning Association* 66, no. 3 (Summer 2000): 243–264; observations in Levittown by June Williamson, October 8, 2004.

23 Whyte, *The Organization Man.*

24 Observations in Park Forest by June Williamson, June 24, 2004.

25 Geoff Mulvihill, "New Numbers: International Migration Is Driving Growth in NJ," *Associated Press,* April 9, 2004.

26 James Barron, "A Classic Suburb Feels Graying Pains," *New York Times,* July 21, 1983.

27 The award is from the American Institute of Architects Committee on the Environment. The library's architect is Croxton Collaborative of New York, experts in green building.

28 Linda Saslow, "Nation's 'First Suburb' Aims to Be Most 'Green.'"

Chapter 4

1 Ray Oldenburg, *The Great Good Place: Cafés, Coffee Shops, Community Centers, Beauty Parlors, General Stores, Bars, Hangouts, and How They Get You through the Day* (New York: Marlowe, 1997), and *Celebrating the Third Place: Inspiring Stories about the "Great Good Places" at the Heart of our Communities* (New York: Marlowe, 2001).

2 Other sociologists have begun correlating the significance of third places with higher rates of civic engagement and positive socioeconomic outcomes, arguing that local differentiations between places factor more than ever in a global capitalist system. See M. Tolbert, Thomas A. Lyson, and Michael D. Irwin, "Local Capitalism, Civic Engagement, and Socioeconomic Well-Being," *Social Forces* 77:2 (1998): 401–428. Similarly, studies have found that absentee-managed industrial plants emit far fewer toxins in communities with more "third places" and other measures of civic engagement than those in locales without them. See Don Grant, Andrew W. Jones, and Mary Nell Trautner, "Do Facilities with Distant Headquarters Pollute More? How Civic Engagement Conditions the Environmental Performance of Absentee Managed Plants," *Social Forces* 83:1 (2004): 189–214.

3 Popular culture frequently reinforces the perception of well-functioning third places in urban and rural locales. Films such as *Barbershop, Diner,* and *Steel Magnolias* chronicle the humor, trust, and support groups that revolve around informal community-building institutions. Those depicted in suburban settings tend to be much more age and class segregated—from the teens congregating in the parking lot of a convenience store in *SubUrbia* to those doing the same at the mall in *Mean Girls,* where "Cady" compares the mall fountain's role as a gathering place to an African watering hole. Academic and cultural critics have increasingly linked the physical environment of contemporary suburbs not just to issues of social alienation (a subject of considerable study in the 1950s and 1960s), but also to questions of infantilization and the acting out of violent fantasies. See Christopher Caldwell, "Levittown to Littleton: How the Suburbs Have Changed," *National Review,* May 31, 1999.

4 Stephan J. Goetz and Anil Rupasingha, "Wal-Mart and Social Capital," *American Journal of Agricultural Economics* (December 2006): 1304–1310.

5 It has been argued that suburbia's lack of designed spaces for informal gathering has encouraged teenagers to make use of derelict suburban industrial areas for stupid but daring forms of recreation. See Andrew M. Shanken, "The Sublime 'Jackass': Transgression and Play in the Inner Suburbs," *Places* 19:3 (2007): 50–55.

6 Anastasia Loukaitou-Sideris, "Inner-City Commercial Strips; Evolution, Decay—Retrofit?" *Town Planning Review* 68:1 (1997): 1–29. This citation references Grady Clay, *Close-Up: How to Read the American City.* (New York: Praeger, 1973) and Larry Sawers and William K. Tabb, eds., *Sunbelt/Snowbelt.* (New York: Oxford University Press, 1984).

7 The earliest shopping centers planned around automobiles, Market Square at Lake Forest, Illinois, from 1916 and Country Club Plaza in Kansas City from 1924, maintained urban street frontage and were anchored by a train station and a new residential suburb, respectively. However, the project that ended up becoming the more influential prototype was the Grandview Avenue Shopping Center in Columbus, Ohio, from 1928. Its thirty stores set behind off-street parking for 400 cars became the continuing model for strip malls and shopping centers.

8 The first commercial neon signs in the United States were installed at a car dealership in Los Angeles in 1923 and spelled "Packard."

9 There were 22,000 strips built between the mid-1950s and late-1970s, and 46,000 by the 1990s. See Dolores Hayden, *Building Suburbia: Green Fields and Urban Growth, 1820–2000* (New York: Pantheon, 2003).

10 International Council of Shopping Centers, "A Brief History of Shopping Centers," ICSC News, June 2000, http://www.icsc.org/srch/about/impactofshoppingcenters/briefhistory.html (accessed December 23, 2007).

11 Brenda Case Scheer, "The Radial Street as a Timeline: A Study of the Transformation of Elastic Tissues," in *Suburban Form: An International Perspective,* ed. Kiril Stanilov and Brenda Case Scheer (New York and London: Routledge, 2004): 115.

12 Ken Jones and Jim Simmons, *The Retail Environment* (London: Routledge, 1990), 169.

13 Ibid., 243.

14 Michael Tubridy, "Defining Trends in Shopping Center History," *Research Review* 13:1 (2006), http://www.icsc.org/srch/rsrch/researchquarterly/current/rr2006131/Defining%20Trends%20in%20Shopping%20Center%20History.pdf (accessed December 29, 2007). As an example of the impact of Triple-A tenant underwriting, when Simon Properties took over ownership from Stanford University of the Stanford Shopping Center, they refused to renew the lease of a highly successful local coffeehouse owner in favor of signing a lease with Starbucks, saying they preferred to rent to a Triple-A tenant with a national chain and national marketing. Najeeb Hasan, "Stanford's Boulevard of Broken Beans: How Los Gatos Coffee Roasting Icon Teri Hope Got Pushed Out of the Increasingly Homogenized Stanford Shopping Center," *Metroactive,* July 26–August 1, 2006. Available at http://www.metroactive.com/metro/07.26.06/stanford-shoping-center-0630.html (accessed December 28, 2007).

15 Jim Hightower, *Eat Your Heart Out* (New York: Crown, 1975); followed later by Stacy Mitchell's *The Home Town Advantage: How to Defend Your Main Street against Chain Stores and Why It Matters* (Minneapolis: Institute for Self-Reliance, 2000).

16 Stacy Mitchell, *Big-Box Swindle: The True Cost of Mega-Retailers and the Fight for America's Independent Businesses* (Boston: Beacon Press, 2006), 5.

17 See Ellen Dunham-Jones, "Temporary Contracts: The Economy of the Post-Industrial Landscape," *Harvard Design Magazine,* (Fall 1997), and "Economic Sustainability in the Post-Industrial Landscape," in *The Green Braid: Towards an Architecture of Ecology, Economy, and Equity,* ed. Kim Tanzer and Rafael Longoria (London: Routledge, 2007), 44–59.

18 See Louise Mozingo, "Campus, Estate, and Park: Lawn Culture Comes to the Corporation," in *Everyday America: Cultural Studies after J. B. Jackson,* ed. Chris Wilson and Paul Groth (Berkeley: University of California Press, 2003).

19 ICSC, "A Brief History of Shopping Centers."

20 Ibid.

21 ICSC members ranked the rise of REITs as the number one defining trend of shopping center history in a major survey on the occasion of the organization's fiftieth anniversary. See Michael Tubridy, "Defining Trends in Shopping Center History."

22 Tom Wolfe's novel *A Man in Full* (New York: Farrar, Straus & Giroux, 1998) is set in Atlanta in the 1990s and describes the strip landscape in these terms. "The only way you could tell you were leaving one community and entering another was when the franchises started repeating and you spotted another 7-Eleven, another Wendy's, another Costco, another Home Depot."

23 Toys"R"Us started in the 1950s but went public in 1978 and started building superstores that made it the first "category killer" big-box store to steal market share from department stores. Home Depot started in 1979, Circuit City in 1981, and Barnes & Noble started its suburban branches in 1991. See Robert Spector, *Category Killers: The Retail Revolution and Its Impact on Consumer Culture* (Boston: Harvard Business School Press, 2005).

24 "The top ten [big-box chains] alone have doubled their market share since 1996 and now capture almost 30 percent of the more than $2.3 trillion Americans spend at stores each year. The largest, Wal-Mart, grew tenfold in fifteen years, and in 2005 accounted for one out of every ten dollars Americans spent." Mitchell, *Big-Box Swindle,* xii.

25 In their book *Urban Space for Pedestrians* (Cambridge MA: MIT, 1975) Boris S. Pushkarev and Jeffrey M. Zupan have shown acceptable walking distances to acquire goods and services in central New York and London to be in the range of 525 to 800 meters. These are similar to routine walking

distances in downtown Winnipeg; however, customers at a Winnipeg power center would not even walk the 200–300 meters between big-box stores. They drove between stores 90% of the time. Brian Lorch, "Auto-Dependent Induced Shopping: Exploring the Relationship between Power Centre Morphology and Consumer Spatial Behaviour," *Canadian Journal of Urban Research* 14:2 (Winter 2005): 364–384.

26 Marlon Boarnet, Randall Crane, Daniel Chatman, and Michael Manville, "Supercenters and the Transformation of the Bay Area Grocery Industry," Bay Area Economic Forum, 2004.

27 Mitchell, *Big-Box Swindle*, 121.

28 Wal-Mart has had a successful strategy of opening several stores in an area and closing them after approximately five years (by which time they are generally very successful and have killed off much of the local competition) in order to open a superstore. See Dunham-Jones, "Temporary Contracts."

29 Mitchell, *Big-Box Swindle*, 10.

30 Jane Jacobs, *The Death and Life of Great American Cities* (New York: Vintage, 1961), 188.

31 Several of these examples came from artist Julia Christensen's website, http://www.bigboxreuse.com. She has a book forthcoming on the subject.

32 Eve M. Kahn, "Thinking Inside the Big Box," *New York Times*, May 12, 2005.

33 Michele Schwartz, "Open on Sundays: When Wal-Mart Moves Out, Churches Move In," *Preservation Online,* April 21, 2006, available at http://www.nationaltrust.org/Magazine/archives/arch_story/042106p.htm.

34 Fred Perpall, telephone interview by Ellen Dunham-Jones, December 13, 2007.

35 In 2005 they also expanded a half mile up the street and opened Chelsea's Kitchen in a former off-track-betting bar. Trading on the fresh, local quality of their food and neighborliness, it will be interesting to see how they survive their latest expansion—into new urbanist projects in Pasadena and Santa Monica. Can third places be franchised?

36 For more on this issue see Thomas H. Sanders, "Social Capital and New Urbanism: Leading a Civic Horse to Water?" *National Civic Review* 91:3 (Fall 2002): 213–234.

37 Erica Sagon, "'La Grande' Eateries to Take Show on Road," *The Arizona Republic*, June 26, 2006.

38 George Homsy, "Making Great Strips Happen: How to Revamp a Strip Mall, or Build One from Scratch," *Planning*, December 1, 2002.

39 Kevin Daly, telephone interview by Ellen Dunham-Jones, December 13, 2007.

40 ICSC Shopping Center Definitions, available at the ICSC website, http://www.icsc.org/srch/lib/SCDefinitions.php (accessed December 20, 2007).

41 Andres Duany, interview by Ellen Dunham-Jones and June Williamson, Miami, Florida, November 21, 2006.

42 The small site may also have factored into the project's very clumsy handling of its rear edges and parking garage.

43 Susan Wachter, "The Determinants of Neighborhood Transformation in Philadelphia—Identification and Analysis of the New Kensington Pilot Study," 2005 (unpublished).

44 The lake had been drained and the shopping center built in anticipation of a never-built highway in the 1960s. The historical marker on the boardwalk in 2005 stated, "Soon other problems surfaced. Stores were frequently flooded, water puddled in the parking lot, and cattails began to break through the asphalt. Ames Lake was fighting to come back!"

45 The detailed plan for the area's revitalization, of which the restored wetlands were only a part, is told in Harrison Fraker, Daniel J. Marckel, Mark Tambornino, and Joseph E. Lambert, "Streets, Parks and Houses: Case Study of a Pedestrian Neighbourhood," *Transport Policy* 1:2 (1994): 160–173. For a more detailed review of the project as implemented, see Jennifer Dowdel, Harrison Fraker, and Joan Nassauer, "Replacing a Shopping Center with an Ecological Neighborhood," *Places* 17:3 (2005): 66–68 .

46 Joan I. Nassauer, "Monitoring the Success of Metropolitan Wetland Restorations: Cultural Sustainability and Ecological Function," *Wetlands* 24:4 (2004): 756–765.

47 Livable Communities Program, Report to Metropolitan Council, October 24, 2007. Available at http://councilmeetings.metc.state.mn.us/council_meetings/2007/102407/1024_2007_LCA%20Report%20to%20Council.pdf (accessed January 1, 2007).

48 Lee Sobel, *Greyfields into Goldfields* (San Francisco: Congress for the New Urbanism, 2002), 51.

49 Quoted in Christopher Swope, "After the Mall," *Governing* (October 2002): 20–25.

50 Quoted in Sandra Tan, "Aging Retail Outlets Present a Dilemma: Developers Struggle to Give Stores New Life," *Buffalo News*, March 15, 2007.

51 Josh Martin, telephone interview by Ellen Dunham-Jones, January 8, 2008.

52 See Michael Dobbins, "Focusing Growth amid Sprawl: Atlanta's Livable Centers Initiative," *Places* 17:2 (Summer 2005): 20–23.

53 Atlanta Regional Commission, 2007 LCI Implementation Report, available at http://www.atlantaregional.com/cps/rde/xbcr/acr/LCI2007ImplReport_v09.pdf (accessed January 1, 2007).

54 TIF and TADs are never without controversy. The redevelopment of Jonquil Plaza has been tied up in a lawsuit charging that the TAD was unnecessary since market pressures would have led to redevelopment anyway. In the meantime, the Livable Communities Coalition of Atlanta sponsored a detailed study of TAD performance and concluded that property values inside TADs outperformed their host communities and climbed an average of more than 14% per year compounded—and in seven cases growth rates were as much as seven times that amount. Those TADs that were not making progress typically experienced delays in securing consent from counties and school districts, identifying developers, and attracting the 90% private investment needed. See Bleakley Advisory Group, *Survey and Analysis of Tax Allocation Districts (TADs) in Georgia: A Look at the First Eight Years* (Atlanta, GA: Livable Communities Coalition, 2007).

55 Michael Brick, "Commercial Real Estate: Fire Destroys More Than a Mixed-Use Project," *New York Times*, December 25, 2002.

56 Sharon Simonson, "Santana Row Model Is Flawed, Its Developers Say," *Business Journal* (Silicon Valley/San Jose), September 17, 2004.

57 Ibid.

58 Quoted in Brick, "Commercial Real Estate: Fire Destroys More Than a Mixed-Use Project."

59 Simonson, "Santana Row Model Is Flawed."

60 Anna Robaton, "Santana Row Bounces Back," *Shopping Center News*, February 2004.

61 Sharon Simonson, "Santana Row Condo Prices Encourage Downtown," *Business Journal* (Silicon Valley/San Jose), December 16, 2005.

62 Based on a presentation given by General Growth Properties executives at the Hotel Developers Conference in March 2007, according to Jim Butler,

"What Is Lifestyle Hotel Mixed-Use Development All About?" March 23, 2007, Hotel Online Special Report, available at http://www.hotel-online.com/News/PR2007_1st/Mar07_Lifestyle.html (accessed January 6, 2008).

63 This information is from the well-informed description of the project at Jim Horne's website, http://www.tndwest.com/santanarow.html.

64 Simonson, "Santana Row Condo Prices Encourage Downtown."

65 Philip Nobel, "Good Malls and Bad Cities," Metropolis, March 2007.

66 Additional consultants on the plan included Robert Charles Lesser & Co., LLC; Hall Planning & Engineering; and King Engineering. Cooper Carry, Inc. has since been hired to implement the first phase of the plan with some modifications.

67 Allan B. Jacobs, Elizabeth Macdonald, and Yodan Rofé, The Boulevard Book: History, Evolution, Design of Multiway Boulevards (Cambridge, MA: MIT Press, 2002), 5.

68 These descriptions are from the Federal Highway Administration website, http://www.fhwa.dot.gov/Environment/flex/cho3.htm, and reflect the distinctly suburban rather than urban orientation of the system.

69 Peter Calthorpe, "From New Regionalism to the Urban Network: Changing the Paradigm of Growth," Harvard Design Magazine 22, (Spring/Summe 2005).

70 Ibid., 65. Critics are concerned that drivers will speed through the one-ways, negating the benefits to pedestrians. The jury is out until build-out is completed in 2010.

71 Ibid., 63.

72 Context Sensitive Solutions in Designing Major Urban Thoroughfares for Walkable Communities is a new Proposed Recommended Practice produced jointly in 2006 by the two organizations under a contract to the Federal Highway Administration. Comments on the manual were taken through 2006 and are now being processed for revisions into a Recommended Practice. The document is available at http://www.cnu.org/node/127.

73 For more information on this transaction, see Sarah Pulleyblank, Civilizing Downtown Highways (San Francisco: Congress for the New Urbanism, 2002). The financing is also described in Bruce Liedstrand and Kristen Paulsen, "Cathedral City Downtown," a Livable Places Profile produced for the Coachella Valley Association of Governments at http://www.scaq.ca.gov/livable/download/pdf/cathedral.pdf (accessed February 3, 2008).

74 Bruce Liedstrand, telephone interview by Ellen Dunham-Jones, February 3, 2008.

75 Liedstrand and Paulsen, "Cathedral City Downtown."

76 Jerry Jack, "Pedestrian-Friendly Redesign: Cathedral City, CA," Case Study No. 21 available at http://www.walkinginfo.org/pedsafe/casestudy.cfm?CS_NUM=21 (accessed January 12, 2008). The author states that a study of pedestrian crashes revealed that from 1993 to1995 there were nine pedestrian accidents, while none have been reported since the roadway opened in 1998.

77 Liedstrand, telephone interview.

78 Michael Freedman, "Restructuring the Strip," Places 17:2 (Summer 2005): 60–67.

79 For a discussion of nodal development along arterials, see Jonathan Barnett, "Redesigning Commercial Corridors," in Redesigning Cities: Principles, Practice, Implementation (Washington, DC: American Planning Association, 2003); see also Geoffrey Booth et al., Transforming Suburban Business Districts (Washington, DC: The Urban Land Institute, 2001).

80 Michael D. Beyard and Michael Pawlukiewicz, Ten Principles for Reinventing America's Suburban Strips (Washington, DC: The Urban Land Institute, 2001).

81 Ibid., 66.

82 Evan Halper, "Turning Old Strip Malls into Housing," Los Angeles Times, June 17, 2001, California Section; Part 2; Page 1; Metro Desk.

83 See Arthur C. Nelson, "America Circa 2030: The Boom to Come," Architect, October 2006, and Robert Steuteville, "Market Trends Favor NU," New Urban News, April/May 2007.

84 See Darren Petrucci, "Stripscape: Pedestrian Amenities along 7th Avenue," Places 17:2 (2005): 42–44.

85 Families who live in auto-dependent neighborhoods spend an average of 25% of their household budget on transportation. Families who live in transit-rich neighborhoods spend just 9%. This is according to a 2007 report by Reconnecting America's Center for Transit-Oriented Development funded by the Federal Transit Administration and the U.S. Department of Housing and Urban Development, titled "Realizing the Potential: Expanding Housing Opportunities near Transit."

86 Transit design experts distinguish between transit-oriented design and transit-adjacent design and point to higher ridership levels associated with the former. See Dena Belzer and Gerald Autler, "Transit-Oriented Development: Moving from Rhetoric to Reality," 2002 report for the Brookings Institution's Center for Urban and Metropolitan Policy and the Great American Station Foundation, http://www.reconnectingamerica.org/public/reports.

87 Although much of the redeveloped properties to date have been underused industrial properties, artists and unique local bars using those spaces have been evicted, contributing to general concerns about rising property values triggering further displacement through gentrification. See Scott Henry, "Memorial Drive, Rising," Creative Loafing, April 12, 2006, and Paul Donsky, "Morphing of Memorial Drive," Atlanta Journal-Constitution, November 23, 2007, G1–4.

88 Another example of a suburban corridor retrofit that is playing up its industrial character is the designation of Route 1 as an arts district where it passes through Mount Ranier, Brentwood, North Brentwood, and Hyattsville, Maryland. The Prince George's County Gateway Arts District identifies seven distinct mixed-use "character areas"—with varied emphases on artist housing, arts production, public art, and entertainment—being developed through overlay guidelines and mixed-use projects developed by local community development corporations. While much of the new development employs a traditional row-house typology and aesthetic (albeit with model units decorated with guitars and Talking Heads posters), the older industrial buildings are being valued and restored as spaces for artists, much as they have been for several years.

89 "Asian Infusion: A Touch of Asia Thrives in Gwinnett," Atlanta Journal-Constitution, July 29, 2006. A follow-up online forum by Beni Dakar asked, "Are you excited about Gwinnett as the 'Asian Mecca'?" Readers' comments were largely negative, not boding well for further social integration. Available at http://www.ajc.com/metro/content/shared-blogs/ajc/duluthtalk/entries/2006/08/08/are_you_excited.html.

90 Ibid.

91 After Byun's financing fell through, Mason relinquished his interest in the property in late 2007 and the new owner has reportedly re-leased the retail sites—at least for now.

92 Michael Gamble and Jude LeBlanc, "Incremental Urbanism: New Models for the Redesign of America's Commercial Strip," *Harvard Design Magazine* 21 (Fall/Winter 2004).

93 The main offices of the Centers for Disease Control are located on Buford Highway, and a researcher at the CDC, Candace Rutt, conducted a Health Impact Assessment of Gamble and LeBlanc's proposal and concluded that it would indeed save lives and improve public health. See Candace D. Rutt, Michael Pratt, Andrew L. Dannenberg, and Brian Cole, "Connecting Public Health and Planning Professionals: Health Impact Assessment," *Places* 17:1 (2005): 86–87.

94 Seth Rosen, "Arlington Undergoes Transformation Thanks to New Development; Growth in Metro Corridors and Shirlington in Recent Years Has Reshaped County," *Arlington Connection*, July 21, 2006.

95 Joe Kohl, interview by Ellen Dunham-Jones and June Williamson, Miami, Florida, November 22, 2006. See also Seth Rosen, "Columbia Pike Ready for Major Facelift," *Arlington Connection*, November 28, 2006.

96 Ryan Gravel, interview by Ellen Dunham-Jones, Atlanta, Georgia, March 8, 2008.

Chapter 5

1 Phrase attributed to Charles C. Bohl.

2 Charles C. Bohl, *Place Making: Developing Town Centers, Main Streets, and Urban Villages* (Washington, DC: The Urban Land Institute, 2002), 168.

3 Douglas Storrs, phone interview by June Williamson, January 28, 2008.

4 After a long period of bureaucratic oversight, the Wampanoag tribe was finally officially recognized in 2007, and tribal leaders are negotiating for casino rights. Jennifer Schwartz, "Gambling with Their Future," *Boston Globe Sunday Magazine,* October 28, 2007.

5 Cape Trends, "Housing Growth, Part I," September 8, 2005, http://www.capecodcommission.org/data/capetrends.htm.

6 Peter Katz, *The New Urbanism* (New York: McGraw-Hill, 1994), 169–177. Participants in the first Mashpee Commons charrette included Alex Krieger, John Massengale, and Anne Tate.

7 Storrs.

8 Bohl, *Place Making,* 168.

9 Duany Plater-Zyberk & Company, Mashpee Commons Code (2002).

10 Town of Mashpee Affordable Housing & Planned Production Plan (Febrary 2005), http://www.mass.gov/?pageID=ehedterminal&L=3&L0=Home&L1=Community+Development&L2=Chapter+40B+Planning&sid=Ehed&b=terminalcontent&f=dhcd_cd_ch40b_planprod&csid=Ehed.

11 For more on suburban morphology see Brenda Case Scheer, "The Anatomy of Sprawl," *Places* 14:2 (Fall 2001): 28–37.

12 Bohl, *Place Making,* 164.

13 Chris Reidy, "Cape Center to Return Part of Boch Donation," *Boston Globe,* July 6, 2006.

14 There have been complaints that the current post office's embedded location in the Commons makes it difficult to provide the drive-through service suburbanites are accustomed to. In response, the developers worked with town officials and the U.S. Postal Service (which has a regressive set of site and building planning requirements that needed to be amended) to find a suitable new location. Construction of a new post office building will begin soon on a site adjacent to the public library; in its new location it will still have a civic presence but will be more easily accessed by car.

15 Cape Cod Metropolitan Planning Organization, "2007 Regional Transportation Plan" (April 2007), http://www.gocapecod.org/rtp/.

Chapter 6

1 See Charles C. Bohl, *Place Making: Developing Town Centers, Main Streets and Urban Villages* (Washington, DC: The Urban Land Institute, 2002).

2 The Road Information Program (TRIP), "Stuck in Traffic: How Increasing Traffic Congestion Is Putting the Brakes on Economic Growth" (May 2001), http://www.tripnet.org/.

3 Geoffrey Booth et al., "Ten Principles for Reinventing America's Suburban Business Districts" (Washington, DC: The Urban Land Institute, 2002), 14.

4 Colin Rowe and Fred Koetter, *Collage City* (Cambridge, MA: MIT Press, 1973).

5 John Chase, Margaret Crawford, and John Kaliski, eds., *Everyday Urbanism* (New York: Monacelli Press, 1999).

6 While suburbs are generally deficient in public spaces, they often compensate with an abundance of community space in the form of sports fields and country clubs. Often requiring membership, these spaces serve important social functions but should be distinguished from public spaces. See Michael Brill, "Mistaking Community Life for Public Life," *Places* 14:2 (2001): 48–55.

7 David Brain, "From Good Neighborhoods to Sustainable Cities: Social Science and the Social Agenda of New Urbanism," *International Regional Science Review* 28:2 (April 2005): 217–238.

8 Since the 1980 Supreme Court decision in Pruneyard v. Robbins, the legal standing of shopping malls (and privately owned new downtowns) has been neither fully public nor fully private and is dependent on state statutes. Except in the five states that have adopted broader protection for free speech, the Court ruled that as privately owned places, they are exempt from the U.S. Constitution's protections of political speech. See Margaret Kohn, *Brave New Neighborhoods: The Privatization of Public Space* (New York: Routledge, 2004).

9 Gregory Randall, *America's Original GI Town: Park Forest, Illinois* (Baltimore: Johns Hopkins University Press, 2000), 140–156.

10 Victor Gruen and Larry Smith, *Shopping Towns USA: The Planning of Shopping Centers* (New York: Reinhold, 1960).

11 Jonathan Miller, foreword to *Greyfields into Goldfields: Dead Malls Become Living Neighborhoods,* by Lee S. Sobel with Ellen Greenberg and Steven Bodzin, (San Francisco: CNU, 2002), 8. Other recent books that examine this phenomenon include David Smiley and Mark Robbins, eds., *Sprawl and Public Space: Redressing the Mall* (New York: NEA/Princeton Architectural Press, 2002) and F. Kaid Benfield, Jutka Terris, and Nancy Vorsanger, *Solving Sprawl: Models of Smart Growth in Communities across America* (New York: National Resources Defense Council, 2001).

12 Steve Laposa, *Greyfield Regional Mall Study* (San Francisco: CNU, 2001), http://www.cnu.org/node/349 (accessed July 23, 2008).

13 Christopher B. Leinberger, "Creating Alternatives to the Standard Real Estate Types," *Places* 17:2 (Summer 2005): 24–29.

14 Miller in Sobel et al., 7.

15 Michael Sorkin, ed., *Variations on a Theme Park: The New American City and the End of Public Space* (New York: Noonday Press, 1992).

16 ICSC, "Shopping Center Definitions," http://www.icsc.org/srch/about/impactofshoppingcenters/ShopCentDef.pdf (accessed August 10, 2007).

17 The International Council of Shopping Centers tracks these statistics carefully. ICSC, "By the Numbers," *Shopping Centers Today*, May 2005, http://www.icsc.org/srch/sct/sct0405/by_the_numbers_042005.pdf.

18 Seth Harry, "The Retail Transect in a Regional Context," *CNU Council Report VI on Retail* (2004): 22–23, 38.

19 Randall, 140–156.

20 Sobel, 68–69; Christopher Swope, "After the Mall," *Governing* 16:1 (October 2002): 20–24.

21 Dennis Hevesi, "Antidotes to Sprawl Taking Many Forms," *New York Times*, October 6, 2003. See also David Smiley, ed., *Sprawl and Public Space: Redressing the Mall* (New York: Princeton Architectural Press, 2002).

22 The Sunnyvale project is being designed for Sand Hill Property Company and RREEF by a team that includes Kenneth Rodrigues & Partners, RTKL Associates, KTGY Group, and the Guzzardo Partnership.

23 The 2000 U.S. Census figures indicate that the median household income in Boca Raton was $38,943 and the median house value was $143,500.

24 Charles C. Bohl, *Place Making: Developing Town Centers, Main Streets, and Urban Villages* (Washington, DC: Urban Land Institute, 2002).

25 Ibid.

26 Ibid.

27 According to the 2000 Census, Winter Park was 10% African American with a median household income of $48,880 and a median house value of $203,700. Incomes and house values are lower in the historically black neighborhoods of Winter Park.

28 Sandra Thompson, "Now This Mall Feels Like Home—and It Is," *St. Petersburg Times*, October 11, 2003.

29 The buildings were designed by Dorsky Hodgson + Partners.

30 Urban Land Institute, "Winter Park Village," *ULI Case Study* #C036024 (October–December 2006).

31 Ibid.

32 Don Martin, "Winter Park Village: Civic Urbanism," *Urban Land* (October 2005): 94.

33 Jill Krueger, "Bellows Preps for More Projects in Hannibal Square," *Orlando Business Journal*, May 13, 2005.

34 The City of Englewood Community Development Department has a low-interest Housing Improvement Loan Program.

35 Harold Stitt, community development manager, City of Englewood, Colorado, interview by June Williamson, Englewood, Colorado, August 8, 2007.

36 Robert Simpson, community development director, City of Englewood, Colorado, presentation at the 2007 conference of the Center for Sustainable Suburban Development, UC Riverside, January 25, 2007, http://cssd.ucr.edu/ (accessed August 6, 2007).

37 The 2000 Census indicates that the median household income in Walnut Creek was $63,238 and the median home value was $391,200.

38 Theresa Harrington, "Walnut Creek Worth Emulating," *Contra Costa Times*, February 10, 2006.

39 Michael Southworth, "Reinventing Main Street: From Mall to Townscape Mall," *Journal of Urban Design* 10:2 (June 2005): 151–170.

40 John King, "Historic Oak Tree Wins Its Battle with Big Business," *San Francisco Chronicle*, September 9, 2000.

41 George Avalos and Blanca Torres, "Upscale Urban Streetscape: Rising Rents Transform Downtown Walnut Creek," *Contra Costa Times*, July 9, 2007.

Chapter 7

1 General Growth Properties press release, April 14, 2005.

2 Reminiscences of the Cottonwood Mall have been gathered at http://www.city-data.com/forum/salt-lake-city-area/36036-holladay-s-cottonwood-mall.html. Contributors recall a rich mix of activities in the mall over the years. It had a dentist's office and lawyers' offices on the second floor, as well as a bank and a grocery store with a lunch counter that was replaced by a food court in the 1980s. It was frequently rented out in the early 1970s for dances on Saturday nights and included a bowling alley near the theaters.

3 Longson oversaw several earlier studies for redevelopment, from simple renovation to a plan designed by ELS Architecture and Urban Design that replaced the mall with a retail-only version of a lifestyle center with some big-box stores.

4 The study concluded that the trade area population was 417,727 persons with an average household income of $73,477 (the highest household income in a five-mile radius within the state).

5 Focusing on 75% of the trade area, the study noted that the area is a family-centered market where 59% of the shoppers are in households with children and 37% of the primary trade households are categorized as upscale households.

6 Matt Shannon, a former employee at DPZ, worked for GGP and facilitated the connection of the two companies.

7 In addition to DPZ staff (including two students on spring break from Andrews University who dropped in and became team members), active participants in the mini-charrette included retail consultants, several GGP professionals from both the Utah office and from headquarters in Chicago, a Holladay-based local residential developer and civil engineer, and the mayor and the city manager of Holladay.

8 Much of the site's eastern border abuts a 10-foot strip of land on the south side of Arbor Lane that prohibits vehicular access (and limits the opportunities for interconnectivity) but affords spectacular mountain views across a cemetery. Memory Lane, at the south of the site, leads to a residential neighborhood concerned about cut-through traffic.

9 Elizabeth Plater-Zyberk, correspondence with Ellen Dunham-Jones, October 2007.

10 Patrick Peterman, telephone interview by Ellen Dunham-Jones, October 2007.

11 Based on the Claritas PRIZM NE cluster system.

12 The target market methodology provides very specific direction for the percentages of housing types, tenure (renter- vs. owner-occupied), unit types, sizes and configurations, values (sales prices or rents), and market capture (absorption forecasts).

13 Based on their consumption patterns and housing preferences, ZVA further characterized the segments of this market as *Urban Achievers*, *e-Types*, *Fast-Track Professionals*, and *New Bohemians*—a not uncommon mix for urban and suburban retrofits.

14 The word *charrette* is French for "cart" or "chariot." Architecture students at the École des Beaux Arts in Paris worked at studios and ateliers some distance from the school. They used carts to bring their drawings to the final presentations, often drawing and

painting en route until the last minute. As a result, the word *charrette* has come to refer to the intense period of developing ideas and producing drawings to represent a design before the deadline. See the publications and website of the National Charrette Institute (http://www.charretteinstitute.org) for more information about contemporary urban design charrette practices and training.

15 The nature of the public involvement in a charrette varies considerably, especially with the scale of the project. Large-scale planning processes often invite the public to work in groups on existing maps of their neighborhood or region and identify the places they value and those they fear and propose activities or connections they would like to see. In other cases, charrettes include regular public presentations of the evolving project, with solicitation of community reaction and ideas to be incorporated as much as possible into the final design.

16 At the time, Hattaway was with Hall Planning & Engineering, although by the final report he was with Glatting Jackson Kercher Anglin.

17 Upper Rock and Mashpee Commons held public charrettes—although the land was privately owned. The cities of Lakewood and Boca Raton, where Belmar and Mizner Park are located, established redevelopment authorities to partner with private developers on the publicly held land and did not hold charrettes. In all of these cases, as at Cottonwood Mall, the developer is beholden to the city to acquire various zoning approvals and often also asks for infrastructure improvements to adjacent public roads and sewers to accommodate the redevelopment, paid for through tax-increment financing. Public charrettes and public-private partnerships can be a useful means of building public support for public investments that will advance improvements to the area.

18 Salt Lake City has particularly wide streets dating back to the Church of Jesus Christ of Latter-Day Saints' historic desire for the streets to be able to accommodate a team of oxen leading a wagon to turn around. Instead of bowing to local custom or proposing the ten-foot-wide travel lanes and seven-foot-wide parking lanes that Hattaway usually recommends, he proposed eleven feet and eight feet, respectively, so as to better accommodate snow removal.

19 Industry standards are documented in *Trip Generation,* 7th edition (Institute of Transportation Engineers, 2003) to calculate new trips and by the *Trip Generation Handbook* (Institute of Transportation Engineers, 2004) to calculate pass-by trips and internal capture. Several studies in 2008 found actual trip generation rates at mixed-use projects and TODs substantially less than ITE-based projections (up to 59% less!) ITE expects to begin the process of revising its standards in 2009."

20 Billy Hattaway, telephone interview by Ellen Dunham-Jones, January 2, 2008.

21 Peterman, telephone interview.

22 The SmartCode correlates form-based coding to the rural-urban transect of particular neighborhoods, towns, or regions (discussed in Chapter 2). For more information see http://www.smartcodecentral.org.

23 The specialty market was interested in the northwest corner site with its prime visibility from both Highland Drive and Murray-Holladay Road, each carrying 22,000 cars per day. However, the retailer was also considering several other sites in and near Holladay for its first presence in the market and had considerable leverage to demand surface parking immediately in front of the store—counter to DPZ's plan to urbanize the corner with a plaza and small retail and office space. Harry Koehler, operating vice president for site planning & traffic, and Carl Goertemoeller, operating vice president for real estate for Macy's, were concerned about having a grocery store abut their department store. Koehler suggested that the specialty market's frontage on Main Street be lined with boutique retail. After consideration of several options and agreement to continue to refine the proposal, the parties at the charrette agreed to provide the market with a surface parking lot, visible from the intersection, but to place a trellised arcade and farmer's market tents along its sidewalk edges to detail it more like a plaza than a parking lot. The Main Street frontage would set back slightly from Macy's with a plaza and café, overlooked by the market's offices on the second floor. However, further modifications were made since the charrette such that Macy's now shares a small plaza with boutique retail and the specialty grocer is off of the Main Street and on Murray-Holladay Drive, although the surface parking lot continues to occupy the prime corner.

24 One of the first exercises in regional planning to employ charrettes at that scale, Envision Utah held over sixty charrette workshops in communities throughout the region and engaged over 18,000 people in online voting for their preferred growth scenario. Peter Calthorpe, a founder of CNU, and his associates led the effort.

25 D'Alesandro recognized the opportunity at Cottonwood and in correspondence with Ellen Dunham-Jones in November 2007 wrote, "The planned transformation of Cottonwood from a declining enclosed shopping center to a vibrant walkable downtown for the surrounding city of Holladay is exciting and reflects our desire to create a special place that integrates shopping, dining, entertainment, employment, and civic uses into a new neighborhood. The leadership that the city has demonstrated here is critical to the reinvention of Cottonwood. We see it as a dynamic new model for many of our shopping centers."

Chapter 8

1 Coinage of the term is attributed to Tim Van Meter, of Van Meter Williams Pollack, designer of several buildings at Belmar. It refers to the common, well-built urban brick commercial buildings, often with industrial sash windows, built in the early twentieth century in many American cities. Tim Van Meter, interview by Ellen Dunham-Jones, January 28, 2005, Denver, Colorado.

2 Mike Rock, interview by June Williamson, Lakewood, Colorado, August 7, 2007.

3 Tom Gougeon, interview by June Williamson, Denver, Colorado, August 8, 2007.

4 Mark Falcone, "Villa Italia, Lakewood, Colorado," in *Sprawl and Public Space: Redressing the Mall,* ed. David Smiley and Mark Robbins (New York: NEA/Princeton Architectural Press, 2002), 51.

5 Paula Moore, "Villa Italia Edges Toward a Revamp," *Denver Business Journal,* June 12, 1998.

6 Christopher Swope, "After the Mall," *Governing,* October 2002.

7 Tom Gougeon.

8 For more on the Alameda and Colfax corridor reinvestment areas in Lakewood, see City of Lakewood, *Lakewood Reinvestment Authority,* http://www.lakewood.org/index.cfm?&include=/CP/lra/LRA-home.cfm.

9 Kieran Nicholson, "Villa Italia Successor Wins Tax: Improvement Fee Will Pay Off Developer's Bonds," *Denver Post,* December 20, 2001, B-02.

10 Quoted in Jason Miller, "Another Greyfield Gone: Belmar in Lakewood, Colorado," *The Town Paper,* Fall 2005.

11 When the green-bonds provision was first added to the 2004 energy bill, critics derided it as "Hooters and polluters" because a Louisiana development that would benefit from the bonds included a Hooters restaurant. Mike Soraghan, "Tax Bill Would Benefit Belmar Developers," *Denver Post,* October 8, 2004, C-01.

12 David Manfredi, interview by Ellen Dunham-Jones, Boston, Massachusetts, October 15, 2007.

13 Donald Shoup, *The High Cost of Free Parking* (Washington, DC: American Planning Association, 2005).

14 For more on suburban morphology, see Brenda Case Scheer, "The Anatomy of Sprawl," *Places* 14:2 (Fall 2001): 28–37.

15 Robert Steuteville, "How to Mitigate the Impact of Big Box Stores," *New Urban News,* July/August 2006.

16 Quoted in Jared Jacang Maher, "Urban Flight: Rents Are Rising on South Broadway. Is Belmar the Solution?" *Denver Westword,* March 30, 2006.

17 Quoted in Kyle MacMillan, "A New Intellectual and Cultural Center," *Denver Post,* September 15, 2006, FF-01.

18 Brian A. Lee, "Building Big in the 'Burbs: Belmar Mixed-Use Development Transforms Lakewood, CO," *Western Real Estate Business,* February 2005.

19 Gougeon.

20 Gougeon.

21 Manfredi.

22 Craig Vickers, landscape architect at Civitas, Inc., interview by June Williamson, Lakewood, Colorado, August 7, 2007.

23 Quoted in Sally Stich, "Belmar: Lakewood District's Bountiful Amenities Help Boost Appreciates of All Varieties," *Denver Post,* May 7, 2006, K-04.

24 Tom, Janis, and Andrew Keating, interview by June Williamson, Lakewood, Colorado, August 6, 2007.

25 Ann Schrader, "Lakewood Targets Panhandling," *Denver Post,* June 21, 2004, B-02. For a probing sociological study of the experiences and motivations of street venders and panhandlers in New York City, see Mitchell Duneier, *Sidewalk* (New York: Farrar, Straus & Giroux, 2000).

Chapter 9

1 Robert Fishman, *Bourgeois Utopias: The Rise and Fall of Suburbia* (New York: Basic Books, 1987).

2 Joel Garreau, *Edge City: Life on the New Frontier* (New York: Doubleday, 1991). See also Brenda Case Scheer and Mintcho Petkov, "Edge City Morphology: A Comparison of Commercial Centers," *Journal of the American Planning Association* 64:3 (Summer 1998): 298–311.

3 Joel Garreau, "Don't Walk," *New Republic* 211:12/13 (September 19, 1994): 24–28.

4 Jonathan Barnett, "Turning Edge Cities into Real Cities," *Planning,* November 2002, adapted from *Redesigning Cities: Principles, Practice, Implementation* (Chicago: APA Press, 2003).

5 Geoffrey Booth et al., *Ten Principles for Reinventing America's Suburban Business Districts* (Washington, DC: The Urban Land Institute, 2002). See also the earlier and larger book by Geoffrey Booth et al., *Transforming Suburban Business Districts* (Washington, DC: The Urban Land Institute, 2001).

6 Christopher Leinberger, "Footloose and Fancy Free: A Field Survey of Walkable Urban Places in the Top 30 U.S. Metropolitan Areas," December 4, 2007, http://www.brookings.edu/papers/2007/1128_walkableurbanism_leinberger.aspx (accessed February 6, 2008).

7 Christopher B. Leinberger, *The Option of Urbanism: Investing in a New American Dream* (Washington, DC: Island Press, 2007), 99.

8 Ibid.

9 Garreau has several articles on the topic at his website, http://www.garreau.com. See Joel Garreau, "The Santa Fe-ing of the Urban and Urbane," April 8, 2006.

10 For research that backs up the argument that the information-rich quality of face-to-face interaction has become even more valued in the context of electronic communication, see Dierdre Boden and Harvey Molotch, "The Compulsion of Proximity," in *NowHere: Space, Time and Modernity*, ed. Roger Friedland and Dierdre Boden (Berkeley: University of California Press, 1994): 257–286, and Barry Wellman, "The Network Community: An Introduction," in *Networks in the Global Village*, ed. Barry Wellmann (Boulder, CO: Westview Press, 1999), 1–48.

11 Garreau, "Don't Walk."

12 The number of daily trips per capita varies from city to city but more or less doubled between 1950 and 2000, with fewer of those trips being nonvehicular. In neighborhoods composed solely of single-family houses, most calculation methods estimate that each household generates approximately ten trips per day. However, that number drops in half or by two-thirds for households of single people, seniors, or lower incomes. Higher density, mixed use, and access to transit correlate with more of those trips being made on foot. For more information, see the U.S. Department of Transportation Travel Model Improvement Program website at http://tmip.fhwa.dot.gov and John S. Miller, Lester A. Hoel, Arkopal K. Goswami, and Jared M. Ulmer, "Borrowing Residential Trip Generation Rates," *Journal of Transportation Engineering* 132.2 (February 2006): 105–113.

13 There is considerable research on walkability. A good survey of this literature is presented in Anne Vernez Moudon et al., "Operational Definitions of Walkable Neighborhood: Theoretical and Empirical Insights," *Journal of Physical Activity and Health* 3: suppl. 1 (2006): S99–S117. See also Michael Southworth and Eran Ben-Joseph, *Streets and the Shaping of Towns and Cities* (New York: McGraw-Hill, 1997).

14 Edge cities often devote 50% or more of surface space to cars, leading to water quality problems from runoff and lack of permeability back to the water table. Air quality is principally compromised from emissions caused by vehicle miles traveled, which has increased at three times the rate of population growth. For a comparison of average energy use and carbon dioxide emissions per person in cities versus suburbs, see Alex Williams, "Don't Let the Green Grass Fool You," *New York Times*, February 10, 2008.

15 See Howard Frumkin, Lawrence Frank, and Richard Jackson, *Urban Sprawl and Public Health: Designing, Planning, and Building for Healthy Communities* (Washington, DC: Island Press, 2004).

16 See Reid Ewing et al., "Relationship Between Urban Sprawl and Physical Activity, Obesity, and Morbidity," *American Journal of Health Promotion* 18:1 (2003); and Lawrence Frank, Martin Andresen, and Tom Schmidt, "Obesity Relationships with Community Design, Physical Activity, and Time Spent in Cars," *American Journal of Preventive Medicine* 27:2 (2004).

17 A useful summary of the wide range of research in this area is presented in "Understanding the Relationship between Public Health and the Built Environment," prepared by Design, Community & Environment; Dr. Reid Ewing; Lawrence Frank and Company; and Dr. Richard Kreutzer for the LEED-ND Core Committee, http://www.cnu.org/sites/files/leed_public_health.pdf.

18 See the writings of William Fulton, "Are Edge Cities Losing Their Edge?" *Planning* 62, May 1996; Charles Lockwood, "Edge Cities on the Brink," *Wall Street Journal* (eastern edition), December 21, 1994, A14; Scheer, "Edge City Monopoly"; and Woody Carter, Robert Frolick, and Tim Frye, "Edge Cities or Edge Suburbs?" presented at the Chicago Meetings of the Midwest Association for Public Opinion Research, November 2, 2002, and available at the website of the Metro Chicago Information Center, http://www.mcic.org.

19 Analysis of Chicago Metro Survey data from 1998 through 2002 reveals that the typical edge-city resident is white, well educated, Catholic, and Republican. The profile is dramatically different from the city of Chicago and represents a more condensed version of suburban patterns. Carter, Frolick, and Frye, "Edge Cities or Edge Suburbs?"

20 Ibid.

21 Ibid. The report also found that "in focus groups, their community's very 'boringness' is a quality residents praise and cherish."

22 Garreau, *Edge Cities,* 5.

23 In *Edge Cities,* Garreau distinguishes three forms of edge cities: the strip, the node, and the pig in the python. The Urban Land Institute book by Geoffrey Booth et al., *Transforming Suburban Business Districts,* uses different categorizations: compact, fragmented, and dispersed. Each has very different implications for strategies to improve walkability and interconnectivity.

24 This list is adapted from Louis G. Redstone, *The New Downtowns: Rebuilding Business Districts* (New York: McGraw-Hill, 1976).

25 Martha Groves, "They're Taking the Walk: Plans Call for a Greener, Less Car-centric Century City That Would Connect New Housing with Shops, Offices, and Restaurants," *Los Angeles Times,* January 13, 2007.

26 Ibid. It is also worth noting that the changes under way have already attracted a new caliber of commercial tenants, specifically top talent agencies who have in turn attracted top restaurateurs, further transforming the edge city's character. See Monica Corcoran, "Let's Do Lunch, Now That There's Somewhere to Do It," *New York Times,* July 22, 2007.

27 Jonathan Barnett, "Turning Edge Cities into Real Cities," in *Redesigning Cities* (Chicago: APA Press, 2003), 169–170.

28 For the first time, S&Ls were allowed to make loans to commercial development and without the usual risk-management precautions, without geographic limitations, and without raising the premiums on their federally insured deposits. The result was a period of easy money (and easy fraud) for high-risk, speculative commercial real estate construction in the already hot suburban markets, especially in the South and West. As the decade progressed, new malls and shopping centers were increasingly upscale, while the class-A, large-floor-plate, glistening office towers were generally designed to lure corporate tenants away from beleaguered downtowns.

29 Bert Ely, "The Resolution Trust Corporation in Historical Perspective," *Housing Policy Debate* 1:1 (1990): 53–78. Corporate mergers, de-acquisitions, and downsizing in the 1990s further rocked the edge-city office market. See also Joel Warren Barna, *The See-Through Years: Creation and Destruction in Texas Architecture and Real Estate 1981–1991* (Houston, TX: Rice University Press, 1992).

30 William H. Whyte first documented the tendency for corporations to relocate in proximity to the CEO's residence in *City: Rediscovering the Center* (New York: Doubleday, 1988). Christopher Leinberger similarly observed this trend as "the favored quarter." Less well known is that Whyte's book also contains a study comparing the stock valuations between 1976 and 1987 of thirty-eight corporations that left New York City against thirty-six that stayed. He found that those that stayed were valued more than two and a half times those that left. The S&L crisis brought these issues to the fore. See Charles Lockwood, "Edge Cities on the Brink," *Wall Street Journal* (eastern edition), December 21, 1994, A14.

31 According to their research, in 1999, in the thirteen largest office markets in the United States, 38% of office space was in downtowns, 37% in edgeless cities, and 25% in edge cities or secondary downtowns. In eleven of those markets (Chicago and New York were the outliers), there was more office space in edgeless cities than in downtowns. By 2006, they claim that edgeless cities accounted for nearly 40% of all office space, half of which is located in "urban" residential areas with more than 3,000 people per square mile, one-third of which is in suburban areas with 1,000–3,000 people per square mile, and the remainder of which is in lower-density exurban areas. Robert E. Lang and Jennifer LeFurgy, "Edgeless Cities: Examining the Noncentered Metropolis," *Housing Policy Debate* 14:3 (2003): 427–460. See also Robert E. Lang, *Edgeless Cities: Exploring the Elusive Metropolis* (Washington, DC: Brookings Institution Press, 2003); and Robert E. Lang, Thomas Sanchez, and Jennifer LeFurgy, "Beyond Edgeless Cities: Office Geography in the New Metropolis," National Center for Real Estate Research report, February 2006.

32 The New York Regional Plan Association's proposed interventions in Somerset County, New Jersey, are an example of such an attempt in an edgeless city. The report is available at http://www.rpa.org.

33 Fulton, "Are Edge Cities Losing Their Edge?"

34 The percentage gains are not always dramatic but are promising considering that the examples studied were not deliberately designed to promote walkability. Several studies are summarized in LEED-ND Core Committee, "Understanding the Relationship Between Public Health and the Built Environment," 21–23. More salient findings include the following: having convenience-oriented retail located near work sites doubled the use of transit from 3.4% to 7.2% (Cambridge Systematics, *The Effects of Land Use and Travel Demand Management Strategies on Commuting Behavior* [Washington, DC: U.S. Department of Transportation, Federal Highway Administration, 1994]); each 10% increase in retail to an employment center resulted in a 3% increase in the mode share of transit and ride-sharing trips (Robert Cervero, "Land Use Mixing and Suburban Mobility," *Transportation Quarterly* 42 (1988): 429–446); residents in communities with a balance of employment and residential uses commute, on average, one-third less distance than do workers living in areas with more housing than employment (Reid Ewing, "Characteristics, Causes and Effects of Sprawl: A Literature Review," in *Environmental and Urban Issues* [Miami: Florida Atlantic University/Florida International University, 1994], 7).

35 Gloria Ohland's 2002 case study of Addison Circle describes the project in some detail and clarifies Robert Shaw's involvement first with Columbus Realty Trust, then Post Properties, and then Amicus Partners. See Hank Dittmar and Gloria Ohland, *The New Transit Town: Best Practices in Transit-Oriented Development* (Washington, DC: Island Press, 2004), 159.

36 A pioneer project in the 1980s, State/Thomas was the Dallas area's first use of tax-increment financing, was the first institution of a new urbanist–based Special Purpose Zoning Code, and incorporated the city's only trolley line. By 2004, its four- to eight-story perimeter-block buildings with lively retail along the highly walkable streets had triggered such a building boom that land prices were higher than downtown and triggered subsequent high-rise condominium development. See Steve Brown, "Urban Renewed," *Dallas Morning News*, November 25, 2004.

37 Quoted in Steve Brown, "Urban-Inspired Development in Addison," *Knight Ridder/Tribune Business News,* Washington, DC, February 11, 2005.

38 Ibid.

39 Town official Carmen Moran was quoted as saying, "One of the reasons we wanted to do Addison Circle is we wanted a center for our town.... We are very proud of how it has turned out." Steve Brown, "Urban-Inspired Development in Addison."

40 "Smart Growth Illustrated: Legacy Town Center, Plano, Texas," available at http://www.epa.gov/piedpage/case/legacy.htm.

41 Neal Templin, "Can a Dull Office Park Give Birth to a Town? EDS Plan for Development Gives 'New Urbanism' a Corporate Ambiance," *Wall Street Journal* (eastern edition), November 24, 1999, B16.

42 Haya El Nasser, "Suburban Office Parks Get Urban Injection," *USA Today*, September 13, 2004.

43 Thaddeus Herrick, "City Lite," *Wall Street Journal*, May 31, 2006, A1.

44 Additional factors include the Perimeter Community Improvement District's success at getting a congestion-relieving new flyover bridge built, as well as extensive improvements to sidewalks and pedestrian crosswalks.

45 Linking two retrofits, the existing buildings on the site were vacated by BellSouth during the company's consolidation described in Chapter 11.

46 Tom Barry, "New Projects Planned for Ashford-Dunwoody," *Atlanta Business Chronicle*, October 15, 2004.

47 Pierre Filion, Kathleen McSpurren, and Nancy Huether, "Synergy and Movement Within Suburban Mixed-Use Centers: The Toronto Experience," *Journal of Urban Affairs* 22:4 (2000): 419–438.

48 For more on the Tukwila plan, see "A Plan for the Heart of the Region: Tukwila, WA" available at www.ftburbandesign.com/files/FTB_Tukwila_Heart_of_the_Region_0.pdf.

49 See "Hacienda Business Park Opportunities," East Bay Community Foundation; Hacienda Business Park Owners Association; Solomon E.T.C, a WRT Company; Nelson/Nygaard, Transportation; Strategic Economics; and UC Berkeley, College of Environmental Design, May 2003, available at http://tod.hacienda.org/SP/HaciendaBusinessParkConceptStudy.pdf.

50 The plan is titled "Coliseum Central Master Plan, Hampton, Virginia, Urban Design Associates, September 2004."

Chapter 10

1   Victor Dover, "The Revitalization of Main Street: Kendall, Florida," in *The Seaside Debates: A Critique of the New Urbanism* (New York: Rizzoli, 2002), 59.

2   Ibid., 62.

3   Jonathan Barnett, *Redesigning Cities: Principles, Practice, Implementation* (Chicago: APA Planners Press, 2003), 170–171.

4   Joseph Kohl, interview by authors, Miami, Florida, November 21, 2006.

5   Shailendra Singh, head of the Miami-Dade County Urban Design Center, interview by authors, Miami, Florida, November 21, 2006.

6   Gilbert DeBlanco, Miami-Dade County planner, email correspondence with authors, November 30, 2006.

7   For more on suburban morphology see Brenda Case Scheer, "The Anatomy of Sprawl," *Places* 14:2 (Fall 2001): 28–37.

8   Subrata Basu, assistant director of planning and zoning, Miami-Dade County, quoted in Robert Steuteville, "A Suburban Agglomeration Becomes a Downtown," *New Urban News*, December 2004.

9   In 2004, Latin American tourists accounted for 40% of the center's gross sales. Shoppers spent $132 per visit, well above the industry average of $80. Shopping center profile by advertising media group JCDecaux, "Dadeland Mall," 2007, http://www.jcdecauxna.com/pages/mall/ViewMarket.aspx?mid=71.

10 Fernando Ibanez, Cervera Real Estate, interview by authors, November 21, 2006. See also Bella Kelly, "Drawn to Dadeland," *Miami Herald*, November 24, 2002, sec. 1H.

11 Karl Ross, "Downtown for Kendall Delayed a Year," *Miami Herald*, April 13, 2001, sec. 3B.

12 Gilbert DeBlanco, interview by authors, Miami, Florida, November 21, 2006.

13 Elizabeth Plater-Zyberk, interview by authors, Miami, Florida, November 22, 2006.

Chapter 11

1   Quoted in Haya El Nasser, "Suburban Office Parks Get Urban Injection," *USA Today*, September 31, 2004.

2   Except for economic and geographic histories, the social role and physical designs of this overlooked history have only recently begun receiving more attention. Examples include Robert Lewis, ed., *Manufacturing Suburbs* (Philadelphia: Temple University Press, 2004); Margaret Crawford, *Building the Workingman's Paradise* (London: Verso, 1996); and Diane Ghirardo, *Building New Communities: New Deal America and Fascist Italy* (Princeton, NJ: Princeton University Press, 1989).

3   Thomas R. Graham, *Satellite Cities: A Study of Industrial Suburbs* (New York: D. Appleton and Company, 1915).

4   Cited in Urban Land Institute, *The Community Builders Handbook* (Washington, DC: The Urban Land Institute, 1968).

5   Kenneth T. Jackson, *Crabgrass Frontier: The Suburbanization of the United States* (New York: Oxford University Press, 1985), 267.

6   Stanford Research Park's influence has extended to Goa, India, where a new office park's red roofs are a deliberate attempt to build up another Silicon Valley. For this and a more extensive history of the Stanford Research Park, see Margaret O'Mara, *Cities of Knowledge, Cold War Science and the Search for the Next Silicon Valley* (Princeton, NJ: Princeton University Press, 2004).

7   See Joel Garreau, *Edge City: Life on the New Frontier* (New York: Doubleday, 1991).

8   Chris Leinberger, "The Favored Quarter: Where the Bosses Live, Jobs and Development Follow," *Atlanta Journal-Constitution*, June 8, 1997.

9   Quoted in Jane Gordon, "Collision of Cultures over a Building," *New York Times*, March 20, 2005.

10 Geoffrey Booth et al., *Transforming Suburban Business Districts* (Washington, DC: The Urban Land Institute, 2001), 7.

11 Robert Lang, "Office Sprawl: The Evolving Geography of Business," http://www.brookings.com.

12 Herschel Abbott, prepared statement to the U.S. Senate Subcommittee on Housing and Transportation's hearing on "TEA-21: Investing in Our Economy and Environment," June 26, 2002.

13 For more on MARTA's role in the Atlanta Metro Plan, see Sharon Feigon and David Hoyt with Gloria Ohlund, "The Atlanta Case Study: Lindbergh City Center," in *The New Transit Town: Best Practices in Transit-Oriented Development,* ed. Hank Dittmar and Gloria Ohlund (Washington, DC: Island Press, 2004).

14 David Goldberg, "BellSouth's Atlanta Metro Plan: A Case Study in Employer-Driven 'Smart Growth,'" Sprawlwatch Clearinghouse, 2000, http://www.sprawlwatch.org/bellsouth.html.

15 See Richard Florida, *The Rise of the Creative Class* (New York: Basic Books, 2002); Richard Florida, *Cities and the Creative Class* (New York: Routledge, 2005); and Richard Florida, *The Flight of the Creative Class* (New York: HarperCollins, 2005).

16 This particular summary comes from Richard Florida, "Response," *Journal of the American Planning Association* 71:2 (Spring 2005): 203.

17 Richard Florida, *The Rise of the Creative Class,* xix.

18 Quoted in Emily Eakin, "Creative Cities and Their New Elite," *New York Times,* June 1, 2002. Florida readily concedes that the masses of software engineers living in Silicon Valley, northern Virginia, and the Seattle suburbs inhabit conventional and relatively homogenous enclaves that are far from eccentric. But he points out that they are located in regions that are known to be amongst the most diverse in the country and offer a wide array of lifestyle amenities. Florida, *The Rise of the Creative Class,* 233.

19 Florida's focus on the ease with which a newcomer can plug into communal activities distinguishes his argument from theories of social capital's role in promoting economic development. Unlike Robert Putnam (see Bowling Alone [New York: Simon & Schuster, 2006]), Florida argues places that foster weak social ties over strong ties are more effective because they are more inclusive (promoting tolerance and broader, networks rather than smaller, in-depth networks). This has positive implications for younger cities and new developments so long as they deliberately foster such opportunities.

20 Florida, *The Rise of the Creative Class,* 232.

21 Wang and Digital are but two examples. Robert Preer, "Route 128 Projects Now Offering More Places to Work—and Live," *Boston Globe,* October 8, 2006.

22 SkySong, http://skysongcenter.com/project_vision.html (accessed November 12, 2006).

23 President Michael Crow's efforts constitute a retrofitting project of their own, nearly doubling ASU's enrollment and adding three new campuses linked by light rail, including one intended to revitalize downtown Phoenix.

24 William H. Whyte, *The Organization Man* (New York: Simon and Schuster, 1956).

25 Florida, *The Rise of the Creative Class,* 201.

26 Philip Nobel, "Living in Zen: The Spa Life, 24/7," *New York Times,* November 2, 2006. Also, Professor Nancy Koehn at Harvard Business School has been studying how Americans are coping with longer work hours and new demands. In an interview on NPR on *Morning Edition* on September 23, 2004, she noted new products that entrepreneurs are coming up with to help us cope in our time-conscious busyness. She also said, "One of the things we lose—and again, there's a business opportunity that's being exploited here, too—is reflection. We also clearly lose civic time, a word that's an old-fashioned word now. But time to be part of a community in an active way. We lose neighborly time. We don't drop in on people because we don't have time for that kind of communal spontaneous fabric that so defined life before the industrial revolution and life all the way into, say, the 1970s. I think finally we're losing time for piddling, time for doing nothing, time to just be and see what comes out of that kind of inactivity, unstimulated time."

27 Wood Partners' proposed nineteen-story residential condominium tower, Horizon, at the entry to the upscale Wildwood Office Park, in the Cumberland Mall area northwest of Atlanta, is but one example.

28 Jim Buchta, "Condos in the Clouds," *Star Tribune* (Minneapolis), August 12, 2004. Note that as of November 2006, the higher-priced units remained on the market.

29 Julie Snow, telephone conversation with Ellen Dunham-Jones, November 8, 2006.

30 The JBG Companies, *Innovations in Livability: Upper Rock District,* large-format promotional project brochure, 4.

31 Thomas C. Palmer, "Huge Development Set to Get State OK," *Boston Globe,* November 2, 2007.

32 David Manfredi, interview by Ellen Dunham-Jones, Boston, MA, October 15, 2007.

33 Ibid.

Chapter 12

1 Quoted in Douglas Fruehling, "Back to the Future," *On Site,* Summer 2007, 24.

2 Herschel Blumberg, interview by June Williamson, Hyattsville, Maryland, February 27, 2006.

3 "Master Plan Concept: Prince George's Town, Maryland," undated report. Edward Durell Stone Papers (MC 340). Special Collections, University of Arkansas Libraries, Fayetteville.

4 Ibid.

5 Jay Parker, telephone conversation with June Williamson, November 12, 2006.

6 Dineene O'Conner, senior planner at the Maryland-National Capital Park and Planning Commission, interview by June Williamson, February 27, 2006.

7 "Descriptive Data/AIA Honor Award Program, 1965," Edward Durell Stone Papers (MC 340), box 82:16. Special Collections, University of Arkansas Libraries, Fayetteville.

8 Parker.

9 Quoted in Steven Overly, "Ehrlich, Johnson Unveil New Town Center for Maryland Students," *The Diamondback,* August 10, 2006.

10 For more on suburban morphology see Brenda Case Scheer, "The Anatomy of Sprawl," *Places* 14:2 (Fall 2001): 28–37.

11 Lonnae O'Neal Parker, "Pr. George's Takes a Bite of the Good Life: Long-Ignored County Now a Retail Magnet," *Washington Post,* June 20, 2006, A01.

12 Overly, "Ehrlich, Johnson Unveil New Town Center for Maryland Students."

Epilogue

1 We are grateful to the Georgia Tech team that participated in the History Channel's 2008 City of the Future competition for helping us develop many of these ideas. The team's vision of Atlanta in one hundred years is entitled "LWARPS—we can reverse sprawl." Thanks to the team members: Ed Akins, Tristan Al-Haddad, Richard Dagenhart, Ellen Dunham-Jones, Janae Futrell, Michael Gamble, Ryan Gravel, David Green, Frances Hsu, Hanyun Huang, Allison Isaacs, Sarah Kiliniski, Swaleha Lalani, Jude LeBlanc, Cassie Niemann, Miharu Morimoto, Brian Peterka, Gernot Riether, Ross Wallace, and Jen Yoon.

IMAGE CREDITS

All images are courtesy of the authors unless otherwise indicated.

INDEX